Behavioral Finance

WHERE DO INVESTORS' BIASES COME FROM?

Behavioral Finance

WHERE DO INVESTORS' BIASES COME FROM?

Itzhak **Venezia**

Tel Aviv Yaffo Academic College, Israel

World Scientific

NEW JERSEY • LONDON • SINGAPORE • BEIJING • SHANGHAI • HONG KONG • TAIPEI • CHENNAI • TOKYO

Published by

World Scientific Publishing Co. Pte. Ltd.

5 Toh Tuck Link, Singapore 596224

USA office: 27 Warren Street, Suite 401-402, Hackensack, NJ 07601

UK office: 57 Shelton Street, Covent Garden, London WC2H 9HE

Library of Congress Cataloging-in-Publication Data
Names: Venezia, Itzhak, editor.
Title: Behavioral finance : where do investors' biases come from? /
[edited by] Emeritus Professor Itzhak Venezia, Tel Aviv Yaffo Academic College and The Hebrew University of Jerusalem, Israel.
Description: New Jersey : World Scientific, 2016.
Identifiers: LCCN 2016015277 (print) | ISBN 9789813100084 (hardcover)
Subjects: LCSH: Investments--Psychological aspects. | Investments--Decision making.
Classification: LCC HG4515.15 .B4389 2016 (print) | DDC 332.601/9--dc23
LC record available at https://lccn.loc.gov/2016015277

British Library Cataloguing-in-Publication Data
A catalogue record for this book is available from the British Library.

Desk Editor: Karimah Samsudin

To my loved ones Dana, Laurie and Irit

Contents

Preface

In early 2015, the Tel Aviv Yaffo Academic College initiated the *First Israel Conference in Behavioral Finance* hoping to start an annual tradition of bringing together in Israel some of the leading researchers in behavioral finance. We thought of beginning this tradition since there are great many Israelis working in this area and we deemed it promising and constructive to gather many of them under one roof to serve as a nucleus for an international conference and since in a way, in light of Kahneman and Tversky's path-breaking contributions, Israel may be considered as the "birthplace of behavioral finance". We invited many leading researchers from around the world to the conference and to our delight, we obtained a large number of submissions of high quality papers to the conference. What we initially planned to be a one day relaxed affair became a very condensed two-day conference. The conference, held in May 2015 in Tel Aviv, organized by Itzhak Venezia (chair), Rachel Gilo Shalom, Doron Kliger, and Roy Zuckerman turned out very successful. Twenty three papers authored by researchers who came from Australia, Holland, Israel, Italy, Russia, Sweden, Switzerland, Taiwan and the USA were presented. We also conducted an experts' panel discussing the application of behavioral finance in investments in Israel. The conference drew quite an extensive audience, and the attendees felt that the lectures were very constructive and opened their eyes to recent advances in the field. It became evident that the conference developed into a center for exchange of ideas and discussions on future research. This convinced me that a book compiling a collection of papers either presented at the conference or by its participants (with a little help from the outside) highlighting the main subjects of the conference will be very useful.

One of the common threads to the papers in the conference which I find extremely intriguing is the question of which factors lead to investors cognitive biases and hence, the book is built around this theme. Most of the articles in this book explore aspects of investors' traits that affect their financial decisions and their cognitive biases, and the exogenous influences which help shape these characteristics. Among the features investigated, which potentially either contribute or limit investors biases, one could find sophistication, professionalism, gender, culture and the media.

The book begins with a review paper *Reference-Based Decisions in Finance* by Fernando Zapatero. The existence of reference points is one of the main issues separating Prospect Theory from traditional decision theory, and their impact on financial decisions is well documented. Zapatero shows that the prevalence of reference points extends much beyond the *status quo* points of Prospect Theory, and argues that they are not always exogenous to the decision making system. According to Zapatero, their pervasiveness can be explained by their benefits to society. A decision making system where the decision makers use reference points, either given to them by nature or by other principals, is quite effective in boosting incentives and providing a positive motivation for economic activity. This argument is supported in this article by examples of reference points in habit formation, relative wealth concerns, benchmarking, relative performance evaluation, managerial compensation, and more.

In addition, if the reference points are not entirely exogenous, there arises the question of the link between the decision makers' persona and the way they determine their reference point, a question that has not been well researched in the extant literature. Since the economic agents can influence the reference points or can choose between several of them, would all make the same choice? And if not, which factors will influence their selection? For example, when the problem posed is whether or not to buy insurance and if so, how much insurance to buy, the reference point is critical. Hence, the decision makers attributes leading some to anchor their decisions to one reference point and others to a different one, may be essential in providing the answer to the problem, but have rarely been researched. Hopefully this paper will attract attention to this issue, to the endogeneity of reference points, and to their important economic role, thereby encouraging future research in these topics.

The next part contains three papers on professionalism and sophistication, or their lack of, on investors' behavior and capital markets (issues touched upon also in other parts of the book). One of the major concerns of researchers in behavioral finance is whether some unscrupulous organizations and individuals can exploit the behavioral biases (or irrationality) of certain groups of investors for their own advantage. If so, there is room to consider the regulation of these organizations, and/or urging for better education of the investors to eliminate or limit their biases. Such concerns are especially severe with regards to complex financial instruments, where in addition to susceptibility to biases, there is a danger of investors being ignorant or misled on the intricacies of the instruments. Ofir and Wiener's article *Individuals Investment in Financial Structured Products from Rational and Behavioral Choice Perspectives* investigates to what extent are individual investors savvy enough to rationally invest in multifaceted instruments such as structured products. They show experimentally that investors in these instruments exhibit several behavioral biases such as loss aversion, the disposition effect, herd behavior, the ostrich effect and the hindsight bias. The tendency of individuals to exhibit the aforementioned biases puts them in danger of being exploited by the issuers and marketers of the structured products. The authors therefore suggest a regulation scheme that will force the issuers and marketers of these financial instruments to reveal their effective fees and thus help even the lesser sophisticated investors achieve better informed decisions.

But wouldn't competition rather than regulation solve this problem better? Some researchers have argued that the issuers of complex instruments are well equipped to reap monopolistic returns, since competition to any existing complex product will be limited due to the difficulty to create and market similar products. Competition therefore will not necessarily drive prices to the level mandated by perfect competition. This point of view leads Ofir and Wiener to conclude that some sort of intervention may be recommended in the case of structured products, undoubtedly one of the more complex instruments available to individuals, and they suggest proper regulatory involvement schemes in their paper.

The disadvantage of unsophisticated individual investors *vis-à-vis* the more sophisticated ones is also exposed in Glode, Hollifield, Kacperczyk and Kogan's paper *Is Investor Rationality Time Varying? Evidence from the Mutual Fund Industry*. They show that performance predictability is more pronounced for funds catering to retail investors than for funds catering to institutional investors, suggesting that unsophisticated investors are more prone to make systematic mistakes in their capital allocation decisions, as they "leave more money on the table". Glode, Hollifield, Kacperczyk and Kogan do not pinpoint at the precise mistakes individuals make, but hint at some alternative theories expounded by the popular press, e.g., that individuals over react in extreme events such as adverse market conditions. The prevalence of over reaction to extreme events has been noted since the early works of Kahneman and Tversky. The lower tendency of professionals to over react than individuals could be explained by their greater confidence (overconfidence). This trait is characterized by the tighter priors of their initial beliefs that make the professionals less prone to change their opinions even in the face of unusual new information. The findings of this paper thus are consistent with the extant behavioral finance premises and reinforce them.

It is hard to find unanimity among researchers on most issues in finance, hence it comes as no surprise to also observe in the behavioral finance literature conflicting statements about the superiority of professionals over amateurs and the sophisticated over the pedestrian. The paper by Swan and Westerholm *Are Domestic Household Investors Better Performers than Foreign Institutions? New Evidence from Finland* is an excellent case in point. They show that domestic households clearly and systematically outperform foreign institutional investors by a very substantial margin of great economic significance, opposite to the findings of Grinblatt and Keloharju[1], who used in their research a similar population and same methodology, but for a shorter period of time. Swan and Westerholm conclude that the inferiority attributed to the individual investor is unjustified and say that "it is no longer possible to classify unambiguously household and individual investors as random 'noise traders' in the behavioral and market microstructure literature". So who are we to believe? It is up to each reader to make his or her own mind, but it seems the paper by Swan and Westerholm makes a dent in the theory of the universality of the dominance

[1] Grinblatt, M., and M. Keloharju. 2000. The investment behavior and performance of various investor types: A study of Finland's unique data set. *Journal of Financial Economics* 55: 43–67.

of professionals over amateurs. It may be rather safe, however, to predict that this discussion will continue to rage.

The next part presents three papers on the effect of culture and gender on decisions. The theory of decision making is usually culture and gender blind. Barring institutional differences, why would decision makers under one culture behave differently than in another if they are all rational? But in behavioral finance, the dominant assumption is that not all decision makers are rational (in the Von Neumann-Morgenstern sense), and there is no reason to expect that all will be irrational in the same way. There are, of course, some well accepted common biases, which probably appear everywhere, but it is interesting to explore to what extent are these biases universal, and to compare their severity and prevalence across gender and culture lines. In their experimental study *The Assessment of Risk Behavior: A Cross-cultural Analysis using the DOSPERT Scale* conducted with Chinese and German subjects, Breuer, Kollath, Salzmann and Nitzsch explore the importance of risk perception relative to expected benefits in a specific risk situation. They compare the behavior of the Chinese students in their sample to that of the German ones. They find, among other results, that their subjects attitudes towards perceived risk are more crucial in explaining their behavior than their subjective evaluation of expected benefits. Furthermore, they demonstrate, using the Domain-Specific Risk-Taking (DOSPERT) scale that nationality is an important factor for explaining risk behavior.

In her paper *Fear of Negative Evaluation, Culture, Gender, and Financial Welfare* Na Young Park focuses on the role of gender in financial decision, and shows that, indeed, there are some features to female Korean decision makers that differ from those of their male counterparts. She shows that female financial consumers are less able to challenge and reject offers and suggestions they receive from financial advisors, which makes them more disposed to abuse. This has important implications on the regulation of financial advisers and on their effects on capital markets.

Rusou, Amar and Ayal's article *Gender and Personal Finance Management* reviews many of the factors that have been shown in prior literature to influence differently men and women's financial behavior such as risk attitudes, financial literacy, confidence in financial knowledge and cognitive style. It also provides explanations and suggests possible determinants of these observed gender differences. The authors argue that gender differences in the area of personal finance did not receive adequate attention in the extant literature, and especially in the area of debt management. From an experiment they conducted to explore the management of multiple debt accounts, they infer possible mechanisms driving gender similarities and differences in behavior.

The next part contains two papers that involve the effects of the media on decision making. The article by Gurevich and Kliger *The Role of Emotions in Decision Making: Theory, Evidence, and Examples from Media Psychology* focuses on the role of emotions on decisions. The authors point to the importance of sentiments on decision making, and note the many social factors that affect decisions via their effects on emotions. Gurevich and Kliger propose that, significant among these factors, is the media in all its forms. Whereas this paper does not concentrate on financial decisions, its generality indicates the applicability of their analysis to such decisions as well. The paper by Kliger and Siev *Firm Disclosure, Media, and the Capital Markets* on the other hand, specifically deliberates on the inter-relationship between media, decisions and the capital markets. Their article explores the effects of the many forms of information, e.g., firm disclosure versus external sources, and differentiates between pricing-relevant and pricing-irrelevant information, and between hard (quantifiable) and soft (qualitative) information. It distinguishes between the various effects of media depending on its form (printed versus electronic) and on volume. As in Gurevich and Kliger, this article also refers to the impact of news stories depending on their effect on emotions (sentiments).

The final part explores some of the more pervasive biases in behavioral finance and discusses the implications of using heuristics in decision making on several financial markets. In their paper *Heuristics and Biases in the Israeli Mortgage Market*, Ofir, Mugerman and Wiener discuss the effects of availability, representativeness, and anchoring on the mortgages market in Israel. More specifically they show, using a unique data on the decisions of borrowers, that the availability and representativeness heuristics play a dominant role in borrowers' choice between fixed rate mortgage (FRM) and adjustable rate mortgage (ARM). Moreover, they show that the borrowers anchor their choices on the regulatory provisions regarding the loan division between FRM and ARM.

In their paper *The Availability Heuristic and other Psychological Aspects of Investors' Reactions to Company-Specific Events*, Kliger and Kudryatsev discuss the effects of the availability heuristic on investors observing firm-specific events. They contend that the company-specific events in their study affect decision makers, and hence prices, not only through the information they provide on future cash flows, but also by their influence on the investors psyche and personal cognitive biases. From three studies the authors have previously conducted on investors' reactions to analyst recommendation revisions, they conclude that mood (which is swayed by the amount of daylight time) affects decisions directly. They argue that changes in contemporaneous stock market index returns and in the VIX index also affect decisions beyond the influence justified by their informative content on future cash flows, by their influence on mood.

Brenner, Galai and Sade in their article *Uniform or Discriminatory Auctions: Endogenizing Bidder's Choice in Divisible Goods Auctions* do not deal with investors' choice of financial products, but in their choice between two alternative pricing mechanisms of auction for government bonds: uniform pricing (where all winners pay the same winning price) versus discriminatory pricing mechanism (where each winner pays his/her bid price). In most previous research, it has been found that the issuer obtains on average higher proceeds under the uniform mechanism. This explains the preference of issuers for this type of auctions, but what about the bidders? Recently, due to increasing competition between diverse auction markets for government bonds, the question of which mechanism buyers prefer became more relevant. The zero sum game nature of the process, and the findings about the higher proceeds for the issuers in uniform auctions, should lead buyers to prefer discriminatory auctions. Brenner, Galai and Sade however, find the opposite in their experiments (surveys). They show that although price plays a major role in determining the participants' decisions, other factors, and especially "fairness" also impact the choice and drive the preference for uniform pricing. One would hate to find out that he or she paid higher prices than others for the same product, an event that could of course also hurt the bidder's reputation. This paper also contributes to two other much debated controversies: the difference between the quality of decisions of the more and the less experienced, and the question of the extent to which monetary rewards are crucial in experimental finance. The authors suggest that in the range of monetary rewards and experience their study covers, these parameters do not considerably affect the results.

Previous research has contended that investors behave myopically, and that this tendency may explain the Equity Premium Puzzle. The closing paper *Factors Affecting the Impact of Investors' Horizon on Asset Allocation Decisions: An Experimental Exploration* by Amar and Kroll revisits experimentally this issue. They investigate in a multi period experiment to what degree investors tend to behave myopically, and find that only one type of participants in their sample, those with an initial low risk-taking level, behave myopically. They also find that investors decision exhibit a fair amount of inertia; there is a tendency among their subjects to avoid unnecessary changes in their asset allocation. In each round of the experiment, subjects are inclined to retain the *status quo* from the previous one. In addition, they show that the investors' education level has a significant influence on their asset allocation, whereas gender, age and wealth do not indicate such effect.

The compilation of all the chapters provides a fresh way of exploring some of the factors that shape the characteristics of the investors and consequently, the effects of these aspects on their biases and decision making. I hope this book provides constructive and stimulating information to all students, researchers, investors and other capital markets participants who are interested in behavioral finance, and will offer a basis for further research and advances in this field.

Acknowledgments The financial support of the Tel Aviv Yaffo Academic College in funding the *First Israel Conference in Behavioral Finance* is gratefully acknowledged. I also thank Professor Shlomo Biderman, President, and Professor Israel Borovich, Dean of the School of Business and Economics, at the Tel Aviv Yaffo Academic College for their encouragement and support.

Itzhak Venezia
Tel Aviv Yaffo Academic College
November 2015

List of Contributors

Moty Amar, Ono College, Israel and Duke University

Shahar Ayal, The Interdisciplinary Center (IDC), Herzliya, Israel

Menachem Brenner, New York University

Wolfgang Breuer, Aachen University, Germany

Dan Galai, College for Academic Studies, Or Yehuda and The Hebrew University of Jerusalem

Vincent Glode, University of Pennsylvania

Gregory Gurevich, University of Haifa, Israel

Burton Hollifield, Carnegie Mellon University

Marcin Kacperczyk, Imperial College, London, and NBER

Doron Kliger, University of Haifa, Israel

Shimon Kogan, The Interdisciplinary Center (IDC), Herzliya, Israel, and the University of Texas at Austin

Jana Anette Kollath, Aachen University, Germany

Yoram Kroll, Ono College, Israel and Ruppin Academic Center, Israel

Andrey Kudryavtsev, Yezreel Valley Academic College, Israel

Yevgeny Mugerman, The Hebrew University of Jerusalem

Rüdiger von Nitzsch, Aachen University, Germany

Moran Ofir, The Interdisciplinary Center (IDC), Herzliya, Israel

Na Young Park, Oxford University, U.K.

Zohar Rusou, The Interdisciplinary Center (IDC), Herzliya, Israel and The Open University of Israel

Orly Sade, The Hebrew University of Jerusalem

Astrid Juliane Salzmann, Aachen University, Germany

Smadar Siev, Carmel Academic Center, Israel

Peter L. Swan, University of New South Wales (UNSW). Australia

P. Joakim Westerholm, University of Sydney, Australia

Zvi Wiener, The Hebrew University of Jerusalem

Fernando Zapatero, University of Southern California

Part I

Reference Points

Chapter 1

Reference-Based Decisions in Finance

Fernando Zapatero*

Abstract

We survey a number of financial settings linked by the importance of a reference point in the decision making process. For each of them, we discuss how the reference points affect the decisions. We conclude that it is not a coincidence that reference points are essential to many financial settings. Reference points boost the incentives of the individuals, which we argue is the reason why they are so prevalent. Stronger incentives lead to more effort, which leads to higher achievement and the desire for more reference point-based decisions.

Keywords: Reference point, utility function, incentives, reputation concerns

JEL Classification: D03, D81, G02

1. Introduction

Prospect Theory, developed by Daniel Kahneman and Amos Tversky in a series of papers (mainly Kahneman and Tversky 1979, and Kahneman and Tversky 1992) is one of the most influential theories in Economics, and is the result of many experiments conducted by them and a large number of collaborators. A key component of Prospect Theory is a reference point that, among other things, splits in two different parts, with different properties each, the decision's space of the economic agents. In particular, when wealth is above the reference point, the economic agent is risk-averse; when wealth is below the reference point, the economic agent is risk-loving. However, this is not the only reference point that affects agents' decisions mentioned

*FBE, Marshall School of Business, USC. E-mail: fzapatero@marshall.usc.edu

in the literature. Rabin (1998) offers a few more examples, mainly related to the *utility function* of the individuals. Utility functions are representations of the preferences of the individuals, and as such, individuals are "born" with them, as if they were assigned by "nature." However, in practice, there are reference points that are given by other economic agents — and not just by *nature*. For example, the benchmarks that are established to evaluate the performance of some economic agents: many funds managers are compensated depending on their performance with respect to a given reference point, typically an index of securities; the compensation of some CEOs depends on their performance with respect to some reference point, like an index or the price of the stock of the company they manage on a given date.

It is possible that there is no other connection among these reference points than the fact that they affect economic agents' decisions, but there is no underlying common reason that justifies why, in so many instances in economics decisions, a reference point is a critical factor in the determination of the optimal choice. However, our conjecture is that there is an ultimate explanation why it is efficient for decision making — at least in economics — to use a reference point, whether it is given by *nature*, possibly as a human trait that improves the *fitness* of the individual (as described by Rayo and Becker, 2007) or established by another *principal* because since we humans are used to reference points, it is an efficient way to motivate economic agents.

Throughout the paper, we analyze some of the main reference points studied in the financial literature. We will conclude with some considerations about the importance of reference points in economic decisions. This is a classification of the reference-dependent decisions we will explore in this survey:

- Maximizing individual utility:
  - Habit formation.
  - Relative wealth concerns.
- Incentives from benchmarking performance.
  - Money managers.

- Relative performance evaluation.
  - — Managerial compensation.
  - — Financial analysts.
- Reputation effects.
  - — Star CEOs.
  - — Financial analysts.

Over the next sections, we will discuss the reference points that affect each decision maker. In the case of CEOs, we will briefly overview two different reference points, one determining their performance evaluation, the other reputation or career concerns. We do not intend this classification to be exhaustive or even fully accurate. We propose it as a convenient starting point for the analysis.

2. Habit Formation

Consider standard utility objectives:

$$\max E\left[\sum_{t=0}^{T} \beta^t \frac{c(t)^{1-\gamma}}{1-\gamma}\right],$$

where $c(t)$ represents consumption at time t. In this model, the utility the individual experiences at a given point in time only depends on consumption realized at that time. This is called the *independence* property of expected utility theory. However, a number of scholars have questioned its validity over the years. The particular deviation from the independence property we consider here was first modeled by Pollak (1970), and Ryder and Heal (1973).

In particular, an individual has habit formation — or *internal* habit formation, as opposed to *external* habit formation, in a terminology we will explain later — when utility of the individual at time t depends on consumption at time t compared to previous consumption. By "previous consumption", we mean the history of consumption of the individual up to time t. For tractability, models use some type of average of past consumption. For example, a popular way to model habit formation considers that the objective of the individual is the following:

$$\max E \sum_{t=0}^{T} \left[\beta^t \frac{(c_t - \alpha z_t)^{1-\gamma}}{1-\gamma} \right]$$

where z is often called the *standard of living*, an average of previous consumption,

$$z_t = \sum_{s=0}^{t-1} \rho^{t-s} c_s$$

α is a measure of the importance of past consumption and $\rho < 1$ is a measure of the *memory* about past consumption, so that the smaller ρ, the more relevant is recent consumption in calculating the average.

The average of past consumption $-z$ in the previous model — is the *reference point*: the value of the contribution of current consumption to utility depends on z. The intuition is straightforward. Take for example two individuals with the same utility function, and both consume an identical amount (say we can measure it as 50) this period (t). Standard utility theory would assign the same value to their utility for the current period t. According to standard utility theory, their previous consumption is irrelevant in the determination of their utility at t. Suppose, though, that one of the individuals is used to a high level of utility in the past (say an average of 100) so that this period is consuming substantially below that level because of a business failure. On the other hand, the other individual was used to a level of consumption lower than the current (say 20), but has received a big promotion that makes the higher consumption possible. Habit formation accounts for the change and assigns a higher level of utility to the second individual.

The notion of habit formation has solid foundations in psychology. In particular, habit formation and the way we model habit formation in finance is closely related to some facts established by psychologists about adaptation. There is plenty of evidence from the research in psychology that the human being is very *adaptive*: Frederick and Loewenstein (1999) analyze the concept of *hedonic adaptation* or "adaptation to stimuli that are affectively relevant" (definition of the authors). Hedonic adaptation happens in both "favorable and unfavorable" circumstances. Hedonic adaptation is pervasive — if not uniform, across people, as Frederick and Loewenstein (1999) discuss. For example, when people experience a positive event in their lives, like a large monetary award as result of winning a lottery, in general, they experience an immediate increase in *happiness*, but it is short-lived, and after a while, they go back to a level of happiness comparable to before the favorable event.[1] The symmetric case is similar: after some unfavorable event, people experience an immediate drop in happiness, maybe associated with depression, for example, but the majority of individuals bounce back after a period of time and recover a level of satisfaction comparable to the one they were enjoying before the event. We also note that adaptation is an efficient way to process information. As Frederick and Lowenstein (1999) state, it "enhances perception by heightening the signal value of changes from the baseline level". The connection to the notion of habit formation we introduced before is straightforward. The formula for z in the habit formation utility described above is a variation of what psychologists call *adaptation level* in terminology introduced by Helson (1947). The difference between the current level of *stimulus* — consumption in our model of habit formation — and the adaptation level is called *hedonic state*, and would correspond to the argument of our utility function.

Habit formation became popular in finance as a possible way to explain some empirical regularities that appeared to be at odds with the predictions of standard utility models. In particular, Mehra and Prescott (1985), in a thought-provoking and very influential paper, showed that the *equity premium* (or difference in return between stocks and bonds) observed from many decades until their study, could not be explained with standard utility unless the degree of risk-aversion of the individuals were unreasonably high.[2] This observation — for which there is not a consensus explanation yet — was called the *equity premium puzzle*, and a large amount of work

[1]Over the last decades, the use of surveys to measure individuals' levels of well-being has exploded. The development of the methodology has reached a point where the majority of scholars accepts and uses the results. See, for example, Kahneman and Krueger (2006) for a survey.

[2]Standard models in macroeconomics and finance use for their analysis degrees of risk aversion ranging between 1 and 10 — the latter is probably already too high. According to Mehra and Prescott (1985), only a risk aversion as 30 or higher could even start to address the size of the equity premium.

has been devoted to try to explain it from the moment Mehra and Prescott (1985) was published. One of the avenues explored in the literature has been habit formation. In particular, Constantinides (1990) studied the possible effects of habit formation on the equity premium and showed that it could help explain the puzzle. On the other hand, Detemple and Zapatero (1992) showed in an equilibrium setting that habit formation could make easier, but also harder, to explain the equity premium puzzle, depending on the specific interaction between consumption and the standard of living z defined before.

Another empirical puzzle around the same time that Mehra and Prescott came up with the equity premium puzzle was the *excess smoothness of consumption.* This refers to the fact that consumption is smooth compared to income. It is a puzzle since income finances consumption, however, for some reason, economic agents' consumption does not fully react to changes (upwards or downwards) in income. This had been known for decades, and addressed through the theory of *permanent income* — individuals use a reference income, the permanent income, to make purchase decision. However, Deaton (1987) showed that this theory did not match the data, and left the question of what explains smoothness of consumption open. Sundaresan (1989) argued that habit forming individual utilities could be an explanation. Certainly, it is a property of habit formation that the individual will not fully react to an increase in income because of the effect it will have on the future standard of living z, given that if it grows too much, it will make harder to keep utility high.

Campbell and Cochrane (1999), in a very influential paper as well, introduce a version of habit formation in an attempt to explain the equity premium puzzle, along with other properties of security prices that the literature had unveiled over that decade: given the large number of attempts to solve the equity premium puzzle, researchers started to look for other properties that the many models proposed should have in order to be credible. For example, historically, interest rates have been low and relatively not volatile. Campbell and Cochrane (1999) consider a representative agent model with habit formation and stochastic risk aversion. The stochastic risk aversion would be the result of aggregating over a population of individuals with different degrees of risk aversion, as shown by Chan and Kogan (2002). Campbell and Cochrane (1999) show the properties that the resulting stochastic discount factor should have to explain all the empirical properties required by the literature. However, Xiouros and Zapatero (2010) show that the parameter values the Campbell and Cochrane (1999) model requires for their representative agent are not supported by the data on individual choices.

In summary, habit formation has received a fair amount of attention in the literature; however, it has failed to be embraced as a first order property of preferences that needs to be including in existing models. At this point, it seems clear that habit formation alone cannot explain a full set of properties of security prices. However, there are many decisions (economic and otherwise) we observe frequently among individuals that are difficult to reconcile with standard utility theory, but fully consistent with habit formation. We have sketched the connection between the economic theory of habit formation and the psychological studies on adaptability. As we argued before, Frederick and Lowenstein (1999) contend that adaptability increases the value of a signal with respect to the reference baseline. The equivalent to that statement in an economic interpretation of habit formation is that habit formation increases the marginal utility of consumption: when the agent gets used to a new level of consumption, the motivation to increase consumption above that level (the marginal utility) increases. Marginal utility is the driver that moves agents to invest money or effort on achieving an extra unit of consumption. How can we explain that many successful entrepreneurs, writers, academics (to mention some examples) keep working as hard as if they were just starting their careers? Fast adaptation (or habit formation) that quickly gets them used to the current level of success and motivates them to work to achieve the next level — as with habit forming utilities — would explain a behavior that seems at odds with standard utility theory.

3. Relative Wealth Concerns

This expression encompasses a number of utility representations and individuals' decision patterns characterized by the the motivation to compete in an economic sense with a reference person or group of persons. In particular, we include here the preferences popularly known as "keeping up with the Joneses". The idea behind this type of preferences is that individuals derive utility from their consumption or wealth compared to the consumption or wealth of the reference group. The latter is a *reference point* that will affect the economic decisions of the individuals who display this type of preferences. This reference group could be neighbors, coworkers, relatives, etc., we elaborate more on this later. More explicitly, with keeping up with the Joneses preferences, individuals experience lower satisfaction for a given level of wealth or consumption the higher is the wealth or consumption of the reference group. In an experiment verified multiple times, participants in a survey are asked whether they would prefer an income (in real terms) of $60,000 in a setting in which the average income is $70,000 or an income of $40,000 in a setting in which the average income is $30,000. Overwhelmingly, the response of the participants is that they would prefer the latter (Solnick and Hemenway 1998). This is at odds with standard utility theory according to which more is always preferable, unconditionally. An earlier paper by Easterlin (1974) conducts an analysis of the level of happiness of Japanese citizens over decades of dramatic economic growth, and argues that the level of happiness has not changed substantially because the relative wealth of most of the people has not changed, despite substantial increases in absolute wealth. Overall, there is overwhelming evidence that relative wealth positioning is a primary determinant of people's happiness.

A possible formalization of a utility function that displays relative wealth concerns is as follows,

$$E\frac{c^{1-\gamma}}{1-\gamma}C^{\alpha}$$

where c is the consumption of the investor, C is the consumption of the *peers*, γ is the risk-aversion, as in the standard expected utility specification, and α measures the *strength* of the relative wealth concerns; it is the keeping up with the Joneses parameter. In the previous specification, C would be the reference point — as z, the standard of living is in the case of utility with habit formation. As in the case of habit formation, the larger the consumption of the peers, the higher the marginal utility of the investor.[3]

[3]The specification of Campbell and Cochrane (1999) we discussed before consists of a representative agent and, therefore, implies both habit formation and relative wealth concerns because the aggregate consumption can be interpreted both as an indicator of

Abel (1990) introduces the notion of relative wealth concerns in academic finance, also as a possible answer to some of the questions finance research was trying to solve at the time, like the equity premium puzzle we discussed before.[4] That research is contemporaneous to the work on habit formation we discussed in the previous section. Keeping up with the Joneses preferences and habit formation were considered as alternative explanations. Campbell and Cochrane (1999) merged both notions. The theory on relative wealth or consumption concerns is very old. Duesenberry (1949) makes relative consumption concerns a central topic of his book *the Theory of Consumer Behavior.* More recently, Robert Frank, in a number of thought-provoking books and papers discusses the reasons and implications of "keeping up with the Joneses" behavior (*Choosing the Right Pond*, 1985 is one of them).

A topic related to relative wealth concerns with vast economic implications is *conspicuous consumption.* In particular, the notion that people will consume expensive goods and services as a way to signal to their peers large wealth. If people care about their wealth with respect to that of a peer group, trying to demonstrate high purchasing power seems a natural consequence. Discussion over the signaling effects of conspicuous consumption is very old, and we already find it in Adam Smith: "A creditable day-labourer would be ashamed to appear in public without a linen shirt, the want of which would be supposed to denote that disgraceful degree of poverty which, it is presumed, nobody can well fall into without extreme bad conduct." Veblen, in his influential book *The Theory of the Leisure Class* (1899), actually introduces the notion of conspicuous consumption. Frank (2008) describes the competition to signal more wealth through positional goods as an "arms race" that leads families to own larger and larger houses, even if that means substantially larger commutes for a few additional square feet that do not compensate for all the time wasted. Charles, Hurst and Roussanov (2009) study different patterns of conspicuous consumption across different ethnic groups in the US but conclude that they are mostly due to differences in income. Lower income groups are more likely to

---

previous consumption of the agent and the average consumption of the peers. Some people use now the terminology *internal* habit formation to denote the former and *external* habit formation for the latter.

[4]Galí (1994) introduces the specific type of utility function we presented above.

spend on traditional conspicuous consumption items like clothes, jewelry and cars.

One recent strand of the financial literature on relative wealth concerns has focused on possible implications of these preferences for the cross-section of stock returns — one of the questions that has attracted the most financial research in the last 25 years. The underlying idea is that investors who care about their wealth level in comparison to other investors will choose securities that help them to keep up with their reference group. For example, an investor with keeping up with the Joneses preferences will optimally buy a security whose return is positively correlated with the wealth of the reference group, as it would be the case with the stock of the company that employs a number of people in the reference group. These choices will affect the demand of particular securities and, through that equilibrium, prices of the securities. In particular, in equilibrium, relative wealth concerns give rise to a multifactor pricing model, where one factor is the market portfolio (as in standard CAPM) and the other factors are the value of the different wealth variables individuals care about. For example, Gómez, Priestley and Zapatero (2009) show that if we consider US and UK investors in a model in which US investors have concerns relative to the average US investor (but not the UK investor), and similarly UK investors with respect to other UK investors, in equilibrium a three-factor model obtains, where the factors are the world market portfolio, the wealth (labor income is the variable used in the paper) of the US investors, and the wealth of UK investors. This is verified at the domestic level for different regions within the US in Gómez, Priestley and Zapatero (2014). This work shows that relative wealth concerns help explain the relation between the cross-section of stock returns and labor income traditionally observed in the literature (for example, Jagannathan and Wang, 1996). In addition, this research presents evidence that the "strength" of the relative wealth concerns is higher in areas of lower population density. That is, in areas of lower population density, an influential peer group is neighbors — as opposed to areas of high population density, where it is difficult to identify who "the neighbors" are. Shemesh and Zapatero (2015) verify this by studying patterns of car purchases: the peer pressure to buy a luxury car is stronger the lower the population density. García and Strobl (2011) study how relative wealth concerns can lead to herding in trading strategies, and subsequent small changes in fundamentals can have a large effect on prices, as a large number of investors rebalance their positions.

As in the case of habit formation, there seems to be overwhelming evidence that relative wealth concern is an important factor in individuals' economic decisions. We discussed in the previous section how habit formation is consistent with the motivation of high performing individuals who seem to quickly get used (*adapted*) to their recent success and find the drive to focus intensely on the next challenge. Formally, habit formation implies higher marginal utility which is a measure of the economic value of effort. Notably, keeping up with Joneses preferences display the same property; however, the reason for the increase in marginal utility is not the standard of living, but the consumption or wealth of the peers — as we have discussed, the model of Campbell and Cochrane (1999) can be interpreted as habit formation or keeping up with the Joneses. Individuals find the drive to exert a high level of effort in their attempt to match or exceed the consumption of their peers. The higher the consumption of their peers, the higher the marginal utility of their consumption. Ferrer-i-Carbonell (2005) corroborates the importance of relative wealth concerns and further finds that when individuals experience an increase in their level of wealth that puts them above their reference group, quickly find a reference group with higher wealth which they now aspire to join. Utility and marginal utility remain at a level similar to that before the wealth increase. This mechanism resembles the adaptation process that habit forming utility models try to capture. However, and despite a substantial increase in research on relative wealth concerns, economic and financial models have not yet embraced keeping up with the Joneses preferences as a first order driver of individuals' economic decisions.

4. Benchmarking in Money Management

An increasing proportion of securities (especially stocks and bonds) is in the hands of institutional investors: mutual funds, pension funds, insurance companies and, more recently, hedge funds.[5] In addition, institutional

[5] Blume and Keim (2012) report an estimated 67% of equities in the hands of institutional investors at the end of 2010.

investors are responsible for even a larger proportion of the daily volume of securities trading. The largest class of institutional investors is mutual funds. There are two types of mutual funds, according to their trading strategy: (i) funds that track an index, that is, hold securities in their portfolio with weights similar to their weights in the index, so that the return of the portfolio mimics as closely as possible the return on the index; this is a *passive* strategy; (ii) funds that *actively* manage their assets to achieve the highest possible return. Nevertheless, the performance of active funds in general is evaluated in comparison to some benchmark, typically a broad index like the S&P 500 — the reference point. This has many important implications, both for the investors in the funds, as well as for financial markets — and arguably all the economy. First, let us consider the implications for the investors in the fund. Suppose that individual investors in the mutual fund have objectives that can be approximated by the maximization of the expected value of a concave utility function whose argument is wealth, including the value of the assets in the portfolio. This is the Expected Utility Paradigm. We then observe that the objectives of the mutual fund manager are not perfectly aligned with the objectives of the investor in the mutual fund, because even if the fund manager has a utility function similar to the investors, the wealth of the fund manager depends on performance with respect to the benchmark. It is a case similar to the comparison between standard utility and utility derived from keeping up with the Joneses preferences. The misalignment of incentives creates an *agency* problem. However, unlike in other agency problems, the investor (*the principal*) has no tools to address the agency problem. The only possible decision is whether to invest in the mutual fund or not. With respect to the financial markets, the mutual funds industry is so large, that the incentives of the fund managers have an effect on equilibrium prices. Next, we elaborate further on these problems.

In two very influential papers, Chevalier and Ellison (1997), and Sirri and Tufano (1998) showed that the flow of money coming in and out of actively managed mutual funds follows a convex pattern around the benchmark: when the fund return on a given year exceeds the return of the index (S&P 500), the fund experiences an inflow of money that depends linearly on the spread between the return on the fund and the benchmark. When the fund underperforms the benchmark, no substantial outflow of money takes place.[6] This implies *convex* incentives with respect to the reference point (the benchmark). This is recently confirmed by Ma, Tang and Gómez (2013), who show that the convex flow of funds around the benchmark translates into a similar type of compensation for the asset managers. In summary, as stated before, mutual fund managers care about the performance of their fund with respect to the index. It is important to note that this comparison happens annually, with the evaluation taking place at the end of the calendar year.

A growing body of research in finance is exploring the effects of these incentives on the investment strategy of fund managers, as well as the possible equilibrium implications for prices, especially stock prices. This literature starts with Brennan (1995). Brown, Harlow and Starks (1996) show that benchmarking can lead to perverse incentives by forcing managers who lag close to the end of the evaluation period (calendar year) to take high risks in an attempt to make up for the difference. Basak, Pavlova and Shapiro (2007) develop a theoretical model to analyze in more detail this problem and confirm that the manager who faces benchmarking will optimally engage in strategies that deviate from what would be optimal for the individual investor. Sotes-Paladino (2015) considers the case of a fund manager who has higher ability or information than other fund managers. He shows that the optimal strategy of the manager consists in trading, taking advantage of the superior information, and when the performance is at some reasonable level above the benchmark (the level depends on the risk aversion of the manager), to lock in the difference by tracking the index. Therefore, the best fund managers will show a performance that is above the benchmark, but not dramatically. Performances that exceed the return of the benchmark by a large amount are probably due to high risk-taking and luck, not ability. This is a thought-provoking result that defies the common wisdom in evaluation of mutual funds performance. There is a vast literature on performance evaluation, but it generally ignores the effect of the convex incentives funds managers face. Also, benchmarking might be partially responsible for the *home bias* observed in the trading strategies of many investors, across many countries. This is the pattern first

[6]The actual kink above which the flow of funds has a positive slope does not exactly match the return on the index.

pointed out in French and Poterba (1991), by which the average investor puts a proportion of portfolio holdings in domestic securities that is higher than what would be optimal in order to take advantage of international diversification opportunities. A large number of papers have tried to explain it. Gómez (2007) shows that this could be the result of benchmarking, which provides incentives for fund managers to tilt their portfolios towards domestic securities.

As we have argued, the holdings of hedge funds and mutual funds are very large, and it is not possible to think of security prices properties without considering the possible effects of fund managers' trading strategies. A recent strand of the literature has focused on the equilibrium implications of the convex incentives of asset managers. Gómez and Zapatero (2003) show that benchmarking leads to a type of multifactor model similar to those that result from relative wealth concerns, and we discussed before. Basak and Pavlova (2013) further show that through the positions of institutional investors, benchmarking leads to an increase in the correlation of the stocks in the index (S&P 500). Buffa, Vayanos and Woolley (2014) show that the trading incentives of fund managers can lead them to push prices away from the equilibrium that would prevail in the absence of these incentives. In the same spirit, Sotes-Paladino and Zapatero (2015) show that the convex incentives around a benchmark can lead to skilled (or better informed) managers to overinvest in overpriced securities, further fueling asset bubbles. This problem can arise with mutual funds, but is more pronounced with hedge funds. The motivation for this study is the widely documented fact that mutual funds, and especially hedged funds, were heavily invested in stock of high-tech companies at the peak of the technology bubble of 2000 (see Brunnermeier and Nagel, 2004, for example). This is puzzling because these asset managers are supposed to be highly skilled and it seems unfitting that they were holding overpriced securities. However, as the previous paper shows, one of the perverse effects of the convex incentives is that holding those assets was the optimal strategy of the hedge fund managers, even if they knew were overpriced.

In summary, as we have briefly discussed, benchmarking translate into convex incentives for the fund managers. These can have substantial effects in the trading strategies of the fund managers and in equilibrium prices. This problem has attracted the interest of a growing number of scholars in recent years. However, as with the previous types of reference-based decisions, these features are still not part of standard models, despite the overwhelming evidence that supports their strong influence in security prices and trading patterns. It is also an open question what are the foundations of the prevalence of the use of reference points — which lead to convex incentives — in the evaluation and compensation of fund managers. In principle, convex incentives can lead to a higher level of effort but, as the literature has discussed, they can lead to perverse effects.

5. Executives Reference-Based Decisions

Over the last forty years — after the publication of the path-breaking Jensen and Meckling (1976) paper — a large body of research has been devoted to the analysis of managerial incentives and the design of contracts that can best align the interest of managers and shareholders. Within this area, we briefly discuss two topics that share the relevance of reference-based decision making.

5.1. *Executive Compensation*

Executive compensation epitomizes the problem of incentive design for an agent in a moral hazard setting. The size of large modern corporations, some worth hundreds of billions of dollars, with many thousands of employees and billions of dollars of revenue, along with the power of their managers — especially their CEOs — and their hefty compensation packages, have made executive compensation a central topic in academic research, and a frequent headline grabber in the financial press. The performance of the top officers of public corporations has large implications for shareholders, creditors, suppliers and employees. However, despite decades of debate about the optimal design of their compensation packages, there is not a lot of common ground among the participants in this debate. One of the few points of agreement is the fact that a substantial part of the compensation package should be linked to the performance of the executive. Also, and that is why we mention this topic here, at least part of the performance-based compensation has to depend on a relative measure of performance, or performance of the company compared to some benchmark, the reference point.

Consistent with the previous foundations, compensation of executives generally consists of two parts, a fixed cash amount, and a component whose value fluctuates with some measure of performance (see Murphy, 2012 for an exhaustive survey on executive compensation). The second component can take several forms — often more than one integrate the compensation package. The most frequent are a cash bonus and/or securities whose value is linked to that of the company, namely stocks and options — or *stock-based compensation.*

The bonus rewards the executive for performance. However, corporations live in a dynamic and complex setting, and its profits and value depend on many factors. Management controls, at least partially, some of these factors, but some others are completely exogenous and management cannot do anything about them. It is essential to the spirit of rewarding the performance of the executive to differentiate between the part that is a result of the effort and ability of the manager from the part that is due to favorable or unfavorable market conditions. For example, the company might operate in an industry that is currently affected as a whole in a positive way by a macroeconomic factor like oil price, but it might be under-performing other companies within the industry. It is outside the spirit of the pay for performance principle to compensate the executive for the *windfall profits* resulting from exogenous positive factors, like oil price in the previous example. For this reason, the literature suggests to compensate the executive for *relative* performance. That is, the particular metric of performance, like earnings, or dividends plus share value increase,[7] is compared to an *internal* or *external standard* — using the terminology of Murphy (2000). Internal standard would be, for example, an average of past realizations of that variable for the company itself. An external standard would be the average value for that variable across all firms in the particular industry in which the firm operates. The standard — internal or external — provides a reference point that will affect the decisions of the executive. The hope is that the decisions of the executive will be aligned with the interests of the shareholders. However, even relative performance compensation does not automatically deliver that alignment of incentives. Murphy (2000) analyzes the choice of the standards. Internal standards bear some similarities

[7] See Murphy (2000) for an exhaustive list.

to the individual habit forming preferences we discussed in a previous section. In particular, an individual with habit forming preferences chooses consumption at a given point factoring in the effect that it will have in the future value of the habit, because this value will be the reference for future consumption and will affect future utility. In similar fashion, the executive of a firm whose performance will be measured on how earnings — for example — compare to past earnings, will take into account that very high current earnings will likely raise the future standard and will make it harder to receive a bonus in the future. In this case, incentives are not perfectly aligned with those of the shareholders. In fact, some scholars claim that traditional mechanisms of pay for performance have not achieved their objectives — for example, Bebchuk and Fried (2004). In addition, they suggest ways to improve the relation between pay and performance, and emphasize the use of external standards.

We now discuss the other standard component of executive compensation, equity-based compensation — mainly stock of the company and/or stock options. Typically, the executive receives the stock and options at the beginning of the contractual period. Stock is typically *restricted*, that is, it cannot be sold for a period of time set in the compensation contract. Similarly, the options cannot be exercised until they *vest*, which happens after a period of time similarly determined in the compensation contract, usually shorter than the maturity of the options. Therefore, the number of shares and/or options the executive receives is fixed from the outset. However, their value changes daily. In the case of restricted stock, the current price is a reference point for the decisions of the executive, concerned about its future value, when the stock can be sold. In the case of options, their strike price provides a reference point. The typical strike price is the price of the stock of the company the day the options are granted. However, equity-based compensation consisting of stock and/or plain vanilla options suffers from the problem we discussed before, that it can provide windfall benefits to the executive, even when the executive has not performed well. Bebchuk and Fried (2004), along with other scholars, suggest the use of indexes to differentiate the part of the increase in price of stock or options due to good performance of the executive from the part due to external trends. This suggestion does not appear to have been embraced in practice so far.

The choice of strike price is especially interesting for our overview of reference points in financial decisions. More precisely, we can think of options as a general class of securities that includes stock in the particular case in which the strike price is zero. Following this line of thought, the literature has studied when it would be optimal for the interests of the shareholders to grant options and when stock would be the optimal choice. The arguments of this debate are as follows. Options, by design, make the compensation of the executive convex, since this is the shape of their payoff with respect to the underlying stock. The lower the strike price, the closer is the option to stock, which has a linear payoff. The convexity of the option has two effects on the incentives of the executive. On one hand, as pointed out early on by Ross (2004), the executive becomes effectively more risk-averse: options embed high leverage (equivalent to a position in stock partially financed with a loan) and small changes in the price of the underlying have big effects in the value of the option. This increase in risk-aversion might force the executive to make decisions that are more conservative and maybe provide less value to shareholders. On the other hand, and also because of the convexity of the payoff, options are more *incentive-loaded* than stock. If the executive is successful in the effort applied to the management of the firm, the resulting payoff will be higher from holding options than stock. Arya and Mittendorf (2005) argue that this trade-off allows firms to select *good* executives: only executives who have high ability and are ready to apply a high level of effort will accept a compensation contract that consists of options. For "low type" executives, options will be too risky. Cadenillas, Cvitanić and Zapatero (2012) argue that the risk effect might trump the incentive effect, and stock might be the only equity-based compensation acceptable to the executive. They further study what factors will determine if options are the optimal compensation to select executives and conclude that this will be the case when the firm has very little information about the candidate to the job — for example, the candidate is young and without a track record — in which case the screening becomes more important; the firm will have to grant a high number of options, but it is worth it. Also, options are the optimal compensation, when the expected return for each additional unit of risk undertaken by the executive is relatively low — so that risky decisions are not as attractive, as it might be the case for value firms, as opposed to growth firms.

5.2. *CEO Reputation Concerns*

We include here a brief discussion on *reputation concerns* as we consider them a variation of reference-based decision making. Reputation concerns affect the decisions of executives who try to build or protect that reputation. In general, reputation is an abstract and complex notion that involves many different aspects. However, in the case of executives, there are a few objective and measurable parameters that arguably affect reputation. In particular, performance measures of the firm that employs the executive are important determinants of the reputation of the executive when compared with similar measures of the competitors. The metrics of performance of the competitors become a reference point that will affect the decisions of the executive concerned about reputation.

In an innovative paper, Malmendier and Tate (2009) study the effect on compensation and company performance of becoming a *superstar CEO* — CEOs who have been awarded some type of high-profile *best CEO of the year* award. They conclude that, upon achieving the new status, superstar CEOs receive higher compensation than otherwise similar executives and their companies under-perform. Following up on this line of research, Shemesh (2015) analyzes the decision-making of the superstar CEOs. He finds strong evidence that supports that CEOs' managerial decisions are driven by an attempt to preserve their recently earned status. In particular, the risk-taking of the companies they run — or help to run — shows a type of *reversion to the mean* in which the beta of the company converges to the beta of the industry to which the company belongs, as if the goal of the risk-taking strategy were to rule out the possibility of conspicuous under-performance that might put in question the value of the award just received. The CEO manages firm decisions in a way that protects the reputation of the superstar CEO.

6. Financial Analysts

Financial analyst is a relatively ambiguous term applied to a large number of assignments. Although some of the issues we discuss in this section might apply to the broader interpretation, here we focus on the professionals who work for financial services companies and follow and study corporations, often within a same industry, and issue reports on them, including forecasts on measures of performance as earnings or sales, and buy/sell recommendations, possibly accompanied by a prediction of the future price of the stock. Typical employers of financial analysts are investment banks, brokerage houses (*sell-side*) and mutual funds (*buy-side*). Most of the research and existing data are about sell-side analysts.

There is a vast literature in finance and accounting that studies the characteristics of the information provided by analysts. In fact, some of the literature concludes that a good amount of information provided by financial analysts is not useful. From a research point of view, a factor that makes the work of financial analysts an interesting topic is that some of the information they provide can be objectively evaluated by comparing it to actual data; for example, earnings forecasts, or buy/sell recommendations. In fact, there are publications (press and digital) that compare the accuracy of the different analysts, and select the most successful, like StarMine for buy/sell recommendations (see Kim and Zapatero, 2015 for more details).

The literature has studied for decades patterns of biases in analysts reports and forecasts, as well as potential reasons that could explain these biases. Of special relevance is the conflict of interest that arises when the employer of the analyst has a business relation with a company covered by the analyst. To at least partially address this problem, since 2003, the SEC requires all analysts, (*regulation AC*, as in *analyst certification*) to certify the truthfulness of their statements, as well as to disclose any possible source of a conflict of interest, like compensation received from the company covered or holdings of the stock of that company by their employer.

More recently, the literature has studied a particular type of incentives analysts face. There is plenty of evidence that the performance of analysts is evaluated on a relative basis: the accuracy of analysts' information is compared with that of other analysts. A consequence of this is that the reports and forecasts of other analysts are a *reference point* that influence their reports and forecasts — the timing of the issuance of the forecast becomes a strategic decision, also studied in the literature. More precisely, analysts clearly would like to do better than their competitor analysts by, for example, issuing more accurate forecasts. Furthermore, they want to avoid that their forecasts are worse than those of other analysts. Since analysts are arguably risk-averse, the incentives to out-perform and not under-perform are asymmetric, with the fear to under-perform by a certain distance "stronger" than the desire to out-perform by the same distance — some type of concavity in preferences for over/under-performance. Abstracting from other factors — many of which are also important and are at play frequently — the combination of these two incentives can end up in *herding*. That is, the analysts issue similar forecasts — maybe following the lead of the first analyst to report.[8] Min and Zapatero (2015) show that when the stock is very volatile and, therefore, deviating from the consensus might lead to substantial under-performance — a forecast very different from the true realization — analysts tend to herd and issue similar recommendations — with low dispersion around the consensus — even if the consensus is inconsistent with analysts' expectations.

Another related incentive with somehow opposing effects stems from the different selections of *star analysts* conducted by some of the trade publications. We mentioned before the case of StarMine — now part of Thomson Reuters — that every year names the analysts with the most "successful" buy/sell recommendations. StarMine came up with an algorithm of a theoretical investment (long or short positions) on the securities rated by an analyst that would monetize the recommendations of the analyst, from *strong buy* to *strong sell*, and therefore provides an objective measure of the accuracy of the predictions.[9] These awards are widely followed, and have a large and positive impact on the reputation of the analysts who receive them. Therefore, analysts have strong incentives to compete for them. This amounts to another type of *tournament*, as those studied in the applied economics literature, following the path-breaking work of Lazear and Rosen (1981). In the previous paragraph, we have discussed how analysts might have incentives to herd around the consensus. However, issuing recommendations close to the consensus is clearly a sub-optimal strategy for analysts who seek to win the tournament. Min and Zapatero (2015) also study this incentive and show that when the stock is not very volatile (relatively predictable), a possible equilibrium consists of some analysts issuing recommendations very different from the consensus — even if the recommendation is not consistent with the

---

[8]The average of the forecasts is called *the consensus* and the standard deviation around the consensus *the dispersion*.

[9]The algorithm is described in www.starmineawards.com.

expectations of the analyst, a "gamble" can lead to a tournament win by pure luck. Therefore, it is possible to have herding when the stock price is very volatile, and a certain degree of dispersion when it is predictable. To be noted, dispersion around the consensus is used some times as an indicator of volatility, but the incentives just discussed bring up another possible interpretation of dispersion — Kim and Zapatero (2015) find in general empirical support for the interpretation resulting from relative performance concerns, except in periods of recession.

As is the case for CEOs, *reputation* is a very important asset for financial analysts and many decisions are guided by the objective to improve it or at least not erode it. In fact, some of our previous discussion about herding to avoid under-performing other analysts, can be attributed to reputational concerns. We analyze next some recent literature about this particular issue. For example, Aharoni, Shemesh and Zapatero (2015) study earnings forecasts, and show that *All-star analysts*[10] issue more accurate forecasts for stocks covered by other All-star analysts — *battleground stocks* — than for stocks that no other All-star analyst covers. This effect is independent of firm characteristics like size or industry. That paper shows that issuing more accurate forecasts than other star analysts on the stocks simultaneously covered by multiple star analysts is a good predictor of the analyst keeping the status as All-star. Arguably, these analysts put more effort in the stocks that seem to have more weight in the minds of the professionals surveyed to select all-stars.

Another line of research that shows evidence of the importance of reputation concerns documents that financial analysts try to avoid covering volatile stocks. Navone and Zapatero (2015) show that increases in volatility are followed by decreases in the number of analysts who cover a stock. In a recent paper, Pan, Wang and Weisbach (2015) show that stock volatility increases after the announcement of a CEO departure, even when it is due to reasons different from performance. That natural experiment permits to verify that analyst coverage drops substantially, both in economic and statistical sense, after an increase in stock volatility.

---

[10]"All-star" is a distinction granted by the influential publication Institutional Investor based on a survey they conduct among hundreds of professionals.

7. Conclusions

Since the work of Kahneman and Tversky (1979, 1992) and their development of Prospect Theory, a large amount of research has been devoted to the analysis of the reference point at the core of Prospect Theory. Prospect Theory was based on a large number of careful experiments that came up with overwhelming evidence that individual economic decisions depend on the relation between possible outcomes and a reference point. In the same spirit, but with a different approach, we discuss several instances in financial decision making where a relatively well identified reference point is a first order factor in the decision — as opposed to try to identify a specific reference point of universal value, as some of the literature following up on Prospect Theory. In some of the cases we consider the reference point is chosen internally: In what we call habit forming preferences, individuals compare their current level of consumption to past consumption; in the particular models we use, we take an average of past consumption, but in practice, it is up to the individual how to compare current and previous consumption. We can make a similar argument for keeping up with the Joneses preferences. In fact, Ferrer-i-Carbonell (2005) shows that the agents adjust their peer group when their wealth changes — therefore, the reference group is at the discretion of the decision maker. We can extend a similar line of argument to the case of reputation concerns. In other cases, the reference point is exogenous and mostly outside the control of the agent. For example, a substantial part of CEOs compensation is based on performance related to an outside measure, like an index of industry returns; it can also be linked to past performance — for example, sales — but in that case, the index is not completely outside the control of the CEO, since the CEO can target a certain level of sales this year, factoring in that it will be the reference next period. Also exogenous is the index to which the performance of asset managers is compared. Then, we also have cases with a reference that is partially endogenous and partially exogenous. For example, the reference financial analysts use to advance their careers — giving rise to career concerns. They will have to compete against the performance of their peers, which is an exogenous reference. However, depending on the career goals of the analysts, they can choose different measures of performance of their peers (the average performance of other analysts, the performance of the star analysts, performance of the top analyst etc.) Overall, though, as discussed by Frederick and Lowenstein (1999) and Rayo and Becker (2007), reference points provide a baseline that increases the value of the signal associated with the decision of the agent.

References

Abel A.B., 1990, Asset prices under habit formation and catching up with the Joneses, American Economic Review 80, 38–42.

Aharoni, G., Shemesh, J. and F. Zapatero, 2015, Star analysts' Rankings and strategic announcements: The case of battleground stocks, working paper, University of Southern California.

Arya, A. and B. Mittendorf, 2005, Offering stock options to gauge managerial talent, Journal of Accounting and Economics 40, 189–210.

Basak, S. and A. Pavlova, 2013, Asset prices and institutional investors, American Economic Review 103, 1728–1758.

Basak, S., Pavlova, A. and A. Shapiro, 2007, Optimal asset allocation and risk shifting in money management, Review of Financial Studies 20, 1583–1621.

Blume, M. and D. Keim, 2012, Institutional investors and stock market liquidity: Trends and relationships, working paper, University of Pennsylvania.

Bebchuk, L. and J. Fried, 2004, Pay without performance: The unfulfilled promise of executive compensation, Harvard University Press, Cambridge, MA.

Brennan, M., 1995, The individual investor, Journal of Financial Research 1, 59–74.

Brown, K., Harlow, W. and L. Starks, 1996, Of tournaments and temptations: An analysis of managerial incentives in the mutual fund industry, Journal of Finance 51, 85–110.

Brunnermeier, M. and S. Nagel, 2004, Hedge funds and the technology bubble, Journal of Finance 59, 2013–2040.

Buffa, A., Vayanos, D. and P. Woolley, 2014, Asset management contracts and equilibrium prices, working paper, London School of Economics.

Cadenillas, A., Cvitanić, J. and F. Zapatero, 2012, Executive stock options as a screening mechanism, working paper, University of Southern California.

Campbell, J., 1996, Understanding risk and return, Journal of Political Economy 104, 298–345.

Campbell, J. and J. Cochrane, 1999, By force of habit: A consumption-based explanation of aggregate stock market behavior, Journal of Political Economy 107, 205–251.

Chan, Y. and L. Kogan, 2002, Catching up with the Joneses: Heterogeneous preferences and the dynamics of asset prices, Journal of Political Economy 110, 1255–1285.

Chevalier, J., and G. Ellison, 1997, Risk taking by mutual funds as a response to incentives, Journal of Political Economy 105, 1167–1200.

Constantinides, G., 1990, Habit formation: A resolution of the equity premium puzzle, Journal of Political Economy 98, 519–543.

Deaton, A., 1987, Life-cycle models of consumption: is the evidence consistent with the theory?" in Advances in Econometrics, Vol II, T. Bewley ed., North-Holland, Amsterdam.

Detemple, J. and F. Zapatero, 1991, Asset pricing in an exchange economy with habit formation, Econometrica 59, 1633–1657.

Duesenberry, J., 1949, Income, Saving and the Theory of Consumer Behavior, Harvard University Press, Cambridge, MA.

Easterlin, R., 1974, Does economic growth improve the human lot?" in Nations and Households in Economic Growth: Essays in Honor of Moses Abramovitz, P. David and M. Reder eds., Academic Press, Inc., New York.

Ferrer-i-Carbonell, A., 2005, Income and well-being: an empirical analysis of the comparison income effect, Journal of Public Economics 89, 997–1019.

Frank, R., 1985, Choosing the right pond: Human behavior and the quest for status, Oxford University Press, New York.

Frank, R., 2008, Should public policy respond to positional externalities?, Journal of Public Economics 92, 1777–1786.

Frederick, S. and G. Loewenstein, G., 1999, Hedonic adaptation, in Well-being: The foundations of hedonic psychology, D. Kahneman, E. Diener, and N. Schwarz eds., Russell Sage Foundation, New York.

French, K. and J. Poterba, 1991, lnvestor diversification and international equity markets, American Economic Review, Papers and Proceedings, 222–226.

Galí, J, 1994, Keeping up with the Joneses: Consumption externalities, portfolio choice, and asset prices, Journal of Money, Credit and Banking 26, 1–8.

García, D. and G. Strobl, 2011, Relative wealth concerns and complementarities in information acquisition, Review of Financial Studies 24, 169–207.

Gómez, J-P., 2007, The impact of keeping up with the Joneses behavior on asset prices and portfolio choice, Finance Research Letters, Volume 4, Issue 2, 95–103.

Gómez, J-P., Priestley, R. and F. Zapatero, 2009, Implications of keeping up with the Joneses behavior for the equilibrium cross-section of stock returns: International evidence, Journal of Finance 64, 2703–2737.

Gómez, J-P., Priestley, R. and F. Zapatero, 2014, Labor income, relative wealth concerns, and the cross-section of stock returns, Journal of Financial and Quantitative Analysis, forthcoming.

Gómez, J-P., and F. Zapatero, 2003, Asset pricing implications of benchmarking: A two-factor CAPM, European Journal of Finance 9, 343–357.

Helson H., 1947, Adaptation level as frame of reference for prediction of psychophysical data, American Journal of Psychology 60, 1–29.

Jagannathan, R. and Z.Wang, 1996, The conditional CAPM and the cross-section of expected returns, Journal of Finance 51, 3–53.

Jensen, M. and W. Meckling, 1976, Theory of the firm: Managerial behavior, agency costs and ownership structure, Journal of Financial Economics 3, 305–360.

Kahneman, D. and A. Krueger, 2006, Developments in the measurement of subjective well-being, Journal of Economic Perspectives 20, 3–24.

Kahneman, D. and A. Tversky, 1979, Prospect Theory: An analysis of decision under risk , Econometrica 47, 263–291.

Kahneman, D. and A. Tversky, 1992, Advances in prospect theory: Cumulative representation of uncertainty, Journal of Risk and Uncertainty 5, 297–323.

Kim, M. and F. Zapatero, 2015, The distorting incentives of relative performance evaluation for equity analysts, working paper, University of Southern California.

Lazear, E. and S. Rosen, 1981, Rank-order tournaments as optimum labor contracts, Journal of Political Economy 89, 841–864.

Ma, L., Tang, Y. and J-P. Gómez, 2015, Portfolio manager compensation in the U.S. mutual fund industry, working paper, IE Business School.

Malmendier, U. and G. Tate, 2009, CEO overconfidence and corporate investment, Journal of Finance 60, 2661–2700.

Mehra, R. and E. Prescott, 1985, The equity premium: A puzzle, Journal of Monetary Economics 15, 145–161.

Murphy, K. J., 2000, Performance standards in incentive contracts, Journal of Accounting and Economics 30, 245–278.

Murphy, K. J., 2012, Executive compensation: Where we are, and how we got there, in Handbook of the Economics of Finance, G. Constantinides, M. Harris and R. Stulz eds., Elsevier Science, North Holland.

Navone, M. and F. Zapatero, 2015, Uncertainty, reputation and analysts coverage, working paper, University of Southern California.

Pan, Y., Wang, T. and M. Weisbach, 2015, Learning about CEO ability and stock return volatility, Review of Financial Studies 28 1623–1666.

Pollak, R., 1970, Habit formation and dynamic demand functions, Journal of Political Economy 78, 745–763.

Rabin, M., 1998, Psychology and Economics, Journal of Economic Literature 36, 11–46.

Rayo, L. and G. Becker, 2007, Evolutionary efficiency and happiness, Journal of Political Economy 115, 302–337.

Ross, S., 2004, Compensation, incentives, and the duality of risk aversion and riskiness, Journal of Finance 59, 207–225.

Ryder, H. and G. Heal, 1973, Optimal growth with intertemporally dependent preferences, Review of Economic Studies 40, 1–31.

Shemesh, J., 2015, CEO Social Status and Risk-Taking, working paper, University of Melbourne.

Shemesh, J. and F. Zapatero, 2015, The intensity of keeping up with the Joneses behavior: Evidence from neighbor effects in car purchases, working paper, University of Southern California.

Sirri, E. and P. Tufano, 1998, Costly search and mutual fund flows, Journal of Finance 53, 1589–1622.

Solnick, S. and D. Hemenway, 1998, Is more always better?: A survey on positional concerns, Journal of Economic Behavior and Organization 37, 373–383.

Sotes-Paladino, J., 2015, Should we expect skilled managers to be stars? (dis)incentive effects of fund flows in money management, working paper, University of Melbourne.

Sotes-Paladino, J. and F. Zapatero, 2015, Riding the bubble with convez incentives, working paper, University of Southern California.

Sundaresan, S., 1989, Intertemporally dependent preferences and the volatility of consumption and wealth, Review of Financial Studies 2, 73–89.

Veblen, T., 1899, The theory of the leisure class: An economic study of institutions, MacMillan, New York.

Xiouros, C. and F. Zapatero, 2010, The representative agent of an economy with external habit-formation and heterogeneous risk-aversion, Review of Financial Studies 23, 3017–3047.

Part II

Professionalism and Sophistication Effects in Finance

Chapter 2

Individuals Investment in Financial Structured Products from Rational and Behavioral Choice Perspectives

Moran Ofir* and Zvi Wiener†

Abstract

Structured products (SP) are synthetic investment instruments specially designed to meet specific needs that cannot be met by acquiring standard financial instruments available in the markets. We argue that many SP currently available to retail investors are designed to exploit several behavioral biases including: loss aversion, the disposition effects, herd behavior, the ostrich effect and the hindsight bias. We perform an experiment that examines investor decision-making in relation to SP investments. Our findings demonstrate that investors tend to be affected by these behavioral biases, which favor SP investments. Accordingly, regulation dealing specifically with SP may be warranted to improve investor protection. We offer a regulation that would compel issuers to reveal the effective fees they charge investors. In disclosing the effective fees, investors will be able to improve their decisions and will be able to evaluate the costs of their behavioral biases.

Keywords: Structured products, behavioral finance, retail investors, sophistication, securities regulation

JEL Classification: D19, G18, K22

*Radzyner School of Law, The Interdisciplinary Center Herzliya, Israel, Corresponding author, e-mail: mofir@idc.ac.il.

†The School of Business Administration, The Hebrew University of Jerusalem, Israel, e-mail: zvi.wiener@huji.ac.il

1. Introduction

Financial innovations have resulted in a variety of complex and innovative financial instruments being offered in the retail marketplace. One type of these innovative financial instruments is structured products. Structured products are pre-packaged financial instruments comprising securities and derivatives bundled into a single derivative instrument. One of the key characteristics of structured products is that the return is determined by a pre-specified formula, which sets out the product's performance in any possible future scenario. Unlike mutual and other types of investment funds, the outcome of a structured product is not a function of on-going active investment.

The structured products were first sold in the U.S. in the 1980s,[1] but the market has grown significantly over the last decade. Large retail markets for structured products exist in all major European countries as well as in North America, Asia, Australia and New Zealand. Structured products have also been introduced in many emerging markets such as Eastern Europe and South Africa[2]. Investors in structured products range from retail investors to individuals, institutional investors, and corporations.

Derivatives constitute an essential ingredient of any structured product, since they enable the customization of return profiles. Accordingly, investment banks active in derivative markets have traditionally driven new product development and have provided retail product vendors the ability to hedge exposure when new products are launched. These include retail banks, building societies, and fund managers, which market financial products either directly to existing customers or via third-party distributors such as financial advisors.

In this paper we focus on retail investors. We define them as individual investors who buy and sell securities for their personal account, and not for another company or organization. Campbell (2006) argues that mistakes in financial decision making are central in the field of household finance. An interesting fact on the structured products market is that about three-fifth of the $68.1 billion structured products sold in 2008 in the U.S. were bought

---

[1] Source: StructuredInvestment.com

[2] Source: Structured Retail Products

by individual investors.[3] The high participation rate of retail investors in the structured products market and their imperfect rationality lead us to focus our analysis on this group of market participates.

While structures contribute to the completeness of modern financial markets by enhancing alternatives open to investors, they have a downside as well. Analyzing typical structured product by figuring out the underlying financial assets and pricing them, demonstrates a transfer of riskless wealth from the investors to the issuers. Section 3 of the paper demonstrates the transfer of wealth from the investor to the issuer for typical structured product.

Figuring out the transfer of riskless wealth, the explanation for the consistent growth of this market cannot be deduced from the neoclassical economic theory. We argue that most structured products available on the market are designed to exploit a number of common behavioral biases observed in the area of decision-making under uncertainty.

We identify several features of structured products, and show how these are associated with specific behavioral biases. The insights are derived from theories associated with various aspects of decision theory: loss aversion, the disposition effect, herd behavior, the ostrich effect and hindsight bias. Section 4 of the paper analyzes the relation between the identified features and the behavioral biases. In this section, we also summarize the existing literature on the chosen behavioral biases. Appendix B summarizes selected structure features and the corresponding behavioral biases.

To examine investor decision-making in relation to the investment in structured products, we conduct an experiment. The experiment tests each bias individually to determine whether investors are influenced by a given bias to such an extent that they favor investment in a structured product over another beneficial alternative. Section 5 of the paper describes the experiment and its results. The experiment is provided in Appendix C.

Following the experiment results, we argue that specific regulation for structured products could be warranted in order to protect investors if the experiment results demonstrate a significant influence of the behavioral biases on investors' decisions. In Section 6 of the paper, we discuss the policy

[3]Source: Bloomberg.

implications of our finding, provide concluding remarks and particularly, offer a specific regulation.

2. Background

Structured products have no exact definition, neither in a business context nor in a regulatory context. U.S. regulators such as the U.S. Securities and Exchange Commission (SEC)[4] and the Financial Industry Regulatory Authority (FINRA)[5] employ a broad definition. Under this definition, a *structured security* is a security derived from or based on another security, basket of securities, index, commodity, or foreign currency. This definition covers a wide range of products, including equity-linked or commodity-linked debt, collateralized debt obligations (CDO), reverse convertibles, and credit-default swaps (CDS).

The European Union's Markets in Financial Instruments Directive (MiFID) defines the concept of 'complex' vs. 'non-complex' financial instruments'. A non-complex product is a liquid investment, which does not comprise any actual or potential liability which exceeds the cost of the instrument and for which adequate information about is publicly available.[6] Any securities not meeting these criteria are considered 'complex' instruments. While this categorically includes all types of non-negotiable securities it also includes derivatives as well as debt instruments with embedded derivatives. European legislation does not offer an exact definition to structured product.

Interest in structured products as a method of portfolio diversification and as a sole investment has grown in the last decade. The global invested assets in structured products between the years 2005–2010 is demonstrated in Figure 1[7].

As demonstrated in Figure 1, the global market experienced a massive growth until 2008. The recent financial crisis influenced the global invested assets in structured products and changed the trend to zero growth in 2009.

---

[4] SEC Rule 434.

[5] FINRA Regulatory Notice 08–81; NASD (National Association of Securities Dealers, now FINRA) Notice to Members 05–59.

[6] MiFID, Article 39.

[7] Source: Structured Retail Products. The Americas data includes the USA, Canada and Latin America.

Figure 1:

In 2010, the market continues to grow and partial evidence for 2011 are showing growing trend as well. Moreover, the European market holds the most significant size of invested assets; in most of the years, the size of the Americas market was approximately one-third of the European market size.

Exchange-traded structures constitute one segment of the structured products market; another important segment is the non-negotiable structures market, distributed primarily by investment and commercial banks. Financial services firms are selling structured products that are wrapped in certificate of deposit. Sales of such products, called "structured CD" or "market-linked CD" have increased in the U.S., especially following Lehman Brothers' bankruptcy.

As debt instruments that use derivatives to achieve various investment objectives, structured products are dependent on the creditworthiness of the issuing firms. In the event of a default, holders of structured products fall in line along with all other creditors. By placing certain structured products strategies inside CDs, the investment is insured in the U.S., like any other bank deposit by the Federal Deposit Insurance Corporation (FDIC).

Standard financial theory is built on the premise that all investors are indifferent among financial products that have identical cash flows. Shefrin and Statman (1993) were the first to apply the idea of combining concepts of arbitrage-theory and behavioral finance when examining a covered-call position (a combination of a stock and a short position in corresponding call option). They show that some of the design features of a covered call are preferable to alternatives with identical cash flows. In general, Shefrin and Statman (1993) argue that investors are not indifferent to the frames of cash flows and propose a behaviorally based framework for the design of financial products. They suggest that behavioral considerations are indispensable in the design of financial products.

Most existing literature of structured products concentrates on pricing issues and not on the investment behavior related to them. Burth *et al.* (2001) analyze the initial pricing of 275 structured products in the Swiss market by comparing them to equivalent strategies in the underlying markets. They find substantial price distortions in favor of the issuing institutions across the various segments of the Swiss structured products market. They also find significant pricing differences between products paying a fixed coupon and those without such a coupon. Structured products with a coupon payment are substantially more mispriced than those without a coupon. An explanation they offer for this finding is that investors may be attracted by the bond-like appearance of products paying a fixed coupon and are therefore ready to pay an additional premium for them.

In addition, Wilkens *et al.* (2003) compare quoted prices of a special class of structured products (reverse convertibles and discount certificates) with the cost of duplicating strategies using exchange-traded options in the German market. They find a strong pricing bias favoring the structures products sellers.

Stimeonov and Wilkens (2005) examine the pricing of equity-linked structured products in the German market. They compared the daily closing prices of a large variety of structured products to the theoretical values derived from the prices of traded options. They find, for the majority of the products, large implicit premiums charged by the issuers of the structured products. Their results suggest that, in the primary market, all types of equity-linked structured products are, on average, priced above their theoretical values and thus favor the issuing institution. The overpricing varies with underlying and product type. In general, more complex products incorporate higher implicit premiums. For example, products with embedded exotic options are subject to even higher premiums, compared to common 'classic' products. In the secondary market, they find that the diagnosed overpricing decreases as the products approach maturity.

Benet *et al.* (2006) focus on reverse-exchangeable securities (RES). They undertake a replication of RES payout with a linear combination of primary securities in order to estimate theoretically "fair" terms of issuance, and contrast these with actual terms. They find a significant pricing bias in favor of the issuing financial institution. More precisely, they show that customers may not be properly rewarded for the volatility risk they bear. Thereby RES coupon rates appear to be set as if these were principally fixed-income products, under-valuing embedded contingent claims features.

Henderson and Pearson (2011) analyze the pricing and expected return of 64 issues of a popular structured equity product in the U.S. Their pricing result imply that, on average, purchasers of the products lock in negative abnormal returns of at least 8% per year relative to the dynamically adjusted portfolio of the underlying stock and bonds with the same risk. The negative abnormal return they find is large enough that under reasonable assumptions about the expected returns of the underlying assets, the mean of the estimates of the expected returns on the structured products is less than zero. They argue that given that the products returns covary positively with the broad market indexes and that the products do not appear to offer tax, liquidity, or other benefits, it is difficult to rationalize their purchase by informed rational investors.

As far as we know, only a very limited number of papers deal with investment behavior related to structured products. Breuer and Perst (2007) analyze discount reverse convertibles (DRC) and reverse convertible bonds (RCB) (both can be interpreted as a combination of a zero coupon bond or a coupon bond with a short position in put options on stocks) by applying cumulative prospect theory and hedonic framing as an example of structured products from a boundedly rational investor's point of view. They find that these structured products are of interest to investors who moderately estimate the expected return of the underlying stock and who underestimate the corresponding return volatility.

Döbeli and Vanini (2010) analyze the investment behavior of retail investors with regard to structured products by using a questionnaire and a field experiment. The real product issued in their field experiment is comparable to the hypothetical product in their questionnaire. They find that the questionnaire participants, on average, behave in a consistent manner within the behavioral finance model and do not behave in accordance with expected utility theory. They focus on the framing effect, and in particular, they find that the description of the structured product in an easily understood form increases the percentage of women and first-time buyers compared to structured products that are described in a technical language.

Our paper belongs to this shortlist of papers focused on the investment behavior of retail investors related to structured products. The paper examines the investment behavior associated with several types of structured products by implementing and testing the influence of several behavioral biases on this investment behavior.

3. An Economic Analysis of a Typical Structured Product

As reviewed, several papers deal with the appropriate method for pricing structured products, and trying to find the estimated hidden costs (e.g. Baule and Tallau (2009), Stoimenov and Wilkens (2005), Wilkens *et al.* (2003), and Burth *et al.* (2001)). However, in this part of the paper, we analyze a typical structured product by figuring out the underlying financial assets and pricing them. This process of reverse engineering demonstrates a transfer of riskless wealth from the investors to the issuers.

The typical structured product has two basic ingredients. The first is a bond, which provides a protection to the principal. The second ingredient is an option which provides an upside potential for the investor. The specific ingredients could vary in different structured products; for instance, the option could vary both with respect to the choice of option, and the choice of underlying asset.

The following example illustrates the riskless transfer of wealth from the investor to the issuer for a typical structured product. This structured deposit provides investors equity exposure with limited principal protection. Its description was translated from the website of one of Israel's leading commercial banks as follows:

> "This structured deposit yields a 9.54% interest rate, payable unconditionally after one year. The principal will either be paid in full or converted to "Teva"[8] shares traded on NASDAQ, if the share price declines as follows:

---

[8]Teva Pharmaceutical Industries Ltd. is a global pharmaceutical company specializing in the development, production and marketing of generic and proprietary branded pharmaceuticals as well as active pharmaceutical ingredients. Teva is among the top 15

At maturity the investor will receive a high, unconditional, 9.54% annual interest rate. The principal will be paid in full if at least one of the following does not occur:

1. The share price of Teva Pharamceuticals decreases at least once during the deposit period by 25% or more, relative to the share price set on the day the deposit is opened.
2. The closing share price of Teva Pharmaceuticals on the deposit's maturity date is lower than its price upon the initial opening of the deposit.

Should *both* of the above-mentioned conditions be fulfilled, the principal will be converted into Teva shares according to the deposit's opening-day share price, and the investor will receive the shares and the 9.54% interest on the principal".[9]

This structured product consists of the following underlying assets:

The issuer sells (writes) a one-year knock-in[10] *put option* triggered at a share price 25% lower than the price on the day the option is issued. The premium to this option, according to Bloomberg's stock option calculator is 11.51%.[11] The premium and the principal are invested in twelve-month T-Bills (annual return on the date of issue was 5.16%).

Assuming an investment of US$100,000:

Premium = 11.51% × US$100,000 = US$11,510
Future Value of T-Bills = US$111,510 × 1.0516 = US$117,264

If	Investor	Issuer
PTEVA decreases within the year by 25% or more and if PTEVA at time 1 < PTEVA at time 0	**Shares** + **US$9, 540**	**US$7, 724**
Otherwise	**US$109, 540**	**US$7, 724**

pharmaceutical companies and among the largest generic pharmaceutical companies in the world. Teva's stock is traded in the Nasdaq.

[9]See appendix A for graphic descriptions of this structured product.

[10]A knock-in option is an option that begins to function as a normal option ("knocks in") once a certain price level is reached before expiration.

[11]This option is not traded; therefore the estimated premium can also compute as 0.9*11.51%=10.36%. In this case, the issuer receives US$ 6,514 on every US$ 100,000 invested in the structured product, regardless of the share price at maturity.

The issuer receives the same amount, regardless of the stock price at maturity, which represents a 7.7% effective fee on the funds invested in the structured product. The investor receives 9.54% and depending on share price movements, either the principal or the shares. The latter alternative is triggered upon a substantial decline in share price and incorporates the losses accrued during the deposit period.

4. A Behavioral Analysis of Structured Products

This paper focuses on five features commonly found in structured products, and the behavioral biases associated with them. In this section, we outline these behavioral biases and analyze the relation between each bias and the corresponding feature.

4.1. *Loss Aversion*

Loss aversion refers to the tendency for people strongly to prefer avoiding losses than acquiring gains. A key conclusion of Kahneman and Tversky's (1979) study of decision-making under uncertainty is that choices are best explained by assuming that the significant carriers of utility are not states of wealth, but rather changes relative to a neutral reference point, such as the *status quo*. In the theory they develop, value is assigned to gains and losses rather than to final assets. The value function is concave for gains, convex for losses, and is steeper for losses than for gains. Empirical estimates of loss aversion demonstrate that the perceived disutility of loss is twice as great as the utility of gain (Tversky and Kahneman, 1991).

Myopic loss aversion, as articulated by Benartzi and Thaler (1995), combines two behavioral concepts — loss aversion (Kahneman amd Tversky, 1979) and mental accounting (Thaler, 1985), and describes the process of mental accounting[12] regarding the flow of information, in which individuals tend to be more sensitive to reductions in the level of well-being than to increases. Myopic loss aversion predicts that dynamic aggregation rules influence investor attitudes toward risk. The frequency with which the information is presented can have an impact on the willingness of

[12] Mental accounting, as presented in Benartzi and Thaler (1995), refers to the implicit methods individuals use to code and evaluate financial outcomes.

an investor to undertake risky investments. Frequent reporting leads to a preference for less risky portfolios. While only a few experimental studies have tested the myopic loss aversion theory, the results were all in the same direction. Thaler *et al.* (1997), Gneezy and Potters (1997), and Gneezy, Kapteyn, and Potters (2003) all observe individual behavior consistent with the predictions of the theory.

Structured products are considered by investors as less risky investments, primarily because most promise principal protection. Principal protection enables loss-averting investors to avoid losses and enjoy gains in certain circumstances. Investors, especially retail investors, consider principal protection a very attractive feature, and their decision whether to invest in a structured product is strongly affected by it.

It is well worth noting in this context that principal protection is usually nominal and not real, and it does not carry any compensation for the time value of money. Moreover, in some structured products, the principal protection is in foreign currency which exposes the principal to foreign currency exchange rate risks. In the structured product analyzed in Section 1, the principle protection is under one possible scenario in cash, but under the other possible scenario in shares, purchased for the investors in a higher price than the market price at maturity. In short, principal protection is not necessarily what one would wish it to be, nor perhaps what retail investors assume it to be.

4.2. *The Disposition Effect*

Identified by Kahneman and Tversky (1979), the disposition effect refers to an aversion to loss realization. Shefrin and Statman (1985) examine this feature within the context of financial markets. Specifically, they examine decisions to realize gains and losses in a market setting. They develop a descriptive theory of capital gain and loss realization in which investors tend to "sell winners too early and ride losers too long", relative to the prescriptions of the normative theory. Using evidence that suggests that this tendency applies in real-life financial markets, Shefrin and Statman demonstrate how the tendency to sell winners and ride losers emerges in prospect theory in the following example:

> Consider an investor who purchased a stock one month ago for $50 and who finds that the stock is now selling at $40. The investor must now

decide whether to realize the loss or hold the stock for one more period. To simplify the discussion, assume that there are no taxes or transaction costs. In addition, suppose that one of two equiprobable outcomes will emerge during the coming period: either the stock will increase in price by $10 or decrease in price by $10. According to prospect theory, our investor frames his choice as a choice between the following two lotteries:

A. Sell the stock now and realize a $10 loss.
B. Hold the stock for one more period, given 50-50 odds between losing an additional $10 or "breaking even".

Since the choice between these lotteries is associated with the convex portion of the S-shaped value function, prospect theory implies that B will be selected over A. That is, the investor will ride his losing stock. An analogous argument demonstrates how prospect theory accounts for a propensity towards profit-taking.

In our research, the relevant behavioral phenomenon is the aversion to loss realization, or in other words, the disposition to "ride losers", as presented in the numerical example. Many structured products include mandatory conversion provisions. Conversion is triggered when the price of the underlying asset falls past a predetermined threshold during the investment period. If the price does not cross this threshold, the investor receives the principal plus a relatively high return. The conversion into the "losing" asset typically reflects a higher price (i.e., the market price at time of issue) than the market price of the asset at the time of the structured product's maturity.

The mandatory conversion feature is activated by the investor tendencies to "ride losers" because the conversion into "losing" assets puts off the realization of losses. Investors will continue to ride the losing asset in the near future and will not realize the loss caused by the investment in the structured product. For instance, in the structured product analyzed in Section 1, the mandatory conversion provision leads to a "purchase" of "Teva" shares at a higher price than the market price at maturity. Investors tend to continue holding the "losing" shares after the structured product matures. This behavior enables then to avoid the loss realization.

4.3. *Herd Behavior*

Herd behavior can explain the phenomenon of large numbers of people acting in the same way at the same time. Large stock market trends, bubbles, and crashes often begin and end with periods in which a large number of investors buy or sell stocks. Individual investors join the crowd of others in a rush to enter or exit the market.

The literature on herd behavior is extensive. Leibenstein (1950) defines it as the extent to which the demand for an asset is increased due to the fact that others also purchase the asset. He explains the motivations underlying herd behavior as "the desire of people to purchase a commodity in order to get into 'the swim of things'; in order to conform with the people they wish to be associated with; in order to be fashionable or stylish; or, in order to appear to be 'one of the boys.'"

Herd behavior is also explained in terms of a network effect. The network effect is first defined by Katz and Shapiro (1985) as follows: "There are many products for which the utility that a user derives from consumption of the good increases with the number of other agents consuming the good. ... The utility that a given user derives from the good depends on the number of other users who are in the same 'network' as he or she." The main assumption underlying the network effect is the existence of complete information. It is assumed that individuals possess identical motivations and expectations regarding the benefits of the goods.

Bikhchandani, Hirschleifer, and Welch (1992) model herd behavior under imperfect information. In their model, herd behavior occurs "when it was optimal for an individual, having observed the actions of those ahead of him, to follow the behavior of the preceding individual without regard to his own information." The decision-maker observes the actions of others and assumes that they hold more valuable information than he or she.

The most common explanation regarding herd behavior in financial markets is this last one. Nonprofessional investors follow the behavior of other investors, assuming that the latter hold more valuable information on the market conditions and trends. Since the assumption of complete information underlying the network effect explanation is not valid in financial markets, we focus on the first explanation.

Investment in structured products enables the investor not only to follow assumingly valuable information held by others, but also to conform to the people with whom they wish to be associated, without risking one's entire funds in a specific investment. If, on the one hand, investors are motivated solely by the information presumably held by other investors, they would invest directly in the underlying asset. If, on the other hand, investors are motivated by a desire to be fashionable and are uncertain about the value of third-party information, they would invest in structured products, which provide only partial exposure to the underlying asset, but leads to the full benefits of conforming to people with whom they wish to.

Structured products, providing investors exposure to commodities, emerging markets and to exotic financial products can exploit herd behavior. For example, structured notes linked to emerging market indices facilitate portfolio diversification in potential growth economies. Investors who purchase these market-linked products can conform to people with whom they wish to be associated, without exposing the entire fund to the risk of the specific emerging market. The structured product analyzed in Section 1 expose the investor to "Teva" share, which is the trendiest share for households in Israel, commonly known as "the share of the crowd".

4.4. *The Ostrich Effect*

The impact of liquidity on the prices of financial assets occupies center stage in the finance literature. The rational pricing of financial assets supports the assessment of a positive correlation between liquidity and prices; i.e., illiquidity has an adverse impact on asset value. When compared with otherwise identical illiquid assets, liquid assets should have a lower yield-to-maturity, given the opportunity to liquidate the position at any stage during the investment horizon and the possibility to realize even a larger return in the market without risking the expected return for holding the investment to maturity.[13]

Galai and Sade (2006) find that investors prefer to hold illiquid assets and are even willing to pay a premium for them. They attribute this

---

[13]Evidence from the finance literature can be found in Brenner, Eldor and Hauser (2001), Amihud, Mendelson and Lauterbach (1997), Kadlec and McConnel (1994), Amihud and Mendelson (1991) and Silber (1991).

seemingly anomalous behavior to an aversion to receiving information on potential interim losses. The ostrich effect is defined as avoiding apparently risky financial situations by pretending they do not exist. In other words, certain individuals, when faced with uncertainty, prefer investments for which the risk is unreported to similar investments (as far as risk and return are concerned) for which the risks are reported frequently. Support for ostrich effect behavior can be found in various types of financial markets and countries[14].

Most structured products are non-negotiable, and hence illiquid. Investors can avoid apparently risky financial situations throughout the lifetime of an illiquid structure by assuming these situations do not exist. The only situation with which the investors are concerned is the one occurring at maturity. The structured product analyzed in Section 1 is illiquid for the investment period of one year. The investors can avoid the existence of risk during the investment period and concern only for the outcome at maturity.

4.5. *Hindsight Bias*

Hindsight and foresight differ formally in the information available to the observer. Hindsightful decision-makers possess knowledge regarding past outcomes. Foresightful decision-makers do not possess this knowledge. Initially documented by Fischhoff (1975), the hindsight bias refers to the tendency to alter perceptions of the inevitability of an event once the outcome is known.

Fischhoff finds that reporting an outcome's occurrence increases its perceived probability of occurrence, and that decision-makers who have received outcome knowledge are unaware of the change in the perceived probability of occurrence. Therefore, reporting an outcome produces an unjustified increase in its perceived predictability, for it seems to have appeared more likely than it actually was.

When the hindsight bias is operating, events that occur are retrospectively seen as having been more likely to occur, and events that did not occur, are retrospectively seen as having been less likely to occur. Investors tend to be unaware of the role that outcome knowledge plays on their perceptions.

---

[14]As demonstrated in Galai and Sade (2006), pp 2757–2758.

Thus, investors tend to believe that seemingly inevitable outcomes were largely apparent in foresight, and these investors tend to invest in products that rely on realized outcomes.

Most structured products rely on an outcome that occurred in the recent past, and are based on the presumed increase in the probability that the same outcome will reoccur in the near future. These structured products guarantee investors relatively high returns should a recent outcome reoccur at maturity. The hindsight investor assesses higher probability to this and tends to favor investing in the structured product. The structured product analyzed in Section 1 was issued two years in a row (as demonstrated in Appendix A), at each time during the year prior to the issuance, the best case scenario occurred. In the second year, this product was issued the worst case scenario has occurred and the issuer did not issue the same product for additional year.

5. Testing Behavioral Biases in Structured Products Investment

We designed a controlled experiment to test our hypothesis concerning the application of behavioral biases to investment decisions involving structured products. The purpose of the experiment is to find the influence of each behavioral bias on the investment decision in structured products. Although a structured product is in fact a bundle of features associated with behavioral biases, in order to show that each single behavioral bias influence the investment decision, each behavioral bias was examined separately. The original experiment was drafted in Hebrew; a translation of the experiment to English is provided in Appendix C.

The experiment comprises seven investment decisions, each involving a binary choice between two mutually exclusive investment alternatives. The distinction between the two investment alternatives is based on the behavioral bias tested in the specific investment decision. The difference between the investment alternatives was marked in order to make it salient for the subjects. The experiment also contains three additional ranking questions in order to neutralize the potential impact of other values on the investment decisions. These ranking questions are relevant only to the part of the experiment which tests the influence of herd behavior on investors' decisions.

The general instructions describe a situation in which the subjects are in possession of a certain amount of money that they wish to invest in the best possible investment. The participants were instructed to choose only one out of the two investment alternatives for each investment decision. They were told that each investment decision should be considered separately, and that in each investment decision, the same amount of money is available to them. The exact initial fund was not specified in order to attain experiment results which are independent of the magnitude of the funds.

Our subject population consists of 122 investment advisor candidates,[15] 104 executive MBA students at the Jerusalem School of Business Administration, and 42 employees from various industries (other than the financial services industry) for a total of 268 subjects. The subject population reflects non-professional investors, households. The sample's population represents retail investors because, on the one hand, it does not include professional investors, and on the other hand, it does not include undergraduate students that do not take investment decisions regularly.

The experiment design and the results for each tested behavioral bias are described as follows:

5.1. *Loss Aversion*

In order to examine the impact of loss aversion on the investment decision in structured products, the subjects face two investment decisions. Both investment decisions offer the investor a choice between a risky investment in a one-year deposit that is dependent on the exchange rate between the Swiss Franc and the Israeli Shekel, and a safe investment in a one-year deposit that ensures the investor a certain return independent of the aforementioned exchange rate.

The two investment decisions can be drawn as illustrated in Figure 2.

One of the risky investments was designed so that with some probability, there is a possibility for loss (a). The other risky investment does not face the investors with a possible loss (A). The outcome of the two risky alternatives is equal and the outcome of the two riskless alternatives is equal. We would expect risk averse investor to prefer the riskless investment

[15]The investment advisor candidates participated in the experiment during their licensing exams, administered by the Israel Securities Authority.

Figure 2:

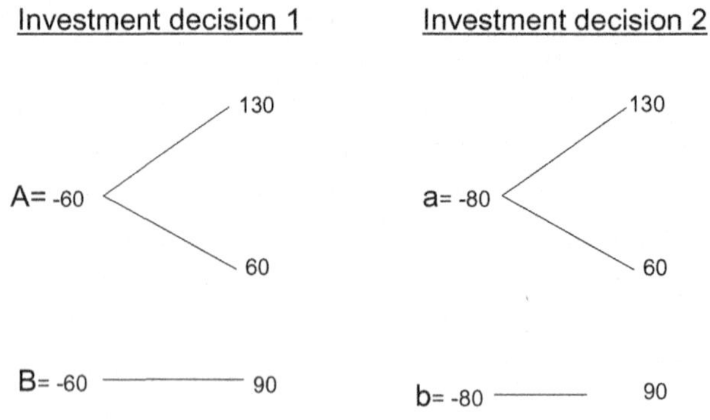

Table 1: Loss Aversion

	a	b
A	27.61%	33.21%
B	8.21%	30.97%

to the risky one in both investment decisions, or in other words, to reduce the variance of their investment's outcomes in both decisions. We would also expect risk-lover investors to prefer the risky investment to the safe one in both decisions. Choosing the risky investment in the first decision and the riskless investment in the second decision can be only explained by loss aversion.

Results

The subjects' choices in the two investment decisions are summarized in Table 1. The rows reflect the choice between a risky investment with no potential losses (denoted as A) and a safe investment (denoted as B). The columns reflect the choice between a risky investment with potential losses (denoted as a) and a safe investment (denoted as b).

The findings show that 33.21% of the subjects preferred the risky investment to the safe one when there were no potential losses, and preferred the safe investment to the risky one when the potential for loss emerged. The results yield a significant chi square statistic $\chi^2(1) = 16.6$,

$p < 0.001$. Consequently, loss aversion did influence a substantial part of the subjects in their decision.

5.2. *The Disposition Effect*

In order to examine the impact of the disposition effect on the investment decision in structured products, the subjects face two investment alternatives. Both alternatives represent two very similarly structured products. The only difference between the alternatives is that in the first, in the worst-case scenario, the initial fund is mandatorily converted into equity, while in the second alternative, in the worst-case scenario the investor is given a cash settlement. The subjects were informed that the implied price of the underlying asset upon conversion exceeds the market price of the share at maturity, i.e., losses while not realized, have been accrued.

Should the majority of investors prefer the mandatory conversion structure to the cash alternative, this would constitute evidence of the prevalence of the disposition effect on investment decision-making.

Results

The subjects' choices are summarized in Table 2. The left column represents the percentage of investors who preferred the mandatory convertible structure product to the nonconvertible one.

As reported in Table 2, 71.27% of the subjects preferred the mandatory conversion to liquidation. The results yield a significant chi square statistic $\chi^2(1) = 48.49$, $p < 0.001$. Apparently, the disposition effect played a role in decision-making for a majority of the subjects.

5.3. *Herd Behavior*

To test the impact of herd behavior on investment decision-making for structured products, the subjects face two investment decisions. Both investment decisions offer the investor a choice between two structured

Table 2: The Disposition Effect

Shares	Cash
71.27%	28.73%

products. In one of the investment alternatives, the return is linked to the performance of a "fashionable" financial asset, and in the other investment alternative, the return is linked to the performance of an "unfashionable" financial asset.

A financial asset is considered "fashionable" due to its appearance in the mass media. We chose two different "fashionable" financial assets. One of them is a "clean-tech" fund that invests in companies that are engaged in technological developments designed to help protect the environment. The other fashionable financial asset is an emerging market index. In each investment decision, the subjects were asked to choose between a "fashionable" structured product and an "unfashionable" one, all the other conditions being equal. The subjects were informed that both underlying assets in every investment decision (the "fashionable" and the "unfashionable") performed equally over the past year.

The experiment also contained three ranking questions in order to ensure that the investment decisions were not affected by other values. The subjects were asked to rank the values appearing in every investment alternative according to importance. We do not find any significant discrepancies between the importance rankings of the different values. Therefore, these values appear not to provide a satisfactory explanation of the investor choice.

Should a majority of investors prefer the "fashionable" over the "unfashionable" structure in each case, this would support the hypothesis that herd behavior comes into play in investor decision-making.

Results

Investment decision preferences are summarized in Tables 3(a) and 3(b). Table 3(a) represents the choice between a structured product specializing in "clean-tech" environmental enterprises and a structured product whose return is linked to the performance of a fund specializing in start-ups, all other conditions being equal. Table 3(b) represents the choice between a structured product tracking an emerging market index and one tracking a developed market index[16], all other conditions being equal.

---

[16]The experiment was conducted before the 2008 financial crisis, at a time when emerging markets investments were extremely popular.

Table 3(a): Herd Behavior-Environmental

Start-up Fund	Environmental Fund
27.61%	72.39%

Table 3(b): Herd Behavior-Emerging Markets

Indian Index	Italian Index
82.46%	17.54%

As reported in Table 3(a), 72.39% of the subjects preferred the "fashionable" clean-tech product to the less fashionable start-up fund. The results yield a significant chi square statistic $\chi^2(1) = 53.73$, $p < 0.001$. As reported in Table 3(b), 82.46% of the subjects preferred the "fashionable" emerging market product to the "less fashionable" developed market alternative. The results yield a significant chi square statistic $\chi^2(1) = 112.97$, $p < 0.001$. Consequently, herd behavior apparently did affect the decision of a majority of subjects.

5.4. *The Ostrich Effect*

To examine the impact of the ostrich effect on structured product investments, the subjects face two alternatives. Both alternatives are similar structured products. The only difference between the two alternatives is that the first is non-negotiable and the second is a highly liquid product, which can be redeemed by the issuer or traded on a secondary market. All the other conditions are equal.

When compared with an otherwise identical illiquid asset, a liquid asset should have a lower yield to maturity, given the opportunity to liquidate the position on demand and the possibility of realizing larger market returns without jeopardizing the locked-in yield-to-maturity. Accordingly, we would expect rational investors to prefer the liquid over non-negotiable structures.

Unlike all the other investment decisions in our experiment, we presented investors with two alternatives to which they should be indifferent;

Table 4: The Ostrich Effect

Illiquid Investment	Liquid Investment
35.58%	64.42%

this investment decision includes a superior alternative. Should any significant segment of investors prefer the inferior illiquid to the liquid structure, this would provide evidence supporting the existence of the ostrich effect on investor decision-making.

Results

Investor selections are summarized in Table 4. The left column represents the percentage of investors who preferred the illiquid structure product to the liquid one.

As reported in Table 4, 35.58% of the subjects preferred the non-negotiable over the liquid structure. This finding yields a significant chi square statistic $p < 0.001$. Consequently, the ostrich effect did have an apparent impact on decision-making for a significant segment of the subjects.

5.5. *Hindsight Bias*

To examine the possible impact of hindsight bias on investments in structured products, the subjects faced two investment alternatives, comprising two similar structured products. The sole distinction between the alternatives is that returns on the first are contingent on an outcome that has occurred in the recent past, while those of the second are contingent on an outcome not recently experienced. All other conditions are equal.

The existence of a hindsight bias is supported if a majority of investors prefer the investment whose returns depends on an outcome that has recently occurred.

Results

Investor selections are summarized in Table 5. The left column represents the percentage of investors who preferred the "hindsighted" structured product over the other.

Table 5: Hindsight Bias

Outcome that has recently occurred	Outcome that did not occur
77.24%	22.76%

Table 5 reveals that 77.24% of the subjects preferred the hindsighted structured. The results yields a significant chi square statistic $\chi^2(1) = 79.53$, $p < 0.001$. Consequently, the hindsight bias does apparently come into play in investor decision-making.

6. Conclusions

Structured products are synthetic investment instruments specially designed to meet specific needs that cannot be met by acquiring standard financial instruments available in the markets. Structured products can be used as an alternative to direct investments in financial assets, as a means to mitigate risk exposure of a portfolio, or as a way of exploiting market trends.

We outlined several key features embedded in various structured products and associated each with specific behavioral bias identified in the literature of decision theory. These include: loss aversion, the disposition effect, herd behavior, the ostrich effect, and hindsight bias.

We performed an experiment to test the possible impact of each behavioral bias on decisions pertaining to investments in structured products. Our findings reveal that, to varying degrees, the examined behavioral biases affect nonprofessional investors.

There are numerous reasons to suspect that the behavior of financial professionals may differ from that of nonprofessional investors — due to training, regulation, market experience, information accessibility, etc. However, it is unclear whether professional investors are really immune to behavioral biases. Hirshleifer (2001) argues that many behavioral finance patterns are so deeply rooted in human behavior that they are difficult to overcome by learning. Moreover, a large number of empirical studies are showing that not only may nonprofessional individuals be subject to such psychological effects, but professional and experts advisors may also be subject to the same biases[17]. If all market players tend to make these errors, the documented behavioral biases may affect market prices and market efficiency substantially. Furthermore, as a result of mispricing, there is a substantial misallocation of resources in the economy.

In demonstrating the impact of these behavioral biases on investors, our results can support the institution of specific regulation for structured products to improve investor protection. The proposed regulation can vary and can be shaped in different forms as sale prohibition or as different levels of mandatory disclosure.

As a modern alternative for household investment, structured products contribute to the completeness of financial markets by enhancing alternatives open to investors. The structured products are offering the investors a different menu of investment alternatives than the traditional financial assets do offer. Therefore, a regulation which includes a sale prohibition can bear a tremendous cost to the completeness of financial markets and to the investors as consumers in this market.

Mandatory disclosure is a less extreme regulatory solution, and it can vary between different levels of disclosure. The optimal level of disclosure is the specific level in which we will get the highest available ratio between the added value to the investor's protection as a result of the disclosure and the cost of disclosure.

We offer a regulation that would compel issuers to reveal the effective fees they charge investors. In disclosing the effective fees, the investors will be able to compare between investment alternatives in a very simple way, and will be able to decide if they are willing to pay this amount for the recognized behavioral bias. This effective value is known to the issuers; therefore its calculation will not bear any additional cost.

In many cases in financial markets, when there are abnormal returns in the market, we can rely on the competitive forces of the economy to drive margins down to marginal cost. We provide a behavioral explanation for the abnormal returns in the structured products market. An additional explanation for the unproductiveness of the competitive forces in the

[17]For example see: Lakonishok, Shleifer and Vishny (1992), Odean (1998), Hirshleifer (2001), Shapira and Venezia (2001), Coval and Shumway (2005), Menkhoff and Nikiforow (2009), Ofir and Wiener (2015).

context of structured products is provided by Carlin (2009). He finds that complexity increases the market power of the firms. In his model, as competition increases, firms tend to add more complexity to their prices as best response, rather than make their disclosures more transparent.

Disclosing the effective fee in structured products can improve the competition in this market. The diversity of the structured products offered in the market and their complexity is creating a difficulty in comparing between any two structured products and a difficulty to issue similar structured product to an existing one. Without a regulatory solution such as mandatory disclosure in the structured products market, issuing firms will continue to raise the complexity of the products and by that raise their profit margins. Therefore, increasing the market competition would enlarge the consumer surplus and contribute to the market efficiency.

Appendix A: A graphic description for the "Teva" structured product

This appendix provides a graphic description of the investment in the "Teva" structured product analyzed in Section 1 of the paper. As demonstrated in the following graphs, at the first year the structured product was issued, both conditions were not met and the investors receive the invested funds in cash. At the second year this structured product was issued, both conditions were met and the invested funds converted into "Teva" shares purchased in the base rate.

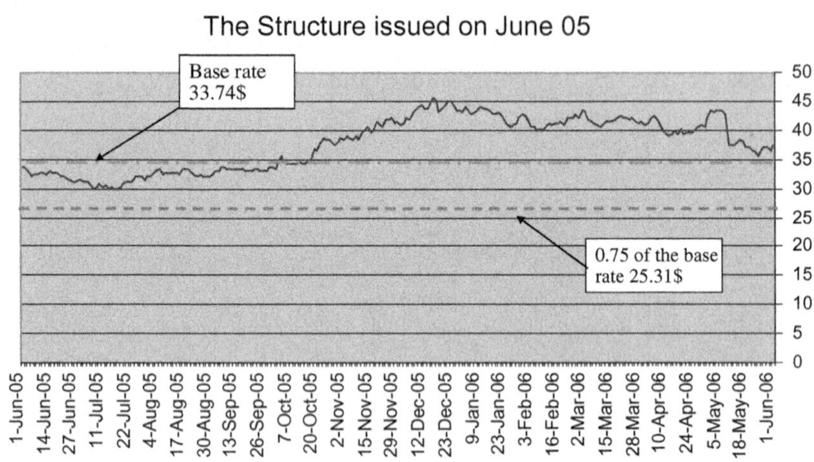

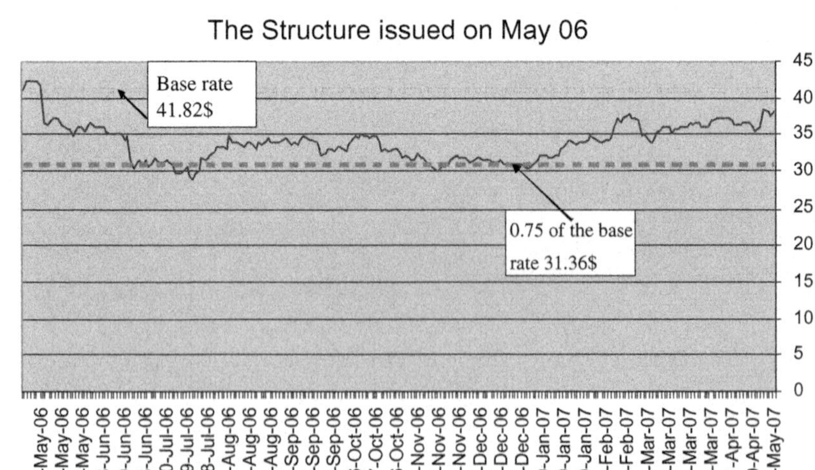

Appendix B: Association between Structured Product Features and Behavioral Biases

Feature	Behavioral Bias	References	Examples
Principal Protection	Loss aversion	Kahneman and Tversky, (1979) Benartzi and Thaler, (1995)	Principal-protected market-linked instruments
Mandatory conversion to a "loser" asset	The disposition effect	Shefrin and Statman, (1985)	Mandatory convertible bonds
Investment in emerging markets and exotic financial products	Herd behavior	Leibenstein (1950) Bikhchandani, Hirschleifer and Welch, (1992)	Market-linked structured notes on emerging market indices
Illiquidity	The ostrich effect	Galai and Sade, (2006)	Non-negotiable structured products
Reliance on outcome that has occurred	Hindsight	Fischhoff (1975) Fischhoff and Beyth, (1975)	Most structured products

Appendix C: The Experiment

The original experiment was drafted in Hebrew; a translation of the experiment to English is followed:
Instructions:

- A given sum of money is at your disposal for investment in the best possible investment.
- You are presented with a number of investment decisions. You must choose only one of the mutually-exclusive investment alternatives for each decision.

- The investment decisions are not related and each should be considered separately.
- The funds available to you are equal for each decision, and hence for each mutually-exclusive investment alternative.

Investment decision 1

a. Investment of the money at your disposal in a one-year deposit that is contingent on the exchange rate between the Israeli Shekel (NIS) and the Swiss franc. For every NIS 60 invested in the deposit, at the end of the year you will receive either NIS 130 if the NIS/ Swiss franc increases, or NIS 60 if the NIS/Swiss franc decreases.
b. Investment of the money in a one-year deposit. For every NIS 60 invested you will receive NIS 90 at the end of the year.

The amount to be remitted at the end of the year includes the principal and no additional amounts shall be received.

Investment decision 2

a. Investment of the money at your disposal in a one-year deposit with a guaranteed interest rate of 9% at the end of the year. The outcome of the principal is contingent on the rate of return on Teva shares during the year. If the price of Teva shares fall by 15% or more in relation to the quoted price of the shares on the date of investment during this period, the principal of the deposit will be converted into Teva shares, based on their value at the beginning of the year. The conversion will take place at the end of the year and you will receive an additional 9% interest. If this condition is not fulfilled, the principal will be returned in full with an additional 9% interest.
b. Investment of the money in a one-year deposit with a guaranteed interest rate of 9% at the end of the year. The outcome of the deposit principal is contingent on the quoted price of Teva shares. If the price of Teva falls over the year by 15% or more in relation to the quoted price of the shares on the date of investment, 85% or less (accordingly) of the initial amount invested will be paid **in cash** with an additional 9% interest. If this condition is not met, the principal will be returned in full with an additional 9% interest.

Investment decision 3

a. Investment of the money at your disposal in a one-year deposit that is linked to the increase in the **Indian** share price index. If the share index increases, the principal shall appreciate in accordance with the relative increase of the Indian share price index. If the index decreases or remains unchanged, the principal will be returned at the end of the year with no additional payments.
b. Investment of the money at your disposal in a one-year deposit that is linked to the increase in the **Italian** Stock Exchange share price index. If the share price index increases, the principal will appreciate in accordance with the relative increase of the index. If the share price index decreases or remains unchanged, the principal will be returned at the end of the year and no additional payments.

The rates of return for the two stock indexes in the previous year were identical.

Investment decision 4

a. Investment of the money that is at your disposal in a one-year deposit that is dependent on the exchange rate of the Swiss franc. For every NIS 80 invested in the deposit, at the end of the year you will receive either NIS 130, if the NIS/Swiss franc exchange rate, or NIS 60 if the exchange rate decreases.
b. Investment of the money that is at your disposal in a one-year deposit. For every NIS 80 invested you will receive NIS 90 at the end of the year.

The amount remitted at the end of the year includes the principal and no additional sums will be paid.

Investment decision 5

a. Investment of the sum at your disposal in a one-year deposit that is linked to the performance of a fund that invests in **technology start-ups**. If the value of the fund increases, the principal invested will appreciate in accordance with the relative increase of the value of the fund. If the value of the fund decreases or remains unchanged, the principal will be returned at the end of the year and no additional payments will be made.

b. Investment of the money that is at your disposal in a one-year deposit that is linked to the performance of a "clean-tech" fund, which invests in companies that are engaged in environmental technologies. If the value of the fund increases, the principal invested will appreciate by the relative increase in the value of the fund. If the value of the fund decreases or remains unchanged, the principal will be returned at the end of the year and no additional sums will be received.

In the previous year both funds yielded the same return.

Investment decision 6

a. Investment of the money at your disposal in a one-year deposit that grants NIS 110 at the end of the year for every NIS 100 invested, **with no option for early withdrawal.**
b. Investment of the money in a one-year deposit that grants NIS 110 at the end of the year for every NIS 100 invested. **The deposit may be withdrawn during the year at the market value on the date of withdrawal, which may be less than NIS 100.**

Investment decision 7

a. Investment of the money at your disposal in a one-year deposit that grants interest at the rate of 10%, provided that the quoted price of a given share increases by at least 10% during the year. **In the previous year the quoted share price increased by 10%.** If this condition is not fulfilled, the money invested is returned in full and no additional amounts shall be received.
b. Investment a one-year deposit that grants interest at the rate of 10% provided that the quoted price of a given share increases by at least 10% during the year. In the preceding year the **quoted share price *did not* increase by 10%.** If this condition is not fulfilled, the money invested is returned in full and no additional sums will be paid.

To what extent do you identify with each of the following statements?
Rank on a scale of 1-10, with 1 = not at all and 10 = very much
Protection of the environment is important _____
Supporting entrepreneurial start-ups is important _____
Investment in markets of developing countries is important _____

Acknowledgements

We would like to thank William Allen, Yakov Amihud, Jennifer Arlen, Oren Bar-Gill, Lucian Bebchuk, Menachem Brenner, Sari Carp, Dan Galai, Assaf Hamdani, Marcel Kahan, Alon Klement, Lewis Kornhauser, Roni Michaely, Uriel Procaccia, Roberta Romano, Orly Sade, Alan Schwartz, Itzhak Venezia, David Yermack and Ro'i Zultan for their helpful comments. For financial support, we thank the Krueger Center at the Hebrew University.

References

Amihud, Y., Mendelson, H., 1991, Liquidity, maturity and the yields on U.S government securities. Journal of Finance 46, 1411–1426.

Amihud, Y., Mendelson, H., Lauterbach, B. 1997, Market microstructure and securities values: evidence from the Tel-Aviv stock exchange. Journal of Financial Economics 45, 365–395.

Baule, R., Tallau, C. 2009, The pricing of path-dependent structured financial retail products. Unpublished working paper. Electronic paper available at: http://ssrn.com/abstract=1254102

Benartzi, S., Thaler, R. 1995, Myopic loss aversion and the equity premium puzzle. Quarterly Journal of Economics 110, 73–92.

Benet, B., Giannetti, A., Pissaris, S., 2006, Gains from structured product markets: the case of reverse-exchangeable securities (RES). Journal of Banking and Finance 30, 111–132.

Bethel, J., Ferrel, A., 2007, Policy Issues Raised by Structured Products, Bookings-Nomura Papers on Financial Services, Yasuki Fuchita, Robert E. Litan, (Eds.) (Brookings Institution).

Bikhchandani, S., Hirschleifer, D., Welch, I., 1992, A theory of fad, fashion, custom and cultural change as informational cascades. Journal of Political Economy 100, 992–1026.

Finance 56, 789–805.

Breuer, W., Perst, A., 2007, Retail banking and behavioral financial engineering: the case of structured products. Journal of Banking and Finance 31, 827–844.

Burth, S., Kraus, T., Wohlwend, H., 2001, The pricing of structured products in the Swiss market. The Journal of Derivatives 9, 30–40.

Campbell, J., 2006, Household Finance. Journal of Finance 61, 1553–1604.

Carlin, B. I., 2009, Strategic price complexity in retail financial markets. Journal of Financial Economics 91, 278–287.

Coval, J. D., Shumway, T., 2005, Do Behavioral Biases Affect Prices, *Journal of Finance* 60, 1–34.

Döbeli, B., Vanini, P., 2010, Stated and revealed investment decisions concerning retail structured products. Journal of Banking and Finance 34, 1400–1411.

Fischhoff, B., 1975, Hindsight ≠ foresight: the effect of outcome knowledge on judgment under uncertainty. Journal of Experimental Psychology 1, 288–299.

Fischhoff, B., Beyth, R., 1975, I knew it would happen- remembered probabilities of once-future things. Organizational Behavior and Human Performance 13, 1–16.

Galai, D., Sade, O., 2006, The 'ostrich effect' and the relationship between the liquidity and the yields of financial assets. Journal of Business 79(5), 2741–2759.

Gneezy, U., Potters, J., 1997, An experiment on risk taking and evaluation periods. Quarterly Journal of Economics 112, 631–645.

Gneezy, U., Kapteyn, A., Potters, J., 2003, Evaluation periods and asset prices in a market experiment. Journal of Finance 58, 821–838.

Henderson, B. J., Pearson, N. D., 2011, The dark side of financial innovation: a case study of the pricing of a retail financial product. Journal of Financial Economics 100, 227–247.

Hirshleifer, D., 2001, Investor Psychology and Asset Pricing, *Journal of Finance* 56, 1533–1597.

Kadlec, G. B., McConnell, J. J., 1994, The effect of market segmentation and illiquidity on asset prices: evidence from exchange listings. Journal of Finance 49, 611–635.

Kahneman, D., Tversky, A., 1979, Prospect theory: an analysis of decision under risk. Econometrica 47(2), 263–291.

Katz, M. L., Shapiro, C., 1985, Network externalities, competition, and compatibility. The American Economic Review 75, 424–440.

Lakonishok, J., Shleifer, A., Vishny, R. W., 1992, The Impact of Institutional Trading on Stock Prices, *Journal of Financial Economics* 32, 23–43.

Leibenstein, H., 1950, Bandwagon, snob, and veblen effects in the theory of consumers' demand. Quarterly Journal of Economics 64, 183–207.

Menkhoff, L., Nikiforow, M., 2009, Professionals' Endorsement of Behavioral Finance: Does It Impact Their Perception of Markets and Themselves?, *Journal of Economic Behavior and Organization* 71, 318–329.

Odean, T., 1998, Are Investors Reluctant to Realize Their Losses?, *Journal of Finance* 53, 1775–1798.

Ofir, M., Wiener Z., 2015, Investor Sophistication and the Effect of Behavioral Biases in Structured Products Investment, *Working Paper.*

Shapira, Z., Venezia, I., 2001, Patterns of Behavior of Professionally Managed and Independent Investors, *Journal of Banking and Finance* 25, 1573–1587.

Shefrin, H., Statman, M., 1985, The disposition to sell winners too early and ride losers too long: theory and evidence. Journal of Finance 40, 777–790.

Shefrin, H., Statman, M., 1993, Behavioral aspects of the design and marketing of financial products. Financial Management 22(2), 123–134.

Silber, W. L., 1991, Discounts on restricted stock: the impact of illiquidity on stock prices. Financial Analyst Journal 47, 60–64.

Stoimenov, P. A., Wilkens, S., 2005, Are structured products 'fairly' priced? An analysis of the German market for equity-linked instruments. Journal of Banking & Finance 29(12), 2971–2993.

Thaler, R. H., 1985, Mental accounting and consumer choice. Marketing Science 4, 199–214.

Thaler, R. H., Tversky, A., Kahneman, D., Schwartz, A., 1997, The effect of myopia and loss aversion in risk taking: an experimental test. Quarterly Journal of Economics 112, 647–661.

Tversky, A., Kahneman, D., 1991, Loss aversion and riskless choice: a reference dependent model. Quarterly Journal of Economics 106, 1039–1061.

Wilkens, S., Erner, C., Röder, K., 2003, The pricing of structured products in Germany. The Journal of Derivatives 11, 55–69.

Chapter 3

Is Investor Rationality Time Varying? Evidence from the Mutual Fund Industry*

Vincent Glode, Burton Hollifield, Marcin Kacperczyk, and Shimon Kogan

Abstract

We provide novel evidence that mutual fund returns are predictable after periods of high market returns but not after periods of low market returns. The asymmetric conditional predictability in relative performance cannot be fully explained by time-varying differences in transaction costs, in style exposures, or in survival probabilities of funds. Performance predictability is more pronounced for funds catering to retail investors than for funds catering to institutional investors, suggesting that unsophisticated investors make systematic mistakes in their capital allocation decisions.

Mutual funds constitute one of the most important investment vehicles in the US. By the end of 2009, 43% of US households owned mutual fund

---

*Glode is at the Wharton School, University of Pennsylvania (vglode@wharton.upenn.edu). Hollifield is at Carnegie Mellon University (burtonh@andrew.cmu.edu). Kacperczyk is at the Imperial College London and NBER (m.kacperczyk@imperial.ac.uk). Kogan is at IDC Herzliya and the University of Texas at Austin (skogan@idc.ac.il). We thank Amit Seru for comments on an earlier draft of the paper. We also thank Michael Cooper, Roger Edelen, Rick Green, Joshua Pollet, Philipp Schnabl, Clemens Sialm, Stijn van Nieuwerburgh, seminar participants at Bank of America, the Interdisciplinary Center Herzliya (IDC), New York University, Tel-Aviv University, Texas A&M University, University of Michigan, University of Texas at Austin, University of Utah, the Rodney L. White Center Conference at Wharton, the EFA meetings, and the WFA meetings for useful comments. Hollifield thanks National Science Foundation grant 0624351 for support. Any opinions, findings, and conclusions or recommendations expressed in this material are those of the authors and do not necessarily reflect the views of the National Science Foundation.

shares and invested a total of $11 trillion in US mutual funds. During the same year, a record-high $883 billion flowed into US mutual funds.[1] In this paper, we ask how efficient are the choices mutual fund investors make across different market conditions. To do that, we look at the cross-sectional performance predictability of mutual funds and ask whether mutual fund investors can benefit by shifting from one subset of mutual funds to another.

A growing number of studies document the presence of skills among fund managers,[2] which leaves the capital-flow explanation relevant for understanding the predictability of fund returns. While the theoretical mechanism through which fund flows might eliminate performance predictability is well understood, empirical evidence on the efficiency of such flows is fairly sparse. Understanding the source and nature of capital allocation seems particularly relevant in the context of mutual funds, which are known to attract a wide spectrum of investors, not always well informed in their investment decisions. Whether capital flows eliminate mispricings in the cross section of fund returns is ultimately an empirical question.

Here, we shed new light on the efficiency of mutual fund investors' decisions by documenting the relationship between fund return predictability and fluctuations in the aggregate stock market. Anecdotal evidence and academic research suggest that swings in economic activity may be related to significant differences in investors' behavior, or composition. For example, the popular press has argued that the recent financial crisis brought about irrationally large downsizing of equity positions in the retirement accounts of retail investors, a fact commonly attributed to investors' overreaction in bad market conditions. Other studies find indirect evidence that unsophisticated investors are more likely to enter the stock market when market returns are high.[3] That similar fluctuations in stock market conditions may also trigger mispricings in the mutual fund sector is worth

---

[1] See the 2009 Investment Company Factbook (http://www.icifactbook.org).

[2] See, Cohen, Coval, and Pástor (2005), Kacperczyk, Sialm, and Zheng (2005), and Kacperczyk and Seru (2007).

[3] This evidence is documented in Grinblatt and Keloharju (2001), Lamont and Thaler (2003), Brunnermeier and Nagel (2004), and Cooper, Gutierrez, and Hameed (2004), among others. In addition, Seru, Shumway, and Stoffman (2010) show that unsophisticated investors learn more and make fewer mistakes in periods of low market returns.

investigating given the recent evidence of time-varying fund returns (see e.g., Mamaysky, Spiegel, and Zhang, 2007).

We study how capital allocation decisions affect asset returns using a large sample of US equity mutual funds over the 1980–2005 period. We examine the conditional cross-sectional predictability of mutual fund returns based on past performance and past flows. Fund performance is known as a useful measure when assessing the skill of a fund manager (see e.g., Chevalier and Ellison, 1999; and Berk and Green, 2004). We sort funds into past performance quintiles and track their subsequent performance. After periods of high market returns, subsequent portfolio rankings are preserved for at least 12 months and the spread in four-factor alphas between high- and low-performance portfolios is about 1.7% on an annualized basis. After periods of low market returns, performance rankings change and the spread in four-factor alphas between high-performance and low-performance portfolios is about zero. Relative performance is persistent after periods of high market returns but not after periods of low market returns.

Fund flows should proxy for investors' information about fund managers' skill and future performance. Funds that receive high capital flows in a given period should be funds for which investors have obtained good news and funds that receive low capital flows in a given period should be funds for which investors have obtained bad news. Building on empirical evidence (e.g., Gruber, 1996; Zheng, 1999) suggesting that funds with high past flows in a given month perform better than funds with low past flows, we separate funds into two groups: funds that received above-median flows, and funds that received below-median flows in that month. When we sort funds based on their past flows, instead of their past performance, we find the same patterns in the cross-section of return predictability. After periods of high market returns the portfolio of high-flow funds earns 1.3% to 2.5% higher annualized abnormal return than the portfolio of low-flow funds. But both portfolios earn practically the same return after periods of low market returns.

Our results are more pronounced when we look at holding-period horizons beyond one month and are robust to the inclusion of momentum and liquidity factors, the use of time-varying factor loadings, and various definitions of market conditions and fund-flow cutoffs. Our results suggest that after high market returns, investors could increase their expected abnormal returns by moving their capital from funds with poor past performance and relatively low flows to funds with good past performance and relatively high flows.

We consider a number of explanations for our findings. First, fund investors may be subject to asymmetric trading frictions across up and down markets, leading them to rationally refrain from switching between funds. Most trading frictions such as load fees and lock-ins appear to be either non-binding for at least one investor or constant across market conditions. Another friction is capital gains taxes — investors may be reluctant to switch capital across funds especially when realized returns are high or in good market conditions. Using fund turnover and the degree of momentum tilt in a fund portfolio to proxy for the average effective capital gains tax liability, we find some support for the capital gains tax explanation, but it appears unlikely to fully explain our results.

Second, the observed patterns in performance predictability could be an artifact of the correlation between the returns on our switching strategy and those on a common passive strategy. For example, if high-flow funds were value funds and low-flow funds were growth funds, then switching between the two types of funds would be equivalent to investors trading a value strategy. To the extent that the profitability of the value strategy is high in up markets and zero in down markets, our results would attain. To explore such an alternative, we calculate the time-varying gains to predictability within various commonly used investment styles. We find evidence of performance predictability within each style category, suggesting that our findings are unlikely to result from mechanically following a common, passive investment strategy. Third, our findings do not result from time-varying differences in survivorship between funds in a high-flow portfolio and those in a low-flow portfolio.

Finally, we provide suggestive evidence that the observed asymmetry in performance predictability may be due to capital allocation mistakes by less sophisticated investors. Comparing retail funds with institutional funds — one proxy for investors' sophistication — the asymmetry in predictability is largely concentrated among funds catering to retail investors. Further, the performance predictability is substantially stronger for young funds, consistent with the idea that young funds cater to less sophisticated investors. Such findings are consistent with the results in Bailey, Kumar, and Ng (2010) who show that more sophisticated investors earn on average higher returns on their mutual fund investments.

Given that after periods of high market returns the fund investors do not seem to process information as efficiently, fund managers' incentives to exert costly effort and acquire information in these states should be weaker. We therefore study cross-sectional differences in the managers' investment strategies across market conditions. We use activeness measures similar to those in Chevalier and Ellison (1999) and show that fund managers are more active after periods of low market returns than they are after periods of high market returns. If fund managers' activeness is costly then it should rationally increase after periods of low market returns, responding to an increase in the fund flows' sophistication.

Our results are related to several strands of literature. First, the notion of predictability in mutual funds' performance is often simplified to the notion of performance persistence. The general finding of the literature is that fund performance does not persist on average, except for the worst performing funds (Carhart, 1997). This result is often interpreted as lack of persistence in managerial skills though this interpretation is largely driven by the measure of skill one uses.[4] We focus on the *time-series* patterns of persistence and show that the predictability varies with changes in stock market conditions.

Second, the paper is also related to studies showing that past flows can predict subsequent fund performance — the "smart money" effect. For example, Gruber (1996) and Zheng (1999) argue that fund flows tend to predict future fund performance. Wermers (2003) and Sapp and Tiwari (2004) cast doubt on the finding by showing that smart money is largely a momentum-driven phenomenon. Using the stock-level data based on mutual fund holdings, Frazzini and Lamont (2008) document that the smart-money effect is very short lasting. Instead, our view of the smart money effect is that smartly allocated money should eliminate any predictable differences in fund returns. We provide evidence that points to

[4]For example, recent studies find strong evidence of persistence in measures of skills that are based on the mix of holdings and return data (e.g., Kacperczyk and Seru, 2007; Kacperczyk, Sialm, and Zheng, 2008; Cremers and Petajisto, 2009).

the importance of market conditions for evaluating the efficiency of fund flows.

Finally, our paper contributes to the literature that considers time-varying conditioning information in aggregate fund performance. Early contributions in this context build on the work by Ferson and Schadt (1996), which emphasizes the role of aggregate stock market predictors in the mutual fund performance evaluation. More recently, the focus has been directly on modeling differences in fund behavior across macroeconomic states. Glode (2011) proposes a model in which mutual fund managers generate good performance in bad states of the economy because investors are willing to pay more for such returns. He shows that such mechanism can lead to negative unconditional performance of the mutual fund industry as a whole. Kacperczyk, van Nieuwerburgh, and Veldkamp (2016) show that fund managers are more active and perform better in recessions because of different returns to learning strategies. Pástor and Stambaugh (2012) argue that uncertainty about the industry-wide returns to scale of delegated asset management and the learning associated with it can drive aggregate fund flows and generate variation in the aggregate performance of the asset management industry. Compared to these studies, our work focuses on the cross-sectional properties of fund performance across different market conditions. We do not seek to understand the aggregate size of the industry or its performance across different market conditions.

The rest of the paper is as follows. In Section 1, we describe the basic economic mechanism that lays out the foundations for our empirical tests. In Section 2, we provide the discussion of the data. In Section 3, we present our main results on the conditional predictability in fund returns. Section 4 entertains a number of potential explanations for the predictability results. In Section 5, we examine the responses of fund managers to predictable variation in fund returns. Section 6 concludes.

1. Hypothesis Development

We use insights developed in the rational model of mutual fund investment of Berk and Green (2004) as the theoretical basis for our empirical tests. Although the predictions we derive are not specific to this model, we use it as a reference because it helps us conceptualize the main elements of our empirical framework.[5] In particular, it provides a useful benchmark of the empirical implications for rational mutual fund flows and how they relate to fund performance.

The main implication of the model we rely on for our empirical work is that future relative performance should not be predictable using information available to investors. Fund size adjusts to make expected abnormal returns equal across all funds. Fund flows reflect investors' decisions, and therefore provide a useful empirical instrument: If the reaction of fund flows to performance changes with market conditions, then accounting for market conditions should provide power in our empirical tests on the predictability of mutual fund performance.

In our empirical tests, we aim to identify situations in which the supply of investors' capital to mutual funds is such that excess returns adjusted for costs are predictable. For example, consider a situation in which a large number of investors participating in the mutual fund sector do not fully exploit emerging profit opportunities. Suppose that such investors were not responsive enough to information about past performance relative to a full-efficiency setting. Then, fund size would not be sensitive enough to past performance and, consequently, mutual funds with good performance in one period would stay too small, their costs would be too small, and such funds would offer a positive expected abnormal return. Similarly, funds with poor performance in one period would stay too big, their costs would be too large, and such funds would offer a negative expected abnormal return. In such a situation, abnormal returns would tend to persist over time.

If fund performance depends on the fund manager's effort as well as ability, then any information that is useful at predicting effort, will also provide predictive power for abnormal returns. We use this to guide our choice of empirical instruments.

---

[5] A classic market efficiency argument suggests that predictability in abnormal returns should disappear before financial markets can reach an equilibrium. Berk and Green (2004) provide mechanisms that describe how such an equilibrium can be reached in the open-end mutual fund industry. The absence of predictability in abnormal performance in equilibrium holds, however, in virtually any environment where investors behave rationally.

2. Data

We define three market conditions: Up, Mid, and Down. A market is *Up* when the three-month average of past market excess returns for this time period is higher than its historical 75th percentile. A market is *Mid* when the three-month average of past market excess returns for this time period is between its historical 25th percentile and 75th percentiles. A market is *Down* when the three-month average of past market excess returns for this time period is lower than its historical 25th percentile. Historical percentiles for time period t are based on the three-month average of S&P 500 index returns from quarter three of 1926 up to period t. We denote the associated indicator functions with $I(MKT_t = Up)$, $I(MKT_t = Mid)$, and $I(MKT_t = Down)$. So, instead of using within-sample percentiles to define up and down markets, we use *out-of-sample* percentiles from 1926 up to each observation date to proxy for the information investors had about market conditions at the time of their trading. Our results are robust to alternative definitions of market conditions such as different percentile cutoffs or longer-term averages of market returns.

Our main tests use monthly data over the period 1980 to 2005. The sample spans 309 months: 39 months are defined as up markets, 38 months are defined as down markets, and the remaining 232 months are defined as mid-markets. Because we use out-of-sample definitions for market conditions, the number of up market and down market months does not equal to 25% of the number of months.

Market conditions tend to cluster over time, as illustrated by the transition probabilities in Table 1. Figure 1 presents the evolution of market conditions over time, along with market returns. The shaded areas in each panel indicate when each particular market condition is attained. Table 2 provides summary statistics of key variables for the different market conditions. The average market return is 4.8% in up markets and –3.0% in down markets.

We merge the CRSP Survivorship Bias Free Mutual Fund Database with the Thomson Reuters holdings database and the CRSP stock price data using the methodology of Kacperczyk, Sialm, and Zheng (2008). The CRSP mutual fund database includes information on fund returns, total net assets, different types of fees, investment objectives, and other fund characteristics.

Table 1: Market Conditions

		MKT Return (per 3m.)		Conditional Probability		
Conditions	N	Mean	S.D.	$I(MKT_{t+1} =$ $Up)$	$I(MKT_{t+1} =$ $Mid)$	$I(MKT_{t+1} =$ $Down)$
$I(MKT_t = Up)$	39	0.048	0.030	0.526	0.474	0.000
$I(MKT_t = Mid)$	232	0.012	0.035	0.084	0.836	0.080
$I(MKT_t = Down)$	38	−0.030	0.065	0.000	0.526	0.474

This table presents means, standard deviations, and transition probabilities for different market conditions. $I(MKT_t = Up)$ equals one when the three-month average of past market excess return is higher than the 75th percentile of the historical three-month average of past market excess returns (starting Q3 of 1926); and zero otherwise. $I(MKT_t = Mid)$ equals one when the three-month average of past market excess return is between the 25th and 75th percentiles of the historical three-month average of past market excess returns (starting Q3 of 1926); and zero otherwise. $I(MKT_t = Down)$ equals one when the three-month average of past market excess return is lower than the 25th percentile of the historical three-month average of past market excess returns (starting Q3 of 1926); and zero otherwise. The sample covers the period 1980–2005.

The Thomson database also provides stock holdings of mutual funds. These data are collected both from reports filed by mutual funds with the SEC and from voluntary reports generated by the funds. We also link reported stock holdings to the CRSP stock database to obtain further information.

We focus our analysis on domestic open-end diversified equity mutual funds, for which the holdings data are most complete and reliable. We eliminate from our sample balanced funds, bond funds, money market funds, international funds, sector funds, and index funds, as well as funds not invested primarily in equity securities. We also exclude funds that hold less than 10 stocks, funds that invest less than 80% of their assets in equity, and funds that in the previous month managed less than \$5 million. We also aggregate funds with multiple share classes into portfolios by value-weighing each share class. Appendix A provides further details on the sample selection. Our sample includes 3,477 distinct funds and 250,219 fund-month observations. The number of funds in each month varies from 158 in May 1980 to 1,670 in July 2001.

Figure 1: Market Return and Conditioning Variables

This figure presents means the monthly market excess returns (solid black line) with the different market conditions. In the upper panel, months defined as $I(MKT_t = Up)$ are shaded gray. These are the months in which the three-month average excess returns is higher than the 75th percentile of the historical three-month average of market excess returns. In the lower panel, months defined $I(MKT_t = Down)$ are shaded gray. These are the months in which the three-month average excess returns is lower than the 25th percentile of the historical market excess return. The data cover the period 1980 to 2005.

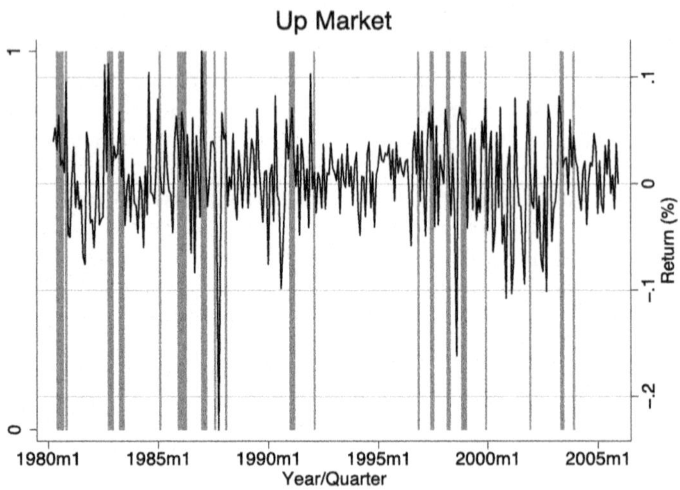

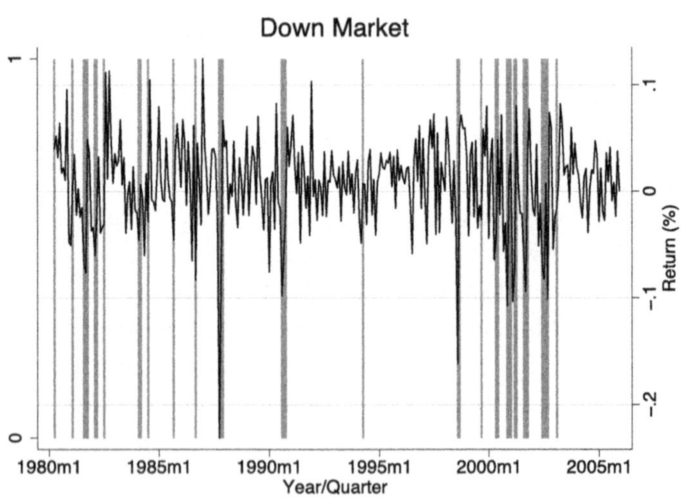

Table 2: Summary Statistics

	Panel A: All Market Conditions				
	Mean	S.D.	Median	p25	p75
Flow	0.0123	0.2381	−0.0003	−0.0147	0.0198
Return	0.0088	0.0549	0.0112	−0.0209	0.0406
Performance	−0.0012	0.0225	−0.0012	−0.0112	0.0087
Age	13.9	14.2	9.0	5.0	17.0
TNA	920.6	3,636.5	153.8	44.9	543.5
Expenses	0.0129	0.0048	0.0123	0.0097	0.0154
Turnover	92.51	132.33	67.00	35.20	115.00
Load	0.0222	0.0261	0.0051	0.0000	0.0475
Value	2.6	0.5	2.6	2.2	2.9
Size	4.1	1.0	4.4	3.5	4.8
Momentum	3.3	0.6	3.3	2.9	3.7
Beta Deviation	0.1428	0.2767	0.1062	0.0505	0.1846
Sector Deviation	0.1875	0.0922	0.1703	0.1265	0.2280
Unsystematic Deviation	0.0084	0.0094	0.0066	0.0033	0.0106

	Panel B: $I(MKT_t = Up)$				
	Mean	S.D.	Median	p25	p75
Flow	0.0147	0.3008	−0.0016	−0.0208	0.0208
Return	0.0474	0.0419	0.0435	0.0183	0.0674
Performance	−0.0025	0.0224	−0.0023	−0.0137	0.0085
Age	14.5	14.5	9.0	5.0	18.0
TNA	884.8	3,457.0	150.8	44.9	529.0
Expenses	0.0126	0.0048	0.0120	0.0095	0.0150
Turnover	92.61	137.04	67.00	35.93	114.21
Load	0.0230	0.0280	0.0022	0.0000	0.0475
Value	2.6	0.5	2.6	2.2	3.0
Size	4.0	1.0	4.4	3.4	4.8
Momentum	3.3	0.6	3.2	2.9	3.7
Beta Deviation	0.1435	0.3822	0.1042	0.0503	0.1795
Sector Deviation	0.1916	0.0900	0.1758	0.1309	0.2334
Unsystematic Deviation	0.0086	0.0083	0.0070	0.0035	0.0109

(*Continued*)

Table 2: (*Continued*)

	Panel C: $I(MKT_t = Down)$				
	Mean	S.D.	Median	p25	p75
Flow	0.0073	0.3897	−0.0025	−0.0163	0.0158
Return	−0.0289	0.0790	−0.0268	−0.0782	0.0200
Performance	−0.0001	0.0296	−0.0002	−0.0139	0.0142
Age	13.4	13.8	8.0	5.0	16.0
TNA	978.1	3,720.3	155.9	43.3	558.9
Expenses	0.0129	0.0047	0.0124	0.0099	0.0155
Turnover	98.65	132.08	72.00	39.00	122.00
Load	0.0212	0.0254	0.0041	0.0000	0.0458
Value	2.5	0.5	2.5	2.2	2.9
Size	4.2	0.9	4.6	3.6	4.9
Momentum	3.3	0.7	3.3	2.8	3.8
Beta Deviation	0.1446	0.1518	0.1102	0.0522	0.1924
Sector Deviation	0.1855	0.0913	0.1686	0.1230	0.2279
Unsystematic Deviation	0.0105	0.0106	0.0083	0.0042	0.0134

Summary statistics are for all market conditions (Panel A), and conditional on either up- (Panel B) or down market (Panel C). *Flow* is defined as $Flow = \frac{TNA_t - TNA_{t-1} * (1+R_t)}{TNA_{t-1}}$. R is the net return of the fund portfolio. *Performance* is the alpha (including residual) from the four-factor model of excess fund returns projected on market premium, size, value, and momentum factors. *Age* is the fund age. *TNA* is the total net assets of a fund (in Millions). *Expenses* is the fund expense ratio. *Turnover* is fund turnover. *Load* is the total fund load. *Value* is the average score of all stocks in the fund portfolio, where each stock is assigned a score (from 1 to 5) based on its book-to-market ratio. *Size* is the average score of all stocks in the fund portfolio, where each stock is assigned a score (from 1 to 5) based on its market capitalization. *Momentum* is the average score of all stocks in the fund portfolio, where each stock is assigned a score (from 1 to 5) based on its past 12-month returns. *BetaDeviation* is the absolute value of the difference between a fund's beta in month t and the average beta in that quarter of all funds in the fund's objective class. Individual fund beta is a market beta from a four-factor model calculated using 36 months of past returns. *SectorDeviation* is the mean square root of the sum of squared differences between the share of a fund's assets in each of ten industry sectors of Fama and French (1997) and the mean share in each sector in month t among all funds in the fund's objective class (aggressive growth, growth, or value). *UnsystematicDeviation* is the absolute value of the difference between a fund's unsystematic risk, *UnsystematicRisk*, and the sample average of this variable over all funds in the fund's objective class in month t. *UnsystematicRisk* is the absolute value of the residual from the Carhart (1997) four-factor model. $I(MKT_t = Up)$ equals one when the three-month average of past market excess return is higher than the 75th percentile of the historical three-month average of past market excess returns (starting Q3 of 1926); and zero otherwise. $I(MKT_t = Mid)$ equals one when the three-month average of past market excess return is between the 25th and 75th percentiles of the historical three-month average of past market excess returns (starting Q3 of 1926); and zero otherwise. $I(MKT_t = Down)$ equals one when the three-month average of past market excess return is lower than the 25th percentile of the historical three-month average of past market excess returns (starting Q3 of 1926); and zero otherwise. The data cover all equity mutual funds for the period 1980 to 2005.

We use the subscripts i, t on a variable to refer to fund i over period t. In order to reduce notational clutter, we only use subscripts when necessary for expositional purposes.

Let $R_{i,t}$ denote fund i's monthly return net of expenses at between t and $t+1$. *Flow* is the fund flow defined as the growth rate of the assets under management (*TNA*), after adjusting for the appreciation of the mutual fund's assets assuming that all cash flows are invested at the end of the period:

$$Flow_{i,t} = \frac{TNA_{i,t} - TNA_{i,t-1} * (1 + R_{i,t})}{TNA_{i,t-1}}. \tag{3.1}$$

To measure *Performance*, we use the factor loadings estimated from a 36-month rolling regression of a fund's returns on the market premium, size, value, and momentum factors and we subtract the required return, given these loadings, from the fund's realized return. *TNA* is the fund's total net assets in millions of dollars. *Expenses* is the fund's expense ratio. *Turnover* is the fund's turnover ratio. *Load* is the total load fee.

Value is the average value score of all stocks in the fund's portfolio, where each stock is assigned a value score from 1 to 5 based on its book-to-market ratio. *Size* is the average size score of all stocks in the fund's portfolio, where each stock is assigned a size score from 1 to 5 based on its market capitalization. *Momentum* is the average momentum score of all stocks in the fund's portfolio, where each stock is assigned a momentum score from 1 to 5 based on its past 12-month returns.

Beta Deviation is the absolute value of the difference between fund i's beta in month t and the average beta in that month of all funds in the fund's objective class. Individual fund beta is a market beta from a four-factor model calculated using 36 months of past returns. *Sector Deviation* is the mean square root of the sum of squared differences between the share of fund i's assets in each of 10 industry sectors of Fama and French (1997) and the mean share in each sector in month t among all funds in the fund's objective class: aggressive growth, growth, or value. *Unsystematic Deviation* is the absolute value of the difference between fund i's unsystematic risk, *Unsystematic Risk*, and the sample average of this variable over all funds in the fund's objective class in month t. *Unsystematic Risk* is the absolute value of the residual from the Carhart (1997) four-factor model.

Table 2 reports summary statistics for our variables; Panel A for the entire sample, Panel B for up markets only, and Panel C for down markets only. Most of the summary statistics in the unconditional sample are consistent with those reported in previous studies, giving us confidence that our analysis is not biased due to sample selection.

Mutual funds in our sample tend to receive more flows after high market returns but they do not necessarily have higher risk-adjusted performance after high market returns. Most other variables do not vary much across the two market conditions, except for measures of deviation which tend to increase in down markets.

3. Evidence on Time-Varying Return Predictability

3.1. *Performance Predictability*

We test the hypothesis that fund investors move capital across funds in an attempt to benefit from future abnormal returns offered by some funds. The resulting capital flows should adjust fund size such that predicted performance going forward is the same for all funds. Fund flows chase past performance but do not help to predict future performance. Similarly, past performance helps to predict fund flows but does not help to predict future performance.

We start by looking at performance persistence. Similar to Carhart (1997), we assign funds into quintile portfolios based on their past four-factor performance and sort observations based on the market condition during the next month. We calculate the equally weighted cumulative performance for these fund quintiles over the subsequent three, six, nine, and 12 months, depending on the market condition when these portfolios are constructed.

Figure 2 depicts the results. The top panel is for portfolios constructed in an up market and the bottom panel is for portfolios constructed in a down market. Persistence patterns differ significantly depending on whether the portfolios are constructed after an up or a down market. After an up market, subsequent alphas are monotonically increasing in past alphas. For example, in the sorting period (labelled $t = 0$), the spread in performance between the top and bottom-quintile funds is around 5.5%. While the spread subsequently narrows, it remains positive and economically significant, ranging from 1.0% after three months to 1.7% after twelve months.

But after a down market, subsequent alphas are not monotonically increasing in past alphas. While the top-quintile funds outperform the bottom-quintile funds by 7.2% in the sorting period, subsequent alphas do not seem to be related to past alphas.[6] Past performance can be used to predict future fund performance after periods of high market returns, but performance cannot be used to predict future performance after periods of low market returns.

Other pieces of information should be used by investors trying to make investment decisions. Unfortunately, we cannot observe all the information available, but we can observe fund flows and proxy for investors' information about fund managers' skill and future performance. For example, funds that receive high capital flows in a given period should be funds for which investors have obtained good news about future returns. Can fund flows be used to predict future performance? How does the predictability depend on market conditions? We construct two equally weighted portfolios — the "High" portfolio includes funds with flows that are higher than the median flow in the past month and the "Low" portfolio includes funds with flows that are lower than the median flow.[7] These portfolios are held for one, three, six, and 12 months.

Let $R_{+,t+1}$ be the excess return on the portfolio of funds with above-median flows and $R_{-,t+1}$ be the excess return on the portfolio of funds with below-median flows. Also, $F_{k,t+1}$ represents the return on factor k, and $\beta_{k,j}$ is the loading on factor k, where $j \in \{+,-\}$. We estimate a conditional

[6]For robustness, we repeat the same analysis with quarterly frequency or based on decile portfolios; the qualitative findings remain unchanged.

[7]This approach deviates slightly from that in Zheng (1999) and Sapp and Tiwari (2004) who sort funds based on positive and negative flows. While the approach these papers take is not as critical in the context of the unconditional framework, it is less desirable in our context given that the distribution of flows may vary systematically across market conditions. Nevertheless, the qualitative aspects of our results remain unchanged if we follow the alternative approach instead.

Figure 2: Performance Persistence vs. Market Conditions

This figure depicts the three, six, nine, and twelve months performance of one-month alpha-sorted funds. Alpha is computed using a standard four-factor model, regressed over a 36-month period. Funds are sorted into five decile groups such that "Quintile 1" ("Quintile 5") refers to the worst (best) past alpha funds. The average alpha during the one month sorting period is reported as "Month 0". The upper panel shows the results for funds sorted following

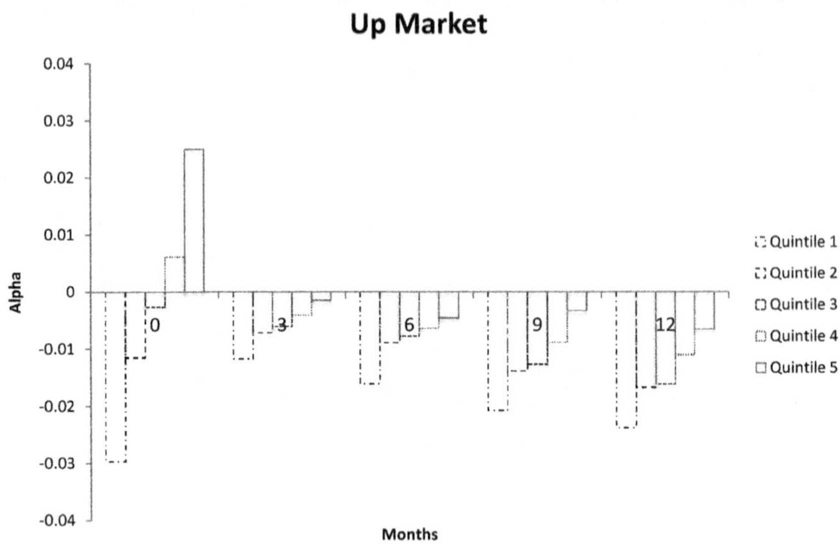

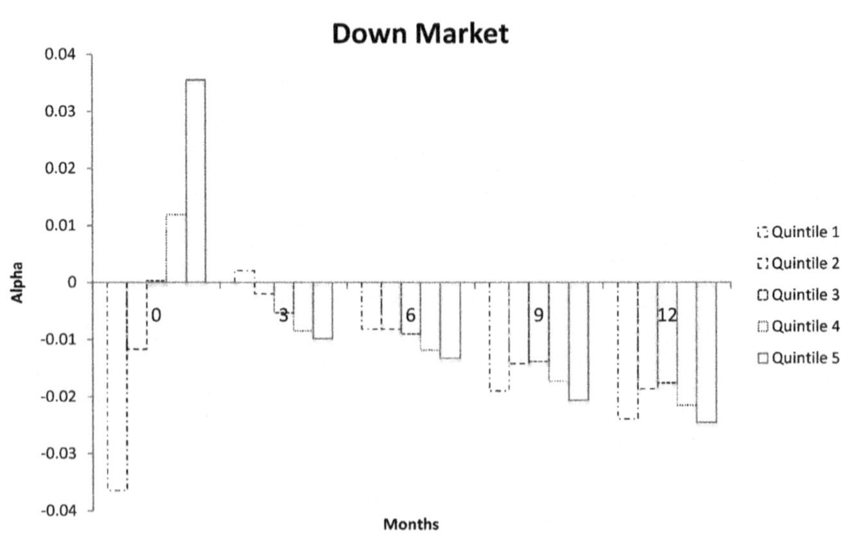

(*Continued*)

Figure 2: months in which $I(MKT_t = Up)$, which are defined as months in which the three-month average excess returns is higher than the 75th percentile of the historical three-month average of market excess returns. The lower panel shows the results for funds sorted following months in which $I(MKT_t = Down)$, which are defined as months in which the three-month average excess returns is lower than the 25th percentile of the historical market excess return. The data cover the period 1980 to 2005.

version of the four-factor model used by Carhart (1997):

$$R_{j,t+1} = \alpha_j^0 + \alpha_j^{Up} I(MKT_t = Up) + \alpha_j^{Down} I(MKT_t = Down) + \sum_{k=1}^{K} \beta_{k,j} F_{k,t+1} + \epsilon_{j,t+1}. \tag{3.2}$$

Table 3 reports the results. The table is divided into four sections, each corresponding to a different investment horizon. The bottom panel of the table reports two sets of results. The first two columns in each section show whether the conditional alpha is different from zero separately for up and down markets. The third column in each section reports tests for the null that the the unconditional alphas of of the two portfolios are equal, and also tests for that the conditional alphas.

Unconditionally, we find no abnormal return from switching between low- and high-flow funds. But the high-flow portfolio generates a substantially higher alpha than the low-flow portfolio after up markets, at horizons of three, six, and 12 months while both portfolios generate statistically indistinguishable performance from each other after down markets. A strategy that buys funds with high past flows after periods of high market returns has a significantly better performance than a strategy that buys funds with low flows after periods of high market returns. A strategy that buys funds with high past flows after periods of low market returns does not, however, have a significantly better performance than a strategy that buys funds with low flows after periods of low market returns.

The asymmetry is consistent with fund investors incorporating information more efficiently after periods of low market returns than after periods of high market returns, or equivalently with a less "sophisticated" mutual fund clientele after periods of high market returns than after periods

Table 3: Performance of Flow-Based Portfolios with Conditional Risk Loadings

	1 Month		3 Months		6 Months		12 Months	
$Flow_{t-1}$	High	Low	High	Low	High	Low	High	Low
MKTPREM	0.979	0.986	0.968	0.990	0.963	0.972	0.958	0.935
	(0.011)	(0.016)	(0.013)	(0.017)	(0.017)	(0.023)	(0.023)	(0.038)
SMB	0.231	0.108	0.234	0.122	0.228	0.186	0.268	0.187
	(0.016)	(0.048)	(0.020)	(0.054)	(0.024)	(0.035)	(0.033)	(0.044)
HML	−0.049	−0.009	−0.055	0.021	−0.057	0.036	−0.055	0.045
	(−0.024)	(−0.047)	(−0.023)	(0.052)	(−0.024)	(0.047)	(−0.025)	(0.064)
UMD	0.022	−0.039	0.020	−0.061	0.037	−0.012	0.074	0.030
	(0.012)	(−0.029)	(0.010)	(−0.031)	(0.014)	(−0.020)	(0.020)	(0.027)
MKTPREM x	−0.056	−0.021	−0.047	−0.028	−0.090	−0.036	−0.009	0.025
$I(MKT_t = Up)$	(−0.032)	(−0.038)	(−0.028)	(−0.021)	(−0.044)	(−0.031)	(−0.030)	(0.040)
MKTPREM x	0.069	−0.011	0.054	0.019	0.073	0.104	0.045	0.107
$I(MKT_t = Down)$	(0.025)	(−0.037)	(0.022)	(0.030)	(0.028)	(0.040)	(0.023)	(0.044)
SMB x	−0.063	0.074	0.017	0.120	0.080	0.063	0.000	0.029
$I(MKT_t = Up)$	(−0.042)	(0.052)	(0.042)	(0.050)	(0.046)	(0.039)	(0.036)	(0.041)
SMB x	−0.027	0.042	−0.003	−0.029	−0.004	−0.134	−0.042	−0.100
$I(MKT_t = Down)$	(−0.032)	(0.054)	(−0.044)	(−0.052)	(−0.052)	(−0.056)	(−0.046)	(−0.064)

HML x	−0.084	−0.103	−0.015	−0.079	−0.090	−0.147	0.073	0.006
$I(MKT_t = Up)$	(−0.066)	(−0.080)	(−0.028)	(−0.061)	(−0.044)	(−0.058)	(0.048)	(0.071)
HML x	0.109	0.099	0.097	0.076	0.117	0.154	0.043	0.088
$I(MKT_t = Down)$	(0.032)	(0.056)	(0.033)	(0.041)	(0.034)	(0.037)	(0.044)	(0.060)
UMD x	−0.019	0.027	−0.031	0.084	−0.060	−0.011	0.006	0.073
$I(MKT_t = Up)$	(−0.068)	(0.058)	(−0.045)	(0.036)	(−0.023)	(−0.022)	(0.066)	(0.105)
UMD x	0.053	0.047	0.044	0.050	0.045	0.035	0.025	−0.001
$I(MKT_t = Down)$	(−0.027)	(0.031)	(0.021)	(0.026)	(0.041)	(0.038)	(0.029)	(−0.029)
$I(MKT_t = Up)$	0.000	−0.001	0.000	−0.002	0.001	−0.001	0.000	−0.002
	(0.002)	(−0.002)	(0.001)	(−0.001)	(0.000)	(−0.001)	(0.001)	(−0.001)
$I(MKT_t = Down)$	−0.001	−0.001	0.000	−0.001	−0.001	−0.001	−0.001	−0.001
	(−0.001)	(−0.001)	(0.001)	(−0.001)	(−0.000)	(−0.001)	(−0.000)	(−0.001)
Constant	0.000	0.000	0.000	0.000	−0.001	−0.001	−0.001	−0.001
	(0.001)	(0.001)	(0.000)	(0.001)	(−0.000)	(−0.001)	(−0.000)	(−0.001)
Observations	307	307	305	305	302	302	296	296
R^2	0.97	0.97	0.97	0.96	0.97	0.97	0.97	0.95

(*Continued*)

Table 3: (*Continued*)

	1 Month			3 Months			6 Months			12 Months		
$Flow_{t-1}$	High	Low	High-Low	High	Low	High-Low	High	Low	High-Low	High	Low	High-Low
Unconditional	−0.033	−0.071	0.038	−0.044	−0.086	0.042	−0.067	−0.103	0.036	−0.117	−0.123	0.006
(in %, per m.)	(0.354)	(0.188)	(0.446)	(0.214)	(0.093)	(0.219)	(0.092)	(0.019)	(0.150)	(0.001)	(0.004)	(0.785)
$I(MKT_t = Up)$	−0.024	−0.148	0.124	−0.058	−0.264	0.206	0.018	−0.141	0.159	−0.142	−0.247	0.105
(in %, per m.)	(0.880)	(0.375)	(0.404)	(0.339)	(0.000)	(0.014)	(0.689)	(0.003)	(0.010)	(0.003)	(0.001)	(0.059)
$I(MKT_t = Down)$	−0.140	−0.146	0.006	−0.058	−0.128	0.070	−0.156	−0.179	0.023	−0.156	−0.156	0.000
(in %, per m.)	(0.019)	(0.206)	(0.960)	(0.359)	(0.000)	(0.398)	(0.000)	(0.000)	(0.705)	(0.000)	(0.010)	(0.997)

Each month we construct portfolios of funds based on their dollar flows. *High* denotes the return on the equally weighted portfolio of funds which received flows that are higher than the median flow in a given period; *Low* is the return on the equally weighted portfolio of funds which received flows that are lower than the median flow in a given period. Both returns are regressed on a set of four factors: market premium (MKTPREM), size (SMB), value (HML), and momentum (UMD), and their interactions with two indicator functions: $I(MKT_t = Up)$ equals one when the three-month average of past market excess return is higher than the 75th percentile of the historical three-month average of past market excess returns (starting Q3 of 1926); and zero otherwise. $I(MKT_t = Mid)$ equals one when the three-month average of past market excess return is between the 25th and 75th percentiles of the historical three-month average of past market excess returns (starting Q3 of 1926); and zero otherwise. $I(MKT_t = Down)$ equals one when the three-month average of past market excess return is lower than the 25th percentile of the historical three-month average of past market excess returns (starting Q3 of 1926); and zero otherwise. Columns (1)–(2) consider monthly returns one month ahead, columns (3)–(4) monthly returns three months ahead, columns (5)–(6) monthly returns six months ahead, and columns (7)–(8) monthly returns twelve months ahead. Standard errors (in parentheses) are adjusted for autocorrelation up to 12 lags using the procedure as in Newey and West (1987). A bottom panel reports monthly returns along with their p-values (in parentheses) on portfolios which condition on both market conditions and fund flows. The panel also reports the results of the F-test of the differences between the respective portfolios. The data cover the period 1980 to 2005.

of low market returns. After periods of low market returns, investors in a low-flow fund would not benefit from switching to a high-flow fund, but these investors would benefit from switching to a high-flow fund after periods of high market returns earning a significantly higher risk-adjusted return. Performance predictability is economically significant, with the magnitude of the spread decreasing monotonically for longer investment horizons. Specifically, the return ranges from 1.3% for a one-year investment horizon to 2.5% on an annualized basis for a three-month horizon. We find similar results when we do not allow for conditional risk factors.

3.2. *Robustness Checks*

We summarize the results of our robustness checks in Table 4. In Panel A, we examine performance predictability from switching between funds whose flows are higher than the 75th percentile of the flow distribution in the past month and funds whose flows are lower than the 25th percentile of the distribution. We still find performance predictability after up markets and no performance predictability after down markets. Moreover, the magnitude of the abnormal return increases and varies between 2% for a one-year investment horizon and 3.9% on an annualized basis for a three-month horizon, consistent with the idea that sorting on more extreme fund flows would generate stronger performance predictability.

In Panel B, rather than sorting based on past one-month fund flows we sort based on the average flows over the past three months using the median flow as a cut-off value. The results, though economically less significant, are qualitatively similar. We find statistically significant predictability after up markets but not after down markets. The results are similar if we use a six-month average flow instead. In Panel C, we condition the strategy on past-month percentage flows rather than on the dollar flows. Again, the results are similar qualitatively and the magnitudes are slightly larger than before.

Finally, in Panel D, we report abnormal returns calculated using the Fama and French three-factor model. The qualitative and the quantitative aspects of our results are similar for strategies after up markets when we use the three-factor model to define abnormal returns. There is statistically significant predictability after down markets, with the economic magnitudes of the spread portfolio becoming slightly larger. The result is

Table 4: Performance of Flow-Based Portfolios: Robustness

	1 Month			3 Months			6 Months			12 Months		
$Flow_{t-1}$	High	Low	High-Low	High	Low	High-Low	High	Low	High-Low	High	Low	High-Low
Panel A: Different Cut-Off Values												
$I(MKT_t = Up)$	0.030	−0.230	0.260	0.043	−0.280	0.323	0.052	−0.151	0.203	−0.069	−0.236	0.167
(in %, per m.)	(0.840)	(0.213)	(0.233)	(0.636)	(0.000)	(0.009)	(0.220)	(0.005)	(0.025)	(0.077)	(0.005)	(0.043)
$I(MKT_t = Down)$	−0.149	−0.169	0.020	−0.095	−0.188	0.093	−0.179	−0.231	0.052	−0.162	−0.184	0.022
(in %, per m.)	(0.043)	(0.202)	(0.913)	(0.198)	(0.000)	(0.447)	(0.000)	(0.001)	(0.562)	(0.000)	(0.008)	(0.833)
Panel B: Based on Past Three Months of Flows												
$I(MKT_t = Up)$	−0.014	−0.174	0.160	−0.105	−0.224	0.119	0.000	−0.119	0.119	−0.156	−0.267	0.111
(in %, per m.)	(0.922)	(0.342)	(0.210)	(0.066)	(0.003)	(0.092)	(0.992)	(0.032)	(0.036)	(0.006)	(0.000)	(0.034)
$I(MKT_t = Down)$	−0.150	−0.133	−0.017	−0.085	−0.089	0.004	−0.168	−0.161	−0.007	−0.176	−0.124	−0.052
(in %, per m.)	(0.017)	(0.248)	(0.874)	(0.057)	(0.090)	(0.957)	(0.000)	(0.002)	(0.900)	(0.000)	(0.072)	(0.429)
Panel C: Percentage Flow Portfolios												
$I(MKT_t = Up)$	0.004	−0.176	0.180	−0.049	−0.273	0.224	0.018	−0.139	0.157	−0.108	−0.285	0.177
(in %, per m.)	(0.978)	(0.336)	(0.340)	(0.566)	(0.002)	(0.043)	(0.680)	(0.006)	(0.057)	(0.048)	(0.000)	(0.012)
$I(MKT_t = Down)$	−0.188	−0.098	−0.090	−0.091	−0.096	0.005	−0.156	−0.183	0.027	−0.162	−0.151	−0.011
(in %, per m.)	(0.012)	(0.431)	(0.576)	(0.117)	(0.047)	(0.964)	(0.000)	(0.001)	(0.734)	(0.000)	(0.017)	(0.900)

Panel D: Three-Factor Model												
$I(MKT_t = Up)$	−0.020	−0.162	0.142	−0.069	−0.241	0.172	0.002	−0.158	0.160	−0.092	−0.184	0.092
(in %, per m.)	(0.609)	(0.226)	(0.337)	(0.212)	(0.000)	(0.034)	(0.967)	(0.001)	(0.008)	(0.002)	(0.000)	(0.060)
$I(MKT_t = Down)$	−0.036	−0.135	0.099	−0.013	−0.135	0.122	−0.082	−0.159	0.077	−0.071	−0.132	0.061
(in %, per m.)	(0.820)	(0.297)	(0.451)	(0.856)	(0.001)	(0.131)	(0.196)	(0.002)	(0.193)	(0.299)	(0.068)	(0.359)

Each month we construct portfolios of funds based on their dollar flows. *High* denotes the return on the equally weighted portfolio of funds which received flows that are higher than the median flow in a given period; *Low* is the return on the equally weighted portfolio of funds which received flows that are lower than the median flow in a given period. Both returns are regressed on a set of four factors: market premium (MKTPREM), size (SMB), value (HML), and momentum (UMD), and their interactions with two indicator functions: $I(MKT_t = Up)$ equals one when the three-month average of past market excess return is higher than the 75th percentile of the historical three-month average of past market excess returns (starting Q3 of 1926); and zero otherwise. $I(MKT_t = Mid)$ equals one when the three-month average of past market excess return is between the 25th and 75th percentiles of the historical three-month average of past market excess returns (starting Q3 of 1926); and zero otherwise. $I(MKT_t = Down)$ equals one when the three-month average of past market excess return is lower than the 25th percentile of the historical three-month average of past market excess returns (starting Q3 of 1926); and zero otherwise. Columns (1)–(2) consider monthly returns one month ahead, columns (3)–(4) monthly returns three months ahead, columns (5)–(6) monthly returns six months ahead, and columns (7)–(8) monthly returns twelve months ahead. Standard errors (in parentheses) are adjusted for autocorrelation up to 12 lags using the procedure as in Newey and West (1987). A bottom panel reports monthly returns along with their p-values (in parentheses) on portfolios which condition on both market conditions and fund flows. The data cover the period 1980 to 2005.

consistent with evidence by Sapp and Tiwari (2004) that momentum is an important part of the observed unconditional predictability in mutual fund returns.

There is predictability in the returns of a strategy in which investors switch capital between high-flow and low-flow funds after periods of high market returns, and no predictability in such a strategy after periods of low market returns. While we believe that fund past flows are a natural choice for a predictive variable because they summarize the information used by investors coming from various sources, we also check if predictability persists using other predictive variables.

Another signal that investors might consider is past raw returns: Lynch and Musto (2003) show that investors' fund flows are sensitive to past raw returns. To allow for this possibility, we use a three-month lagged fund return as a predictive variable and sort funds into two groups: a group with positive returns and a group with negative returns. We repeat the analysis in Table 3 using raw returns.

The results using raw returns are qualitatively similar to those reported in Table 3. There is a significant degree of relative performance predictability after periods of high market returns but no relative performance predictability after periods of low market returns. Moreover, there is little performance predictability for the very short, one-month investment horizon and strong performance predictability for the three-month, six-month, and 12-month investment horizons. The economic magnitudes are comparable to that of a strategy that conditions on past fund flows. All the portfolio returns are statistically significant at the 1% level.

Finally, the predictability results might be due to the use of equally weighted portfolios. By using equally weighted portfolios in our tests, we assign a greater weight to smaller funds. To the extent that small funds systematically differ from large funds, the differences in composition of funds across different portfolios and times could produce biased results. We therefore repeat the analysis using value-weighted fund portfolios. The economic and statistical magnitudes of the results remain unchanged. The predictability results are therefore unlikely to be driven by differences between small and large funds.

The information in raw returns, in risk-adjusted returns, and in fund flows might be processed differently by investors after periods of high market returns than it is processed after periods of low market returns. Or equivalently, the investors trading mutual fund shares after periods of high market returns might process this information less diligently than the investors trading mutual fund shares after periods of low market returns. Overall, capital appears to be allocated more efficiently after periods of low market returns than after periods of high market returns. Boundedly rational investors might overreact to information, but our empirical evidence instead suggests that mutual fund investors under-react to information after periods of high market returns, and react appropriately after periods of low market returns. Funds with low past performance and low flows tend to remain too large after periods of high market returns, giving rise to subsequent abnormally low performance for up to a year.

4. Possible Explanations for the Empirical Results

We now entertain possible explanations for the time-varying predictability in fund returns. Our candidates include time-varying transaction costs, predictable variation in stock returns, differences in survivorship rates, and capital allocation mistakes.

4.1. *Transaction Costs*

Asymmetric predictability could result from time-varying transaction costs. The transaction costs would have to offset any abnormal gains unexplained by the common risk factors we use, implying that transaction costs are significantly higher after up markets than after down markets. We know of no evidence that direct trading costs or fund expenses change much over time, but transaction costs arising from differences in investors' taxation bases may generate such time variation. For example, after up markets, investors who invest in high-flow funds may be more likely to have accrued higher taxable income than those investing in low-flow funds. As a result, the gap in their returns might simply be offset by their tax liability.

Although it is generally difficult to directly measure tax impacts on each mutual fund investor, tax liabilities are likely to be positively correlated with the degree of momentum trading and turnover a fund exhibited in the past (e.g., Bergstresser, Poterba, and Zarutskie, 2003). To this end, we test the tax story in two ways. We condition our tests on funds' momentum loadings and on funds' turnover ratios. We sort funds according to their momentum loading: High-momentum funds are defined as those in which the *Momentum* indicator is greater than three; funds with *Momentum* below three are low-momentum funds. Subsequently, we evaluate the performance predictability of the two portfolios after up and down markets.

Panels A and B of Table 5 report the results for the momentum-sorted portfolios. Consistent with the tax story, we find that the magnitude of the predictability is larger for high-momentum funds than low-momentum funds. Still, the difference in alphas for high-flow and low-flow low-momentum funds is at least 1% on an annualized basis. The patterns of performance predictability are qualitatively consistent with our previously reported findings for both low-momentum and high-momentum portfolios of funds. There is statistically significant return predictability after up markets but not after down markets.

Similarly, Panels C and D of Table 5 report the results for portfolios of funds sorted by turnover ratios — above and below the sample median. There is strong performance predictability in both low-turnover and high-turnover portfolios of funds after up markets and no performance predicability after down markets. The economic magnitude of this phenomenon is only slightly larger for the high-turnover funds.

Our results are supportive of taxes affecting investors' behavior. But since the findings hold for both low-momentum and high-momentum portfolios and both low-turnover and high-turnover portfolios, our results are unlikely to be entirely driven by differences in transaction costs from capital gains taxation.

4.2. *Style-Based Predictability*

Perhaps the returns on our switching strategy occur because the strategy is correlated with some well-know passive strategies. For example, if high-flow funds were value funds and low-flow funds were growth funds, then switching between high-flow funds and low-flow funds would be the same as following a value strategy. To the extent that the profitability of the value strategy were high in up markets and zero in down markets, it would generate observationally equivalent results to ours. Although our empirical approach controls for any systematic differences in factor exposure, our

Table 5: Performance of Flow-Based Portfolios: Impact of Transaction Costs

$Flow_{t-1}$	1 Month			3 Months			6 Months			12 Months		
	High	Low	High-Low	High	Low	High-Low	High	Low	High-Low	High	Low	High-Low
Panel A: Low-Momentum Funds												
$I(MKT_t = Up)$	−0.144	−0.284	0.140	−0.117	−0.289	0.172	−0.097	−0.206	0.109	−0.311	−0.400	0.089
(in %, per m.)	(0.300)	(0.031)	(0.194)	(0.140)	(0.000)	(0.005)	(0.105)	(0.005)	(0.046)	(0.002)	(0.001)	(0.140)
$I(MKT_t = Down)$	0.110	0.099	0.011	0.204	0.137	0.077	0.144	0.074	0.070	−0.073	−0.132	0.059
(in %, per m.)	(0.450)	(0.437)	(0.906)	(0.047)	(0.135)	(0.180)	(0.279)	(0.510)	(0.192)	(0.622)	(0.299)	(0.256)
Panel B: High-Momentum Funds												
$I(MKT_t = Up)$	0.137	−0.073	0.210	−0.013	−0.216	0.203	0.038	−0.160	0.198	−0.095	−0.199	0.104
(in %, per m.)	(0.380)	(0.707)	(0.141)	(0.854)	(0.004)	(0.010)	(0.430)	(0.000)	(0.001)	(0.037)	(0.011)	(0.074)
$I(MKT_t = Down)$	−0.268	−0.346	0.078	−0.173	−0.244	0.071	−0.252	−0.288	0.036	−0.176	−0.188	0.012
(in %, per m.)	(0.006)	(0.032)	(0.523)	(0.023)	(0.000)	(0.364)	(0.000)	(0.000)	(0.545)	(0.000)	(0.001)	(0.870)
Panel C: Low-Turnover Funds												
$I(MKT_t = Up)$	−0.085	−0.152	0.067	−0.136	−0.322	0.186	−0.063	−0.241	0.178	−0.247	−0.332	0.085
(in %, per m.)	(0.510)	(0.349)	(0.601)	(0.020)	(0.000)	(0.011)	(0.138)	(0.001)	(0.020)	(0.000)	(0.000)	(0.096)
$I(MKT_t = Down)$	−0.118	−0.147	0.029	−0.033	−0.071	0.038	−0.107	−0.139	0.038	−0.164	−0.194	0.030
(in %, per m.)	(0.038)	(0.115)	(0.787)	(0.534)	(0.049)	(0.604)	(0.010)	(0.061)	(0.576)	(0.000)	(0.000)	(0.639)

(*Continued*)

Table 5: (*Continued*)

$Flow_{t-1}$	1 Month			3 Months			6 Months			12 Months		
	High	Low	High-Low	High	Low	High-Low	High	Low	High-Low	High	Low	High-Low
Panel D: High-Turnover Funds												
$I(MKT_t = Up)$	0.034	−0.111	0.145	−0.001	−0.195	0.194	0.085	−0.128	0.213	−0.044	−0.170	0.126
(in %, per m.)	(0.881)	(0.571)	(0.419)	(0.993)	(0.011)	(0.061)	(0.179)	(0.029)	(0.005)	(0.443)	(0.036)	(0.066)
$I(MKT_t = Down)$	−0.194	−0.148	0.046	−0.068	−0.194	0.126	−0.187	−0.220	0.033	−0.149	−0.159	0.010
(in %, per m.)	(0.030)	(0.357)	(0.766)	(0.444)	(0.000)	(0.223)	(0.011)	(0.001)	(0.663)	(0.041)	(0.122)	(0.910)

We divide all funds with respect to their characteristics. Panel A reports results for low-momentum funds, Panel B for high-momentum funds, Panel C for low-turnover funds, and Panel D for high-turnover funds. For each sample separately, each month, we construct portfolios of funds based on their dollar flows. *High* denotes the return on the equally weighted portfolio of funds which received flows that are higher than the median flow in a given period; *Low* is the return on the equally weighted portfolio of funds which received flows that are lower than the median flow in a given period. Both returns are regressed on a set of four factors: market premium (MKTPREM), size (SMB), value (HML), and momentum (UMD), and their interactions with two indicator functions: $I(MKT_t = Up)$ equals one when the three-month average of past market excess return is higher than the 75th percentile of the historical three-month average of past market excess returns (starting Q3 of 1926); and zero otherwise. $I(MKT_t = Mid)$ equals one when the three-month average of past market excess return is between the 25th and 75th percentiles of the historical three-month average of past market excess returns (starting Q3 of 1926); and zero otherwise. $I(MKT_t = Down)$ equals one when the three-month average of past market excess return is lower than the 25th percentile of the historical three-month average of past market excess returns (starting Q3 of 1926); and zero otherwise. Columns (1)–(2) consider monthly returns one month ahead, columns (3)–(4) monthly returns three months ahead, columns (5)–(6) monthly returns six months ahead, and columns (7)–(8) monthly returns twelve months ahead. Standard errors (in parentheses) are adjusted for autocorrelation up to 12 lags using the procedure as in Newey and West (1987). Each panel reports monthly returns along with their p-values (in parentheses) on portfolios which condition on both market conditions and fund flows. Each panel also reports the results of the F-test of the differences between the respective portfolios. The data cover the period 1980 to 2005.

adjustment may be imprecise. Hence, we examine the predictability results within different investment styles. Table 6 reports the results.

In Panels A and B, we split funds into broad classes of value and growth funds. Value funds are defined as those in which the *Value* indicator is greater than 3; funds with *Value* indicator below 3 are growth funds. We find qualitatively similar patterns within both classes of funds. The magnitude of the observed predictability is slightly stronger for value funds for shorter horizons and stronger for growth funds at longer horizons. In Panels C and D, we compare smaller-cap and larger-cap funds. Smaller-cap funds are defined as those in which the *Size* indicator is below 3; the funds with *Size* indicator above 3 are larger-cap funds. We find no significant difference in economic magnitudes between the two categories of funds. However, the statistical significance is much stronger for larger-cap funds. This difference may occur because our sample is tilted towards larger-cap funds, which might help the precision of our estimates.

We conclude that our results are unlikely to be due to investors trading based on well-known passive investment strategies.

4.3. *Differences in Survivorship*

The design of our performance predictability tests requires that the mutual funds included in each portfolio are present in the sample throughout the entire evaluation period of up to twelve months. Our tests could be biased if some funds dropped out of the sample before the end of the evaluation period. This would produce a survivorship bias (Brown *et al.*, 1992; Carpenter and Lynch, 1999). The survivorship bias issue would not be important if the attrition process randomly affected both portfolios. In such a case, any performance difference would be offset by the difference in the long-short portfolio. On the other hand, our results could be explained by survivorship bias if for example funds in high-flow portfolio were subject to more attrition, and thus had better average performance, than funds in low-flow portfolio, especially after up markets.

We evaluate such a possibility by explicitly looking at the survival rates of different portfolios while also conditioning on market returns. In addition, we calculate survival rates separately for each investment horizon. Table 7 reports the results. As expected, we find that the survival rates decrease with an increase in investment horizon. Nevertheless, the

Table 6: Performance of Flow-Based Portfolios: Within-Style Analysis

	1 Month			3 Months			6 Months			12 Months		
$Flow_{t-1}$	High	Low	High-Low	High	Low	High-Low	High	Low	High-Low	High	Low	High-Low
Panel A: Value Funds												
$I(MKT_t = Up)$	−0.007	−0.138	0.145	−0.067	−0.263	0.196	−0.004	−0.122	0.118	−0.286	−0.319	0.033
(in %, per m.)	(0.974)	(0.284)	(0.214)	(0.548)	(0.003)	(0.003)	(0.940)	(0.055)	(0.014)	(0.001)	(0.001)	(0.349)
$I(MKT_t = Down)$	−0.012	−0.045	0.033	0.182	0.093	0.089	0.077	0.034	0.043	−0.016	−0.011	−0.005
(in %, per m.)	(0.947)	(0.778)	(0.706)	(0.173)	(0.395)	(0.171)	(0.495)	(0.745)	(0.369)	(0.881)	(0.917)	(0.917)
Panel B: Growth Funds												
$I(MKT_t = Up)$	0.002	−0.143	0.145	−0.107	−0.258	0.141	−0.015	−0.174	0.159	−0.160	−0.242	0.082
(in %, per m.)	(0.988)	(0.444)	(0.328)	(0.135)	(0.000)	(0.071)	(0.796)	(0.001)	(0.014)	(0.002)	(0.002)	(0.166)
$I(MKT_t = Down)$	−0.171	−0.180	0.009	−0.088	−0.152	0.064	−0.183	−0.208	0.025	−0.188	−0.183	−0.005
(in %, per m.)	(0.024)	(0.119)	(0.938)	(0.163)	(0.000)	(0.436)	(0.000)	(0.000)	(0.690)	(0.000)	(0.002)	(0.950)
Panel C: Small-Cap Funds												
$I(MKT_t = Up)$	−0.152	−0.257	0.105	−0.233	−0.406	0.173	−0.078	−0.185	0.107	−0.291	−0.390	0.099
(in %, per m.)	(0.558)	(0.225)	(0.580)	(0.032)	(0.001)	(0.124)	(0.276)	(0.018)	(0.164)	(0.016)	(0.002)	(0.196)
$I(MKT_t = Down)$	−0.047	−0.289	0.242	0.135	0.013	0.122	−0.130	−0.144	0.014	−0.189	−0.250	0.061
(in %, per m.)	(0.226)	(0.297)	(0.451)	(0.000)	(0.001)	(0.131)	(0.001)	(0.002)	(0.193)	(0.000)	(0.068)	(0.359)

Panel D: Large-Cap Funds												
$I(MKT_t = Up)$	0.038	−0.086	0.124	0.022	−0.179	0.201	0.083	−0.086	0.169	−0.053	−0.185	0.132
(in %, per m.)	(0.797)	(0.508)	(0.383)	(0.736)	(0.000)	(0.013)	(0.037)	(0.023)	(0.006)	(0.109)	(0.002)	(0.011)
$I(MKT_t = Down)$	−0.132	−0.092	−0.040	−0.109	−0.142	0.033	−0.157	−0.167	0.010	−0.162	−0.142	−0.020
(in %, per m.)	(0.026)	(0.433)	(0.742)	(0.010)	(0.001)	(0.683)	(0.000)	(0.000)	(0.863)	(0.000)	(0.010)	(0.762)

We divide all funds with respect to their investment style. Panel A reports results for value funds, Panel B for growth funds, Panel C for small-cap funds, and Panel D for large-cap funds. For each sample separately, each month, we construct portfolios of funds based on their dollar flows. *High* denotes the return on the equally weighted portfolio of funds which received flows that are higher than the median flow in a given period; *Low* is the return on the equally weighted portfolio of funds which received flows that are lower than the median flow in a given period. Both returns are regressed on a set of four factors: market premium (MKTPREM), size (SMB), value (HML), and momentum (UMD), and their interactions with two indicator functions: $I(MKT_t = Up)$ equals one when the three-month average of past market excess return is higher than the 75th percentile of the historical three-month average of past market excess returns (starting Q3 of 1926); and zero otherwise. $I(MKT_t = Mid)$ equals one when the three-month average of past market excess return is between the 25th and 75th percentiles of the historical three-month average of past market excess returns (starting Q3 of 1926); and zero otherwise. $I(MKT_t = Down)$ equals one when the three-month average of past market excess return is lower than the 25th percentile of the historical three-month average of past market excess returns (starting Q3 of 1926); and zero otherwise. Columns (1)–(2) consider monthly returns one month ahead, columns (3)–(4) monthly returns three months ahead, columns (5)–(6) monthly returns six months ahead, and columns (7)–(8) monthly returns twelve months ahead. Standard errors (in parentheses) are adjusted for autocorrelation up to 12 lags using the procedure as in Newey and West (1987). Each panel reports monthly returns along with their p-values (in parentheses) on portfolios which condition on both market conditions and fund flows. Each panel also reports the results of the F-test of the differences between the respective portfolios. The data cover the period 1980 to 2005.

Table 7: Survival Rates in Flow-Based Portfolios

	1 Month			3 Months			6 Months			12 Months		
$Flow_{t-1}$	High	Low	High-Low	High	Low	High-Low	High	Low	High-Low	High	Low	High-Low
$I(MKT_t = Up)$	98.58	98.52	0.06	96.60	96.64	−0.05	94.45	94.00	0.45	88.51	87.49	1.02
(in %, per m.)	(2.43)	(2.40)	(0.735)	(3.45)	(2.76)	(0.906)	(4.56)	(3.53)	(0.461)	(4.47)	(3.82)	(0.258)
$I(MKT_t = Down)$	98.17	98.71	−0.54	94.87	95.26	−0.38	89.93	90.53	−0.60	84.74	85.66	−0.92
(in %, per m.)	(2.19)	(1.77)	(0.035)	(5.17)	(4.47)	(0.393)	(5.93)	(5.84)	(0.385)	(5.91)	(6.26)	(0.241)

Each month we construct portfolios of funds based on their dollar flows. *High* denotes the portfolio of funds which received flows that are higher than the median flow in a given period; *Low* is the portfolio of funds which received flows that are lower than the median flow in a given period. Both portfolios are tracked over one, three, six, and twelve months, conditional on two indicator functions:$I(MKT_t = Up)$ equals one when the three-month average of past market excess return is higher than the 75th percentile of the historical three-month average of past market excess returns (starting Q3 of 1926); and zero otherwise. $I(MKT_t = Mid)$ equals one when the three-month average of past market excess return is between the 25th and 75th percentiles of the historical three-month average of past market excess returns (starting Q3 of 1926); and zero otherwise. $I(MKT_t = Down)$ equals one when the three-month average of past market excess return is lower than the 25th percentile of the historical three-month average of past market excess returns (starting Q3 of 1926); and zero otherwise. We estimate average survival rates as a time-series average of the ratio of the number of funds that appear in the beginning and the end of the investment period and the number of funds that appear in the beginning of the investment period. We report the differences in average survival rates along with their p-values (in parentheses). The data cover the period 1980 to 2005.

average survival rates are generally quite high: In the portfolio with a one-year investment horizon these rates approach 90%. Moreover, we find no evidence of significant differences in survivorship across the different conditional portfolios. If anything, the difference in survival rates is slightly higher for portfolios after down markets. Hence, the asymmetric predictability in performance we document is unlikely to be driven by differences in funds' survivorship.

4.4. *Investors' Capital Allocation Mistakes*

One plausible mechanism behind our findings is that mutual fund investors — as a group — are more prone to making mistakes when allocating capital after periods of high market returns than after periods of low market returns. Our results suggest that after periods of high market returns, mutual fund investors leave too much capital in poor performing funds and move too little capital into good performing funds. Lamont and Thaler (2003) and Brunnermeier and Nagel (2004) provide empirical evidence of irrational investment decisions by individual or retail investors. Consequently, if capital allocation mistakes are driving our findings of asymmetric predictability in mutual fund performance, we expect the observed differences in fund predictability to be more pronounced for retail investors than for institutional investors.

We estimate equation (3.2) separately for retail and institutional investors. Panel A of Table 8 presents the results for retail investors. We observe patterns similar to those presented in Table 3: strong predictability in the performance earned by switching capital across funds after up markets but no predictability in performance after down markets. The magnitude is economically significant and varies from 1.8% for a one-year horizon to 3.2% on an annualized basis for a three-month horizon. In Panel B, we present the results for institutional investors. We find no predictability in the performance earned from switching across funds after up or down markets.

Another instrument we use is the fund age. Young funds may be regarded by investors as new and fashionable and so may attract fund flows from less sophisticated investors. Simultaneously, such funds are also less known to investors, making it more likely for investors to make mistakes in their investments such funds. To this end, we consider two groups of funds:

Table 8: Performance of Flow-Based Portfolios: Based on Investors' Type

Panel A: Retail Investors

	1 Month		3 Months		6 Months		12 Months	
$Flow_{t-1}$	High	Low	High	Low	High	Low	High	Low
MKTPREM	0.982	0.998	0.972	0.999	0.966	0.975	0.961	0.937
	(0.012)	(0.016)	(0.016)	(0.017)	(0.019)	(0.025)	(0.025)	(0.041)
SMB	0.230	0.097	0.229	0.120	0.226	0.180	0.253	0.178
	(0.015)	(0.049)	(0.019)	(0.055)	(0.022)	(0.038)	(0.034)	(0.049)
HML	−0.062	−0.009	−0.076	0.028	−0.073	0.038	−0.073	0.051
	(−0.025)	(−0.049)	(−0.023)	(0.053)	(−0.023)	(0.050)	(−0.024)	(0.067)
UMD	0.031	−0.039	0.027	−0.058	0.044	−0.008	0.080	0.041
	(0.013)	(−0.030)	(0.010)	(−0.033)	(0.015)	(−0.022)	(0.021)	(0.030)
MKTPREM x	−0.032	−0.028	−0.049	−0.009	−0.101	−0.018	−0.015	0.021
$I(MKT_t = Up)$	(−0.034)	(−0.039)	(−0.031)	(−0.022)	(−0.048)	(−0.033)	(−0.034)	(0.042)
MKTPREM x	0.074	−0.014	0.055	0.013	0.084	0.120	0.042	0.129
$I(MKT_t = Down)$	(0.023)	(−0.039)	(0.025)	(0.029)	(0.030)	(0.042)	(0.027)	(0.047)
SMB x	−0.080	0.071	−0.004	0.092	0.062	0.045	−0.007	0.030
$I(MKT_t = Up)$	(−0.045)	(0.056)	(−0.042)	(0.052)	(0.053)	(0.041)	(−0.040)	(0.046)
SMB x	−0.032	0.049	−0.004	−0.040	−0.023	−0.139	−0.067	−0.107
$I(MKT_t = Down)$	(−0.034)	(0.057)	(−0.048)	(−0.053)	(−0.050)	(−0.058)	(−0.052)	(−0.069)
HML x	−0.058	−0.102	−0.013	−0.075	−0.086	−0.155	0.063	−0.012
$I(MKT_t = Up)$	(−0.067)	(−0.080)	(−0.029)	(−0.063)	(−0.046)	(−0.061)	(0.052)	(−0.072)
HML x	0.115	0.099	0.107	0.063	0.125	0.152	0.045	0.093
$I(MKT_t = Down)$	(0.033)	(0.059)	(0.034)	(0.041)	(0.032)	(0.038)	(0.044)	(0.063)
UMD x	−0.018	0.032	−0.040	0.081	−0.067	−0.016	−0.013	0.067

$I(MKT_t = Up)$	(−0.076)	(0.062)	(−0.047)	(0.038)	(−0.030)	(−0.023)	(−0.071)	(0.105)
UMD x	0.048	0.051	0.041	0.046	0.040	0.035	0.018	−0.004
$I(MKT_t = Down)$	(0.029)	(0.033)	(0.020)	(0.027)	(0.041)	(0.039)	(0.030)	(−0.030)
$I(MKT_t = Up)$	0.000	−0.001	0.000	−0.002	0.001	−0.001	0.000	−0.001
	(0.002)	(−0.002)	(0.001)	(−0.001)	(0.001)	(−0.001)	(0.001)	(−0.001)
$I(MKT_t = Down)$	−0.001	−0.001	0.000	0.000	−0.001	−0.001	0.000	−0.001
	(−0.001)	(−0.002)	(0.001)	(0.001)	(−0.000)	(−0.001)	(0.001)	(−0.001)
Constant	0.000	0.000	0.000	0.000	0.000	−0.001	−0.001	−0.001
	(0.000)	(0.001)	(0.000)	(0.001)	(0.000)	(−0.001)	(−0.000)	(−0.001)
Observations	307	307	305	305	302	302	296	296
R^2	0.97	0.97	0.97	0.96	0.97	0.97	0.97	0.95

Panel A: Retail Investors

	1 Month			3 Months			6 Months			12 Months		
$Flow_{t-1}$	High	Low	High-Low	High	Low	High-Low	High	Low	High-Low	High	Low	High-Low
$I(MKT_t = Up)$	0.040	−0.101	0.141	0.032	−0.235	0.267	0.106	−0.110	0.216	−0.046	−0.200	0.154
(in %, per m.)	(0.819)	(0.577)	(0.361)	(0.653)	(0.001)	(0.002)	(0.020)	(0.024)	(0.001)	(0.396)	(0.010)	(0.010)
$I(MKT_t = Down)$	−0.065	−0.111	0.046	0.015	−0.070	0.085	−0.084	−0.135	0.051	−0.085	−0.124	0.039
(in %, per m.)	(0.297)	(0.394)	(0.726)	(0.842)	(0.143)	(0.320)	(0.122)	(0.017)	(0.430)	(0.112)	(0.052)	(0.605)

(*Continued*)

Table 8: (*Continued*)

Panel B: Institutional Investors

	1 Month		3 Months		6 Months		12 Months	
$Flow_{t-1}$	High	Low	High	Low	High	Low	High	Low
MKTPREM	0.974	0.963	0.958	0.975	0.959	0.966	0.949	0.935
	(0.012)	(0.019)	(0.011)	(0.020)	(0.018)	(0.020)	(0.025)	(0.032)
SMB	0.230	0.132	0.237	0.131	0.228	0.196	0.292	0.206
	(0.025)	(0.047)	(0.027)	(0.051)	(0.032)	(0.032)	(0.034)	(0.033)
HML	−0.021	−0.005	−0.013	0.010	−0.023	0.034	−0.019	0.039
	(−0.024)	(−0.047)	(−0.024)	(0.050)	(−0.028)	(0.042)	(−0.030)	(0.056)
UMD	0.002	−0.035	0.000	−0.060	0.018	−0.017	0.053	0.010
	(0.014)	(−0.028)	(0.014)	(−0.029)	(0.016)	(−0.017)	(0.023)	(0.023)
MKTPREM x	−0.098	−0.009	−0.052	−0.057	−0.073	−0.060	0.012	0.028
$I(MKT_t = Up)$	(−0.044)	(−0.033)	(−0.035)	(−0.026)	(−0.050)	(−0.031)	(0.035)	(0.039)
MKTPREM x	0.056	−0.005	0.068	0.020	0.065	0.063	0.060	0.050
$I(MKT_t = Down)$	(0.035)	(−0.036)	(0.029)	(0.032)	(0.031)	(0.036)	(0.024)	(0.039)
SMB x	−0.040	0.097	0.078	0.166	0.114	0.111	0.005	0.025
$I(MKT_t = Up)$	(−0.043)	(0.050)	(0.048)	(0.050)	(0.050)	(0.038)	(0.040)	(0.040)
SMB x	−0.021	0.034	−0.003	−0.002	0.026	−0.109	−0.012	−0.066
$I(MKT_t = Down)$	(−0.030)	(0.052)	(−0.044)	(−0.051)	(0.058)	(−0.054)	(−0.043)	(−0.053)
HML x	−0.150	−0.093	−0.033	−0.067	−0.072	−0.142	0.091	0.048
$I(MKT_t = Up)$	(−0.078)	(−0.081)	(−0.030)	(−0.061)	(−0.055)	(−0.056)	(0.053)	(0.069)
HML x	0.098	0.098	0.082	0.102	0.108	0.159	0.058	0.072
$I(MKT_t = Down)$	(0.031)	(0.057)	(0.036)	(0.043)	(0.043)	(0.036)	(0.047)	(0.054)
UMD x	−0.044	0.034	−0.025	0.108	−0.039	0.007	0.027	0.094
$I(MKT_t = Up)$	(−0.055)	(0.054)	(−0.045)	(0.036)	(−0.023)	(0.024)	(0.069)	(0.104)
UMD x	0.060	0.042	0.055	0.056	0.068	0.031	0.043	0.007
$I(MKT_t = Down)$	(0.025)	(0.028)	(0.021)	(0.029)	(0.040)	(0.039)	(0.033)	(0.028)
$I(MKT_t = Up)$	0.000	−0.002	−0.001	−0.002	0.000	−0.001	−0.001	−0.002
	(0.002)	(−0.002)	(−0.001)	(−0.001)	(0.001)	(−0.001)	(−0.001)	(−0.001)

	(1)	(2)	(3)	(4)	(5)	(6)	(7)	(8)
$I(MKT_t = Down)$	−0.002	−0.001	−0.001	−0.001	−0.002	−0.001	−0.001	−0.001
	(−0.001)	(−0.001)	(−0.001)	(−0.001)	(−0.001]	(−0.001)	(−0.000)	(−0.001)
Constant	−0.001	−0.001	−0.001	−0.001	−0.001	−0.002	−0.002	−0.002
	(−0.001)	(−0.001)	(−0.000)	(−0.001)	(−0.000)	(−0.000)	(−0.001)	(−0.000)
Observations	307	307	305	305	302	302	296	296
R^2	0.97	0.97	0.97	0.96	0.97	0.97	0.97	0.95

	1 Month			3 Months			6 Months			12 Months		
$Flow_{t-1}$	High	Low	High-Low	High	Low	High-Low	High	Low	High-Low	High	Low	High-Low
$I(MKT_t = Up)$ (in %, per m.)	−0.081	−0.318	0.237	−0.228	−0.348	0.120	−0.171	−0.216	0.055	−0.324	−0.360	0.038
	(0.597)	(0.020)	(0.146)	(0.002)	(0.000)	(0.176)	(0.003)	(0.000)	(0.493)	(0.000)	(0.000)	(0.534)
$I(MKT_t = Down)$ (in %, per m.)	−0.292	−0.251	−0.041	−0.249	−0.244	−0.005	−0.333	−0.283	−0.050	−0.315	−0.243	−0.072
	(0.001)	(0.027)	(0.763)	(0.000)	(0.000)	(0.954)	(0.000)	(0.000)	(0.442)	(0.000)	(0.000)	(0.327)

We divide all funds into retail and institutional categories. For each category separately, each month, we construct portfolios of funds based on their last month dollar flows. *High* denotes the return on the equally weighted portfolio of funds which received flows that are higher than the median flow in a given period; *Low* is the return on the equally weighted portfolio of funds which received flows that are lower than the median flow in a given period. Both returns are regressed on a set of four factors: market premium (MKTPREM), size (SMB), value (HML), and momentum (UMD), and their interactions with two indicator functions:$I(MKT_t = Up)$ equals one when the three-month average of past market excess return is higher than the 75th percentile of the historical three-month average of past market excess returns (starting Q3 of 1926); and zero otherwise. $I(MKT_t = Mid)$ equals one when the three-month average of past market excess return is between the 25th and 75th percentiles of the historical three-month average of past market excess returns (starting Q3 of 1926); and zero otherwise. $I(MKT_t = Down)$ equals one when the three-month average of past market excess return is lower than the 25th percentile of the historical three-month average of past market excess returns (starting Q3 of 1926); and zero otherwise. Columns (1)–(2) consider monthly returns one month ahead, columns (3)–(4) monthly returns three months ahead, columns (5)–(6) monthly returns six months ahead, and columns (7)–(8) monthly returns twelve months ahead. Standard errors (in parentheses) are adjusted for autocorrelation up to 12 lags using the procedure as in Newey and West (1987). Panel A reports the results for retail investors and Panel B presents the results for institutional investors. A bottom panel of each Panel reports monthly returns along with their p-values (in parentheses) on portfolios which condition on both market conditions and fund flows. The panel also reports the results of the F-test of the differences between the respective portfolios. The data cover the period 1980 to 2005.

Funds that are not more than three years old, and funds that are nine or more years old, which is the median fund age in our sample. For each group, we again consider predictability patterns in the model in which investors can switch across different types of funds. Table 9 reports the results.

We find a significant degree of performance predictability in both groups of funds after up markets but not after down markets. The magnitude of the abnormal returns is quite different between the two groups. The abnormal returns are significant for young funds, especially for short-term, one-month and three-month horizons, and slightly weaker for longer horizons. The abnormal returns are significant only for old funds for the middle-term horizons. The results are consistent with the explanation that less sophisticated investors channel their funds extensively and quickly to new mutual funds and such investors tend to repeat the same capital allocation mistakes over time.

The results in this section suggest that the primary factor for the observed differences in predictability across market conditions could be that retail investors rather than institutional investors make more investment mistakes after up markets than after down markets.

5. Variations in Fund Managers' Strategies

Investors seem to incorporate information more efficiently after periods of low market returns than they do after periods of high market returns. Do fund managers respond to that by altering their behavior across market conditions? Following high market returns, fund managers should have weaker incentives to exert costly effort to acquire unique information, while following periods of low returns fund managers should have stronger incentives to exert effort. The type of information collected, processed, and used by mutual fund managers to form portfolios should vary with market conditions.

One way in which such time variation in incentives may show up is that when more unique information is known, funds should pursue investment strategies that are cross-sectionally more distinct. Here, we examine how the level of cross-sectional dispersion in investment strategies moves with market conditions. We use measures similar to those of Chevalier and Ellison (1999) to capture dispersion in managers' portfolios with respect to a typical fund portfolio at time t.

Table 9: Performance of Flow-Based Portfolios: Based on Fund Age

Fund Age<= 3

	1 Month			3 Months			6 Months			12 Months		
$Flow_{t-1}$	High	Low	High-Low	High	Low	High-Low	High	Low	High-Low	High	Low	High-Low
$I(MKT_t = Up)$	0.046	−0.553	0.599	0.176	−0.289	0.465	−0.024	−0.043	0.019	−0.085	−0.275	0.190
(in %, per m.)	(0.855)	(0.000)	(0.015)	(0.185)	(0.000)	(0.001)	(0.808)	(0.704)	(0.892)	(0.394)	(0.054)	(0.075)
$I(MKT_t = Down)$	−0.076	−0.168	0.092	−0.132	−0.250	0.118	−0.247	−0.278	0.031	−0.205	−0.241	0.036
(in %, per m.)	(0.595)	(0.302)	(0.661)	(0.029)	(0.005)	(0.382)	(0.003)	(0.042)	(0.812)	(0.006)	(0.031)	(0.783)

Fund Age>= 3

	1 Month			3 Months			6 Months			12 Months		
$Flow_{t-1}$	High	Low	High-Low	High	Low	High-Low	High	Low	High-Low	High	Low	High-Low
$I(MKT_t = Up)$	−0.024	−0.112	0.088	−0.075	−0.228	0.153	0.016	−0.126	0.110	−0.168	−0.246	0.078
(in %, per m.)	(0.877)	(0.432)	(0.550)	(0.216)	(0.000)	(0.060)	(0.677)	(0.006)	(0.026)	(0.004)	(0.001)	(0.193)
$I(MKT_t = Down)$	−0.152	−0.172	0.020	−0.066	−0.123	0.057	−0.133	−0.163	0.030	−0.179	−0.187	0.008
(in %, per m.)	(0.016)	(0.175)	(0.873)	(0.336)	(0.010)	(0.482)	(0.006)	(0.003)	(0.647)	(0.000)	(0.002)	(0.912)

We divide all funds with respect to their age. Panel A reports results for funds younger than three years and Panel B for funds older than nine years (median value of the fund sample). For each sample separately, each month, we construct portfolios of funds based on their dollar flows. *High* denotes the return on the equally weighted portfolio of funds which received flows that are higher than the median flow in a given period; *Low* is the return on the equally weighted portfolio of funds which received flows that are lower than the median flow in a given period. Both returns are regressed on a set of four factors: market premium (MKTPREM), size (SMB), value (HML), and momentum (UMD), and their interactions with two indicator functions: $I(MKT_t = Up)$ equals one when the three-month average of past market excess return is higher than the 75th percentile of the historical three-month average of past market excess returns (starting Q3 of 1926); and zero otherwise. $I(MKT_t = Mid)$ equals one when the three-month average of past market excess return is between the 25th and 75th percentiles of the historical three-month average of past market excess returns (starting Q3 of 1926); and zero otherwise. $I(MKT_t = Down)$ equals one when the three-month average of past market excess return is lower than the 25th percentile of the historical three-month average of past market excess returns (starting Q3 of 1926); and zero otherwise. Each panel reports monthly returns along with their p-values (in parentheses) on portfolios which condition on both market conditions and fund flows. Columns (1)–(2) consider monthly returns one month ahead, columns (3)–(4) monthly returns three months ahead, columns (5)–(6) monthly returns six months ahead, and columns (7)–(8) monthly returns twelve months ahead. Standard errors (in parentheses) are adjusted for autocorrelation up to 12 lags using the procedure as in Newey and West (1987). Each panel also reports the results of the F-test of the differences between the respective portfolios. The data cover the period 1980 to 2005.

We consider three dispersion measures. The first one, *Beta Deviation*, measures boldness in the sense of taking a large bet on the direction of the market. The variable is calculated as the absolute value of the difference between fund *i*'s beta in month *t* and the average beta in that month across all funds in the fund's objective class. Individual fund beta is a market beta from a four-factor model calculated using 36 months of past returns:

$$BetaDeviation_{i,t} = |Beta_{i,t} - \overline{Beta}_{g,v}|. \tag{3.3}$$

The second one, *Sector Deviation*, measures boldness in the style of a manager. The measure captures how much a manager concentrates her portfolio in sectors that differ from those that are most popular at the time. Specifically, *Sector Deviation* is defined as the mean square root of the sum of squared differences between the share of fund *i*'s assets in each of 10 industry sectors of Fama and French (1997) and the mean share in each sector in quarter *t* among all funds in fund *i*'s objective class: aggressive growth, growth, or value.[8]

$$SectorDeviation_{i,t} = \frac{1}{J}\left(\sum_{j}\sqrt{\sum_{k}(w_{kj} - \overline{w}_{g,v})^2}\right), \tag{3.4}$$

where w_k is the weight of stock *k* in industry *j*, and $\overline{w}_{g,v}$ is the weight of a fund objective (growth, value) in the same industry *j*; *J* is the number of distinct industries.

The third dispersion variable is *Unsystematic Deviation*, which measures fund boldness in terms of a departure from a typical portfolio, based on the level of its unsystematic risk. Specifically, the variable is calculated as the absolute value of the difference between a fund's unsystematic risk, *Unsystematic Risk*, and the sample average of this variable over all funds in fund *i*'s objective class in month *t*. *Unsystematic Risk* is the absolute value of the residual from the Carhart (1997) four-factor model:

$$UnsystematicDeviation_{i,t} = |UnsystematicRisk_{i,t} - \overline{UnsystematicRisk}_{g,v}|. \tag{3.5}$$

[8]To identify investment objectives we use CDA style categories 2, 3, and 4. Industry sectors are defined using a modified 10-industry classification of Fama and French, as in Kacperczyk, Sialm, and Zheng (2005).

By construction, a smaller value for each of these variables corresponds to less dispersion in the managers' portfolios and thus possibly less unique information being acquired.

We relate the measures of dispersion of investment strategies to market conditions by estimating the regression model:

$$Dispersion_{i,t} = \lambda_0 + \lambda_1 I(MKT_t = Up) + \lambda_2 I(MKT_t = Down) + \lambda_3 X_{i,t} + FundF.E. + \epsilon_{i,t}. \quad (3.6)$$

Here, *Dispersion* denotes the degree of similarity in investment strategy of fund i at time t and it is proxied by *Beta Deviation*, *Sector Deviation*, and *Unsystematic Deviation*. $I(MKT_t = Up)$ and $I(MKT_t = Down)$ represent the state of the market, and X defines the set of control variables. Our controls include *Performance*, *Log(Age)*, *Log(TNA)*, *Expenses*, *Turnover*, *Flow*, *Value*, *Size*, and *Momentum*. In addition, some specifications include fund-fixed effects.

The coefficients of interest are λ_1 and λ_2. We expect these coefficients to vary systematically if the fund strategies differ after up and down markets. For instance, if the fund managers' strategies are similar after up but different after down markets, λ_1 will be negative and λ_2 will be positive.

The results, presented in Table 10, show that fund strategies are generally more dispersed after down markets than after up markets.

Table 10: Fund Strategies and Market Conditions

	Beta Deviation		Sector Deviation		Unsystematic Deviation	
Performance	−0.196	−0.167	0.056	0.024	−0.139	−0.099
	(0.054)	(0.032)	(0.052)	(0.024)	(0.192)	(0.159)
Log(Age)	0.001	0.007	−0.022	−0.022	−0.011	−0.031
	(0.002)	(0.003)	(0.002)	(0.001)	(0.005)	(0.007)
Log(TNA)	−0.001	−0.005	−0.007	−0.003	−0.009	−0.001
	(0.001)	(0.001)	(0.001)	(0.001)	(0.002)	(0.002)
Expenses	2.161	−0.428	1.739	−0.674	4.835	0.040
	(0.513)	(0.193)	(0.326)	(0.187)	(0.851)	(0.788)
Flow	−0.015	0.001	0.011	−0.014	0.029	0.024
	(0.012)	(0.008)	(0.012)	(0.007)	(0.037)	(0.029)

(*Continued*)

Table 10: (*Continued*)

	Beta Deviation		Sector Deviation		Unsystematic Deviation	
Turnover	0.015	0.003	−0.002	−0.003	0.048	0.028
	(0.003)	(0.001)	(0.002)	(0.001)	(0.007)	(0.004)
Value	0.004	0.003	0.011	0.002	−0.026	−0.025
	(0.005)	(0.001)	(0.004)	(0.001)	(0.009)	(0.006)
Size	−0.010	−0.007	−0.013	−0.007	−0.029	−0.036
	(0.002)	(0.002)	(0.002)	(0.001)	(0.005)	(0.007)
Momentum	−0.002	−0.009	0.002	0.002	0.003	0.002
	(0.003)	(0.002)	(0.003)	(0.001)	(0.008)	(0.006)
$I(MKT_t = Up)$	−0.002	−0.002	0.003	0.003	−0.005	−0.007
	(0.005)	(0.004)	(0.005)	(0.003)	(0.006)	(0.006)
$I(MKT_t = Down)$	0.011	0.010	0.003	0.003	0.011	0.010
	(0.004)	(0.004)	(0.005)	(0.004)	(0.006)	(0.005)
Constant	0.146	0.199	0.219	0.281	0.787	0.897
	(0.026)	(0.010)	(0.022)	(0.007)	(0.048)	(0.042)
Observations	167,584	167,584	58,144	58,144	167,584	167,584
R^2	0.03	0.39	0.07	0.64	0.02	0.10
Fund Fixed-Effects	No	Yes	No	Yes	No	Yes
	F-test: $I(MKT_t = Up) = I(MKT_t = Down)$					
Difference	−0.013	−0.012	−0.000	0.000	−0.016	−0.018
	(0.000)	(0.032)	(0.821)	(0.894)	(0.001)	(0.017)

The dependent variables are *BetaDeviation* in Columns (1) and (2), *SectorDeviation* in Columns (3) and (4) and *UnsystematicDeviation* in Columns (5) and (6). Bottom row provides the F-test along with its p-values of the differences between coefficients on $I(MKT_t = Up)$ and $I(MKT_t = Down)$. Our controls include Performance, Log(Age), Log(TNA), Expenses, Flow, Turnover, Value, Size, and Momentum. Flow, Performance, and Turnover have been winsorized at the 1% level. All variables are defined in Table 2. $I(MKT_t = Up)$ equals one when the three-month average of past market excess return is higher than the 75th percentile of the historical three-month average of past market excess returns (starting Q3 of 1926); and zero otherwise. $I(MKT_t = Mid)$ equals one when the three-month average of past market excess return is between the 25th and 75th percentiles of the historical three-month average of past market excess returns (starting Q3 of 1926); and zero otherwise. $I(MKT_t = Down)$ equals one when the three-month average of past market excess return is lower than the 25th percentile of the historical three-month average of past market excess returns (starting Q3 of 1926); and zero otherwise. Standard errors (in parentheses) are clustered by fund and time. A bottom panel reports an F-test of differences in coefficients on $I(MKT_t = Up)$ and $I(MKT_t = Down)$ along with their p-values (in parentheses). The data cover the period 1980 to 2005.

The difference between up markets and down markets is statistically significant for measures of *Beta Deviation* and *Unsystematic Deviation* and is statistically insignificant for *Sector Deviation*. The results hold when we include fund-fixed effects. Moreover, the coefficient on $I(MKT_t = Up)$ is negative and the coefficient on $I(MKT_t = Down)$ is positive for two out of the three measures of dispersion. Fund managers appear to internalize the behavior of fund investors in their trading strategies.

6. Conclusion

We show evidence of time-varying predictability in the cross section of mutual fund returns. Our evidence suggests that investors in the mutual fund sector do not always react efficiently to information and leave significantly more money on the table after periods of high market returns than after periods of low market returns. Investing in funds with high fund flows when market returns are high produces future abnormal returns (compared with investing in funds with low fund flows), while investing similarly when market returns are low does not produce future abnormal returns. Similarly, investing in funds with good performance when market returns are high produces future abnormal returns (compared with investing in funds with poor performance), while investing in funds with good performance when market returns are low does not produce future abnormal returns. The return predictability is robust to the inclusion of standard risk and style controls, as well as the time-series variation in factor loadings.

The differential response in fund flows across market conditions is largely confined to retail funds, rather than institutional funds, consistent with the observed differences in returns result across these two groups of investors. Fund managers seem to recognize that investors behave differently in up and down markets — their investment strategies are more dispersed cross-sectionally after periods of low market returns than after periods of high market returns.

Our results suggest the presence of relative mispricings in the equity mutual fund industry after periods of high returns, exactly when industry size is large. The finding, in turn, has strong implications for mutual fund investors — mostly individual households — as well as for the overall market efficiency debate and asset pricing. Indeed, recent work by Vayanos and Woolley (2010) examines implications of institutional trading for asset prices. Studying the implications of our findings in such a setting is a fruitful area for future research.

References

Bailey, Warren, Alok Kumar, and David Ng, Behavioral Biases of Mutual Fund Investors, 2010, *Journal of Financial Economics*, forthcoming.

Bergstresser, Daniel, James Poterba, and Rebecca Zarutskie, 2003, Mutual Fund Portfolio Turnover and the Effective Tax Burden on Taxable Investors, Working Paper, Duke University.

Berk, Jonathan B. and Richard C. Green, 2004, Mutual Fund Flows and Performance in Rational Markets, *Journal of Political Economy* 112: 1269–1295.

Brown, Stephen, William Goetzmann, Jonnathan Ingersoll, and Stephen A. Ross, 1992, Survivorship Bias in Performance Studies, *Review of Financial Studies* 5: 553–580.

Brunnermeier, Markus and Stefan Nagel, 2004, Hedge Funds and the Technology Bubble, *Journal of Finance* 59: 2013–2040.

Carhart, Mark, 1997, On Persistence in Mutual Fund Performance', *Journal of Finance* 52: 57–82.

Carpenter, Jennifer and Anthony W. Lynch, 1999, Survivorship Bias and Attrition Effects in Measures of Performance Persistence, *Journal of Financial Economics* 54: 337–374.

Chen, Joseph, Harrison Hong, Ming Huang, and Jeffrey Kubik, 2004, Does Fund Size Erode Mutual Fund Performance?, *American Economic Review* 94: 1276–1302.

Chevalier, Judith and Glenn Ellison, 1999, Career Concerns of Mutual Fund Managers, *Quarterly Journal of Economics* 114: 389–432.

Christoffersen, Susan, 2001, Why do Money Fund Managers Voluntarily Waive their Fees?, *Journal of Finance* 56: 1117–1140.

Cohen, Randolph, Joshua D. Coval, and Ľuboš Pástor, 2005, Judging Fund Managers by the Company that They Keep, *Journal of Finance* 60: 1057–1096.

Cooper, Michael J., Roberto C. Gutierrez, and Allaudeen Hameed, 2004, Market States and Momentum, *Journal of Finance* 59: 1345–1366.

Cremers, Martijn and Antti Petajisto, 2008, How Active is Your Fund Manager? A New Measure that Predicts Performance, *Review of Financial Studies* 22: 3329–3365.

Edelen, Roger M., Richard Evans, and Gregory B. Kadlec, 2007, Scale Effects in Mutual Fund Performance: The Role of Trading Costs, Working Paper, University of Virginia.

Elton, Edwin J., Martin J. Gruber, and Christopher R. Blake, 2001, A First Look at the Accuracy of CRSP Mutual Fund Database and a Comparison of the CRSP and the Morningstar Mutual Fund Database, *Journal of Finance* 56: 2415–2430.

Fama, Eugene F. and Kenneth R. French, 1997, Industry Costs of Equity, *Journal of Financial Economics* 43: 153–193.

Ferson, Wayne E. and Rudi W. Schadt, 1996, Measuring Fund Strategy and Performance in Changing Economic Conditions, *Journal of Finance* 51: 425–461.

Frazzini, Andrea and Owen A. Lamont, 2008, Dumb Money: Mutual Fund Flows and the Cross-Section of Stock Returns, *Journal of Financial Economics* 88: 299–322.

Glode, Vincent, Why do Mutual Funds 'Underperform'?, *Journal of Financial Economics* 99: 546–559.

Grinblatt, Mark and Matti Keloharju, 2001, What Makes Investors Trade?, *Journal of Finance* 56: 589–616.

Gruber, Martin. J., 1996, Another Puzzle: The Growth in Actively Managed Mutual Funds, *Journal of Finance* 51: 783–810.

Kacperczyk, Marcin and Amit Seru, 2007, Fund Manager Use of Public Information: New Evidence on Managerial Skills, *Journal of Finance* 62: 485–528.

Kacperczyk, Marcin, Clemens Sialm and Lu Zheng, 2005, On the Industry Concentration of Actively Managed Equity Mutual Funds, *Journal of Finance* 60: 1983–2011.

Kacperczyk, Marcin, Clemens Sialm and Lu Zheng, 2008, Unobserved Actions of Mutual Funds, *Review of Financial Studies* 21: 2379–2416.

Kacperczyk, Marcin, Stijn van Nieuwerburgh, and Laura Veldkamp, 2016, A Rational Theory of Mutual Funds' Attention Allocation, *Econometrica* 84: 571–626.

Lamont, Owen A. and Richard H. Thaler, 2003, Can the Market Add and Subtract? Mispricing in Tech Stock Carve-Outs, *Journal of Political Economy* 111: 227–268.

Lynch, Anthony W. and David K. Musto, 2003, How Investors Interpret Past Returns, *Journal of Finance* 58: 2033–2058.

Mamaysky, Harry, Matthew Spiegel, and Hong Zhang, 2007, Estimating the Dynamics of Mutual Fund Alphas and Betas, *Review of Financial Studies* 21: 233–264.

Newey, Whitney K. and Kenneth D. West, 1987, A Simple Positive-Definite Heteroskedasticity and Autocorrelation Consistent Covariance Matrix, *Econometrica* 55: 703–708.

Pástor, Ľuboš and Robert Stambaugh, 2012, On the Size of the Active Management Industry, *Journal of Political Economics* 120: 740–781.

Sapp, Travis and Ashish Tiwari, 2004, Does Stock Return Momentum Explain the "Smart Money" Effect?, *Journal of Finance* 54: 2605–2622.

Seru, Amit, Tyler Shumway, and Noah Stoffman, 2010, Learning by Trading, *Review of Financial Studies*, 23: 705–739.

Vayanos, Dimitri, and Paul Woolley, 2010, Fund Flows and Asset Prices: A Baseline Model, Working Paper, London School of Economics.

Wermers, Russell, 2000, Mutual Fund Performance: An Empirical Decomposition into Stock-Picking Talent, Style, Transactions Costs, and Expenses, *Journal of Finance* 55: 1655–1703.

Wermers, Russell, 2003, Is Money Really 'Smart'? New Evidence on the Relation between Mutual Fund Flows, Manager Behavior, and Performance Persistence, Working Paper, University of Maryland.

Zheng, Lu, 1999, Is Money Smart? A Study of Mutual Fund Investors' Fund Selection Ability, *Journal of Finance* 54: 901–933.

Appendix A. Sample Selection

We base our selection criteria on the objective codes and on the disclosed asset compositions. First, we select funds with the following ICDI objectives: AG, GI, LG, or IN. If a fund does not have any of the above ICDI objectives, we select funds with the following Strategic Insight objectives: AGG, GMC, GRI, GRO, ING, or SCG. If a fund has neither the Strategic Insight nor the ICDI objective, then we go to the Wiesenberger Fund Type Code and pick funds with the following objectives: G, G-I, AGG, GCI, GRI, GRO, LTG, MCG, and SCG. If none of these objectives are available and the fund has the CS policy (Common Stocks are the mainly held securities by the fund), then the fund will be included. We exclude funds that have the following Investment Objective Codes in the Spectrum Database: International, Municipal Bonds, Bond and Preferred, and Balanced. Since the reported objectives do not always indicate whether a fund portfolio is balanced or not, we also exclude funds that, on average, hold less than 80% in stocks.

Elton, Gruber, and Blake (2001) identify a form of survival bias in the CRSP mutual fund database, which results from a strategy used by fund families to enhance their return histories. Fund families might incubate several private funds and they will only make public the track record of the surviving incubated funds, while the returns for those funds that are terminated are not made public. To address this incubation bias, we exclude the observations where the year for the observation is prior to the reported fund starting year and we exclude observations where the names of the funds are missing in the CRSP database. Incubated funds also tend to be smaller, which motivates us to exclude funds that had in the previous month less than $5 million in assets under management.

In the next step, we are able to match about 94% of the CRSP funds to the Thomson database. The unmatched funds tend to be younger and smaller than the funds for which we find data in Spectrum. Wermers (2000) mentions that the Spectrum data set often does not have any holdings data available during the first few quarters listed in the CRSP database.

Mutual fund families introduced different share classes in the 1990s. Since different share classes have the same holdings composition, we aggregate all the observations pertaining to different share classes into one observation. For the qualitative attributes of funds (e.g., name, objectives, year of origination), we retain the observation of the oldest fund. For the total net assets under management (TNA), we sum the TNAs of the different share classes. Finally, for the other quantitative attributes of funds (e.g., returns, expenses, loads), we take the weighted average of the attributes of the individual share classes, where the weights are the lagged TNAs of the individual share classes.

For most of our sample period, mutual funds are required to disclose their holdings semi-annually. A large number of funds disclose their holdings quarterly, while a small number of funds have gaps between holding disclosure dates of more than six months. To fill these gaps, we impute the holdings of missing quarters using the most recently available holdings, assuming that mutual funds follow a buy-and-hold strategy. In our sample, 72% of the observations are from the most recent quarter and less than 5% of the holdings are more than two quarters old. We exclude funds that have fewer than 10 identified stock positions and funds that did not disclose their holdings during the last year. This final selection criterion reduces the number of mutual funds used in this study to 3,261 funds.

Chapter 4

Are Domestic Household Investors Better Performers than Foreign Institutions? New Evidence from Finland*

Peter L. Swan[†] and P. Joakim Westerholm[‡]

Abstract

We replicate and extend the methodology of Grinblatt and Keloharju (2000) to find that foreign institutional investors in Finland no longer achieve superior performance. This is despite their persistence in adopting 'positive feedback' trading strategies. We find that individuals and households outperform over most horizons even though they adopt contrarian negative feedback trading strategies. Foreign institutions appear to suffer from incentive and informational disadvantages that encourage 'trend-chasing.' The informationless strategy of buying past winners and selling past losers can no longer be associated with superior performance. Moreover, it is no longer correct to classify unambiguously household and individual investors as random 'noise traders.'

Keywords: Positive feedback trading, agency problems, home bias, noise trading

JEL Classification: G10

---

*The authors wish to thank the Euroclear Finland Limited and the Swedish School of Economics and Business Administration (Hanken) for provision of the data and the Australian Research Council (ARC) for financial support. We thank participants at the Paul Woolley (UTS) Workshops and Banking and Finance seminars, UNSW, Karl Anderson, Ning Gong, Élise Payzan-LeNestour, Matthew Spiegel, Maxwell Stevenson, Avi Wohl and an anonymous referee.

[†]UNSW Australia Business School, University of New South Wales, Sydney NSW 2052 Australia. Email: peter.swan@unsw.edu.au

[‡]University of Sydney Business School. Correspondence Address: University of Sydney Business School, NSW, 2006, Australia. Tel: +61 2 9351 6454. Fax: +61 2 9351 6461. Email: joakim.westerholm@sydney.edu.au.

This paper aims to clarify the often-conflicting literature on persistent trading patterns and the resulting performance of specific investor classes, e.g., domestic vs. foreign, and households vs. institutional investors. Compare, for example, Grinblatt and Keloharju (2000), Hau (2001), Dvořák (2005), and Barber, Odean, and Zhu (2009). With comprehensive daily data on the trading behavior of every investor in the Finnish economy over a decade, we show that domestic households clearly and systematically outperform foreign institutional investors by a very substantial margin of great economic significance. Grinblatt and Keloharju (2000), who introduce the methodology we adopt, show exactly the opposite outcome for the same data and a much shorter two-year period that overlaps with the period of concern to this study. Thus, our findings are immune to challenges on methodological grounds without also rejecting the original study. In this paper, we show that both agency and locational issues seem to play a crucial role in explaining the success or otherwise of investor trading performance. Based on these findings, we conclude that it is no longer possible to classify unambiguously household and individual investors as random 'noise traders' (Black, 1986) in the behavioral and market microstructure literature.[1]

The influential[2] study by Grinblatt and Keloharju (2000) introduced researchers to one of the first comprehensive analyses of the behavior and performance of investor groups. Their main conclusion is that there is a clear negative relationship between feedback and trading performance over the six-month future horizon — positive feedback foreign investors outperform negative feedback domestic households.

There are, however, strong grounds for revisiting this topic. Grinblatt and Keloharju (2000) confine their study to only a two-year sample of investor behavior from which they draw very strong conclusions. We believe that this is far too short a period for a thorough analysis of trading patterns

---

[1]According to Black (1986), 'noise trading' is trading on noise as if it were information. In the behavioral literature, 'noise traders' play a fundamental role as the source of sentiment driving prices away from fundamentals. In the microstructure literature, noise traders appear in a more benign light as investors that systematically lose money when they provide liquidity to informed — largely institutional — trades.

[2]The paper has considerable impact with 1,186 citations in Google Scholar as of August 2015. The number of citations has more than doubled in the last five years and is still growing rapidly.

and trader performance, particularly given that the period from 1995 to 1996 is in proximity to the 1993 opening of the Finnish stock market to foreign investors, making it potentially unrepresentative. This choice of sample period induces bias towards displaying foreigners as 'smart' traders (in the terminology of Grinblatt–Keloharju), even though locals reaped capital gains from foreigner buy-pressure as both parties benefitted from global diversification. This trend may explain why foreign investors trade more effectively in the two-year Grinblatt–Keloharju data period than over the entire ten-year sample period we examine herein that is inclusive of their two-year period.[3]

In this paper, we first attempt to replicate the methodology of Grinblatt and Keloharju (2000) for the same database. We extend their single forward-looking investment horizon of six months to a range of one day to 12 months. Recent studies have demonstrated interest in both short- and long-run patterns.[4] We also extend their data sample period by eight years to provide a more robust ten-year sample in place of the original two-year sample.[5] We find that behavioral results are persistent in that foreign investors continue to use 'positive feedback' (i.e., buying (selling) past winners (losers)) strategies[6] and households continue to use 'negative

[3]The purchase of domestic stocks by foreign investors occurs from approximately January 1993 due to the relaxation of the ban. Price-pressure in the form of purchases by foreigners drove up the price of Nokia tenfold over the two-year period 1993–94, just prior to the commencement of the Grinblatt–Keloharju sample period. This price increase makes sense as it permitted both local and foreign investors to better diversify globally. Buying pressure over the subsequent two-year Grinblatt and Keloharju sample period helped to push Nokia up by a further tenfold, but there was then a temporary decline prior to the stock gaining another five-fold by 1997. By 1997, the total Nokia gain was 25-fold after the opening up to foreigners, as the stock became a significant constituent of international indices and in more demand by global investors.

[4]For example, on the assumption that small trades represent the trades of retail investors, Barber, Odean, and Zhu (2009) find that small-trade order imbalances outperform over one month but underperform a year later.

[5]Seru, Shumway, and Stoffman (2010) provide one of the few published studies of Euroclear Finland data based on a lengthy sample of nine years. They find that unsuccessful individual investors largely learn by ceasing to trade once they discover a lack of ability. Linnainmaa (2010) matches up Euroclear data over eight years with limit order data to argue that apparently poor household performance could arise because they tend to place limit orders.

[6]While Grinblatt and Keloharju (2000) refer throughout to 'positive feedback strategies' as 'momentum' trading, we do not adopt this terminology as Berk, Green, and Naik (1999),

feedback' (i.e., buying (selling) past losers (winners)) strategies. Why then should an extension be of interest? We find that, consistent with Grinblatt-Keloharju, over the original two-year dataset and an identical methodology, foreign investors perform well and households perform badly in the relative short term (i.e., the six-month period examined by Grinblatt and Keloharju); however, over the twelve-month horizon not examined by Grinblatt-Keloharju, household performance is systematically neither good nor bad. More importantly, we find that over the entire 10-year period, households significantly outperform foreign investors over horizons ranging from six months to 12 months. We also find that the two very small categories,[7] nonprofit organizations and general government, which are most likely to face severe agency problems, considerably underperform over all horizons and periods. Thus, we find that, contrary to Grinblatt and Keloharju (2000), households appear more 'sophisticated' and 'smart' than do foreign investors and, consistent with their locational advantage, appear better informed.[8] It is notable that the authors appear confident about the robustness of their findings despite the very short trading history reflected in their data:

> "The results, although based on only two years of data, are too strong to be altered by methodological tweaking. In part, the power of our statistical tests arises from their ability to exploit the relative independence of the daily decisions of investors to buy and sell stocks. More importantly, the highly significant results are generated by economic significance: these daily decisions predict future stock returns with surprising frequency."

Johnson (2002) and Sagi and Seasholes (2007) make clear that 'momentum' is a particular pattern in stock returns that is not necessarily generated by positive feedback strategies. In fact, 'rational' momentum returns could arise from the changing risk profile of a company over time. Both 'contrarian' and 'positive feedback' trading 'profits' could simply be due to a willingness to bear certain kinds of risks.

[7]Only for these small categories do our results differ significantly from those of Grinblatt and Keloharju. Both programs and computers have significantly improved since Grinblatt and Keloharju undertook their original study, and these improvements might account for some of the discrepancies.

[8]Using a sample of 35 stocks, Kalev, Nguyen, and Oh (2008) adopt a different methodology to show that domestic investors outperform foreign investors in the long term in all stocks, with the one exception of Nokia.

Our contribution in the present paper is both simple and elementary in the extreme. We do not purport to advance theory or methodology, or improve empirical outcomes by discovering new data sources. To the contrary, what we achieve herein is limited but nonetheless significant: we replicate the methodology of Grinblatt and Keloharju (2000) for the same database but extend their data by eight years to provide a more robust 10-year sample instead of the original two-year.[9] We find that their behavioral results are persistent in that foreign investors continue to use positive feedback strategies and households are still contrarian. Why then is our "trivial" extension of interest? We find that over the entire 10-year period, households *outperform* foreign investors over virtually every horizon from one day to six months. Moreover, households also outperform every subsequent two-year period over most horizons. Thus, with no more than a simple extension of the dataset, we find that, contrary to Grinblatt and Keloharju (2000), households appear more sophisticated than foreign investors, their investment strategy is more compelling and rational, and, consistent with their locational advantage, households appear to be far better informed.

Ours is not the only study to revisit the findings of Grinblatt and Keloharju (2000). Lu, Swan and Westerholm (2015) adopt an entirely different methodology from Grinblatt and Keloharju (2000) in which they match the trades of three aggregate Finnish groups — households, domestic institutional investors, and foreign investors — as counterparties in a zero-sum trading game. They find both for the two-year Grinblatt and Keloharju (2000) period and over the inclusive 17-year horizon 1995–2011 that households outperform foreign institutional investors. Thus, the real contribution of the present paper lies in making an "apples for apples" comparison with Grinblatt and Keloharju (2000) in which their methodology is exactly preserved. Consequently, we can rule out methodological differences as the basis for our reversal of their basic findings once we extend their very limited sample period.

[9]Seru *et al.* (2009) provide one of the few published studies of depository data from Finland based on a lengthy sample of nine years. They find that individual investors largely learn by ceasing to trade once they discover a lack of ability.

Unlike the earlier results, our findings in the present paper do not support a behavioral story, on the contrary they are consistent with a rational home bias based on informational advantage. The information disadvantage hypothesis explains the tendency for foreign investors to underweight the international component of their portfolios. French and Poterba (1991) dubbed this issue the home bias puzzle, while Cooper and Kaplanis (1994) and Tesar and Werner (1995) proposed information disadvantage as a potential explanation. Coval and Moskowitz (1999, 2001) hypothesize that investors are subject to the same locational biases, related to the geographic proximity of firm headquarters, both within an international and domestic context. Halling *et al.* (2008) show that US trading in ADRs is more intensive the closer the geographic proximity of the stock. Teo (2009) finds that hedge funds with a physical presence in the country in which they invest outperform by 3.72% per year. Baik, Kang and Kim (2010) and Seasholes and Zhu (2010) also find a local advantage within the US.

Bernile, Kogan and Sulaeman (2015) address an alternative behavioral hypothesis: investors with limited cognitive ability use familiarity as a screening device to overweight local stocks. Because both the informational and screening advantage explanations can result in excess local returns, Bernile *et al.* (2015) attempt to show that non-local stocks generally contain more public than private information. Thus, they favor the local private information explanation over the behavioral explanation. Coincidently, our findings are inconsistent with the behavioral explanation as Finnish investor outperformance is not due to a preference for local stocks. By contrast, their relative trading performance indicates either location-based informational advantage or an ability to exploit the trend-following nature of foreign investor trades to determine fundamental values and thus to trade profitably by being able to predict future price movements.

In light of our new results, it is clear that it is important to revisit this topic now when we have access to more data. In addition to extending the original article by investigating a longer time period and more trading horizons, we analyze the same dataset using alternative methodologies. We utilize the widely accepted methodology known as 'holdings-based calendar-time portfolios' (see, e.g., Odean, 1999, and Seasholes and Zhu, 2010, but also see Lu, Swan, and Westerholm, 2015, for a critique), in which a time series of each group's portfolio returns is regressed on the market's excess returns and other risk factors including size, book-to-market, and momentum factors. We find that households outperform foreign investors over the ten-year data period but that outperformance is not statistically significant once these risk factors are taken into account. Consistent with bias towards higher beta stocks induced by positive feedback trading identified by Jegadeesh and Titman (1993), the CAPM beta of foreign investors exceeds both unity and the household beta. This finding implies under-diversification and bias towards stocks that perform well in rising markets.

We also implement a variant of these holding portfolios, 'transactions-based calendar-time portfolios,' used in Odean (1999) and Seasholes and Zhu (2010), among others. We form calendar-time portfolios of buys and sells separately. We use these to analyze the difference in buy and sell returns over an annual buy-and-hold time horizon on both an equal- and value-weighted basis. Contrary to our results using the Grinblatt and Keloharju methodology and holdings-based analysis, we find no evidence of foreign investor trading outperformance over the Grinblatt-Keloharju two-year period. This is true for either equal- or trade-weighted returns. We do find evidence, however, that small and medium households (by value of portfolio at the start of 1995) outperform over this two-year period. The results for all and small households are similar over the entire 10-year period. Domestic investors outperform with outperformance relative to foreign investors on both an equal and value-weighted basis. There is evidence of foreign investor outperformance in comparison to the outcomes of large and medium household categories. Statistically, performance differences are not significant.

This paper proceeds as follows. Section 1 details the data used in this study. Section 2 describes the trading pattern methodology and results. Section 3 examines future performance. Section 4 discusses the significance and interpretation of the findings, while the final section concludes.

1. Data

The primary data source is Euroclear Finland Limited (formerly Finnish Central Securities Depository). Euroclear maintains a record of the holdings in Finnish stock of every shareholder. As such, the database contains every transaction that occurred between 1 January 1995 and 31

December 2004. With a look-back period of six months and a look-forward period of 12 months, market stock return data to complement Euroclear data cover a longer period.

1.1. *Characteristics of the Dataset*

Every investor trading in the Finnish market is required to register with Euroclear and obtain a unique account number that the investor must continue to use at all times. Records for each transaction include date, ISIN stock code, unique account number, business sector code, ownership type, reference code, buy/sell indicator, volume and price.

Dates are, however, not time-stamped, and as such, the dispersion of trading throughout the day is not examinable. Moreover, the record of transactions is not limited to those trades that occur during regular trading hours. The ISIN field allows the sample to be limited to the sixteen stocks with the highest market capitalization as of 1 January 1995. In this, we follow Grinblatt and Keloharju (2000) with the aim of ensuring that adequate liquidity is available in the stocks of interest. There are five stocks de-listed or merged during the ten-year sample. These stocks are Cultor I, Huhtamaki K, Nokia K, Partek, and Valmet. In unreported results available from the authors on request, we control for possible effects of using a static sample. We perform the same analysis using a sample of the top 25 stocks by market capitalization included in the OMXH 25 index available for the period 1998–2004. This index represents most of the market capitalization and is the basis for the index futures and options market. The rebalancing of this sample occurs twice a year to replicate the index composition exactly. We also analyze a sample of all sufficiently active stocks during the entire 1995–2004 period. These results do not materially change the conclusions expressed in this paper.

The sector field displays one of 42 numbers that classify the business sector to which the account belongs. We aggregate sector codes into the nine classes adopted by Grinblatt and Keloharju. These classes are 'all households' with a portfolio during the investigated period: 'small,' 'medium,' and 'large households' with an existing portfolio at the start of 1995; 'non-profit organizations' such as foundations; 'general government' made up of central and municipal funds; 'non-financial corporations'; 'finance and insurance institutions'; and 'foreign investors.'

There is one exception to the account field providing a unique investor identifier. Foreign investors are able to register under a nominee account. Hence, such accounts can link with multiple foreign investors. The unfortunate consequence is that, while nominee accounts have a distinct ownership number, it is not possible to break the foreign investor category down into types that are more specific. Consequently, we record all nominee accounts as foreign investors.

One highly desirable feature of the dataset is that it maintains a record of the initial holdings of every investor registered by 1 January 1995. The dataset allows almost perfect accuracy in replicating the holdings of any investor class over time as the cumulative sum of buying and selling transactions.

To preserve commonality with Grinblatt and Keloharju (2000), we construct household subsamples (i.e., small, medium, and large) based on portfolio market capitalization as of 1 January 1995. We complete this process for all stocks listed in the Euroclear dataset, not simply for the sixteen stocks of interest in the study. For each account number, adhering to a household sector code, it is possible to calculate the value of the portfolio holdings. We break accounts into three categories of equal market capitalization as of that date. Subsamples contain only accounts registered prior to 1995, while the all-household sample also contains newer accounts.

The dataset only uniquely identifies direct holdings. Holdings through mutual funds or American Depository Receipts (ADRs) do not reflect holdings of the underlying constituents. The database is comprehensive in that it includes records of trades in all Finnish stocks regardless of the exchange or trading platform on which the stock has traded. We obtain the official closing prices for all stocks on the Helsinki Stock Exchange from the Swedish School of Economics and Business Administration from 3 January 1994 to 30 December 2004. To compute future return horizons for up to twelve months for daily buy-order imbalances in 2004, it is necessary to use a 2005 price series from Datastream. The Helsinki Stock Exchange supplies the history of dividends on all stocks for the years 1993–2004. To adjust for stock splits, we utilize adjustment factors from Datastream and manually check their accuracy.

1.2. *Summary Statistics*

Table 1 uses monthly returns unadjusted for market movements computed from the official closing price series. Monthly returns include dividend allocations and adjustments for stock splits. The table reports details of the stock market capitalization in Euros. We report monthly arithmetic returns and return standard deviations for both a two-year sample (i.e., 1995–1996) and a ten-year sample (i.e., 1995–2004). We also report returns and standard deviations for an equally weighted portfolio formed with the sixteen stocks.

Table 2 provides descriptive statistics displaying differences in the investor classes disaggregated between the initial two-year period and the overall 10-year period from 1995 to 2004. The initial number of small household accounts is large relative to the much smaller number of large household accounts. Volume, value, and the number of trades report average daily buy and sell positions by investor class. The 'holdings' category reports the average daily fraction of holdings by investor class. 'Return' refers to the average daily return, inclusive of the change in portfolio value as well as trading gains and losses expressed in basis points. We adjust all data for stock splits with values recorded in Euros. One of the most striking aspects of the table is the very considerable rise in the holdings of foreign investors, particularly as the general government class sells down. Foreign investors hold on average 29% of total holdings in the sixteen stocks in 1995–1996; however, over the entire period, their average holdings are much higher at 61%.

Table 3 reports the mean share of buy volume for each of the nine investor groups for each of the 16 stocks. The market share of trading activity is computed for each investor group for each stock by dividing the number of shares bought by that investor class by the total number of shares bought by all investor classes in that stock. As Grinblatt and Keloharju (2000) mention, the benefit of this equal weighting is to diminish the dominance of Nokia. We repeat this analysis for both the two- and 10-year samples. We retain stocks that merge or de-list during the 10-year sample in the analysis until they no longer trade. In addition, we compute the mean share of buy value and mean share of buy-trades for each of the 16 stocks. Panel A examines the 1995–1996 subsamples, while Panel B examines the full 10-year period.

Table 1: Initial Market Capitalization of Sample and Arithmetic Returns

	Market Cap Jan 1, 1995 Mill. Euro	Market Cap Dec 31, 1996 Mill. Euro	Market Cap Dec 31, 2004 Mill. Euro	Mean Monthly Arithmetic Returns		Standard Deviation of Returns	
				95-96	95-04	95-96	95-04
Nokia A	4,787.4	9,387.6	54,192.9	0.028	0.026	0.133	0.146
Nokia K	4,241.0			0.028	0.056	0.132	0.129
Outokumpu	1,841.7	1,644.1	2,383.4	−0.001	0.038	0.076	0.471
Rautaruukki	808.8	859.39	1,213.87	0.007	0.037	0.080	0.430
Enso R	741.6	674.53	7,417.86	0.000	0.027	0.071	0.398
Enso A	726.5	638.38	2,068.00	0.001	0.038	0.073	0.376
Metsä-Serla B	724.4	595.68	1,371.58	0.000	0.005	0.091	0.107
Valmet	643.2	575.28		0.001	0.038	0.100	0.560
Kesko V	546.0	632.8	1067.6	0.009	0.038	0.070	0.440
Finnair	397.8	459.52	471.26	0.001	0.034	0.076	0.424
Kone B	454.1	427.29	3,089.43	0.000	0.036	0.083	0.532
Huhtamaki I	463.1	622.5	1,227.3	0.018	0.084	0.096	0.706
Stockmann A	337.4	390.4	518.3	0.007	0.046	0.051	0.532
Partek	332.3	463.16		0.011	0.025	0.082	0.241
Huhtamaki K	326.5	442.60		0.018	0.033	0.084	0.476
Cultor I	326.0	638.32		0.028	0.058	0.057	0.466
Totals	17,697.8	18,451.6	75,021.5	0.010	0.031	0.085	0.402

This table reports market capitalization, returns and standard deviations in returns for each of the sixteen largest Helsinki Stock Exchange stocks by market capitalization as of 1 January 1995. We report market capitalization for the beginning of 1995, end of 1996, and end of 2004; the cutoffs of the two investigated samples, the first period being identical to the period investigated by Grinblatt and Keloharju (2000). We report figures in Euros for the whole period, converting values prior to 1999. We report monthly arithmetic mean returns using official closing prices and the standard deviation of these returns. The 'totals' row reports the total of market capitalization and the mean of monthly returns and standard deviations for all shares. A merger of Nokia K, Valmet, Partek, Huhtamaki K and Cultor occurs in the other company series or they delist during the investigated period.

We conclude from Tables 2 and 3 that foreign investors consistently overweight the three largest stocks by market capitalization — the two Nokia share series, and Outokumpu[10] — as they have the largest holdings and are the most active traders in these stocks.

[10]These companies are also among the oldest in the sample. Nokia was founded in 1865 (listed 1915) and Outokumpu was founded in 1932 (listed 1988), in comparison to an average founding year of 1936 for the rest of the sample. Analyst coverage recorded in

Table 2: Characteristics of Investor Categories, 1995–2004

	Households–All	Households–Small	Households–Medium	Households–Large	Non-Profit Organizations	General Government	Finance and Insurance	Non-Financial	Foreign Investors
Initial No Accounts	474,948	451,487	21,289	2,172	4,697	432	466	10,939	2,150
1995–1996:									
Volume	0.31	0.10	0.11	0.08	0.10	0.44	1.31	1.31	117.1
Value Traded	30.7	1.5	2.0	1.3	8.8	31.0	135.8	138.7	2268.9
Number Trades	739	488	162	37	29	7	250	259	1760
Share Holdings	0.092	0.031	0.038	0.022	0.067	0.377	0.091	0.084	0.289
Return	2.8	3.7	3.8	4.0	1.1	0.02	3.8	−0.8	5.5
1995–2004:									
Volume	0.94	0.30	0.21	0.14	0.34	0.66	7.86	2.99	117.1
Value Traded	45.9	7.8	8.7	6.6	18.2	11.3	270.8	167.8	4012.2
Number Trades	1274	565	186	44	35	7	1370	645	7538
Share Holdings	0.064	0.018	0.024	0.017	0.045	0.172	0.053	0.053	0.613
Return	1.5	1.7	1.6	1.7	0.7	0.3	1.8	0.5	2.4

This table examines the characteristics of nine different investor categories over the two investigated samples, 1995–1996 and 1995–2004. The nine investor-categories are households (i.e., all, small, medium, and large), nonprofit organizations, general government agencies, finance and insurance institutions, non-financial corporations, and foreign investors. Following Grinblatt and Keloharju (2000), we classify the households by size based on the portfolio values of 1 January 1995. This means that the 'all' category includes accounts created after January 1995 and the number of accounts in the other categories is frozen. Hence, the sum of the household category statistics do not necessarily sum to the 'all' category values. The table reports the number of unique accounts recorded in the Euroclear dataset on 1 January 1995. We report the average daily volume, value traded, and number of transactions traded by investor type as the sum of buy and sell transactions. We express volume in millions of shares, value in millions of Euros and number of trades in thousands. We report the average daily holdings of each investor class as a proportion of total market holdings in the 16 stocks. We calculate average daily return on the previous day's closing portfolio, adding trading and holding gains as the sum of realized profits and changes in portfolio value corrected for purchases and sales, and report these in basis points.

Table 3: Fraction of Daily Buy-Volume for Nine Investor Classes

	Households–All	Households–Small	Households–Medium	Households–Large	Non-Profit Organizations	General Government	Finance and Insurance	Non-Financial	Foreign Investors
Panel A: 1995–1996									
Nokia A	0.009	0.002	0.003	0.002	0.001	0.004	0.055	0.045	0.887
Nokia K	0.011	0.003	0.005	0.002	0.004	0.022	0.097	0.047	0.819
Outokumpu	0.007	0.002	0.003	0.002	0.003	0.026	0.070	0.026	0.867
Rautaruukki	0.083	0.021	0.035	0.016	0.030	0.068	0.176	0.126	0.517
Enso R	0.041	0.011	0.014	0.010	0.019	0.018	0.133	0.085	0.705
Enso A	0.185	0.063	0.074	0.030	0.035	0.044	0.204	0.183	0.349
Metsä-Serla B	0.041	0.014	0.015	0.006	0.006	0.019	0.108	0.060	0.766
Valmet	0.024	0.007	0.009	0.003	0.012	0.019	0.099	0.038	0.808
Kesko V	0.061	0.029	0.014	0.007	0.011	0.052	0.162	0.167	0.547
Finnair	0.063	0.018	0.027	0.010	0.017	0.053	0.144	0.093	0.630
Kone B	0.052	0.015	0.015	0.010	0.007	0.036	0.113	0.086	0.706
Huhtamaki I	0.018	0.007	0.004	0.005	0.009	0.014	0.121	0.040	0.798
Stockmann A	0.170	0.072	0.058	0.021	0.160	0.012	0.087	0.129	0.442
Partek	0.110	0.035	0.036	0.029	0.032	0.088	0.222	0.191	0.355
Huhtamaki K	0.255	0.080	0.110	0.028	0.039	0.092	0.302	0.154	0.154
Cultor I	0.039	0.015	0.009	0.009	0.009	0.020	0.189	0.069	0.674
Mean	0.072	0.024	0.027	0.012	0.024	0.037	0.142	0.096	0.629
Median	0.011	0.001	0.001	0.000	0.000	0.000	0.058	0.027	0.755

(*Continued*)

Table 3: (*Continued*)

	Households–All	Households–Small	Households–Medium	Households–Large	Non-Profit Organizations	General Government	Finance and Insurance	Non-Financial	Foreign Investors
Panel B: 1995–2004									
Nokia A	0.006	0.002	0.001	0.001	0.001	0.003	0.055	0.028	0.906
Nokia K	0.010	0.003	0.004	0.002	0.003	0.017	0.110	0.047	0.813
Outokumpu	0.021	0.007	0.005	0.002	0.004	0.022	0.086	0.030	0.838
Rautaruukki	0.059	0.019	0.016	0.009	0.013	0.033	0.143	0.068	0.684
Enso R	0.014	0.004	0.004	0.003	0.006	0.012	0.073	0.037	0.858
Enso A	0.151	0.059	0.036	0.010	0.014	0.040	0.201	0.090	0.504
Metsä-Serla B	0.026	0.009	0.007	0.003	0.004	0.013	0.074	0.034	0.850
Valmet	0.018	0.005	0.006	0.003	0.009	0.018	0.079	0.035	0.841
Kesko V	0.058	0.023	0.012	0.006	0.010	0.035	0.130	0.085	0.682
Finnair	0.171	0.061	0.035	0.012	0.015	0.037	0.107	0.085	0.585
Kone B	0.031	0.010	0.007	0.005	0.006	0.019	0.091	0.046	0.806
Huhtamaki I	0.030	0.010	0.007	0.005	0.014	0.026	0.112	0.043	0.775
Stockmann A	0.231	0.096	0.050	0.016	0.077	0.008	0.113	0.091	0.480
Partek	0.176	0.061	0.044	0.028	0.046	0.051	0.169	0.172	0.386
Huhtamaki K	0.222	0.074	0.082	0.029	0.055	0.099	0.324	0.140	0.158
Cultor I	0.037	0.016	0.007	0.006	0.007	0.021	0.125	0.052	0.757
Mean	0.078	0.029	0.019	0.008	0.017	0.026	0.118	0.066	0.695
Median	0.013	0.003	0.001	0.000	0.000	0.000	0.052	0.015	0.825

This table reports the average fraction of daily buy-volume for nine investor classes in sixteen stocks. We calculate the fraction on each trading day as the number of shares purchased in a stock by an investor class divided by the total number of shares bought by all investors in that same stock. Panel A reports figures for the two-year subsample spanning 1995–1996. Panel B reports corresponding figures spanning 1995–2004.

2. Methodology and Detected Trading Patterns

The general methodology reported herein follows the approach used by Grinblatt and Keloharju (2000) for a two-year sample period (i.e., 1995–1996). Without such commonality in methodology, we could not convincingly address either whether it is possible to replicate the results in Grinblatt and Keloharju (2000) or whether they are representative. An exception arises because we think it important to examine more than just the future six-month performance horizon. We examine future investor horizons from one day to 12 months. We also extend the analysis in the time series by investigating the original 1995–1996 period plus the ten-year period covering 1995–2004. We extend the analysis in the cross section by analyzing the same top 16 stocks as Grinblatt and Keloharju (2000), the top 25 constituents in the major futures index OMXH-25, and all common stock listed during the investigated period. Finally, the original analysis is complemented using alternative methodologies: (a) 'holdings-based calendar-time portfolios' in which we regress a time series of each group's portfolio returns on the market's excess returns and other risk factors including size, book-to-market and momentum factors and (b) 'transactions-based calendar-time portfolios' used in several studies, most recently by Seasholes and Zhu (2010). Here, we mimic the buying and selling behaviors of investors. To do so, we form calendar-time buy and sell portfolios, analyzing the difference in returns between these based on an annual buy-and-hold time horizon.

2.1. *Buy Ratios and Past Returns*

To determine whether on a particular trading day t an investor class i in a particular stock j is a net buyer, we calculate a ratio — termed a 'buy ratio' — as the number of shares bought divided by the number of shares bought plus the number of shares sold. That is:

$$BuyRatio_{i,j,t} = \frac{Buy_{i,j,t}}{Buy_{i,j,t} + Sell_{i,j,t}} \tag{4.1}$$

Thomson Financial IBES at the start of 2000 is 43 analysts for Nokia and 21 analysts for Outokumpu compared to 15 analysts on average for the rest of the sample.

A 'buy ratio' greater than one-half indicates an investor's order imbalance in favor of buys and thus net purchases.

It is possible to examine positive feedback and contrarian behavior by exploring whether an investor class on average exhibits positive 'buy ratios' on stocks with strong past performance. A positive feedback investor is defined by their inclination to buy based on strong past returns, whereas a contrarian investor buys based on weak (negative) past returns. To analyze this relationship, it is necessary to link 'buy ratios' with past returns for both the two-year and the 10-year samples.

We construct return series for sixteen stocks for various past horizons. The past periods considered follow Grinblatt and Keloharju (2000) and are akin to the periods in Jegadeesh and Titman (1993) and Rouwenhorst (1998). The five periods are:

- [−1D, 0] — the return on the previous trading day;
- [−1W,−D] — the return on the previous trading week excluding the previous day;
- [−1M,−W] — the return on the previous month excluding the previous week;
- [−6M,−M] — the return on the previous six months excluding the previous month;
- [−6M, 0] — the return on the previous six months.

We construct both the arithmetic and natural logarithm returns over these horizons. We report results only for the arithmetic return series as the natural logarithm series produces quantitatively similar findings. On each day between 2 January 1995 and 30 December 2004, there exist returns for each of the sixteen stocks over five different horizons. Ranking occurs for each horizon's returns for each day in descending order. This ranking by return breaks stocks into one of three classes. The first class — the 'past winner' or 'positive feedback' class — consists of the stocks with the four highest returns over the relevant horizon. The second class — the 'past loser' or contrarian class — refers to the stocks with the four lowest returns over the relevant horizon. The remaining class — the 'past neutral' class — refers to the stocks not ranked in either the 'past winner' or 'past loser' class and thus not subject to trading behavior based on past returns. The 'past neutral' class ideally consists of the remaining eight stocks. We note that the 'past neutral' class only consists of eight stocks in those circumstances whereby all sixteen stocks trade on that particular day.

We define the 'buy ratio difference' as:

$$BuyRatioDiff_{i,t} = \sum_{j \in Winners} BuyRatio_{i,j,t} - \sum_{j \in Losers} BuyRatio_{i,j,t}. \quad (4.2)$$

On each day, we match 'buy ratios' for the nine investor-classes with the five return rankings in order to calculate the 'buy ratio difference,' as defined above, for each day for each of the nine investor-classes. This calculation is the sum of the 'buy ratios' of the four 'past-winner' class stocks minus the sum of the 'buy ratios' of the four 'past-loser' class stocks. We then compare the 'buy ratio difference' to a value of zero. If the 'buy ratio difference' is greater than zero, the investor class exhibits positive feedback behavior on that trading day. The intuition is that an investor class with a positive 'buy ratio difference' is buying a disproportionate number of stocks from the 'past-winner' class.

For each investor class, we calculate the fraction of days that the 'buy ratio difference' is positive. An investor whose portfolio choice is independent of past returns should have a positive 'buy ratio difference' on half of the trading days. A positive feedback investor should have a positive 'buy ratio difference' on more than half of the trading days. If the reverse is true, however, the investor class is a contrarian trader.

Table 4 and Figure 1 display the fraction of days for which each of the nine investor-classes has positive 'buy ratio differences.' Results for the two-year sample are similar to Grinblatt and Keloharju (2000). Hence, we are able to replicate their results in our past-return analysis. Small numerical discrepancies in buy ratio differences and significance levels are likely to be due to minor differences in the composition of investor types. Almost without exception, domestic investors of all types have a fraction of positive 'buy ratio differences' that are less than one-half, thus signifying contrarian behavior. Foreign investors for all horizons have a fraction of positive 'buy ratio differences' greater than one-half, signifying positive feedback behavior. Trader behavior is dependent on the time horizon. Domestic households — and particularly small and medium households — become more contrarian as the time horizon extends, while foreign investors become more positive feedback biased. The single exception to the basic

Table 4: Fraction of Days Displaying Positive Buy ratios and Past Returns

	1995–1996					1995–2004				
	[−1D, 0]	[−1W, −1D]	[−1M, −1W]	[−6M, −1M]	[−6M, 0]	[−1D, 0]	[−1W, −1D]	[−1M, −2W]	[−6M, −1M]	[−6M, 0]
Households										
All	0.43	0.33	0.29	0.25	0.17	0.36	0.34	0.33	0.31	0.24
	(0.00)	(0.00)	(0.00)	(0.00)	(0.00)	(0.00)	(0.00)	(0.00)	(0.00)	(0.00)
Small as of 1995	0.43	0.39	0.34	0.26	0.20	0.38	0.38	0.36	0.35	0.26
	(0.00)	(0.00)	(0.00)	(0.00)	(0.00)	(0.00)	(0.00)	(0.00)	(0.00)	(0.00)
Medium as of 1995	0.43	0.38	0.33	0.30	0.25	0.40	0.38	0.37	0.37	0.30
	(0.00)	(0.00)	(0.00)	(0.00)	(0.00)	(0.00)	(0.00)	(0.00)	(0.00)	(0.00)
Large as of 1995	0.42	0.44	0.38	0.43	0.36	0.41	0.38	0.39	0.42	0.38
	(0.00)	(0.01)	(0.00)	(0.00)	(0.00)	(0.00)	(0.00)	(0.00)	(0.00)	(0.00)
Nonprofit Organizations	0.37	0.39	0.37	0.44	0.39	0.41	0.42	0.40	0.41	0.39
	(0.00)	(0.00)	(0.00)	(0.01)	(0.00)	(0.00)	(0.00)	(0.00)	(0.00)	(0.00)
General Government	0.35	0.40	0.40	0.44	0.38	0.38	0.42	0.39	0.41	0.36
	(0.00)	(0.00)	(0.00)	(0.01)	(0.00)	(0.00)	(0.00)	(0.00)	(0.00)	(0.00)
Finance and Insurance	0.47	0.49	0.53	0.47	0.48	0.49	0.49	0.51	0.50	0.51
	(0.24)	(0.59)	(0.24)	(0.24)	(0.42)	(0.32)	(0.42)	(0.14)	(0.87)	(0.40)

Nonfinancial Corporations	0.39	0.44	0.50	0.47	0.42	0.41	0.43	0.44	0.46	0.41
	(0.00)	(0.02)	(0.93)	(0.18)	(0.00)	(0.00)	(0.00)	(0.00)	(0.00)	(0.00)
Foreign Investors	0.55	0.58	0.52	0.54	0.57	0.55	0.55	0.55	0.56	0.58
	(0.03)	(0.00)	(0.42)	(0.07)	(0.00)	(0.00)	(0.00)	(0.00)	(0.00)	(0.00)

This table reports the fraction of volume-based positive buy ratio difference days for both a two-year sample and a ten-year sample. We create buy ratios by measuring the ratio of volume bought to total volume transacted for each trading day for each stock for each investor class. On each day, we assign the available buy ratios a ranking based on historical returns. We examine five past return horizons. These horizons consist of the previous day [−1D, 0], the previous week excluding the previous day [−1W, −1D], the previous month excluding the previous week [−1M, −1W], the previous six months excluding the previous month [−6M, −1M], and the previous six months [−6M, 0]. We use the horizons to rank buy ratios independently. We add together the buy ratios of the four stocks with the highest return over the relevant horizon. We then add together the buy ratios of the four stocks with the lowest return over the relevant horizon and subtract from the previous sum to construct the (unreported) buy ratio difference. A positive buy ratio difference signifies positive feedback behavior on that day. We take averages over all days in order to report the fraction of days exhibiting positive feedback behavior. An investor whose trades are independent of past returns should exhibit a fraction of one-half. An investor exhibiting negative feedback should exhibit a fraction of less than one-half. We use tests based on a two-tailed binomial probability distribution to report statistical significance from 0.5 as a p-value in parentheses below the fractions of positive buy ratio difference days.

Figure 1: Buy Ratios as a Function of Past Stock Performance Based on Table 4

This figure describes the average fraction of daily buy-volume for nine investor classes in sixteen stocks. We report the fractions on the x-axis as a difference from 0.5, and each column represents one past time horizon, ranging from one day to six months.

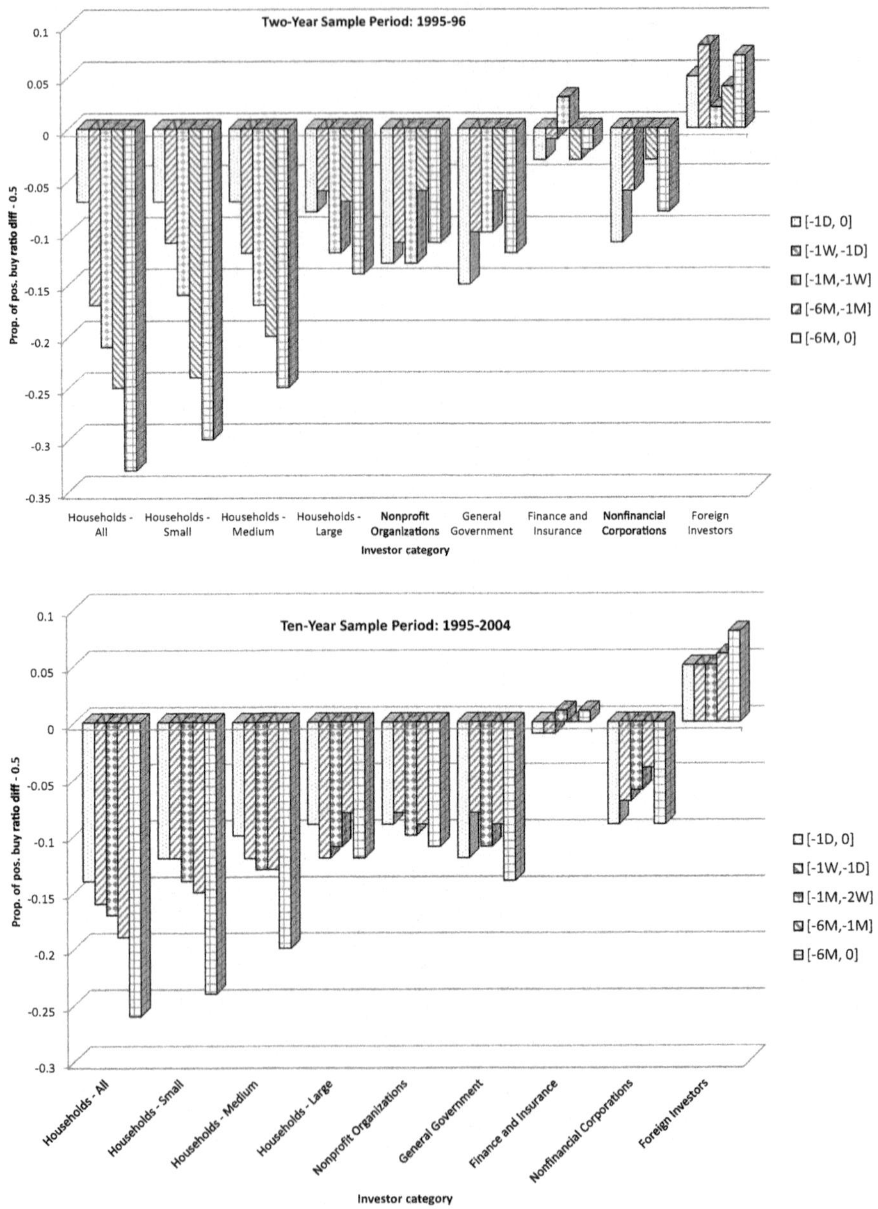

pattern is the finance and insurance institution class. While they exhibit a fraction of positive 'buy ratio' days that are mostly less than one-half, the result is insignificant. Consequently, finance and insurance institutions behave as if they believe in efficient markets such that past price changes are irrelevant.

Grinblatt and Keloharju (2000) identify a highly questionable negative association between contrarian behavior and investor 'sophistication.' The most contrarian (i.e., small households) are poor performers, while the largest (i.e., foreign (US) investors) are the most highly successful positive feedback traders, according to their findings. Small households are also the least sophisticated in that they are supposedly inclined to hold on to losers and cash in on winners early. We respond that while extreme contrarian behavior could have an association with this 'disposition effect,' it need not do so. Contrarian behavior does not imply a bias between selling winners and hanging onto losers. Second, the proof of the sophistication pudding is in the eating. Below, we find that total, small and medium households do about as well as domestic institutions over most horizons from six months and upwards over the full data period. These two groups dominate all other investor classes, including foreign investors. Hence, our findings contradict the Grinblatt and Keloharju negative association between contrarian behavior and sophistication over our longer data period.

Table 4 and Figure 1 also display the results of a 10-year sample spanning 1995-2004 for 'buy ratios' calculated using buying and selling volume. Domestic investors pursue contrarian strategies, while foreign investors pursue positive feedback strategies. As in the two-year sample, we find that the fraction of positive 'buy ratio differences' for finance and insurance institutions is insignificantly different from one-half.

2.2. *Robustness Tests*

We conduct robustness checks[11] using the two additional ratio types.[12] Such results at least confirm earlier results and, in most cases, strengthen

---

[11]The results from these robustness tests are available from the authors upon request.

[12]The first alternative is the ratio of value bought to the sum of value bought and value sold. The second is the ratio of the number of buy transactions to the number of buy transactions plus the number of sell transactions.

them. We repeat tests for the three types of ratios using two subsamples. The first subsample excludes Nokia A and Nokia K, which experience extreme return volatility during the 10-year period. The second subsample excludes the stocks that de-list or merge. If we remove either Nokia A or Nokia K, it shows that foreign investors follow weaker positive feedback patterns. This trend is indicative of particularly strong positive feedback trading for the two stocks that weight highest in the market index. All earlier results remain intact in the two subsamples.

3. Buy Ratios and Future Stock Performance

We now extend the analysis to examine stock selection and future returns by proposing that investor classes with 'buy ratios' that are positive on average in future winning stocks generate superior returns and are thus more informed.

3.1. *Modified original methodology*

The intuition is simple. When an investor class buys a disproportionate number of stocks with better than average future performance, it outperforms an average benchmark to display its informational advantage.

We use the 'buy ratios' from previous analysis with the future return series. The six future periods, including the two new nine-month and 12-month horizons, are as follows:

- [0, +1D] — the return on the following trading day;
- [+1D, +1W] — the return for the following trading week excluding the following day;
- [+1W, +1M] — the return for the following month excluding the following week;
- [0, +6M] — the return for the following six months, the only horizon reported by Grinblatt and Keloharju;
- [0, +9M] — the return for the following nine months;
- [0, +12M] — the return for the following 12 months.

As before, we calculate future returns as both arithmetic returns and natural logarithm returns but only report arithmetic returns.

We rank the six return series, separating them into three 'performance classes.' The 'future winners' consist of the four stocks with the highest returns for that horizon. The 'future-losers' consist of the four stocks with the lowest future returns. The remaining stocks belong in the 'future-neutral' class such that portfolio choice is unaffected by the stock's future returns. The number of stocks in the 'neutral-class' varies depending on the number of stocks trading on that day. Stocks that de-list, merge, or do not trade on a particular day are not included in the ranking on that day.

We match the ranked returns with the 'buy ratio' data and calculate the 'buy ratio difference' for each day. This buy ratio difference is equal to the sum of the 'buy ratios' of the four 'future-winners' minus the sum of the 'buy ratios' of the four 'future-losers.' If the 'buy ratio difference' is positive on a particular day, we consider the investor-class a superior performer on that trading day. We report the fraction of days for which the 'buy ratio difference' is positive.

We examine the propensity of different investor classes to buy stocks that prove to be superior performers over various future horizons up to twelve months. This means, for example, that in analyzing the two-year period 1995–1996, we include daily return data for the subsequent twelve-month period, i.e., 1997. The results presented in Table 5 and Figure 2 show the fraction of days for which an investor group exhibits a positive 'buy ratio difference.' A fraction greater than one-half indicates an ability to buy future superior performers. A fraction less than one-half indicates a propensity to buy future inferior performers. We are careful to optimize the runs for every investor class. Hence, if they have days for which there is sufficient rank to perform the normal ranking, we decrease the number of stocks used for ranking. This enables us to include these days, rather than to simply discard all observations for that investor-class on that day. These adjustments affect small classes such as subsamples of non-profit organizations and general government agencies that consistently underperform for both two-year and 10-year horizons. Large classes are not affected. All estimations include only days when the particular class has traded.

First, we consider volume-based 'buy ratios' during the two-year sample including 1995 and 1996 in Panel A. Examining the six-month horizon, as reported by Grinblatt and Keloharju (2000), foreign investors indicate a significant ability to buy future winning stocks. Finance and insurance (i.e., domestic institutions) also tend to buy stocks that outperform. Other investor categories tend to buy stocks that underperform over a six-month

Table 5: Fraction of Days Displaying Positive Buy ratios and Future Returns

Panel A	1995–1996					
	[0, +1D]	[+1D, +1W]	[+1W , +1M]	[0, +6M]	[0, +9M]	[0, +12M]
Households						
All	0.45	0.48	0.43	0.45	0.44	0.46
	(0.02)	(0.16)	(0.00)	(0.02)	(0.00)	(0.03)
Small as of 1995	0.45	0.49	0.45	0.49	0.46	0.50
	(0.02)	(0.30)	(0.02)	(0.36)	(0.04)	(0.50)
Medium as of 1995	0.50	0.47	0.44	0.45	0.48	0.51
	(0.46)	(0.12)	(0.00)	(0.02)	(0.16)	(0.33)
Large as of 1995	0.41	0.39	0.38	0.36	0.40	0.42
	(0.00)	(0.00)	(0.00)	(0.00)	(0.00)	(0.00)
Nonprofit Organizations	0.30	0.30	0.27	0.27	0.28	0.30
	(0.00)	(0.00)	(0.00)	(0.00)	(0.00)	(0.00)
General Government	0.30	0.2912	0.29	0.30	0.31	0.31
	(0.00)	(0.00)	(0.00)	(0.00)	(0.00)	(0.00)
Finance and Insurance	0.54	0.57	0.54	0.57	0.56	0.57
	(0.04)	(0.00)	(0.05)	(0.00)	(0.00)	(0.00)
Nonfinancial Corporations	0.50	0.50	0.47	0.48	0.54	0.54
	(0.50)	(0.50)	(0.10)	(0.19)	(0.05)	(0.04)
Foreign Investors	0.49	0.51	0.54	0.56	0.54	0.53
	(0.33)	(0.39)	(0.03)	(0.00)	(0.05)	(0.04)

Panel B	1995–2004					
	[0, +1D]	[+1D, +1W]	[+1W , +1M]	[0, +6M]	[0, +9M]	[0, +12M]
Households						
All	0.45	0.49	0.50	0.53	0.52	0.55
	(0.00)	(0.12)	(0.39)	(0.00)	(0.06)	(0.00)
Small as of 1995	0.46	0.48	0.51	0.53	0.53	0.55
	(0.00)	0.06	(0.16)	(0.00)	(0.00)	(0.00)
Medium as of 1995	0.47	0.497	0.49	0.53	0.54	0.55
	(0.00)	(0.24)	(0.07)	(0.00)	(0.00)	(0.00)
Large as of 1995	0.39	0.39	0.41	0.46	0.48	0.47
	(0.00)	(0.00)	(0.00)	(0.00)	(0.02)	(0.00)

(*Continued*)

Table 5: (*Continued*)

Panel B	1995–2004					
	[0, +1D]	[+1D, +1W]	[+1W , +1M]	[0, +6M]	[0, +9M]	[0, +12M]
Nonprofit Organizations	0.35 (0.00)	0.37 (0.00)	0.35 (0.00)	0.33 (0.00)	0.34 (0.00)	0.33 (0.00)
General Government	0.36 (0.00)	0.38 (0.00)	0.37 (0.00)	0.42 (0.00)	0.42 (0.00)	0.41 (0.00)
Finance and Insurance	0.53 (0.00)	0.54 (0.00)	0.52 (0.00)	0.53 (0.00)	0.53 (0.00)	0.53 (0.00)
Nonfinancial Corporations	0.50 (0.34)	0.49 (0.24)	0.50 (0.45)	0.52 (0.02)	0.53 (0.00)	0.54 (0.00)
Foreign Investors	0.52 (0.05)	0.49 (0.73)	0.51 (0.22)	0.50 (0.64)	0.49 (0.26)	0.49 (0.14)

This table reports the fraction of volume-based positive buy ratio difference days for both the 1995-1996 two-year and 10-year samples. We create buy ratios as in previous sections. We examine six return horizons. The horizons are the following day [0, +1D], the following week excluding the following day [+1D, +1W], the following month excluding the following week [+1W, +1M], the following six months [0, +6M], nine months [0, +9M], and 12 months [0, +12M]. We use the horizons to rank the buy ratios of each investor class independently, excluding days when there is no trading by the analyzed investor class. We add together the buy ratios of the four stocks with the highest return over the relevant horizon. We then add together the buy ratios of the four stocks with the lowest return over the relevant horizon and subtract from the previous sum to construct the (unreported) buy ratio difference. A positive buy ratio difference signifies superior stock selection. We compute the average fraction of positive buy ratios for each investor class over all days in the investigated period. An investor class that neither under- nor overperforms should exhibit a fraction of one-half. We use tests based on a two-tailed binomial probability distribution to report statistical significance from 0.5 as a *p*-value in parentheses below the reported fractions of positive buy ratio difference days.

horizon. We are thus able to replicate reasonably well the Grinblatt and Keloharju (2000) results in the future return analysis. In Column 5 of Panel A of our Table 5, foreign investors have a proportion of positive buy ratios of 0.561 comparable to 0.556 in Grinblatt and Keloharju (2000). We report an exceedingly high significance level of 0.00 of the difference from 0.5, while Grinblatt and Keloharju (2000) report a lower significance level of 0.022. Note that we use a two-tailed unadjusted binomial probability distribution to determine the significance of our results, while Grinblatt and Keloharju

Figure 2: Future Performance as a Function of Current Buy Ratios Based on Panels A and B of Table 5

This figure describes the average fraction of daily buy-volume for nine investor classes in sixteen stocks. We report the fractions on the x-axis as a difference from 0.5, and each column represents one future time horizon, ranging from one day to 12 months.

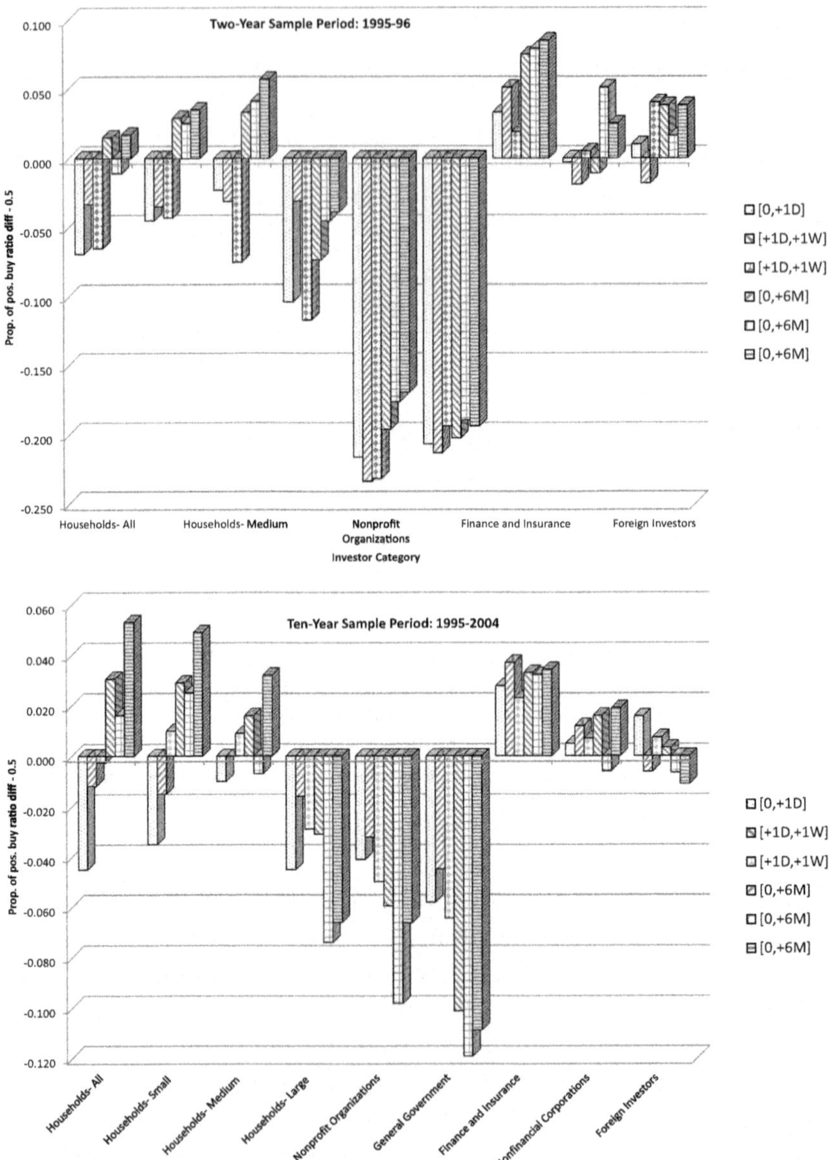

employ their own modified testing methodology, which is difficult to replicate fully.[13] Similarly, comparing our results to those of Grinblatt and Keloharju (2000), in regard to positive buy ratios, all households exhibit a proportion of 0.455 vs. 0.448, while finance and insurance institutions exhibit a proportion of 0.565 vs. 0.552. We thus report a proportionally higher significance level: 0.02 vs. 0.044 for households and 0.00 vs. 0.026 for finance and insurance institutions. Our results for the relationship of investor class-specific future performance to buy ratios are thus both statistically and economically significant. Replicating the Grinblatt and Keloharju (2000) significance testing methodology does not change the signs of the results or make them insignificant. We expect to generate significant differences in returns between the investor classes because the fraction of positive buy ratios on a daily level is sufficiently large.

Domestic institutional investors (i.e., finance insurance and non-financial corporations) exhibit a greater ability to select stocks that perform well over both short- and long-term future horizons. Foreign investors exhibit good performance over all horizons, with stronger long-term performance. Households underperform on all horizons during the investigated two-year sample period but do relatively better over longer-term horizons.

Second, we report in Panel B of Table 5 and in Figure 2 that the 'fraction of days' for the nine investor-types exhibit a positive 'buy ratio difference' for the 10-year sample period 1995–2004. This entire period shows, in some respects, quite different results from the first two years of

---

[13]Grinblatt and Keloharju (2000) perform an AR(4.1) adjustment to the binomial sign test controls for the possibility that some of the orders placed by different investors within a class on day t will be executed on different days. The residuals from a regression of buy ratio differences on lagged buy ratio differences should not exhibit time-series patterns (probably first-order autocorrelation) if an AR (4.1) specification reasonably characterizes the time series of buy ratio differences. If the buy ratio differences of foreign investors have first-order autocorrelations that are insignificant, irrespective of the horizon for the past or future return, the autocorrelation adjustment is not necessary. To make sure our binominal test statistics are not too high, we analyze the first-order autocorrelation in buy ratio differences. We find that for the past-return analysis the results hold, while for the future-return analysis, some results are already insignificant and any further correction is not necessary. The significant results retain their significance, as the first-order autocorrelations are insignificant, irrespective of the horizon for future return.

the sample. Foreigners are now poor performers over every horizon with the exception of one-day returns. These findings indicate that every investor group, with the exception of domestic institutions, provides liquidity to impatient foreign investors as they have matching negative one-day returns. We believe that their better performance in the first two years of the study is due to their proximity to the opening up of the market for foreign investors in 1993. Previously, foreigners outperformed households; however, now households outperform foreign investors over every horizon from six months to 12 months, with supposedly the least sophisticated small households performing the best. The 'all household,' 'small as of 1995,' and 'medium as of 1995' categories are all highly statistically significantly better performers than a 0.5 score consistent with random selection. The typical household score of 0.55 is exceedingly high from the perspective of economic significance.

For the one-week and one-month horizon, there is little difference between households and foreign investors. We find that non-profit organizations and general government agencies perform exceedingly poorly throughout, regardless of the period examined. Comparing results for the ten-year period to the two-year period, the statistical significance is somewhat weaker. The difference in fraction of positive buy ratio days is similar for households (i.e., turning from less than 0.5 to greater than 0.5) and finance and insurance institutions (i.e., remaining greater than 0.5), while the difference is weaker for foreign investors (i.e., turning from significantly greater than 0.5 to statistically insignificant).

3.2. *Robustness Tests*

Removing Nokia A and Nokia K from the sample does not alter the ranking between the investor classes for the two-year period 1995–1996. However, the performance of foreign investors is lower across all horizons without Nokia (not reported). The performance of finance and insurance institutions is intact over shorter horizons and lower in the longer horizons. Exclusion of Nokia improves performance of households in the shorter term and falls over longer-term horizons. This outcome supports the explanation that Nokia largely drives foreign investor returns — more so than do domestic investors.

3.3. *Alternative Methodology and Extended Cross Sectional Sample of Companies*

For the two-year period analyzed by Grinblatt and Keloharju (2000, p. 61), the authors reject as inappropriate the estimation of a factor model to perform a standard 'holdings-based calendar-time portfolios' test due to data limitations. Because we do not agree on the severity of data limitations, we attempt this for both the two-year and 10-year periods using daily, weekly, and monthly observations for all[14] actively trading shares during the period. Using Finnish data, we construct market return, high minus low book-to-market, small minus big market capitalization factor loadings following Fama and French (1993), and a Carhart (1997) momentum factor loading. We report the results in Table 6. While the factors are not significant for all investor groups investigated above, we are able to estimate factors with reasonable accuracy for four main classes of investors: domestic households, domestic institutions, foreign investors and a residual group of investors. These four factors explain why a significant proportion of the returns and intercepts (alphas) in the estimated model are slightly negative for the main investor classes and slightly positive for the residual class of investors. During the 1995–1996 period, domestic households exhibit the lowest alpha. By contrast, the alpha of domestic households is highest (i.e., least negative) in the 1995–2004 period, followed by domestic institutions and foreign investors. The results confirm that when conventional methodology is used, domestic investors outperform foreign investors. These results are robust using daily and weekly data (not reported).

As indicated above, we also implement 'transactions-based calendar-time portfolios'. We form calendar-time buy and sell portfolios to analyze the difference in buy and sell returns over annual buy and hold time horizons. Unlike the Grinblatt-Keloharju methodology based on a binary difference between buys and sells, the new methodology takes into account the actual return differences reflecting volumes. We report equally weighted return estimates in Table 7 and trade weighted return results

---

[14] To be able to estimate a factor model we need more than 16 stocks. During the investigated period, 1995–96, there were 107, and during 1995–2004, there were 209 sufficiently actively traded main classes of common stock.

Table 6: Alternative Methodology: Holdings-Based 'Calendar-Time Portfolios' — Monthly Data

	1995–1996				1995–2004			
Coefficient	Agg Hholds	Dom Inst	Foreign Inv	Resid Inv	Agg Hholds	Dom Inst	Foreign Inv	Resid Inv
Alpha	−1.298**	0.069	−0.570	−0.412*	0.005	−0.0007	−0.01727	0.085**
	(0.02)	(0.46)	(0.22)	(0.08)	(0.89)	(0.83)	(0.60)	(0.05)
CAPM Beta	2.399**	0.863***	2.55***	1.484***	1.051***	0.940***	1.282***	0.982***
	(0.04)	(0.00)	(0.00)	(0.00)	(0.00)	(0.00)	(0.00)	(0.00)
HML Bk to Mkt	12.453*	0.692	3.085	5.771*	0.486	0.306	−2.590	1.506
	(0.09)	(0.60)	(0.627)	(0.09)	(0.790)	(0.856)	(0.13)	(0.50)
SMB Mcap	−11.668**	−0.923	−14.746**	−5.338**	−2.471	−1.424	−2.427	4.988**
	(0.03)	(0.33)	(0.01)	(0.04)	(0.20)	(0.42)	(0.18)	(0.04)
Momentum 1 Yr	5.891**	−0.338	3.092	1.925*	−0.202	−0.015	0.233*	−0.213**
	(0.01)	(0.37)	(0.109)	(0.050)	(0.878)	(0.91)	(0.08)	(0.02)
Observations	12	12	12	12	108	120	108	108
R^2	0.87	0.93	0.08	0.89	0.56	0.61	0.67	0.49

This table reports results from estimations of a four-factor model to explain excess monthly stock returns. As the market return, we use the OMXH all share-capped index, as a risk-free rate and one-month CD rate. We construct high minus low book-to-market and small minus big market capitalization factor loadings following Fama and French (1993) and a 'one year' momentum factor loading based on Carhart (1997) using Finnish data. We estimate the model for four main classes of investors: domestic households, domestic institutions, foreign investors and a residual group of investors. The significance of coefficients are tagged with * at the 10%, ** at the 5% and *** at the 1% level of significance; p-values are reported in parentheses.

Table 7: Alternative Methodology: Equally Weighted Transactions-Based 'Calendar-Time Portfolios' — Daily Data

	1995–1996							1995–2004						
	Returns (bp/day)			Diff		Alpha		Returns (bp/day)			Diff		Alpha	
	Buys	Sells	Diff.	%	t-st	Ann%	t-st	Buys	Sells	Diff.	%	t-st	Ann%	t-st
Households														
All	177.7	178.0	−0.3	−0.03	0.0	8.6	0.8	8.1	6.8	1.3	0.13	1.1	3.1	0.5
Small as of 1995	179.6	174.8	4.8	0.48	0.5	6.0	0.6	76.3	55.0	21.3	2.13	1.8	2.3	0.4
Medium as of 1995	175.0	166.2	8.8	0.88	0.7	8.9	0.9	75.6	76.6	−1.0	−0.10	0.1	3.0	0.5
Large as of 1995	177.0	180.1	−3.1	−0.31	0.1	8.7	0.8	78.9	85.6	−6.7	−0.67	0.4	5.4	0.8
Nonprofit Org.	159.2	156.6	2.6	0.26	0.1	12.1	1.0	39.0	48.0	−9.0	−0.90	0.6	1.8	0.3
General Gov.	305.6	305.7	−0.1	−0.01	0.0	41.9	1.5	−2.6	−6.5	4.0	0.40	0.1	18.5	1.1
Finance and Ins.	−1059	−979	−79.9	−7.99	5.1	9.3	0.9	−1972	−1948	−24.0	−2.40	1.2	2.7	0.4
Nonfinancial Corp.	194.0	190.2	−3.8	−0.38	0.3	6.6	0.7	120.2	121.8	1.6	0.16	0.1	0.0	0.6
Foreign Investors	188.5	192.7	−4.2	−0.42	0.3	5.9	0.6	123.3	123.3	0.016	0.00	0.0	3.3	0.5

This table reports the average returns of equal-weighted transactions-based 'calendar-time portfolios'. Portfolios are formed by mimicking the trades of all investors in each of the nine investor's classes for the periods 1995–1996 and 1995–2004. We hold stocks in a 'calendar-time portfolio' for one year. For a given investor class, we form one 'calendar-time portfolio' based on stocks bought ('buys') and another portfolio based on stocks sold ('sells'). An equal-weighted 'calendar-time portfolio' refers to initially buying (selling) $1 of each stock bought ('sold'). We show the difference of returns between the buys and sells portfolios ('diff') in both basis points per day and annualized in percentages. The 'alpha' reports the annualized constant from a regression of the buys-minus-sells portfolio returns on the market's excess returns. We report t-statistics for tests of difference in mean returns between the 'buys' and 'sells' portfolios and for the estimated 'alpha' coefficient.

in Table 8.[15] Contrary to our results using the Grinblatt and Keloharju methodology and holdings-based analysis, we find no evidence of foreign investor trading outperformance over the Grinblatt-Keloharju two-year period based on either equal- or value-weighted returns. We do find evidence, however, that small and medium households outperform the two-year period. Over the 10-year period, household outperformance is more tightly restricted to small households that are both equal- and value-weighted.

These results are consistent with two propositions: (a) that the two-year Grinblatt-Keloharju period is more representative of the entire ten-year period than our reworking of their methodology in Table 5 would suggest, and (b) there may never have been foreign investor outperformance relative to small households. In a statistical sense, none of the transaction-based findings using alternative methodology is significant. As such, it is difficult to establish the notion that entire investor classes are either under- or over-performers with the far more ambitious holding-period approach that takes into account trade size and direction. Note that the CAPM alpha results we report in Tables 7 and 8 are not statistically significant.

Finally, we provide the buy ratio analysis from Sections 3 and 4 for a sample of the top 25 constituent companies included in the OMXH 25 futures index and additionally for all 800 common stocks listed at least during a part of the investigated period 1995–2004. We analyze the fraction of volume-based positive buy ratio difference days using the backward-looking six-months and forward looking six-month horizon for the three main investor classes, households, finance and insurance and foreign investors. These results are available from the authors upon request. In the long run, the top 25 share results support our previous results, showing that domestic households together with domestic institutions (i.e., finance and insurance) are contrarian and superior performers. The all-share results also support the view that households are contrarian and foreigners are momentum investors. The future performance results indicate that for equally weighted portfolios across all stocks, households

[15]An equal-weighted calendar-time portfolio refers to initially buying (selling) $1 of each stock bought (sold). A value-weighted calendar-time portfolio refers to buying or selling the same number of shares that individual investors buy or sell. In this way, large transactions initially receive more weight than small transactions.

Table 8: Alternative Methodology: Value Weighted Transactions-Based 'Calendar-Time Portfolios' — Daily Data

	1995–1996							1995–2004						
	Returns (bp/day)			Diff		Alpha		Returns (bp/day)			Diff		Alpha	
	Buys	Sells	Diff.	%	t-st	Ann%	t-st	Buys	Sells	Diff.	%	t-st	Ann%	t-st
Households														
All	230.2	213.9	16.3	1.63	1.6	9.0	0.9	147.6	152.6	−5.0	−0.50	0.4	3.6	0.6
Small as of 1995	234.3	213.5	20.8	2.08	2.1	9.6	0.9	132.0	125.7	6.3	0.63	0.5	4.3	0.7
Medium as of 1995	228.0	210.0	17.9	1.79	1.2	8.6	0.8	148.5	164.1	−15.6	−1.56	1.1	4.0	0.6
Large as of 1995	260.6	264.3	−3.7	−0.37	0.1	7.7	0.7	206.1	229.1	−23.0	−2.30	1.2	4.3	0.7
Nonprofit Org.	227.1	221.5	5.6	0.56	0.2	13.1	1.0	148.8	172.7	−23.8	−2.38	1.3	0.0	0.5
General Gov.	420.3	423.8	−3.5	−0.35	0.0	0.4	1.5	144.9	145.4	−0.5	−0.05	0.0	14.5	0.9
Finance and Ins.	−656.0	−651.6	−4.4	−0.44	0.6	6.2	0.6	−827.1	−825.6	−1.5	−0.15	0.4	3.2	0.5
Nonfinancial Corp.	230.2	218.3	−11.8	−1.18	0.7	5.7	0.6	235.4	240.0	4.6	0.46	0.3	3.5	0.6
Foreign Investors	230.3	231.4	−1.1	−0.11	0.1	6.9	0.7	257.3	254.8	2.5	0.25	0.1	3.4	0.5

This table reports average returns of value-weighted transactions-based calendar-time portfolios. Portfolios are formed by mimicking the trades of all investors in each of the nine investors' classes for the periods 1995–1996 and 1995–2004. We hold stocks in a calendar-time portfolio for one year. For a given investor class, we form one 'calendar-time portfolio' based on stocks bought ('buys') and another portfolio based on stocks sold ('sells'). A value-weighted 'calendar-time portfolio' refers to buying or selling the same number of shares that individual investors buy or sell. In this way, large transactions initially receive more weight than small transactions. We show the difference in returns between the buys and sells portfolios ('diff') in both basis points per day and annualized percentages. The 'alpha' reports the annualized constant from a regression of the buys-minus-sells portfolio returns on the market's excess returns. We report t-statistics for tests of difference in mean returns between the 'buys' and 'sells' portfolios and for the estimated 'alpha' coefficient.

and foreigners exhibit neutral performance. Domestic institutions become positive feedback traders and underperform when all shares are included.

For none of these results can we rule out the possibility that patient households in Finland provide liquidity to impatient institutional investors — and foreign investors in particular. According to our implementation of the Grinblatt-Keloharju methodology, compensation occurs for this risk-taking by out-performance over virtually all horizons except for the very short term. Superior local knowledge makes households less expensive liquidity providers.[16]

4. Significance and Interpretation of the Findings

To understand the significance of our contribution, it is helpful to view this reassessment of the main findings of Grinblatt and Keloharju (2000) in the context of the behavioral literature. Much of this literature relies on the belief that individual investors (i.e., households) are 'naïve' and 'unsophisticated' relative to delegated portfolio managers (i.e., institutional investors).[17] For example, Grinblatt and Keloharju (2002) find that foreign investors made up a large part of US institutional investors (i.e.,

---

[16]Our findings are thus consistent with those of Kaniel and Liu (2006), who found that for small and medium orders on the NYSE, limit-orders are more likely to contain information than is the case for market orders.

[17]For example, De Long, Shleifer, Summers, and Waldman (1991) rely on experimental evidence of cognitive biases to suggest that individuals are consistently poor assessors of probabilities with a tendency to underestimate variances and to be overconfident. They examine in the context of a partial equilibrium model the evolution of individual investors termed 'noise traders' and an alternative group, 'rational' investors. Assuming that noise traders cannot affect stock prices, their model indicates that such investors taking excessive risks can survive and dominate the market. Kogan, Ross, Wang, and Westerfield (2006) arrive at similar conclusions within a general equilibrium context. While the behavioral literature emphasises the role of cognitive biases in an effort to explain seemingly puzzling price patterns, such biases need not be ubiquitous. For example, Payzan-LeNestour and Bossaerts (2011) provide experimental evidence to show that subjects are capable of very sophisticated Bayesian updating involving complex jump processes, and thus, complexity need not be a barrier to rational learning. De Long, Shleifer, Summers, and Waldman (1990a) examine positive feedback investors. They point out that in the presence of such investors, rational speculative trades can be destabilizing. Anticipating future buying when investors receive good news, rational investors will push up prices even higher than the good news warrants. De Long, Shleifer, Summers, and Waldman (1990b) assume that individual noise traders falsely believe they have information such that stock prices depart significantly

delegated portfolio managers), systematically outperforming households while, importantly, adopting positive feedback strategies. Furthermore, causal association has several implications. While the literature has until recently been mixed,[18] the richness of the Finnish data in terms of coverage has lent weight to the view that households are inferior investors.

This richness combined with our reversal of previous findings of striking differences in the performance of different investor groups enables us to arrive at new insights concerning information and agency. Unlike institutions, individuals do not face agency issues with respect to delegated portfolio management.[19] We find that delegated portfolio managers in

---

from fundamental values even when there is no fundamental risk. Sophisticated rational arbitrageurs cannot eliminate the mistaken mispricing that could get worse before it gets better. Noise traders who underestimate risk can earn higher returns than sophisticated investors due to their own destabilizing influence.

[18]Barber and Odean (2000) for the US detect no signs of superior performance amongst households based on data from a discount broker. Seasholes (2000) finds that foreign investors buy (sell) ahead of good (bad) earnings announcements in Taiwan while domestic investors do the opposite. Lin and Swanson (2003) and Barber, Lee, Liu, and Odean (2009), and Chen, Johnson, Lin, and Liu (2009) find foreign investors perform better than domestic investors in Taiwan. Froot and Ramadorai (2008), examining twenty-five countries, reach the same conclusion, as do Froot, O'Connell, and Seasholes (2001). Hau (2001) and Dvořák (2005) find that domestic investors are superior performers at intra-month horizons but foreigners are superior performers at horizons beyond one month. Hvidkjaer (2008) finds that small trades, and thus presumably small investors, systematically underperform large trades in the US. Finally, using rigorous calendar-time holding and trading portfolios and a dataset of individual investor holdings and trades for a large US discount internet broker, Seasholes and Zhu (2010) find no evidence of local investor informational advantage. These findings are not universal. Choe, Kho and Stulz (2005) for Korea and Chan, Menkveld and Yang (2004) for China find domestic investors are superior performers, as do Agarwal, Faircloth, Liu and Rhee (2009) for Indonesia. Kang and Stulz (1997) find that foreign investors in Japan exhibited a preference for large firms such that performance was poor. Kaniel, Saar, and Titman (2008) find that US stocks experience statistically significant excess returns of 0.80% in the 20 days following a week of intense buying by individuals, and −0.33% following a week of intense individual selling. They attribute their finding to individuals providing liquidity to institutional investors. Jackson (2003) obtains similar results for Australia. Ivković and Weisbenner (2005) show the importance of the flow of value-relevant information regarding local companies for individual investors and Ivković and Weisbenner (2007) indicate word-of-mouth effects for individual investors. Ivković, Sialm, and Weisbenner (2008) show that more concentrated individual portfolios outperform more diversified ones.

[19]Massa and Patgiri (2009) find that mutual funds with higher incentives and thus fewer agency problems systematically outperform. Individuals trading on their own behalf

the form of domestic institutional investors perform as well as small and medium households in the longer term and better in the very short term. Hence, the inferior performance of foreign investors would not seem to be due to their ownership status *per se*. What distinguishes foreign investors from local institutions, other than the latter's proximity to company headquarters, is reliance on positive feedback trading. Thus, the trading strategy employed by foreigners may be an important factor in long-term under-performance. Consequently, negative feedback trading — buying more after price reductions and less after price increases — may be a profitable strategy but only for relatively well-informed and motivated investors. Contrarian investors consisting of nonprofit organizations such as foundations and government agencies inclusive of municipalities have the same locational advantages as households and institutional investors yet nevertheless still systematically underperform. For these groups, agency considerations appear to dominate any locational advantages that they may possess.

To minimize their informational disparity when US investors invest overseas, one should expect them to index-weight their investments. Such a procedure would ensure that Nokia holdings are proportional to their large size and are not overly weighted. As noted above, what we actually see is more concentrated investments in the largest stocks by established and widely followed companies with the greatest analyst coverage. This is consistent with the 'information disadvantage' hypothesis of Cooper and Kaplanis (1994) and Tesar and Werner (1995). Brennan and Cao (1997) suggest that foreign investors pursue positive feedback-trading strategies, not because they are smart but because they think it an optimal strategy for uninformed investors. Index weighting would seem preferable. Erb,

obviously incur no agency costs at all. Stoughton, Wu, and Zechner (2011) model investment advisors who managed $42.3 trillion in the US as of its peak in April 2008. They point out that often sizeable 'kickbacks' are paid, as was the case of feeder funds to the Bernard Madoff scam. They argue that unsophisticated investors are often the victims of such kickbacks. Kelley and Tetlock (2013) find that for retail investors both aggressive and passive net buying positively predict firms' monthly stock returns with no evidence of return reversal. Only aggressive orders correctly predict firm news, including earnings surprises, suggesting they convey novel cash flow information. Only passive net buying follows negative returns, consistent with traders providing liquidity and benefiting from the reversal of transitory price movements.

Harvey, and Viskanta (1996) show that political, financial, and economic risk factors relate to returns on international investments. Hence, they affect how aggressively investors weight a market in their portfolio. Our findings are also consistent with the view that foreign institutions are 'glamor investors' leading to poor performance (see Lakonishok, Shleifer and Vishny, 1994, for US domestic institutions) while contrarian households are better performing 'value investors.'

5. Conclusions

In this paper, we replicate and extend the analysis of Grinblatt and Keloharju (2000) for both their initial two-year sample period and for an extended 10-year sample period. We confirm most of their reported six-month horizon results for the initial sample period: foreign investors and domestic finance and insurance corporations outperform with statistical and economic significance. However, foreign investors underperform the extended sample period, especially for longer horizons, whether we use the original Grinblatt and Keloharju methodology or the more conventional calendar-time holdings portfolios approach incorporating a momentum factor. Households, households with small portfolios, households with medium portfolios, non-financial corporations and finance and insurance institutions are superior stock selectors and appear better informed. The 'transaction-based calendar-time portfolios' approach once again finds evidence that small households in particular are superior traders, thus rejecting the finding by Grinblatt and Keloharju that foreign investors are always superior traders relative to small households, even over the original two-year period of analysis.

Far from appearing more 'sophisticated' and 'informed' as stated by Grinblatt and Keloharju (2000), foreign investors seem less informed, and their behavior seems to recognize this disadvantage in a variety of ways. Foreign investors focus on the largest stocks with high company age and analyst coverage where this disadvantage is not as great and adopt positive feedback strategies that require minimal local knowledge. However, adopting index weights would seem to be a better strategy for minimizing a lack of local knowledge. By contrast, households — and in particular, small and medium households — appear to access superior information and adopt contrarian-trading strategies with negative feedback properties that may help to stabilize markets.

The results in this paper support nine major observations. (a) It is still possible to classify foreigners as 'positive feedback traders' in Finland, as reported by Grinblatt and Keloharju (2000). (b) Households still fall into the category of 'negative feedback traders' in Finland. (c) Finnish institutions no longer remain negative feedback traders, nor are they positive feedback traders, as they display 'neutral' characteristics. (d) Finnish institutional investors continue to outperform relative to all other investor classes with the exception of small and medium households and do so over all horizons investigated herein. (e) Both small- and medium-sized households outperform over longer-term horizons from six months to twelve months using the full ten-year dataset. (f) It is no longer possible to consider foreign investors as the best performing investors in Finland. (g) Positive feedback trading behavior can no longer be associated with superior performance. (h) Insofar as households have a tendency to hold onto losers for too long and cash out on winners too early, this behavioral trait can no longer be associated with underperformance. (i) It is no longer possible to unambiguously classify household and individual investors as purely random 'noise traders' in the behavioral and market microstructure literature, as there is now evidence of better candidate groups such as foreign investors and nonprofit organizations (e.g., foundations and government agencies, inclusive of municipalities).

References

Agarwal S., S. Faircloth, C. L. Liu, and S. G. Rhee. 2009. Why do foreign investors underperform domestic investors in trading activities? Evidence from Indonesia. *Journal of Financial Markets* 12: 32–53.

Baik, B., J-K. Kang, and J-M. Kim. 2010. Local institutional investors information asymmetries, and equity returns. *Journal of Financial Economics* 97: 81–106.

Barber, B. M., and T. Odean. 2000. Trading is hazardous to your wealth: The common stock investment performance of individual investors. *Journal of Finance* 55: 773–806.

Barber, B. M., T. Odean, and N. Zhu. 2009. Do Retail Trades Move Markets? *Review of Financial Studies* 22: 151–186.

Barber, B. M., Y. Lee, Y. Liu, and T. Odean. 2009. Just How Much Do Individual Investors Lose by Trading? *Review of Financial Studies* 22: 609–632.

Bernile, G., S. Kogan, and J. Sulaeman. 2015. Information Environment and the Geography of Firms and Investors. Unpublished Working Paper, Singapore Management University.

Berk, J. B., R. C. Green, and V. Naik. 1999. Optimal Investment, Growth Options, and Security Returns. *Journal of Finance* 54: 1553–1607.

Black, F. 1986. Noise. *Journal of Finance* 41: 529–543.

Brennan, M., and H. Cao. 1997. International Portfolio Flows. *Journal of Finance* 52: 1851–1880.

Carhart, M. M. 1997. On persistence in mutual fund performance, *Journal of Finance* 52: 57–82.

Chan, K., A. Menkveld, and Z. Yang. 2004. Are domestic investors more informed than foreign investors? Evidence from the Perfectly Segmented Market in China. Unpublished Working Paper. Hong Kong University of Science and Technology, Discipline of Finance.

Chen, L., S. A. Johnson, J. Lin, and Y. Liu. 2009. Information, sophistication, and foreign versus domestic investors' performance. *Journal of Banking and Finance* 33: 1636–1651.

Choe, H., B. Kho, and R. Stulz. 2005. Do Domestic Investors Have an Edge? The Trading Experience of Foreign Investors in Korea. *Review of Financial Studies* 18: 795–829.

Cooper, I., and E. Kaplanis. 1994. Home Bias in Equity Portfolios, Inflation Hedging, and International Capital Market Equilibrium. *Review of Financial Studies* 7: 45–60.

Coval, J., and T. Moskowitz. 1999. Home Bias at Home: Local Equity Preference in Domestic Portfolios. *Journal of Finance* 54: 2045–2073.

Coval, J., and T. Moskowitz. 2001. The Geography of Investment: Informed Trading and Asset Prices. *Journal of Political Economy* 109: 811–841.

De Long J. B., A. Shleifer, L. H. Summers, and R. J. Waldman. 1991. The survival of noise traders in financial markets, *Journal of Business* 64: 1–19.

De Long J. B., A. Shleifer, L. H. Summers, and R. J. Waldman. 1990a. Noise trader risk in financial markets. *Journal of Political Economy* 98: 703–738.

De Long J. B., A. Shleifer, L. H. Summers, and R. J. Waldman. 1990b. Positive Feedback Investment Strategies and Destabilizing Rational Speculation, *Journal of Finance* 45: 379–395.

Dvořák, T. 2005. Do Domestic Investors Have an Information Advantage? Evidence from Indonesia. *Journal of Finance* 60: 817–839.

Erb, C., C. Harvey, and T. Viskanta. 1996. Political risk, financial risk and economic risk. *Financial Analyst Journal* 52: 29–46.

Fama, E., and K. French. 1993. Common risk factors in the returns on stocks and bonds. *Journal of Financial Economics* 33: 3–56.

French, K., and J. Poterba. 1991. Investor Diversification and International Equity Markets. *American Economic Review* 81: 222–226.

Froot, Kenneth A., and T. Ramadorai. 2008. Institutional Portfolio Flows and International Investments. *Review of Financial Studies* 21: 937–971.

Froot, K., P. O'Connell, P., and M. S. Seasholes. 2001. The portfolio flows of international investors. *Journal of Financial Economics* 59: 151–193.

Grinblatt, M., and M. Keloharju. 2000. The investment behaviour and performance of various investor types: A study of Finland's unique data set. *Journal of Financial Economics* 55: 43–67.

Halling, M., M. Pagano, O. Randl, and J. Zechner. 2008. Where Is the Market? Evidence from Cross-Listings in the United States. *Review of Financial Studies* 21: 725–761.

Hau, H. 2001. Location Matters: An Examination of Trading Profits. *Journal of Finance* 56: 1959–1983.

Hvidkjaer, S. 2008. Small Trades and the Cross-Section of Stock Returns. *Review of Financial Studies* 21: 1123–1151.

Ivkovié, Z., C. Sialm, and S. J. Weisbenner. 2008. Portfolio Concentration and the Performance of Individual Investors. *Journal of Financial and Quantitative Analysis* 43: 613–55.

Ivkovié, Z., and S. J. Weisbenner. 2005. Local Does as Local Is: Information Content on the Geography of Individual Investors Common Stock Investments. *Journal of Finance* 60: 267–306.

Ivkovié, Z. Z., and S. J. Weisbenner. 2007. Information Diffusion Effects in Individual Investors' Common Stock Purchases: Covert Thy Neighbours' Investment Choices. *Review of Financial Studies* 20: 1327–57.

Jackson, A. 2003. The aggregate behavior of individual investors. Working paper, London Business School.

Jegadeesh, N., and S. Titman. 1993. Returns to Buying Winners and Selling Losers: Implications for Stock Market Efficiency. *Journal of Finance* 48: 65–91.

Johnson, T. C. 2002. Rational Momentum Effects. *Journal of Finance* 57: 585–608.

Kalev, P. S., A. H. Nguyen, and N. Y. Oh. 2008. Foreign versus local investors: Who knows more? Who makes more? *Journal of Banking & Finance* 32: 2376–2389.

Kaniel, R., G. Saar, and S. Titman. 2008. Individual Investor Trading and Stock Returns. *Journal of Finance* 63: 273–310.

Kaniel, R., and H. Liu. 2006. So What Orders Do Informed Traders Use? *Journal of Business* 79: 1867–1913.

Kang, J., and R. Stulz. 1997. Why is there a home bias? An analysis of foreign portfolio equity ownership in Japan. *Journal of Financial Economics* 46: 3–28.

Kelley, E. K., and P. C. Tetlock. 2013. How wise are crowds? Insights from retail orders and stock returns. *Journal of Finance* 68. 1229–1265.

Kogan, L., S. A. Ross, J. Wang, and M. M. Westerfield. 2006. The survival and price impact of irrational traders. *Journal of Finance* 61: 195–229.

Lakonishok, J., A. Shleifer, and R. W. Vishny. 1994. Contrarian Investment, Extrapolation, and Risk, *Journal of Finance* 49: 1541–1578.

Lin, A., and P. Swanson. 2003. The Behaviour and Performance of Foreign Investors in Emerging Equity Markets: Evidence from Taiwan. *International Review of Finance* 4: 189–210.

Linnainmaa, J. T. 2010. Do Limit Orders Alter Inferences about Investor Performance and Behavior? *Journal of Finance* 65: 1473–1506.

Lu, W. Swan, P. L. and Westerholm, P. J. 2015, 'Other People's Money': Mum and Dad Investors vs. the Professionals, UNSW Working Paper.

Massa, M., and R. Patgiri. 2009. Incentives and Mutual Fund Performance: Higher Performance or Just Higher Risk Taking? *Review of Financial Studies* 22: 1777–1815.

Odean, T. 1999. Do Investors Trade Too Much? *American Economic Review* 89: 1279–1298.

Payzan-LeNestour, E. and P. Bossaerts, 2011. Risk, Unexpected Uncertainty, and Estimation Uncertainty: Bayesian Learning in Unstable Settings. *PLOS Computational Biology* 7, 1–14. http://journals.plos.org/ploscompbiol/article?id=10.1371/journal.pcbi.1001048

Rouwenhorst, G. 1998. International Momentum Strategies. *Journal of Finance* 53, 267–284.

Sagi, J. S. and M. S. Seasholes. 2007. Firm-specific attributes and the cross-section of momentum. *Journal of Financial Economics* 84: 389–434.

Seasholes, M. S. 2004. Re-examining Information Asymmetries in Emerging Stock Markets. Unpublished Working Paper. University of California, Berkeley.

Seasholes, M. S. 2000. Smart foreign traders in emerging markets. Unpublished working paper. Harvard University.

Seasholes, M. S., N. Zhu. 2010. Individual Investors and Local Bias. *Journal of Finance* 65: 1987–2010.

Seru, A., Shumway,T., and N. Stoffman. 2010. Leaning by Trading. *Review of Financial Studies* 23: 705–739.

Stoughton, N. M., Y. Wu, and J. Zechner, 2011. Intermediated Financial Management. *Journal of Finance* 66: 947–980.

Teo, M. 2009. The Geography of Hedge Funds. *Review of Financial Studies* 22: 3531–3561.

Tesar, L., and I. Werner. 1995. Home bias and high turnover. *Journal of International Money and Finance* 14: 467–492.

Part III

Culture and Gender Effects

Chapter 5

The Assessment of Risk Behavior: A Cross-cultural Analysis using the DOSPERT Scale

Wolfgang Breuer[a], Jana Anette Kollath[*,b], Astrid Juliane Salzmann[c] and Rüdiger von Nitzsch[d]

Abstract

Using modified versions of the Domain-Specific Risk-Taking (DOSPERT) scale, we conducted surveys among German and Chinese university students. Our tests confirm previous findings that risk taking is indeed domain-specific. More importantly, our results show that differences in risk behavior are attributable more to perceived risk than to expected benefits. Risk behavior is almost entirely predictable by differences in the attitude towards perceived risk, but less so by differences in the subjective evaluation of expected benefits. Additionally, our study measures risk attitude through two distinct methodologies: on an individual-subject level and on a group-level. We find that the individual-subject risk attitude can lead to inadequate conclusions. Furthermore, our research highlights the relevance of national culture as an important factor for explaining risk-taking propensity. Our findings yield substantial support for the 'cushion hypothesis' and highlight the usefulness of the cultural

[a]Chair of Business Administration and Finance, School of Business and Economics, Department of Finance at RWTH Aachen University, Templergraben 64, 52056 Aachen, Germany.

[b]Research Associate, School of Business and Economics, Department of Decision Theory and Financial Services at RWTH Aachen University, Templergraben 64, 52056 Aachen, Germany.

[c]Research Associate, School of Business and Economics, Department of Finance at RWTH Aachen University, Templergraben 64, 52056 Aachen, Germany.

[d]Chair of Decision Theory and Financial Services, School of Business and Economics at RWTH Aachen University, Templergraben 64, 52056 Aachen, Germany.

*Corresponding author. Email: kollath@efi.rwth-aachen.de

dimension of individualism versus collectivism in order to explain risk behavior.

Keywords: Risk behavior, risk attitude, risk perception, domain specificity, psychometric scale, culture

JEL Classification: C91, D03, D81, G02, Z10

1. Introduction

Decision-making significantly shapes people's lives and the way they interact with each other. In almost every decision, risk and uncertainty loom large — even if this perhaps does not always appear as obvious as in economic decision making. As empirical evidence suggests considerable between-person variation in risk behavior, the understanding of risk behavior provides insights into choice behavior and a precise definition of the determining factors of human actions. This might eventually provide the possibility to reconstruct and — more relevantly — to predict individual investment behavior.

Against this background, an understanding of the antecedents of individual risk-taking propensity is particularly rewarding. Researchers try to explain the between-person variation in risk behavior on the one hand by demographic variables such as age, gender or cultural background. On the other hand, other studies assume risk factors such as risk perception and risk attitude as driving factors of this variation. The literature proposes manifold approaches for a reliable assessment of individual differences in the attitude towards risk. This paper focuses on risk behavior of individuals, and particularly elaborates on basic determinants of individual content in a cross-country cultural analysis. Our approach rests on the Domain-Specific Risk-Taking (DOSPERT) scale, which we apply to German and to Chinese nationals. Specifically, we focus on the determinants 'perceived risk' and 'expected benefits', assessed by means of a risk-return framework, and on the measurement of risk attitude through two distinct methodologies. We measure risk attitude on an individual-level and within groups, which allows us to examine whether risk attitude varies by domains, i.e., for financial versus non-financial decision-making, and cultures.

The distinction between decisions under risk and uncertainty lays in the possibility to assess objective probabilities to probabilistic outcomes in risky situations, whereas in decision situations under uncertainty, the decision maker only knows the possible outcomes (Knight, 1965). Thus, defining risk as the variation of outcomes in terms of gains and losses, prospect theory claims that people are risk averse over gains and risk-seeking over losses (Kahneman and Tversky, 1979). Moreover, prospect theory implicates that most individuals put more effort into avoiding losses than into achieving gains, an artefact known as loss aversion, and people tend to overweight small probabilities. Hence, individuals do usually not behave rationally when it comes to risky situations and show very different reactions towards risk. People can behave in risk-seeking, risk-neutral, or risk-avoidance ways, even if the situational factors of the respective decision do not differ. So-called risk behavior can be directly measured through the actions that people choose in decision situations. Despite the advantage of risk behavior being directly observable, the issue of predicting risk behavior remains unsolved. Risk behavior is generally explained through a distinction of the parameters of risk perception and risk attitude.

Risk perception is the personal assessment of the extent and controllability of risk in a decision situation (Sitkin and Pablo, 1992). A specific valuation can differ strongly from individual to individual due to varying interpretations of reality. Therefore, an individual might perceive exactly the same risk differently at distinct moments or in distinct circumstances, which results in very diverse behaviors (Knight, 1965). Recent work in behavioral finance shows the influence of risk perception on risk behavior (see for example, Sitkin and Pablo, 1992, or Nosic and Weber, 2007). It is commonly assumed that risk perception in turn is vastly influenced by the personal reference point (Weber and Milliman, 1997), characterized by values, feelings, and experiences of individuals. According to Sitkin and Pablo (1992), the reference point includes the situational problem-frame, and cultural and social influences as well as psychological aspects. Cultural aspects are abstract values a group of people formed to evaluate behavior through the perception of the situational characteristics (Hofstede, 2009). These common values lead to common fears that partly define the individual risk perception (Douglas and Wildavsky, 1982). The other part that determines risk perception are personal values based on personal experiences. Therefore, risk perception is the subjective response towards objective risk (Beck, 2007). Thus, risk perception, which can be described as a dynamic process, is on the one hand quantifiable and measurable, but on the other hand, not uniquely definable regarding the influencing parameters. The same features hold true for the extent of the involved effects on risk behavior (Soane, Dewberry and Narendran, 2010).

Risk attitude is the chosen state of mind towards risk, and needs to be observed independently of risk perception or a specific decision situation (von Nitzsch, 2008). It describes the preferences of a decision maker towards risk in general, and in the same way, as risk behavior itself, it can be characterized as risk-seeking, risk neutral, or risk averse. An individual with an exceptional risk-seeking attitude is very attracted to risk and usually shows a high willingness to take risks. On the contrary, a person with a very risk-averse attitude tries to avoid any risks as far as possible.

In contrast to risk behavior and risk perception, the measurement of risk attitude is rather problematic. This is particularly true if one wants to rely on expected utility theory or the measurement of the so-called relative risk attitude (Weber, Blais and Betz, 2002). The first approach shows different results when different measurements of expected utility are used, while the second approach has weaknesses regarding the assessment of the utility function through lotteries in non-material domains. A more promising approach goes back to Sarin and Weber (1993), and measures risk attitude by means of a risk-return framework. In traditional finance, the risk-return trade-off goes back to Markowitz (1952) and describes the investors' selection of their portfolios based on the expected return and expected risk in order to maximize their expected utility. To apply this framework to all decision domains, risk behavior (i.e., the preference for an option X) is generated through the more general trade-off between expected benefit (hope) and perceived risk (fear) of a situation. The following equation describes this content:

$$\text{Preference (X)} = a \times \text{Expected Benefit (X)} + b \times \text{Perceived Risk (X)} + c$$

Parameter a describes the effect of the marginal value of the expected benefit of an option X on risk behavior. The second parameter b describes the marginal effect of the perceived risk of an option X on risk behavior, and thus represents the risk attitude. Parameter c is the error coefficient (Weber, Blais and Betz, 2002). Figure 1 shows the described risk-return framework. Several studies have demonstrated that the expected benefit and the perceived risk as determinants of risk behavior vary situationally.

Figure 1: Risk-Return Framework

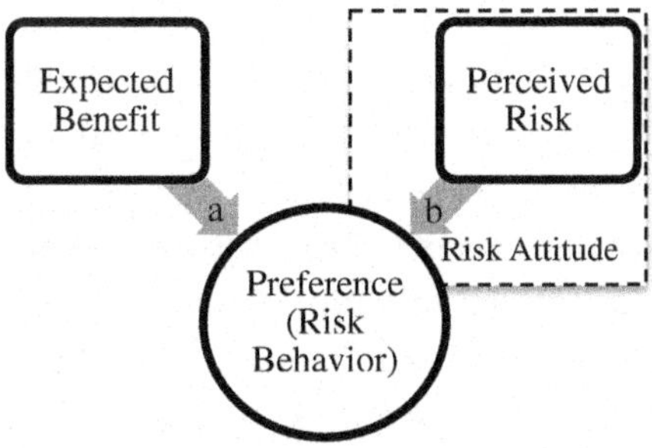

Nevertheless, the risk attitude given through parameter *b* is expected to be domain-independent and therefore cross-situationally constant. Summarizing, the last approach focuses on the relationship between risk perception and the final decision to determine the individual risk attitude (Weber and Milliman, 1997).

A practical application of the latter approach is the Domain-Specific Risk-Taking (DOSPERT) scale, inaugurated in Weber, Blais and Betz (2002), which evaluates risk behavior and its determinants 'expected benefit', 'perceived risk' and 'risk attitude' in five different domains. While the more traditional assessments based on the expected utility framework have only limited success in predicting individual risk attitude, the DOSPERT scale has demonstrated its usefulness in a range of empirical studies, and is well established (see for example, Harrison *et al.*, 2005, or Wu and Cheung, 2014). However, previous analyses provide inconclusive evidence for the importance of risk perception and expected benefits for predicting risk-taking behavior within the risk-return framework. Weber, Blais and Betz (2002), maintain that perceived benefits are more important in determining risk propensity than is perceived risk, whereas Hu and Xie (2012) demonstrate the importance of risk perception to explain risk behavior. Our analysis aims to shed some light on this issue and evaluates the explanatory power of both variables in a cross-country setting in order to arrive at more robust findings. The first aim of this study is thus to find out whether differences in risk behavior are more attributable to perceived risk than to expected benefits, and whether there are cross-cultural peculiarities. Second, we test the empirical power of the risk-return framework to assess risk attitude with two different methodologies, i.e., we compare the assessment of the parameter b at an individual-subject level and at a group level. We do so in order to find out whether risk attitude is indeed domain-independent when assessed at an individual-subject level or at a group level based on the above risk-return framework and the DOSPERT scale. Because risk propensity appears to be highly context-dependent, we study the effects in two distinct cultures, i.e., we study the differences between a Western and non-Western population in financial and non-financial risk taking: Germany and China. The adapted scale within this empirical study was extended and customized to fit the international context and includes participants from both countries.

2. Method

2.1. *Procedure*

The DOSPERT scale proposed by Weber, Blais and Betz (2002) is a psychometric scale for analyzing risk behavior and its determinants in different material and non-material areas. The scale contains items from a chosen amount of risky activities. The covered domains include social, ethics, health/safety, recreational, and financial risks. The last area separates further into 'investment' and 'gambling', which can essentially be analyzed as independent domains. In each of the five areas, expected benefit, perceived risk, risk attitude as well as resulting risk behavior are examined with the help of the risk-return approach. The original survey includes 40 items that represent risky behaviors from all five domains, distributed equally across all domains. The items were generated and validated through factor analysis and repeated practice with American students based on a beta version of the DOSPERT scale by Weber, Blais and Betz (2002). Each participant has to answer three questions on each of 50 items. The first subscale measures the risk behavior, i.e., the risk taking intention, using the instruction: 'For each of the following statements, please indicate the likelihood that you would engage in the described activity'. The corresponding five-stage answering scale ranges from 'very unlikely' (1) to 'very likely' (5). The second scale measures the perceived risk and employs the following instruction: 'For each of the following statements, please indicate how risky you perceive each situation'. The answering scale ranges from 'not at all risky' (1) to 'extremely risky' (5). The third and last subscale for measuring expected benefits asks the respondent to answer the question: 'For each of the following statements, please indicate the benefits you would obtain from each situation'. This five-stage answering scale ranges from 'no benefits' (1) to 'great benefits' (5). Coefficients from the last two scales can be used to measure sensitivities to perceived risk and to expected benefits within the risk-return approach. Therefore, to determine the coefficients *a* and *b* of the risk-return equation, the expected benefit and risk perceptions of each test person need to be imputed to the risk behavior of the respective test person using the corresponding item scores. In particular, a positive coefficient *b* implies a risk-seeking attitude, while a negative coefficient indicates a risk-averse attitude.[1]

The DOSPERT scale has been applied and modified in numerous studies. Within this study, the DOSPERT scale bases mainly on the original DOSPERT scale of 2002 with some amplifications in order to allow for our special intercultural research approach. In total, the questionnaire includes 50 items and seven domains. An additional financial domain, namely personal finance, was added that comprises financial items dealing with general financial decision making in everyday life. This additional financial domain is required, because not everyone can identify him/herself with investment or gambling risks. Twenty-two of the items originate from the original DOSPERT scale of 2002, 11 from the beta version of the DOSPERT scale, and three items have been added from the modified DOSPERT scale of 2006. Additionally, 14 items have been newly-generated to support the intercultural comparison of a highly collectivistic culture, Chinese, with a moderately collectivist culture, German. The 14 items focus mainly on the social domain which is of particular interest with regards to the cushion hypothesis. The items are presented to the participants in mixed order, independently of the associated domains. The complete set of items is listed in the Appendix.

2.2. *Participants*

The first group of participants consists of German students from RWTH Aachen University, Germany, and the second group comprises Chinese students from the Tsinghua University in Beijing, China. The first group

[1] See http://www.dospert.org for further information about scoring instructions.

receives a German version of the questionnaire and the second participant group an English one. Though it would have been preferable to conduct the Chinese survey in the students' native language, this appeared difficult to manage, as students originated from many different provinces, each with its own specific dialect. Nevertheless, we do not believe that formulating the questionnaire in English results in severe sample flaws. First, translation problems would only occur if the survey questions could not be properly understood by the participants. This seems however unlikely, as classes in the premier Chinese universities are typically held in English and all students are fluent in that language. Second, survey answers are simply marked with a cross, so language is not an issue. The consistency of our results with Hu and Xie (2012), who used the Chinese version of DOSPERT, supports this reasoning. The items and answering scales are back-translated to ensure that contents remain the same, and that comparability is granted. We only include fully completed questionnaires of students with German or Chinese citizenship in our sample. In total, 211 surveys are completed in China by students with Chinese citizenship including 110 women and 101 men. The average age is 21.5 years (standard deviation: 1.64; range: 18–25). In Germany, 196 questionnaires are completed by students with German citizenship, including 68 women and 128 men. The average age of the sample is 22.4 years (standard deviation: 2.18; range: 19–30). We control for age and gender in the following analysis in order to account for the different sample composition.

3. Results

To answer our research questions, we follow the basic instructions of Weber, Blais and Betz (2002). Therefore, we conduct a reliability analysis before we examine the results in the three subscales to derive differences in risk behavior in both participant groups. Then we estimate several regression models in order to generate the risk attitude. We proceed on an individual-subject level first and then continue on a group level. The group-level regression models also allow us to examine the influence of culture by using a dummy variable. Finally, we assess whether differences in risk behavior are more attributable to risk perception or to perceived benefits.

3.1. *Reliability*

We consider Cronbach's alphas and average item-total correlations in order to evaluate the reliability of the study in the following.

Table 1 gives an overview of Cronbach's alphas and item-total correlations for scales 1 and 2 separately for the five domains and

Table 1: Cronbach's Alphas and Item-Total Correlations

Germany	Cronbach's alphas		Item-total correlations	
	Risk behavior	Risk perception	Risk behavior	Risk perception
Sub-scale	Scale 1	Scale 2	Scale 1	Scale 2
Finance	0.76	0.79	0.40 (0.17–0.59)	0.44 (0.14–0.70)
Investment	0.76	0.65	0.51 (0.42–0.59)	0.43 (0.33–0.55)
Gambling	0.73	0.81	0.40 (0.22–0.56)	0.63 (0.41–0.76)
Personal Finance	0.15	0.42	0.21 (0.17–0.27)	0.26 (0.20–0.29)
Health/safety	0.44	0.55	0.12 (−0.98–0.32)	0.26 (0.05–0.40)
Recreational	0.68	0.65	0.44 (0.25–0.55)	0.40 (0.23–0.52)
Ethics	0.67	0.70	0.36 (0.14–0.50)	0.40 (0.21–0.52)
Social	0.58	0.80	0.18 (−0.38–0.52)	0.40 (0.16–0.55)
Total	0.84	0.89		
China	**Cronbach's alphas**		**Item-total correlations**	
	Risk behavior	Risk perception	Risk behavior	Risk perception
Sub-scale	Scale 1	Scale 2	Scale 1	Scale 2
Finance	0.78	0.72	0.43 (−0.11–0.67)	0.30 (−0.73–0.56)
Investment	0.74	0.34	0.53 (0.44–0.66)	0.19 (0.12–0.29)
Gambling	0.86	0.81	0.68 (0.57–0.76)	0.60 (0.47–0.82)
Personal Finance	0.24	−0.18	0.33 (−0.17–0.34)	0.06 (−0.18–0.15)
Health/safety	0.50	0.72	0.25 (−0.67–0.41)	0.41 (−0.18–0.75)
Recreational	0.63	0.14	0.40 (0.09–0.69)	0.07 (−0.07–0.21)
Ethics	0.57	0.82	0.28 (0.02–0.47)	0.54 (0.39–0.77)
Social	0.60	0.83	0.24 (−0.17–0.69)	0.40 (−0.68–0.71)
Total	0.80	0.86		

participant groups. The highest average item-total correlations for the Germans show up in the domains investment in scale 1 and gambling in scale 2 with 0.51 and 0.63. The lowest average item-total correlations exist in scales 1 and 2 in the domain health/safety with 0.12 and 0.26. Weber, Blais and Betz (2002) suggest including only items with an item-total correlation of 0.3 or above to obtain a reliable questionnaire. Hence, items with an item-total correlation of less than 0.3 in all scales and across both participant groups are excluded. In this study, all item-total correlations exceed 0.3 in at least one sub-scale for at least one of the two participant groups, and are therefore included in this analysis. The highest average item-total correlations for the Chinese participants occur in the gambling domain in both scales with 0.68 and 0.6. The lowest scores occur in scale 1 in the social area with 0.24 and in scale 2 in the personal finance domain with 0.06. In total, most correlations are above or close to 0.3, so that the reliability of the results is well acceptable. The least reliable domains for both groups are the personal finance domain as well as health/safety.

Moreover, the total Cronbach's alphas, which express the internal consistency of a scale, exceed 0.8 for all domains, both scales, and both participant groups. We can therefore assume a high internal consistency. For both groups and both scales the personal finance domain is the least reliable. Highly reliable are the domains finance and investment with 0.76 for the German participants in scale 1, and the gambling domain with 0.81 in scale 2. For the Chinese participants, the domains gambling in scale 1 with 0.86 and the social domain with 0.83 in scale 2 are the most consistent. Summarizing the reliability analysis on item-total correlations and Cronbach's alphas, our results show that the domains gambling and investment are the most reliable ones. On the contrary, personal finance, which has been newly added, is the least reliable domain, but still included for the following regression analysis, because it contains financial items that cannot be analyzed through the sub-scales investment or gambling, but are important to obtain a comprehensive assessment of the finance domain.

3.2. *Subscale Means*

Figures 2, 3, and 4 show the subscale means for the Chinese and German samples. The Germans and the Chinese differ considerably in all subscales. Chinese individuals show a higher willingness to conduct risky financial

Figure 2: Means of Risk Behavior Rating

Figure 3: Means of Risk Perception Rating

activities than the German sample. Moreover, in all non-financial domains, the Chinese show rather risk-averse behavior, whereas the Germans are more willing to take these risks. The Germans are most risk-seeking in the social domain with a mean of 3.5, and the Chinese in investment risk with 3.23. The risk perception rating in Figure 3 supports these findings. The Chinese participants perceive activities in financial domains to be not as risky as those in non-financial domains, while the Germans perceive the riskiness of the activities exactly contrarily. Figure 4 finally shows the differences between the two samples in expected benefits. Both samples reveal rather small benefits in all domains. The Chinese observe higher benefits than Germans in all domains except in the ethics domain. The

Figure 4: Means of Expected Benefit Rating

Germans have the highest benefits in the ethics domain with 2.98, and the Chinese in the investment domain with a mean of 3.16. These findings indicate that German and Chinese individuals differ to a great extent in their risk attitude, their perception of risk, and the expected benefits of all risk categories. The Chinese display rather risk-seeking results in financial and rather risk-averse results in non-financial domains, whereas the results of German respondents demonstrate exactly obverse views.

3.3. *Individual-Subject Level Regression Analysis*

In the following, we examine the risk attitude of both participant groups more rigorously. To measure risk attitude on the individual-subject level, we regress risk behavior on expected benefits and perceived risk with a separate regression for each domain and each participant. An individual is classified as risk seeking if his/her regression coefficient for perceived risk is significant (at a significance level of 0.10) and positive. Conversely, an individual is classified as risk averse if its regression coefficient is significant and negative. If the regression coefficient does not differ significantly from zero, the individual is classified as risk neutral. Table 2 shows the results for German participants and Table 3 for Chinese participants. The upper parts of the Tables 2 and 3 give the respective distribution of risk attitudes across respondents by risk domain. The lower parts of the two tables present the number of individuals with consistent or inconsistent risk attitudes across the five domains. Commonly, both groups show rather risk averse

Table 2: Risk Attitude (in %) of the German Sample

	Risk attitude		
Domain	Averse	Neutral	Seeking
Finance	77.04	16.84	6.12
Health/Safety	66.33	23.98	9.69
Recreational	63.27	25.51	11.22
Ethics	73.47	16.84	9.69
Social	82.14	14.80	3.06

	Risk attitude
Averse for all domains	40.31
Averse or neutral	42.35
Neutral for all domains	0.00
Neutral or seeking	3.06
Seeking for all domains	0.00
Seeking or averse	14.29
Seeking, neutral or averse	0.00

Table 3: Risk Attitude (in %) of the Chinese Sample

	Risk attitude		
Domain	Averse	Neutral	Seeking
Finance	59.72	29.38	10.9
Health/Safety	74.41	19.43	6.16
Recreational	53.55	29.86	16.59
Ethics	79.62	12.8	7.58
Social	82.94	11.37	5.69

	Risk attitude
Averse for all domains	28.91
Averse or neutral	46.45
Neutral for all domains	2.37
Neutral or seeking	8.53
Seeking for all domains	0
Seeking or averse	13.74
Seeking, neutral or averse	0

attitudes and less neutral or seeking risk attitudes in all domains, whereas only a minority of each group shows risk-seeking attitudes in the examined domains. Thus, the distribution of the attitudes from risk averse to risk-seeking is rather similar across all domains for both groups. With regard to the measured individual-subject risk attitudes, the lower part of the two tables suggests rather constant averse or neutral attitudes in all domains for each individual and for both participant groups. 42.35% of all the German and 46.45% of all the Chinese participants display an averse or neutral risk attitude in all five risk categories. Hence, the frequency of risk attitude categories is rather similar in both participant groups with few individuals exhibiting risk-seeking attitudes and the great majority possessing risk averse or neutral attitudes, and therefore does not differ much across cultures. Furthermore, indicating attitudes ranging from averse to neutral, the results show that risk attitude is indeed domain-independent from the individual-subject perspective.

3.4. *Group Level Regression Analysis*

We perform further regression analyses on a group level to explore the usefulness of expected benefits and perceived risk for explaining risk behavior and for assessing the average risk attitudes of both groups. Specifically, for each domain, we predict behavioral scores with a linear model including the perceived risk and expected benefit scores as predictor variables. We further include age and gender (male = 0, female = 1) of participants in the regression models. We estimate the regression models separately for the German and the Chinese sample. Table 4 shows the regression coefficients for the intercept term, expected benefits, and perceived risk, as well as the adjusted R^2 in each domain.

Regarding our first research question, differences in risk taking seem to be associated primarily with differences in the way that individuals translate perceived risks of some options into actions rather than differences in the evaluation of expected benefits. The coefficient of expected benefits is insignificantly positive throughout almost all regression models. This result is in line with Hu and Xie (2012), who find that perception of risk is better than expected benefits as a predictor of risk behavior. Therefore, the respective subscale of the DOSPERT instrument will most often suffice to predict risk taking in most applications (Weber, Blais and Betz, 2002).

With respect to our second research question, our tests of the risk-return model now confirm that risk taking is indeed domain-dependent, as risk attitude coefficients vary substantially across domains. The results show considerable cross-group and cross-situational consistency. Risk perception and risk behavior are generally negatively correlated, suggesting perceived risk aversion. Considering the methodology of the individual-subject level risk attitude, the coefficients denote risk-averse attitudes in all domains in the German group. For the Chinese group, the coefficients indicate risk-averse attitudes in all domains except in the financial domains (i.e., personal finance, gambling, and investment), in which neutral risk attitudes occur. Apparently, this finding is in stark contrast to the individual-subject analysis, and demonstrates important differences to the previous results of Tables 2 and 3. Although, even for China, most individuals exhibit a risk-averse attitude towards financial risks, the overall assessment on the group level is a neutral attitude. The reason for this result in comparison to the risk attitude of the German students is that, not only are there fewer Chinese students with averse risk attitudes in the financial domains than German students, but also that the risk-averse Chinese students are characterized by lower average levels of risk attitude in these domains. In this respect, the analysis of Table 4 offers additional insights in comparison to the results of Tables 2 and 3. Considering solely the individual-subject level analyses of Section 3.3 would therefore circumvent adequate conclusions with regard to domain-specific as well as to cultural peculiarities.

The finding of risk perception being significantly negatively related to risk behavior for the three financial domains in the German sample only is consistent with the 'cushion hypothesis' proposed in Hsee and Weber (1999). The strong social bonding among individuals in a collective culture like that of China allows jointly developing mechanisms to hedge against risk. If someone is in need, he/she can turn to his/her social network for support. Members of a collectivistic society can receive substantial material and financial assistance, as they have a large and close social network to count on. The collectivist network would 'cushion' its members in case they were to 'fall'. Thus, the collectivist network is of particular importance for society members, so that social risks, which could threaten the network, are mainly avoided, and risks are taken only in non-social areas like the financial

Table 4: Regression Coefficients and Adjusted R^2

Germany							
	Intercept	Perceived Risk	Perceived Benefit	Age	Gender	R^2	N
Finance	3.59***	−0.40***	0.05	0.01	−0.31***	0.20	196
Investment	4.7***	−0.66***	0.01	0.02	−0.43***	0.28	196
Gambling	3.36***	−0.33***	0.11	−0.01	−0.32***	0.18	196
Personal Finance	3.81***	−0.49***	0.03	0.02	−0.08	0.22	196
Health/Safety	5.03***	−0.58***	−0.12	0.01	−0.10	0.29	196
Recreational	5.89***	−0.72***	0.03	−0.02	−0.45***	0.34	196
Ethics	5.27***	−0.46***	0.02	−0.05**	−0.10	0.21	196
Social	3.74***	−0.22***	0.00	0.01	−0.07	0.10	196

China							
	Intercept	Perceived Risk	Perceived Benefit	Age	Gender	R^2	N
Finance	2.03**	0.11	0.11	0.00	−0.10	0.03	211
Investment	2.22**	0.04	0.14	0.02	−0.11	0.02	211
Gambling	1.64	0.10	0.03	0.00	−0.12	0.02	211
Personal Finance	4.71***	−0.44***	0.07	-0.02	−0.11	0.07	211
Health/Safety	4.65***	−0.48***	0.02	-0.02	−0.07	0.35	211
Recreational	4.44***	−0.90***	0.05	0.05	0.23**	0.30	211
Ethics	3.24***	−0.29***	0.06	0.01	−0.10	0.17	211
Social	3.14***	−0.12*	0.05	0.01	−0.01	0.03	211

Germany & China								
	Intercept	Perceived Risk	Perceived Benefit	Age	Gender	R^2	Dummy Nationality	N
Finance	3.04***	−0.18***	0.08	0	−0.20***	0.12	−0.24***	407
Investment	3.93***	−0.35***	0.06	0.02	−0.27***	0.16	−0.39***	407
Gambling	2.6***	−0.13**	0.04	−0.01	−0.20**	0.04	−0.01	407
Personal Finance	4.33***	−0.47***	0.05	0.01	−0.09	0.24	−0.34***	407
Health/Safety	4.61***	−0.51***	−0.02	−0.01	−0.08	0.38	0.23***	407
Recreational	5.61***	−0.80***	0.01	0	−0.11	0.31	0.02	407
Ethics	4.27***	−0.35***	0.05	−0.03*	−0.12*	0.3	0.24***	407
Social	3.28***	−0.16***	0.03	0.01	−0.04	0.25	0.28***	407

Note: $^{*}p < 0.05$, $^{**}p < 0.01$, $^{***}p < 0.001$.

area. Therefore, the cushion feature serves only as a security against non-social, but not against social and relational risks.

We finally merge both samples and reestimate the regression model. We also include a dummy variable which indicates the nationality of the participants (China = 0, Germany = 1). This additional variant of the group-level analysis enables us to identify further significant differences in risk attitude in Germany and China, which are difficult to determine for simple country-specific examinations.

The previous results generally hold; perceived risk is highly significant throughout all domains, but the corresponding risk attitude coefficients also vary strongly across domains. The explanatory power of expected benefits is limited. Gender also provides a useful determinant in four domains.

After accounting for differences in the perceived risk and expected benefits, the country dummy has considerable explanatory power for risk behavior. This finding is particularly interesting, as it demonstrates the importance of the national background when explaining risk-taking behavior. Individuals from different countries reveal significantly diverging behavior in risky situations, the roots of which can be notably ascribed to country-specific factors. National culture emerges as the critical factor at the roots of such cross-country differences (Guiso, Sapienza and Zingales, 2006).

The results indicate that Chinese and German nationals exhibit different risk behavior even if perceived risk and expected benefits are held constant across countries. The German participants react in a less risk-taking manner with regard to monetary consequences. This effect reinforces our findings from above, where the coefficients in the single country regressions show that the Chinese exhibit less risk aversion in the financial domains. This outcome eventually reveals that differences in risk behavior arise from differences in risk attitude in different countries. This finding supports recent research focusing on cultural differences in order to understand risk perceptions, because uniform reality and risk attitude cannot be assumed across countries or cultures (Breuer, Riesener and Salzmann, 2014).

4. Discussion

Our results acknowledge the use of the DOSPERT scale, as Chinese nationals act particularly less risk aversely in finance-related matters than Germans do. The findings for the other areas are exactly the opposite, as Germans appear less risk-averse therein. Our results strongly support previous findings that risk-taking is indeed domain-specific. Our results also show that differences in risk behavior are predictable almost entirely by differences in the way that individuals translate perceived risks of some options into actions but less so by the influence of the expected benefits.

Our work further confirms the existence of differences in risk attitudes across countries and domains when using the group-level regression. When using the individual-subject-level regression for measuring risk attitudes, these do not differ substantially across countries and domains, because this approach only indicates a too vague distribution of attitudes, whereas the group-level regression considers the actual value of the perceived risk coefficients on an aggregated level. For a similar reason, the group-level approach itself can be refined by adding a country dummy to the regression. When including this dummy in the regression model, nationality emerges as an important domain-dependent factor for explaining risk behavior. Our findings do not support the conjecture that Germans are generally more risk averse than the Chinese (Hsee and Weber, 1999; Statman and Weng, 2010). In fact, our analysis indicates that individuals from the two different countries are risk averse in distinct ways. Risk behavior can be influenced through a variety of factors, and the 'cushion hypothesis', which traces such differences back to national culture, delivered a useful explanation for our case. Such findings support previous studies on the relationship between culture and economics, and again highlight the importance of incorporating cultural differences into future analyses (Weber and Hsee, 1998). It is therefore necessary to decompose risk behavior into an individual-specific as well as a cultural-specific component. Due to differences in risk attitude, individuals translate perceived risk into different behavior, depending on their cultural background, and this fact should not be neglected (Wang and Fischbeck, 2008).

Previous studies often suggest employing data on cultural values to proxy for cross-cultural differences in risk perception. The question of obtaining suitable and reliable measures is hence of peculiar concern. A wide range of frameworks measuring national culture exist, and each framework comprises certain measures related to risk taking. The cultural dimension of uncertainty avoidance from the Hofstede (1980) model have received utmost attention in this field (Bontempo, Bottom and Weber, 1997). Our analysis calls attention to another cultural dimension, namely the dimension of individualism versus collectivism, when explaining risky choice behavior. The usefulness of the 'cushion hypothesis' for explaining our results demonstrates that the cultural dimension of individualism cannot be neglected if we are to understand risk behavior. Thus, the cultural dimensions of uncertainty avoidance and individualism versus collectivism should always be included simultaneously in such analyses. The omission of one dimension may lead to incomplete inference and severe contortion of results (Antonczyk and Salzmann, 2012).

References

Antonczyk, R. C., and A. J. Salzmann. 2012. "Venture Capital and Risk Perception." *Zeitschrift für Betriebswirtschaft* 82: 389–416. DOI:10.1007/s11573-012-0556-1

Beck, U. 2007. *Weltrisikogesellschaft* (1st ed.), Frankfurt am Main: Suhrkamp Verlag.

Blais, A.-R. and E. U. Weber. 2006. "A Domain-Specific Risk-Taking (DOSPERT) Scale for Adult Populations." *Judgment and Decision Making* 1: 33–47.

Bontempo, R. N., W. P. Bottom, and E. U. Weber. 2006. "Cross-cultural Differences in the Perception: A Model-based Approach." *Risk Analysis* 17: 479–488. DOI:10.1111/j.1539-6924.1997.tb00888.x

Breuer, W., M. Riesener, and A. J. Salzmann. 2014. "Risk Aversion vs. Individualism: What Drives Risk Taking in Household Finance?" *The European Journal of Finance*, forthcoming.

Douglas, M., and A. Wildavsky. 1982. "How can we know the risks we face? Why risk selection is a social process." *Risk Analysis* 2: 49–58.

Guiso, L., P. Sapienza, and L. Zingales. 2006. "Does Culture affect Economic Outcomes?" *Journal of Economic Perspectives* 20: 23–48.

Harrison, J. D., J. M. Young, P. Butow, G. Salkeld, and M. J. Solomon. 2005. "Is it worth the risk? A systematic review of instruments that measure risk propensity for use in the health setting." *Social Science and Medicine* 60: 1385–1396.

Hofstede, G. 2002. *Cultural Consequences: Comparing Values, behaviors, institutions, and organizations across nations.* (2nd ed.), USA: Sage Publications.

Hsee, E. U., and C. K. Weber. 1999. "Cross-national Differences in Risk Preference and Lay Predictions." *Journal of Behavioral Decision Making* 12: 165–179.

Hu, X., and X. Xie. 2012. "Validation of the Domain-Specific Risk-Taking Scale in Chinese College Students." *Judgment and Decision Making* 7: 181–188.

Kahneman, D., and A. Tversky. 1979. "Prospect Theory: An analysis of decision under risk." *Econometrica* 47: 263–291.

Knight, F. H. (1965): *Risk, uncertainty & profit* (1st ed.), New York: Harper Torchbooks.

Markowitz, H. 1952. "Portfolio Selection." *The Journal of Finance* 7: 77–91.

von Nitzsch, R. 2008. *Entscheidungslehre* (5th ed.), Mainz: Wissenschaftsverlag Mainz.

Nosic, A., and M. Weber. 2007. "Determinants of risk taking behavior: the role of risk attitudes, risk perceptions and beliefs." Available at SSRN: http://ssrn.com/abstract.

Sarin, R. K., and M. Weber. 1993. "Risk-value Models." *European Journal of Operations Research* 70: 135–149.

Sitkin, S. B., and A. L. Pablo. 1992. "Reconceptualizing the Determinants of Risk Behavior." *Academy of Management Review* 17: 137–153. DOI:10.5465/AMR.1992.4279564

Soane, E., C. Dewberry, and S. Narendran. 2010. "The Role of Perceived Costs and Perceived Benefits in the Relationship between Personality and Risk-related Choices." *Journal of Risk Research* 13: 303–318.

Statman, M., and J. A. Weng. 2010. "Investment across Cultures: Financial Attitudes of Chinese-Americans." *Journal of Investment Consulting* 11: 37–44.

Wang, M., and P. S. Fischbeck. 2008. "Evaluating Lotteries, Risks, and Risk-mitigation Programs." *Journal of Risk Research* 11: 775–795.

Weber, E. U., and C. K. Hsee. 1998. "Cross-cultural Differences in Risk Perception, but Cross-cultural Similarities in Attitudes towards Perceived Risk." *Management Science* 44: 1205–1217.

Weber, E. U., and R. A. Milliman. 1997. "Perceived Risk Attitudes: Relating Risk Perception to Risky Choice." *Management Science* 43, 123–144.

Weber, E. U., A.-R. Blais, and N. E. Betz. 2002. "A Domain-Specific Risk-Attitude Scale: Measuring Risk Perceptions and Risk Behaviors." *Journal of Behavioral Decision Making* 15: 263–290. DOI:10.1002/bdm.414.

Wu, J., and H. Y. Cheung. 2014. "Confirmatory Factor Analysis of Dospert Scale with Chinese University Students." *Psychology Reports: Mental & Physical Health* 114: 185–197.

Appendix

Domains	Items
Finance	
F1	Investing 10% of your annual income in a moderate growth mutual fund.*
F2	Investing 5% of your annual income in a very speculative stock.*
F3	Investing 5% of your annual income in a conservative stock.*
F4	Investing 10% of your annual income in a new business venture.***
F5	Betting a day's income at a horse race.*
F6	Betting a day's income in a high-stake poker game.*
F7	Betting a day's income on the outcome of a sporting event (e.g., soccer).*
F8	Gambling a week's income at a casino.*
F9	Purchasing a lottery ticket.
F10	Lending a friend an amount of money equivalent to one month's income for you.**
F11	Spending money impulsively without thinking about the consequences.**
F12	Taking a job where you get paid exclusively on a commission basis.**
Health/Safety	
H1	Not wearing a helmet when riding a motorcycle.*
H2	Never wearing a seatbelt.*
H3	Walking home alone at night in a somewhat unsafe area of town.*
H4	Regularly eating unhealthy food.*
H5	Usually consuming a lot of alcohol and/or cigarettes in your free time.*
H6	Regularly riding your bicycle without a helmet.**
H7	Eating expired food products that still look okay.**
H8	Engaging in environmental activities e.g., to halt the climate change.
Recreational	
R1	Trying Bungee Jumping.*
R2	Going camping in the wilderness, beyond civilization.*
R3	Going down a ski run that is too difficult.*
R4	Going whitewater rafting at high tide in the springtime.*
R5	Playing soccer/basketball/tennis.
Ethics	
E1	Cheating in exams.*
E2	Forging somebody's signature e.g., on an attendance list.*
E3	Copy and pasting information together from various internet sources to create your own piece of work.**
E4	Using office supplies for your personal business.**

(*Continued*)

Appendix (*Continued*)

Domains	Items
E5	Not returning a wallet you found that contained 2000 $\bar{\pi}$/200€.***
E6	Revealing a friend's secret so someone else.***
E7	Telling a lie for your best friend.
E8	Telling a lie for a classmate that you do not know so well.
Social	
S1	Admitting that your tastes are different from those of your friends.*
S2	Arguing with a friend who has a very different opinion on an issue.*
S3	Asking your boss for a raise.*
S4	Taking a job that you enjoy over one that is prestigious but less enjoyable.*
S5	Dating someone that you are working with.**
S6	Openly disagreeing with your boss.**
S7	Moving to a new town.**
S8	Deciding to share an apartment with someone you do not know well.**
S9	Openly showing your frustration and anger when things does not working out.
S10	Placing a lot of trust in family members to rescue you if were to be in (financial) trouble.
S11	Accepting a job which you do not prefer, just because that would please your family.
S12	Preferring to work on a task on your own than within a group.
S13	Disagreeing with your group at a group project.
S14	Saying 'No' when a person that you do not know so well asks you to do him/her a favor.
S15	Saying 'No' when a friend asks you to do him/her a favor.
S16	Providing private information, such as photos and status updates in social networks.
S17	Communicating with people in different countries on the World Wide Web.

Note. (*) DOSPERT scale 2002. (**) Beta version DOSPERT scale 2002. (***) Modified DOSPERT scale 2006.

Chapter 6

Fear of Negative Evaluation, Culture, Gender, and Financial Welfare

Na Young Park*

Abstract

This paper examines whether financial consumers are able to challenge and reject offers and suggestions from financial advisors. Survey data of Korean financial consumers shows that only 11% of the participants answered that they are completely able to ask the questions they want to ask to financial advisors about financial products and services they are considering, and only 30% answered that they are able to reject offers and suggestions by financial advisors. Many subjects attributed fear of negative evaluation as the reason for not asking questions, i.e., to be seen polite and knowledgeable. Furthermore, controlling for education and age effects, female subjects tend to reject others' offers and suggestions significantly less than male subjects in financial settings. This could result in suboptimal financial welfare for women. This paper attempts to provide explanations by addressing the notions of fear of negative evaluation and social value constructs of politeness and obedience imposed in Confucian cultures particularly for women, as well as the social value constructs of the 'good girl' making it more difficult for women to hold their hands up and say no to others.

Keywords: Fear of negative evaluation and decision makings, confucianism, social value constructs, aggression, economics of gender

JEL Classification: Z19, C93, D01

This paper addresses the interesting question of whether financial consumers are able to ask and reject, through a survey with financial consumers in South Korea. The survey data of Korean financial consumers show that

*University of Oxford, current address (affiliation): Incheon National University

only 11% and 30% of the participants answered that they are completely able to ask questions to, and reject by others, suggestions and offers i.e., financial advisors, in settings associated with financial decisions. Many subjects attributed the fear of negative evaluation by others as the reason for not asking questions, i.e., to be seen as polite and knowledgeable. This paper attempts to explain how such a fear of negative evaluation may be more apparent in Confucian cultures, and also among women. Social value constructs in Confucian culture, i.e., emphasizing groups rather than individuals, female subordination, as well as value constructs of 'good girls' could attribute to making it more difficult for women to raise their hands up and reject other's suggestions and requests. The survey results show that female subjects tend to reject others' suggestions significantly less compared to male subjects in both financial as well as non-financial decisions. This paper has a very modest goal in providing an initial examination of such ideas and to provide a foundation for more thorough and developed tests going forward.

1. Fear of Negative Evaluation, Culture, Social Value Constructs

Fear of negative evaluation was first defined by Watson and Friend (1969) as "apprehension about others' evaluations, distress over negative evaluations by others, and the expectation that others would evaluate one negatively". It is related to the desire of seeking others' approval and avoiding others' disapproval. Moreover, it can result in higher degree of sensitivity in response to situational factors, and can be associated with submissiveness and conformity in social behavior. It is reasonable to suspect that fear of negative evaluation can affect financial welfare, i.e., financial consumers' behavior of avoiding asking questions to financial advisors about financial products and services and avoiding refusal of suggestions made by financial advisors in attempts to seek their approval. To my knowledge, this is the first paper addressing an interesting question of whether financial consumers are able to ask and reject offers and suggestions by others, i.e., financial advisors, following one's own wills. Also, the paper examines whether the fear of negative evaluation lies behind such a behavior.

The standard economic model of expected utility suggests that one should be able to ask and reject following one's own wills at all times, if asking and rejecting should result in better economic outcomes. However, people act in social settings, and they care about other people's opinion about them. This notion of fear of negative evaluation is related to the desire of seeking others' approval and avoiding others' disapproval, and can result in a higher degree of sensitivity in response to situational factors, and can be associated with submissiveness and conformity in social behavior.

There are many studies supporting that gender differences in aggression follow from different placement in social structure between men and women. (e.g., Eagly, 1987; Eagly and Wood, 1998; Eagly and Steffen, 1986; Hyde, 1984; and Wood, 1987). In particular, they argue that inherited psychological disposition in terms of aggression is similar across gender, but differences in social behavior comes from the division of labor across gender and related economic and social structure of societies producing gender hierarchy. This viewpoint implies that roles with less status and power in societies are associated with subordinate behavior. This is because people with greater access to power and status would find it more likely to obtain positive outcomes by displaying dominance, i.e., when displaying direct verbal aggression. In contrast, people with lower access to power and status would find subordinate behavior to be more expected by others, and find little success with displaying dominance and aggression in the roles they occupy. That is, women's typically weaker power and status in society somehow make women to carry behavior of low aggression. On the other hand, there are some studies showing that gender difference in aggression also lies in different inherited mechanisms (i.e., Campbell, 1999).

Studies exist on related topics such as gender difference in persuasion and social influence (Cooper, 1979; Eagly and Carli, 1981; Johnson and Eagly, 1989), self-disclosure (Dindia and Allen, 1992), leadership style and effectiveness (Eagly and Johnson, 1990; Eagly and Karau, 1991; Eagly, Makhijani and Klonsky, 1992; Eagly, Karau and Makhijani, 1995). In addition, there is a large literature on gender difference in preferences and biased beliefs, i.e., risk aversion and overconfidence. Many studies support that men are generally more risk-taking than women (i.e., Jianakoplos and Bernasek, 1998, Barsky, Juster, Kimball, and Shapiro, 1997, and Byrnes, Miller and Schafer, 1999). Jianakoplos and Bernasek (1998) find from the 1989 Survey of Consumer Finances that 60% of the female survey participants and 40% of the male participants responded that they were not willing to take financial risks, respectively. Similarly, Barsky, Juster, Kimball, and Shapiro (1997) find that men tend to take more risks than women, from their survey of 5200 men and 6400 women. Similarly, men are generally more overconfident than women (i.e., Barber and Odean, 2000; Deaux and Farris, 1977; Lundeberg, Fox and Punccohar, 1994).

The gender difference in aggression arising from social structure would not be the same across cultures. For example, consider the country where the survey was conducted, Korea, which is often characterized by Confucianism. Korea had undergone a transformation to the patriarchal family system from a much more bilateral family system during the early and middle Choson Dynasty (1392–1910). The patriarchal family system was central to a strategy in neo-Confucianism, which emphasized a tightly structured system of kinship designed to promote loyalty to and stability of a series of groups, i.e., family and state. Neo-Confucianism made authority, i.e., of the male head of the family, the lineages, the state, unchallenged through prescribing the roles and states of each member of groups. The ideas of individual self-realization and salvation of Buddhism was considered as detraction from groups. Obedience to groups, in particular to the leaders of groups, was considered mandatory. Doing things differently from the group according to an individual's own will could be considered as a rebellion to the group and even impoliteness. The safest strategy in a social group with such value constructs would then be adherence to groups. Thus, in Confucian cultures, people are often taught to be, expected to be, and rewarded for adhering to both told and untold rules of the groups to which they belonged. In such a collectivist society, one's evaluation of oneself gets heavily affected by evaluations by others. People consciously and unconsciously seek approval of others in groups to be felt worthy. Thus, the suppression of aggressive behavior in social structure is more likely to arise in Confucian cultures. Particularly, the typically weaker power and status of women in Confucian cultures encourage them to exert lower level of aggression, since they find subordinate behavior to be more expected by others and find little success with displaying dominance and aggression in the roles they occupy. Subordination of women in the system of kinship in Confucianism exerts such pressure on women to an even higher degree through both explicitly told rules as well as downward pressure on self-esteem and self-regard of females who end up tying their self-worth to others' opinions.[1]

Furthermore, a related mechanism of social pressure is social control over women through social value constructs such as 'good girl' or 'lady'. These terms connote gentle, chaste, gracious, virtuous, ingenuous, good, clean, kind, noncontroversial, and above suspicion and reproach, and exert normative restriction on how social behavior of women should be according to Fox (1977). This is linked to the idea of gender-role which individuals start to learn in early childhood; that girls are taught and expected to be and rewarded for being quieter, more passive, more controlled, and kinder, compared to boys. Furthermore, aggressiveness, independence of action and thought, self-determination, self-evaluation of women get curtailed by continual pressure from peers, parents, and even the girls themselves. That is, one is under pressure to demonstrate femininity through behaviors in social interactions. This idea of value constructs of being noncontroversial and adhering to requests could potentially attribute to gender differences in the ability to say no to offers and suggestions by others.

2. Survey and Results

I conducted a paper-based survey involving adult financial consumers in South Korea in winter 2014, with the help of a nation-wide commercial bank at the bank's various branches. The subjects are randomly recruited. In total, 243 subjects have participated. Of the participants, 38% are male, 70% have above college education. Their ages ranged from 18 to 79, with a mean of 44. Of the participants, 15%, 25%, 21%, 21%, 19% are in 18–20s, 30s, 40s, 50s, 60s and above respectively.

This survey questions addressed an interesting question of whether financial consumers feel that they are able to ask questions about financial products they are considering, and say no to offers and suggestions by financial advisors. Also, it tests whether the fear of negative evaluation lies behind such behaviors. Moreover, the survey tests gender differences.

[1]The discussions on Confucianism and women in Confucian society follow Deuchler (1992, 2003)

The following questions are designed to measure the ability to ask questions to others and say no to offers and suggestions by others, in both general and financial settings. The responses are from 1 to 5, with 1 being 'Not at all' and 5 being 'Very able'.

[*Questions Measuring Ability to Ask Questions to and Say No to Others*]

Q1. Are you able to ask what you want to ask?
Q2. Are you able to say no or reject other's offers or suggestions when you want to?
Q3. Are you able to ask what you want to ask in financial settings, i.e., during investment advisory services offered by financial advisors?
Q4. Are you able to say no or reject other's offers or suggestions when you want to during financial transactions, i.e., offers and suggestions made by financial advisors?

And I have following predictions:
[*Predictions*]

Prediction 1: People are not completely able to ask questions they want to ask to others in both general and financial settings.
Prediction 2: People are not able to say no to others' offers and suggestions in both general and financial settings.
Prediction 3: The reason behind such behavior would be fear of negative evaluation by others.
Prediction 4: Females tend to be less able to say no to others compared to males.

As shown in Table 1, subjects on average scored higher on the ability to say no during financial transactions, compared to in settings associated with non-financial transactions. Approximately 30% of the subjects answered that they are completely able to say no to others in financial settings, whereas only 9% of the subjects answered that they are completely able to say no to others in general non-financial settings. This is consistent with the prediction of the standard model of expected utility theory.

In contrast, it is surprising to observe that subjects on average scored lower on the ability to ask questions they want to ask to others during financial transactions, compared to the ability to ask questions in non-financial transactions. 26% of the subjects answered that they are

Table 1: Ability to Ask and Reject

Reasons	Mean Score	Percentage of Subjects with Full Score
Ability to Ask and Rejeect — Total [Q_R_Ability]	3.52	
Are you able to ask what you want to ask? [Q]	3.72	25.51%
Are you able to say no when you want to? [R]	3.04	8.64%
Are you able to ask what you want to ask during financial transitions? [Q_fin]	3.38	11.11%
Are you able to say no when you want to during financial transactions? [R_fin]	3.90	29.63%

Q, R, Q_fin, R_fin range from 1 to 5 with 1 being 'Not at all' and 5 being 'Very able.' Q_R_Ability is the sum of the score of the answers to the aforementioned four questions, divided by four.

completely able to ask questions they want to ask to others in general non-financial settings, whereas only 9% of the subjects answered that they are completely able to ask questions they want to ask to others in financial settings. This cannot be explained by the standard model, since not asking questions they need or want implies foregoing information acquisition opportunities. And this can result in having to make financial decisions with a smaller set of information, and the outcome from the smaller set of information may be different and could potentially be worse than the outcome from the larger complete set of information.

Then one would wonder what the underlying causes of such a behavior suppressing one's questions and saying yes to others. One could reckon that one of the commonsensical reasons for not asking questions, in general or/and financial settings, must be the lack of financial knowledge and the resulting difficulty to formulate appropriate questions, and/or the lack of trust placed on the information provided by the counterparty, i.e., financial advisor. However, the survey results, as seen in the Table 2, show that many more subjects answered that they avoid asking questions because '[they] do not want to be seen impolite or annoying to the financial advisor' and '[they] do not want to let others know [their] lack of understanding of financial products and transactions'. These reasons are associated with the notion of fear of negative evaluation: subjects answered that they avoid asking questions to financial advisors because they want

Table 2: Reasons of Not Asking

The following questions are asked to identify the reasons of not asking. The participants are asked to checkmark if the following reason applies.

Reasons	Percentage Answering √ to
I do not want to be seen impolite or annoying to the financial advisor.	23.46%
I do not want to let other know my lack of understanding.	10.29%
I do not understand what the financial advisor says.	7.00%
I believe that the financial advisor would give wrong information anyway.	5.35%

to be seen as polite and knowledgeable, even when this implies that they would forego potentially valuable information and can make them worse-off in their financial welfare. These results are consistent with my earlier predictions.

Furthermore, it is possible to conjecture that subordination of women in the system of kinship in Confucianism exerts such pressure on women to an even higher degree through both explicitly told rules as well as indirect effects, i.e., exerting downward pressure on their self-esteem and self-regard, and end up tying their self-worth to others' opinions. In addition, another related social value constructs of 'good girl' or 'lady' may exert normative restriction on how desirable behavior of women should be.

Table 3 shows difference across gender. It is not surprising to see that female subjects scored lower for all questions associated with the ability to ask questions and say no to others compared to male subjects. And some of the differences are robust to controlling education and age effects. Female subjects are significantly less able to say no to others in both general and financial settings compared to male subjects. The regression coefficient estimate of a binary variable recorded one for male subjects is 0.24 for the regression with R_fin as the dependent variable. This implies that female subjects tend to have R_fin scores lower by 0.24 compared to male subjects. Given the complete score of 5, 0.24 is not a negligible difference at all. Similarly, the regression coefficient estimate of a binary variable recorded one for male subjects is 0.34 for the regression with R as the dependent variable. This implies that female subjects tend to have R scores lower by 0.34 compared to male subjects. Again, given the complete score of 5,

Table 3: Gender Difference

	Two Sample T-Test			Regression (Controls: Education, Age)	
	Female	Male	*Difference t[F-M]*	Coefficient Estimate	T-Statistic (Robust)
Q_R_Ability	3.43	3.66	*−2.42***	0.21	1.99**
Q	3.64	3.85	*−1.44*	0.24	1.43
R	2.88	3.24	*−2.52***	0.34	2.03**
Q_fin	3.29	3.55	*−1.75**	0.12	0.73
R_fin	3.81	4.07	*−1.93**	0.24	1.72*

Two Sample T-Tests, and Regressions with Q_R_Ability, Q, R, Q_fin, R_fin as the dependent variables. *, **, *** indicate significance at 10%, 5%, and 1%, respectively.

0.34 is not a negligible difference at all. In sum, consistent with my earlier prediction, female subjects are significantly less able to say no to others in both general and financial settings compared to male subjects.

3. Conclusion

This paper makes an important contribution by showing fear of negative evaluation can result in lower financial welfare through suppression of one's questions and not being able to say no to others. Specifically, the survey with Korean financial consumers shows that (1) average scores on various questions on the ability to ask questions to others and say no to others following one's wills in both general and financial settings are far from complete scores, (2) non-negligible portion of these subjects particularly pointed desire to be seen as polite and knowledgeable as reasons behind of not asking questions to financial advisors, (3) such tendencies of avoiding asking questions to others and saying no to others are much more apparent among female subjects. These behaviors cannot be explained by the standard economic model, but by the notions of the fear of negative evaluation and value constructs of politeness and obedience imposed in certain cultures. Furthermore, female subjects reject financial offerings and suggestions significantly less compared to male subjects. This could be due to the fear of negative evaluation and value constructs of politeness and obedience working at a greater degree through social expectation and enforcement of subordination of women in Confucian culture. In addition, the value constructs of 'good girl' being kind, noncontroversial, and adhering to requests, could also help in explaining gender differences. Going forward, it would be interesting and meaningful to do cross-culture comparisons to derive a more concrete conclusion. Also, it would be meaningful to estimate the economic loss to the society as a whole generated through the mechanisms addressed in this paper. Moreover, it would be helpful for individuals, firms, policymakers to find remedies to the problem of passivity and subordination in social structure in certain cultures. The cultures and social structures exerting pressure on people to behave more adherently and subordinately to others, limiting freedom of expression, putting too much weight on others' opinions may not be optimal at least when economic performance is considered. We need to consider how to ensure freedom and capability of expression, and thus improve our economic welfare at home, at work, and in a society as a whole.

References

Barber, Brad and Terrance Odean. 2000. "Boys will be Boys: Gender, Overconfidence, and Common Stock Investment". *Quarterly Journal of Economics* 116: 261–292.

Barsky, R. B., Juster, F. T., Kimball, M. S., M. Shapiro. 1997. "Preference parameters and behavioral heterogeneity: An experimental approach in the Health and Retirement Study". *Quarterly Journal of Economics* 112: 537–579.

Byrnes, James, David C. Miller, William D. Schafer. 1999. "Gender differences in risk taking: a meta-analysis". *Psychological Bulletin* 125: 367–383.

Campbell, A. 1999. "Staying alive: Evolution, culture, and women's intrasexual aggression". Behavioral and Brain Science 22: 203–252.

Cooper, H. M. 1979. "Statistically Combining Independent Studies: A Meta-Analysis of Sex Differences in Conformity Research". *Journal of Personality and Social Psychology* 37: 131–146.

Deaux, Kay and Elizabeth Farris. 1977. "Attributing Causes for One's Own Performance: The Effects of Sex, Norms, and Outcome". *Journal of Research in Personality* 11: 59–72.

Deuchler, Martina. 1992. The Confucian Transformation of Korea: A Study of Society and Ideology. Cambridge, MA and London: Council on East Asia Studies, Harvard University (Harvard-Yenching Institute Monograph Series 36).

Deuchler, Martina. 2003. "Propagating female virtues in Choson Korea," In Dorothy Ko, JaHyun Kim Haboush, and Joan R. Piggott (eds.), Women and Confucian

Cultures in Premodern China, Korea, and Japan. Berkeley: University of California Press

Dindia, Kathryn and Michael Allen. 1992. "Sex Differences in Self-Disclosure: A Meta-Analysis". *Psychological Bulletin* 112: 106–124.

Eagly, Alice and Linda Carli. 1981. "Sex of Researchers and Sex-Typed Communications as Determinants of Sex Differences in Influenceability: A Meta- Analysis of Social Influence Studies". *Psychological Bulletin* 90: 1–20.

Eagly, Alice and Blair T. Johnson. 1990. "Gender and Leadership Styles: A Meta-Analysis". *Psychological Bulletin* 108: 233–256.

Eagly, Alice, S. J. Karau and M. G. Makhijani. 1995. "Gender and the Effectiveness of Leaders: A Meta-Analysis". *Psychological Bulletin* 117: 125–145.

Eagly, A. H. 1987. "Sex differences in social behavior: A social-role interpretation". Erlbaum.

Eagly, A. H., Karau, S. J. 1991. "Gender and the emergence of leaders: A meta-analysis". *Journal of Personality and Social Psychology* 60: 685–710.

Eagly, A. H., Makhijani, M. G. & Klonsky, B. G. 1992. "Gender and the evaluation of leaders: A meta-analysis". *Psychological Bulletin* 111: 3–22.

Eagly, A. H., Steffen, V. J. 1986. "Gender and aggressive behavior: A meta-analytic review of the social psychological literature". *Psychological Bulletin* 100: 309–30.

Eagly, A. H., Wood, W. 1998. "The origins of sex differences: Evolution versus social structure". Unpublished manuscript.

Fox, Greer Litton. 1977. "Nice Girl: Social Control of Women through a Value Construct". *Signs* 2: 805–817.

Hyde J. S. 1984. "How Large are Gender Differences in Aggression?: A Developmental Meta-Analysis". *Developmental Psychology* 20: 722–736.

Jianakoplos, N., A. Bernasek. 1998. "Are women more risk averse?" *Economic Inquiry* 36: 620–630.

Johnson, Blair T. and Eagly, Alice. 1989. "Effects of Involvement on Persuasion: A Meta-Analysis". *Psychological Bulletin* 106: 290–314.

Lundeberg, M. A., P. W. Fox, and J. Punccohar. 1994. "Highly Confident but Wrong: Gender Differences and Similarities in Confidence Judgments". *Journal of Educational Psychology* 86: 114–121.

Watson, D., R Friend. 1969. "Measurement of Social-evaluative Anxiety". *Journal of Consulting and Clinical Psychology* 33: 448–57.

Wood, W. 1987. "Meta-Analytic Review of Sex Differences in Group Performance," *Psychological Bulletin* 102: 53–71.

Chapter 7

Gender and Personal Finance Management

Zohar Rusou*,‡, Moty Amar† and Shahar Ayal‡

Abstract

The chapter reviews gender related differences in saving and investment behavior and in debt management, and the major factors that have been identified in previous research as influencing the quality of financial decisions making, such as risk attitudes, financial literacy, confidence in financial knowledge and cognitive style. In addition, we analyze preliminary data from our laboratory studies on men and women's management of multiple debt accounts. Based on our findings, we suggest possible mechanisms that drive gender similarities and differences in behavior.

Keywords: Debt repayment, financial decision making, financial literacy, gender differences, investment and saving behavior, risk attitudes

JEL Classification: G02

1. Introduction

The ability of both men and women to effectively manage their personal and household finances has important consequences on individuals' lives in modern society. For instance, the implications of making sound savings and investment decisions and efficiently managing open debt accounts are considerable, both at the personal level of financial well-being and psychological well-being (Lusardi and Mitchell, 2008, 2011) and at the public level of welfare policy and economic growth. Therefore, it is not surprising that researchers as well as financial institutions are interested in

*Department of Psychology and education, The Open University of Israel, Israel
†School of Business Administration, Ono Academic College, Israel
‡School of Psychology, Interdisciplinary Center Herzliya (IDC), Israel

understanding how individuals make monetary decisions. The challenge is to better understand the psychological forces that lead people to irrational financial decisions, and then redirect these forces to design public policy interventions to improve the financial capabilities of individuals such as encouraging people to employ financial planning and save more for tomorrow, (Thaler and Benartzi, 2004).

The need to improve financial behavior gains additional impetus, when we take into account gender differences and inequality. A relatively broad range of empirical literature has documented that the economic well-being of men and women differ significantly. Women tend to have lower working-life incomes (Bajtelsmit, Bernasek and Jianakoplos, 1999), save less for retirement (Kelly and Gong, 2010), own fewer investment products (Atkinson and Messy, 2012) and have lower levels of wealth as compared to men (Hui, Vincent and Woolley, 2011; Schmidt and Sevak, 2006; Siermiska, Frick and Grabka, 2010). According to an OECD report (2013), women tend to live longer than men, but have a weaker labor market position, shorter working lives and lower average income. Thus women are at higher risk than men of facing financial hardship. Consequently, women's ability to effectively participate in economic activities, manage their financial accounts and control their decision-making processes is crucial.

An essential aspect of attempts to improve the financial well-being of individuals is understanding the factors that influence the quality of their financial decisions, and uncovering which factors have a differential effect on men and women's financial behavior. In section 2, we elaborate on several such factors that have been identified in previous research including risk attitudes, financial literacy, confidence in financial knowledge and cognitive style. This section also reviews explanations and possible determinants of these observed gender differences.

The remainder of the chapter is organized as follows: Section 3 examines the impact of gender related differences on the quality of investment decisions. Section 4 reviews the current literature on the effect of gender on debt management behavior, and then analyzes data from our laboratory on men and women's management of multiple debt accounts. Based on these preliminary data, we suggest possible mechanisms behind gender similarities and differences in the observed behavior.

It should be noted however, that the existing body of research on gender differences in financial decision making has focused mostly on investments and gambling. Although we acknowledge that the ability to make appropriate saving and investments decisions has a profound impact on individuals' overall wealth and their future financial well-being, we also stress in this chapter that additional financial activities such as open debt management (Novailitis 2006), might also play a major role in determining financial wealth and well-being. Our data analysis on gender differences in debt management is thus a first step in exploring this unchartered route.

2. Factors that Differentially Impact Men and Women's Financial Decisions

Research on gender and financial behavior has highlighted several factors that differentially influence men and women's financial decision-making. The most extensively examined determination factors in the literature on gender differences in financial behavior are risk attitudes (Croson and Gneezy, 2009; Eckel and Grossman, 2002, 2008), financial knowledge (Fonseca *et al.*, 2012; Lusardi and Mitchell, 2008, 2011), overconfidence (Barber and Odean, 2001; Goldsmith and Goldsmith, 1997; Hira and Mugenda, 2000; Powell and Ansic, 1997; Webster and Ellis, 1996) and cognitive style (experiential–intuitive versus rational–analytical: Epstein, 2003; Pacini and Epstein, 1999; Sladek, Bond and Phillips, 2010).

2.1. *Attitudes Toward Risks*

Different risk preferences by men and women have been documented in many studies across a wide range of domains. A substantial body of research suggests that in most areas females tend to be more averse to risk than males (see a meta-analysis by Byrnes, Miller & Schafer, 1999). A similar pattern of higher propensity for risk taking in men as compared to women was also found by most of the studies in the domain of investing and gambling. (Berggren and Gonzalez, 2010; Croson and Gneezy, 2009; Eckel and Grossman, 2002, 2008; Graham *et al.*, 2002; Hallahan, Faff, and McKenzie, 2004; but see also Kunnanatt and Emiline, 2012). This association has been detected both in experimental laboratory studies and in field surveys. For instance, field studies that have looked at the structure of individuals' actual investments found consistent support for gender-related differences in risk preferences. Women report lower levels of risk tolerance, tend to have less risky asset portfolios, exhibit greater relative risk aversion in their allocation of wealth into defined contribution pension assets and exhibit lower willingness to accept financial risk as compared with men (Agnew, Balduzzi and Sunden, 2003; Arano, Parker and Terry, 2010; Bajtelsmit *et al.*, 1999; Halko, Kaustia and Alanko, 2012; Hinz, McCarthy and Turner, 1997; Jianakoplos and Bernasek, 1998; Siva, 2012; Watson and McNaughton, 2007).

Laboratory studies that have presented participants with settings designed to mimic investment behavior have generally reverberated the same pattern of gender related differences. For example, Charness and Gneezy (2012) found strong evidence for gender differences in risk preferences. They collected data from 15 sets of experiments with a similar design that involved a single simple investment game. These experiments were conducted by different researchers in different countries, with different instructions, durations, payments, subject pools and such. The analysis of the actual investment behavior of the participants yielded a consistent result. Women made smaller investments in risky assets as compared to men. Thus, the researchers concluded that women are financially more risk-averse. Eckel and Grossmann (2002) found significant gender differences in risk preferences. In their study, participants chose between alternative gambles with different expected returns and variances. They found that women indicated a preference for the less risky prospect. Women also reported a lower risk propensity than men when asked about their attitudes towards financial risks.

It should be noted that although gender-related disparities in risk perception are widely acknowledged, there is less agreement about their causes and their underlying mechanisms. In addition, some studies have found contradictory evidence under specific settings. For example, Schubert *et al.* (1999) found gender differences in risk preferences when the task involved abstract gambling decisions; however, the differences disappeared when an investment decision context was presented. Schubert *et al.* (1999) found that under specific situations men might be more risk-averse than women. Eckel and Grossman (2008) reviewed several studies that examined differences in risk-related behavior of men and women. They made a distinction between laboratory studies that presented abstract gambles, laboratory studies that presented contextual environments of investments or insurance decisions, and field studies that measured men and women's actual gambling behavior and real-life investment allocation decisions. While the majority of the laboratory experiments in their review showed that women are less risk-tolerant than men, some studies that involved investment and insurance frames presented counterevidence. In addition, some cross-cultural studies have found gender differences among whites, but not among other ethnic groups (Feng and Seasholes, 2008), although women tended to be more risk averse than men in most countries (OECD, 2013; Zinkhan and Karande, 1991).

2.1.1. *Why do men and women differ in their attitudes toward risk?*

Although gender-related disparities in risk preferences have been demonstrated across a wide variety of domains and specifically in financial arenas, the mechanisms underlying these differences have been less well explored. Researchers have suggested several possible explanations for the gender gap in risk preferences.

One explanation was put forward by Eckel and Grossman (2008) who contended that the contradictory results in the literature might stem from a failure to control for intervening factors such as, wealth, marital status and other demographic factors that might bias the measures of males and female differences in risky choices. In line with these concerns, some authors have proposed socio-cultural explanations, including that women's tendency for risk aversion is a result of factors such as marital status, self-perception as knowledgeable, and age (Gerrans and Clark-Murphy, 2004). For example, the gender effect in Gerrans and Clark-Murphy's study was not uniform and some notable reversals of the gender effect were found. In their study, single females in the younger age category emerged as more likely to select lower risk investment choices, but married females in the younger age category had a greater likelihood of choosing the riskier option relative to married males in the older age category.

A second explanation has to do with disparities in the levels of financial knowledge and financial experiences of women and men (Beckmann and Menkhoff, 2008; Brokešová, 2013; Dwyer, Gilkeson, and List, 2002;

Eckel and Grossman, 2008; Menkhoff, Schmidt and Brozynski, 2006). Several researchers have presented empirical evidence that demonstrates a direct link between financial knowledge and risk tolerance. For example, in a sample of undergraduate students, women were inclined to choose safer options in financial decisions, but these differences were statistically significant only when experience and knowledge were very high (Brokešová, 2013). Similarly, the impact of gender on risk-taking was significantly weakened when investor knowledge of financial markets and investments was controlled for (Dwyer, Gilkeson, and List, 2002). In addition, men were more risk-seeking among low knowledge individuals, while women were more risk-seeking among high knowledge individuals (Gysler and Kruse, 2002).

One plausible way to examine whether women's risk aversion stems from a lack of relevant knowledge is to look at the behavior of knowledgeable women in risky financial settings. However, the results from several sources suggest that women's tendency toward risk aversion is also present in professional financial analysts. For example, gender was still a strong predictor of risk-taking when the study included participants who had extensive personal and professional experience with financial matters, such as wealthy private banking investors, investment advisors and managers and finance students (Halko, Kaustia and Alanko, 2012). In addition, female professional investors placed more emphasis on the safety of an investment than male professional investors (Olsen and Cox, 2001). Furthermore, female fund managers were found to be more risk-averse and more likely to shy away from competition than male fund managers (Beckmann and Menkhoff, 2008).

Other explanations cite biological factors such as gender differences in testosterone levels (Sapienza, Zingales and Maestripieri, 2009), or cognitive or emotion-based factors, such as women's relative insensitivity to probabilities combined with their tendency for pessimism (Fehr-Duda, De Gennaro and Schubert, 2006), a tendency for optimists of a specific subgroup of males (Felton, Gibson and Sanbonmatsu, 2003), and gender differences in self-reported emotions (Johnson and Weber, 2009).

Finally, an evolutionary explanation was put forward by Eckel and Grossman (2002). They claimed that gender differences in risk-behavior patterns stem from evolved strategies that reflect differences in the costs and benefits of sex-linked alternative investments in reproductive success. Interestingly, evolutionary accounts are also used to explain gender related differences in the importance placed in financial security in the domain of sexual attraction. Financial security was found to be one of the three qualities women most often sought in men. Woman were more than twice as likely as men to seek financial security, and women placed much more emphasis on financial security as compared to physical attractiveness, while men were more likely than women to seek attractiveness (Harrison and Saeed, 1977). This explanation seems quite compelling and relevant, since, historically, women across many different countries have been dependent on men for financial security (Schmidt and Sevak, 2006).

2.2. *Financial Literacy*

Recently, financial literacy has been widely acknowledged as a basic skill that is essential for individuals who need to make financial decisions in today's modern multifaceted financial environment. An extensive amount of empirical studies provides evidence that men have higher levels of financial literacy (Chen and Volpe, 2002; Fonseca *et al.*, 2012; Lusardi and Mitchell, 2008, 2011; Zissimopoulos, Karney and Rauer, 2008). For example, Zissimopoulos *et al.*, (2008) found that less than 20% of middle-aged college-educated women could answer a basic compound interest question compared to about 35% of college-educated males of the same age. Chen and Volpe (2002) found that women have lower financial knowledge in personal finance than men. Women scored lower than men in 22 out of 36 questions and had a higher score on only one question. These patterns were obtained across different countries (OECD, 2013), and a wide range of age groups (Agnew and Harrison, 2015; Chen and Volpe, 2002).

Although the evidence on gender-related disparities in financial literacy are quite robust, less is known about the mechanisms that may produce this gap (Fonseca *et al.*, 2012). The studies on the mechanisms that underlie the observed gender gap offer some insights on possible determining factors, including differences in tendencies, attitudes, and experiences (OECD, 2013). Chen and Volpe (2002) argued that gender differences in financial literacy are related to education and experience. Their study shows that factors such as *major field* and years of education had a significant effect on knowledge. Business majors knew more than non-business majors, and knowledge increased with years of education. They also argued that men and women have different attitudes to financial matters, and that women have less interest in finance, as more men than women in their study rated personal finance as an important topic. Whereas men chose to study mathematics and other number-oriented subjects, women had a preference for English and word-related subjects. Other researchers who have specifically examined how financial decisions, are made within households, have reported that men, more often than women, make the financial decisions and consequently acquire more financial knowledge (Fonseca *et al.*, 2012).

2.3. *Confidence and Overconfidence in Financial Knowledge and Skills*

The evidence indicate that men have more confidence in their financial skills than females (Chen and Volpe, 2002; Fonseca *et al.*, 2012; Lusardi and Mitchell, 2008, 2011; Zissimopoulos, Karney and Rauer, 2008). Research focusing on gender-related differences in investment patterns suggests that female investors tend to have less confidence in their investment decisions than male investors in similar settings (Agnew *et al.*, 2003; Barber and Odean, 2001; Webster and Ellis, 1996), even when there was no apparent difference in actual knowledge (Goldsmith and Goldsmith, 1997) or when both genders had a similar level of prior experience and education (Powell and Ansic, 1997). Females less than males tend to feel that they are better off in comparison with others (Hira and Mugenda, 2000), and are more likely to attribute their performance to good luck (Powell and Ansic, 1997) and to indicate that they do not know the answer to a question on a financial knowledge test rather than attempt to answer it (Bengtsson, Persson and Willenhag 2005; OECD, 2013). However, some studies have not found a difference in men and women's level of confidence in financial decision-making (Berggren and Gonzalez, 2010).

2.4. *Thinking Style*

Another factor that was highlighted as affecting investment behavior is the prevalence of analytic versus intuitive thinking styles (for a recent review, see Ayal *et al.*, 2015). The dominance of the two thinking styles is measured by the Rational-Experiential Inventory (REI) developed by Epstein *et al.*, (1996) which consists of two subscales, the rational thinking style (which measures individual differences in relying on a conscious, analytical, and relatively affect-free information processing system) and experiential thinking style (faith in intuition). Studies have reported small but significant gender differences in thinking styles. Males are more likely than females to identify themselves as rationally able, and females were more likely than males to identify themselves as experiential (having higher faith in intuition) (Epstein, 2003; Pacini and Epstein, 1999; Sladek, Bond and Phillips, 2010).

Glaser and Walther (2013) argued that high faith in intuition might diminish the positive effect of financial literacy on reasonable investment decisions, since individuals might rely on their hunches rather than on thorough explorations. On the other hand, Wong, Kwong, and Ng (2008) examined the relationship between the rational thinking style and decision quality in an escalation situation, and reported a positive relationship between a tendency for rational thinking and escalation bias. They concluded that rational thinking increases confidence in previous decisions, and accordingly increases escalation.

3. Gender Differences in Saving and Investment Behavior

Given the relative robustness of the evidence on gender differences in risk attitudes, financial literacy, confidence in financial matters and thinking style, there appears to be implications for men and women's investment patterns and financial outcomes. For instance, some researchers have claimed that the lower levels of knowledge, lower confidence and reduced willingness to accept risks can be costly to women investors, and lead them to less profitable investments, due to their higher reliance on safer low return saving products and less reliance on high return investments (Brokešová, 2013; Graham *et al.*, 2002).

These claims are reinforced by a substantial body of literature on the relationship between gender and investment behavior, which has shown that women invest their financial resources more conservatively compared to men. For example, Halko, Kaustia and Alanko (2012) studied the relationship between gender and stock holdings in Finland, and found that men have riskier portfolios than women, even after controlling for financial knowledge and financial resources. They also found that the strongest predictor of this gender gap is women's higher risk aversion. Watson and McNaughton (2007) examined the impact of gender on the retirement fund preferences of staff in an Australian university. Their data revealed that women chose more conservative investment strategies than men. This result remained significant after controlling for age (which was negatively related to risk-taking) and income (which was positively related to risk-taking). Similar patterns have emerged in studies that analyzed allocations of wealth into defined contribution pension assets (Bajtelsmit *et al.*, 1999), and data of the 1990 survey of participants in the federal government's Thrift Savings Plan in the USA (Hinz *et al.*, 1997). In both studies, women invested their pension assets more conservatively than men. Hinz *et al.* (1997) also found that a large percentage of women invested in the minimum-risk portfolio available to them. A portion of the pattern could be explained by women's lower incomes, but the result persisted after controlling for economic and demographic variables.

However in specific situations, women's lower confidence can be beneficial (Barber and Odean, 2001; Willows and West, 2015). For example, research by Barber and Odean (2001) provides evidence that men trade more excessively than women. They analyzed the trading records of approximately 35,000 households and found that men traded 45% more than women, and that this excessive trading led to significantly lower returns for men as compared to women. These differences were the most prominent between single men and single women. The authors suggested that because of their tendency toward less overconfidence, women tend to be more careful, rely on information that is more comprehensive, and are likely to ask more questions than men do.

To summarize, the picture that emerges from the ample research on the relationship between gender and investing behavior highlights several factors that differentially affect men and women's behavior patterns of personal finance management, and specifically suggest that there are advantages and disadvantages associated with the fact that women invest their financial resources more conservatively. Nevertheless, there are also studies that do not find these expected gender differences (Bliss and Potter,

2002; Powell and Ansic, 1997; Willows and West, 2014).The implications of these differences on overall portfolio performance are inconclusive and have yet to be explored.

4. Gender Differences in the Management of Open Debts

The ability to manage open debts efficiently (or inefficiently) directly affects the risk of accumulating high levels of debts and the total amount of wealth possessed by an individual. In addition, the amount of individual debt has psychological and social implications. The empirical evidence shows that high levels of debt are associated with increased levels of psychological distress (Bridges and Disney, 2010; Brown, Taylor and Price, 2005; Norvilitis, Szablicki, and Wilson, 2003), and mental disorders (Jenkins *et al.*, 2008). High levels of debt are also associated with individuals' lower self-perceptions of their ability to control their financial situation (Lange and Byrd, 1998), and with higher probabilities of dropping out of college (Dwyer, Hodson and McCloud, 2013). Thus, in order to develop effective approaches to improve financial well-being, it is essential to understand how people handle their multiple debts, and whether women differ from men in this regard.

To date, however, there has been very little exploration of gender differences in debt management, and the few studies that have addressed this issue report inconclusive results. Some studies show that women own more credit cards (Goldsmith and Goldsmith, 2006), report spending more than they should, buy things they do not need, make unplanned purchases (Hira and Mugenda, 2000; Hira and Loibl, 2008), and carry more debt than men (Davies and Lea, 1995; Goldsmith and Goldsmith, 2006). On the other hand, other studies did not find gender differences in credit-card debt (Novailitis *et al.*, 2006) or in individuals' satisfaction with their debt levels (Hira and Mugenda, 2000) and some studies demonstrated that more women than men are likely to have a budget (Henry, Weber and Yarbrough, 2001), and that the majority of both men and women did not engage in excessive or problem buying behavior (Hira and Mugenda, 2000). Thus, the role of gender in debt management is unclear and calls for further research (c.f., Novailitis *et al.*, 2006).

4.1. *Data From Our Laboratory*

One important component of debt management is the repayment of open debts. Since many individuals have several debt accounts (Experian, 2009), a key element in the attempt to reduce open debt is by developing of strategies of debt repayment (i.e., developing schemes to determine which of their open debt accounts to repay first). From a normative perspective, it is quite clear that in order to minimize the total amount of debt across loans, the best approach is to pay the minimum payment for each debt first (to avoid surcharges and penalties) and then use all available cash to pay down the loan with the highest interest rate. After this loan has been paid off, people should move to the loan with the next highest interest rate, and so on. However, previous research suggests that people stray from normative principles when managing debts. Rather than adhering to the financially optimal strategy of repaying first the debts with the highest interest rates, many individuals prefer to repay the smallest debts first. That is, they prioritize reducing the number of debt accounts over reducing the total amount of debt across accounts, and thus exhibit "debt account aversion" (Amar *et al.*, 2011).

To tackle the issue of which gender-related differences in behavior are likely to emerge in an environment of multiple debt accounts, we reanalyzed a database from an experiment that simulated a real-life situation of recurring repayment decisions in an environment of multiple open debts. To this end, we employed the "Debt Management Game" (Experiment 1, Amar *et al.*, 2011 — see box below). One hundred and ninety two undergraduate students (55% female; mean age: 21.5) participated in the experiment.

We extended this basic paradigm and used two experimental conditions, each designed to shed light on a different aspect of debt repayment behavior. The first condition ("No-saving"), in which participants were required to allocate all of their available cash to debt repayment, examined gender differences in debt account aversion. The second condition, ("Saving Allowed") in which participants could determine the amount of the money to repay debts and store the rest in a "checking" account (with lowest interest rate than all open debt), examined how the opportunity to irrationally keep some of the available cash differentially affected men and women's repayment strategies.

Overview of the "Debt Management Game"

In the Debt Management Game, participants were saddled with multiple debt accounts that varied in amount and annual interest rate (see Table 1 below), and were asked to make recurring decisions on how to repay these debts over 25 rounds, which represented 25 years. In each round, participants received a $5,000 cash allotment that they could use to pay down one or more of the open debt accounts. In addition, participants occasionally received cash bonuses that could also be used to pay off their debts ($20,000 in round 6, $15,000 in round 12, and $40,000 in round 19). Participants repaid debts by typing in the amount they wanted to allocate to each debt account and then approving it (see Appendix A). After participants approved their decision, the program presented the updated balance of each debt and a graph displaying the past and current standing of each debt (to illustrate, appendix A presents a screen example of the debt management game). At the end of the game, the total debt of each participant was calculated. In the "No Saving" condition, total debt was calculated by summing debt amounts in the participant's open debt accounts. In the "Saving Allowed" condition, total debt was calculated by reducing the amount of cash remaining in the checking account (if any) from the sum of debts in the open debt accounts.

Table 1: The Interest Rate and Initial Size of Each Debt

	Annual Interest Rate (%)	Initial Amount ($)
Debt 1	2.50	3,000
Debt 2	2.00	8,000
Debt 3	3.50	11,000
Debt 4	3.25	13,000
Debt 5	3.75	52,000
Debt 6	4.00	60,000
Checking account*	2.00	0

*The checking account was used in the "Saving Allowed" condition, in order to store cash that was not used for debt repayment

A financially optimal player who (in each round) allocates all available cash to the open debt with the highest interest rate would first pay off

Debt 6, then Debt 5, and then Debt 3 and then begin to repay Debt 4 (the game would end before Debt 4 could be completely repaid). The financially optimal player would never allocate any cash toward Debts 1 and 2 and would conclude the game with three open debts that sum to $29,428 in total (appendix 2 shows the final screen of Debt Management Game for a financially optimal player). Importantly, because the interest rate on savings in the "Saving Allowed" condition was less than or equal to the interest rates of all the debts (all debt interest rates were 2% or greater), a participant who adopted the normative approach in the "Saving Allowed" condition would not allocate any money to saving. Thus, the total debt of a financially optimal player at the end of the game should be $29,428 in both conditions (see Appendix B).

The game was incentive compatible. Participants received a bonus based on their performance: specifically, they received $4.00 if their total debt at the end of the game was $30,000 or less, $3.00 if their total debt was between $30,001 and $35,000, $2.00 if their total debt was between $35,001 and $40,000, and $1 if their total debt was greater than $40,000.

4.1.1. *Working hypotheses on gender differences*

The findings presented in this chapter suggest two main predictions with regard to gender differences in debt management. First, a relatively extensive literature on the gender gap in financial literacy yields the general finding that women have less financial knowledge than men (Fornero and Monticone, 2011; Lusardi and Mitchell, 2008, 2011; Sekita, 2011). Thus, we anticipated that women would show a higher bias toward reducing the number of debt accounts over reducing the total amount of debt across accounts. Based on this rationale we formulated our first hypothesis:

Hypothesis A — women will allocate less money to the highest interest debt, compared to men.

Second, women's tendency to exhibit intolerance to risk has been attributed by researchers to an evolved mechanism that reflects differences in the costs and benefits of sex-linked alternative investments in reproductive success (Eckel and Grossman, 2002). Hence, we expected that when being able to determine how much cash to keep versus allocating for debt repayment, women more than men might want to keep money for "a rainy day" and consequently, would allocate less money to the closing of open debts. Based on this rationale, we formulated our second hypothesis:

Hypothesis B — Women will keep more cash money (irrationally saving) compared to men, and as a result, women will end the game with higher total debt amounts.

4.1.2. *Results and discussion*

First, we examined whether participants adopted a normative strategy for debt repayment (i.e., whether they used the money to repay the open debts with the highest interest rates). Mean total debt in both conditions was significantly greater than the total debt of a (hypothetical) financially optimal player (both $p < 0001$). Across both conditions, the average participant lost $12,903 because of non-optimal debt repayment decisions. As reported in Amar et al. (2011), the total debt in the saving-allowed condition was significantly larger than total debt in the no-saving condition ($39,513 vs. $33,939; $t(79) = 44.12, p < 0001$). However, it remained unclear what prompted this increase in irrationality when saving was allowed and whether this effect was similar in both men and women.

In order to examine the first hypothesis that women would show a higher bias toward reducing the number of debt accounts over reducing the total amount of debt across accounts, we examined gender differences in the average amount of money which were used to pay off the debt with the highest interest (i.e., rational money). When saving was not allowed and all the money was allocated directly to open debts, no significant difference was found between women and men in their amount of money that was allocated to the debt with the highest interest rate (Mwomen $=$ $86,665$ vs. Mmen $= 86,060$; $t(78) = .323, p > .05$) or their aggregate debt at the end of the game (Mwomen $= 34,473$ vs. Mmen $= 33,216$; $t(78) = -1.134, p > .05$). Thus, the first hypothesis was not supported since we did not find evidence for higher irrationality or debt account aversion (DAA) among women in this condition. These findings corroborate the mixed results that have been obtained in previous research, and might suggest that gender has a null effect on rationality in debt management decisions. However, the findings may also stem from the fact that debt management does not require extensive financial knowledge (i.e., interest rate comparisons are sufficient) compared to investment decisions.

Most interestingly, our analyses also revealed a potential gender difference when saving was allowed. In line with the second hypothesis, the data demonstrated that when able to determine how much money to keep versus how much money should be allocated for debt repayment, women chose to keep more cash than men, and consequently allocated less money to close open debts (Mwomen $= 12,196$ vs. Mmen $= 15,560$ vs.; $t(110) = -2.09$, $p = .039$). As a result, their aggregate debt at the end of the game was higher than that of men (Mwomen $= 39,124$ vs. Mmen $= 35,128$; $t(110) = -2.42$, $p = .017$). In addition, a comparison between the "Saving Allowed" and "No Saving" conditions revealed that the option to keep cash had a negative impact on women's debt repayment performance. Specifically, the women's aggregate debt at the end of the game in the "Saving Allowed" condition was significantly higher than in the "No Saving" condition ($M = 39,124$ vs. $34,473$; $t(110) = -2.42$, $p = .001$). In contrast, no negative impact was observed on men's debt repayment performance as no significant difference was observed between men's aggregate debt at the end of the game in the "Saving Allowed" condition and the "No Saving" condition (Msaving allowed $= 33,216$ vs. M no saving $= 35,128$; $t(110) = -1.02$, $p > .05$).

These results lend initial credence to the supposition that women save more money for 'a rainy day' and consequently, they end up with a higher total debt than men. While more direct research and field data are required to put this assertion to a direct test, it supports theoretical approaches that explain gender differences in financial decisions by evolutionary related differences, rather than cognitive skills such as rationality and financial literacy.

5. Concluding Remarks

The evidence and the experiments reviewed in this section highlight the existence of substantial gender disparities in factors that have differential implications for men and women's management of personal finance. Although much is known about gender differences in factors related to general saving behavior such as risk attitudes, financial literacy, confidence in financial knowledge and thinking styles, less is known about how these factors differentially affect personal finance management of men and women. In particular, the evidence on the relationship between gender and monetary decisions in the loss domain such as debt management is still scarce and limited. Initial data from our laboratory did not support the claim that gender differences in financial performance stem from individual differences in thinking styles, knowledge or financial literacy but rather from women's greater need for financial security, which is reflected in a tendency to save more for a rainy day (even when this saving is irrational). These results emphasize the great importance of further studies to shed more light on this topic, and design effective interventions to promote more optimal financial decisions while considering gender differences and inequalities in economic wellbeing.

Acknowledgments

This research was supported by an Israel Science Foundation (ISF) Grant # 1566/2012 to SA and MA.

References

Agnew, J., Balduzzi, P., & Sunden, A. (2003). Portfolio choice and trading in a large 401 (k) plan. *American Economic Review*, 193–215.

Agnew, S., & Harrison, N. (2015). Financial literacy and student attitudes to debt: A cross national study examining the influence of gender on personal finance concepts. *Journal of Retailing and Consumer Services*, 25, 122–129.

Amar, M., Ariely, D., Ayal, S., Cryder, C. E., & Rick, S. I. (2011). Winning the battle but losing the war: The psychology of debt management. *Journal of Marketing Research*, 48(SPL), S38–S50.

Arano, K., Parker, C., & Terry, R. (2010). Gender-based risk aversion and retirement asset allocation. *Economic Inquiry*, 48(1), 147–155.

Atkinson, A., & Messy, F. A. (2012). Measuring financial literacy.

Ayal, S., Rusou, Z., Zakay, D., & Hochman, G. (2015). Determinants of judgment and decision making quality: the interplay between information processing style and situational factors. *Frontiers in psychology*, 6.

Bajtelsmit, V. L., Bernasek, A., & Jianakoplos, N. A. (1999). Gender differences in defined contribution pension decisions. *Financial Services Review*, 8(1), 1–10.

Barber, B. M., & Odean, T. (2001). Boys will be boys: Gender, overconfidence, and common stock investment. *Quarterly journal of Economics*, 261–292.

Beckmann, D., & Menkhoff, L. (2008). Will women be women? Analyzing the gender difference among financial experts. *Kyklos*, 61(3), 364–384.

Bengtsson, C., Persson, M., & Willenhag, P. (2005). Gender and overconfidence. *Economics letters*, 86(2), 199–203.

Berggren, J., & Gonzalez, R. (2010). Gender difference in financial decision making.

Bliss, R. T., & Potter, M. E. (2002). Mutual fund managers: does gender matter?. *The Journal of Business and Economic Studies*, 8(1), 1.

Bridges, S., & Disney, R. (2010). Debt and depression. *Journal of health economics*, 29(3), 388–403.

Bokešová, Z. (2013, April). Gender Differences in Financial Decisions. In *GV-CONF 2013: proceedings in Global Virtual Conference* (119–122).

Brown, S., Taylor, K., & Price, S. W. (2005). Debt and distress: Evaluating the psychological cost of credit. *Journal of Economic Psychology*, 26(5), 642–663.

Byrnes, J. P., Miller, D. C., & Schafer, W. D. (1999). Gender differences in risk taking: A meta-analysis. *Psychological Bulletin*, 125(3), 367.

Charness, G., & Gneezy, U. (2012). Strong evidence for gender differences in risk taking. *Journal of Economic Behavior & Organization*, 83(1), 50–58.

Chen, H., & Volpe, R. P. (2002). Gender differences in personal financial literacy among college students. *Financial Services Review*, 11(3), 289–307.

Croson, R., & Gneezy, U. (2009). Gender differences in preferences. *Journal of Economic literature*, 448–474.

Davies, E., & Lea, S. E. (1995). Student attitudes to student debt. *Journal of Economic Psychology*, 16(4), 663–679.

Dwyer, P. D., Gilkeson, J. H., & List, J. A. (2002). Gender differences in revealed risk taking: evidence from mutual fund investors. *Economics Letters*, 76(2), 151–158.

Dwyer, R. E., Hodson, R., & McCloud, L. (2013). Gender, debt, and dropping out of college. *Gender & Society*, 27(1), 30–55.

Eckel, C. C., & Grossman, P. J. (2002). Sex differences and statistical stereotyping in attitudes toward financial risk. *Evolution and Human Behavior*, 23(4), 281–295.

Eckel, C. C., & Grossman, P. J. (2008). Differences in the economic decisions of men and women: Experimental evidence. *Handbook of Experimental Economics Results*, 1, 509–519.

Epstein, S. (2003). Cognitive-experiential self-theory of personality. *Handbook of psychology.*

Epstein, S., Pacini, R., Denes-Raj, V., & Heier, H. (1996). Individual differences in intuitive–experiential and analytical–rational thinking styles. *Journal of Personality and Social Psychology*, 71(2), 390.

Experian (2009), With age comes wisdom and a higher credit score. Experian Marketing Insight Snapshot, [available at http://www.experian.com/business-resources/insight-form-agewisdom.html].

Fehr-Duda, H., De Gennaro, M., & Schubert, R. (2006). Gender, financial risk, and probability weights. *Theory and decision*, 60(2–3), 283–313.

Felton, J., Gibson, B., & Sanbonmatsu, D. M. (2003). Preference for risk in investing as a function of trait optimism and gender. *The Journal of Behavioral Finance*, 4(1), 33–40.

Feng, L., & Seasholes, M. S. (2008). Individual investors and gender similarities in an emerging stock market. *Pacific-Basin Finance Journal*, 16(1), 44–60.

Fonseca, R., Mullen, K. J., Zamarro, G., & Zissimopoulos, J. (2012). What explains the gender gap in financial literacy? The role of household decision making. *Journal of Consumer Affairs*, 46(1), 90–106.

Fornero, E., & Monticone, C. (2011). Financial literacy and pension plan participation in Italy. *Journal of Pension Economics and Finance*, 10(04), 547–564.

Gerrans, P., & Clark-Murphy, M. (2004). Gender differences in retirement savings decisions. *Journal of Pension Economics and Finance*, 3(02), 145–164.

Glaser, M., & Walther, T. (2014). Run, Walk, or Buy? Financial Literacy, Dual-Process Theory, and Investment Behavior. *Financial Literacy, Dual-Process Theory, and Investment Behavior* (April 16, 2014).

Goldsmith, E., & Goldsmith, R. E. (1997). Gender differences in perceived and real knowledge of financial investments. *Psychological Reports*, 80(1), 236–238.

Goldsmith, R. E., & Goldsmith, E. B. (2006). The effects of investment education on gender differences in financial knowledge. *Journal of Personal Finance*, 5(2), 55–69.

Graham, J. F., Stendardi Jr, E. J., Myers, J. K., & Graham, M. J. (2002). Gender differences in investment strategies: an information processing perspective. *International journal of bank marketing*, 20(1), 17–26.

Gysler, M., & Kruse, J. B. (2002). *Ambiguity and gender differences in financial decision making: An experimental examination of competence and confidence effects.* Swiss Federal Institute of Technology, Center for Economic Research.

Halko, M. L., Kaustia, M., & Alanko, E. (2012). The gender effect in risky asset holdings. *Journal of Economic Behavior & Organization*, 83(1), 66–81.

Hallahan, T. A., Faff, R. W., & McKenzie, M. D. (2004). An empirical investigation of personal financial risk tolerance. *Financial Services Review-Greenwich*, 13(1), 57–78.

Harrison, A. A., & Saeed, L. (1977). Let's make a deal: An analysis of revelations and stipulations in lonely hearts advertisements. *Journal of Personality and Social Psychology*, 35(4), 257.

Henry, R. A., Weber, J. G., & Yarbrough, D. (2001). Money management practices of college students. *College Student Journal*, 35(2), 244.

Hinz, R. P., McCarthy, D. D., & Turner, J. A. (1997). Are women conservative investors? Gender differences in participant-directed pension investments. *Positioning Pensions for the Twenty-first Century*, 91, 103.

Hira, T. K., & Loibl, C. (2008). *Gender differences in investment behavior* (253–270). Springer New York.

Hira, T. K., & Mugenda, O. (2000). Gender differences in financial perceptions, behaviors and satisfaction. *Journal of Financial Planning-Denver-*, 13(2), 86–93.

Hui, T. S. W., Vincent, C., & Woolley, F. (2011). Challenges to Canada's Retirement Income System: Understanding Gender Differences in Retirement Saving Decisions. *Social Research and Demonstration Corporation.*

Jenkins, R., Bhugra, D., Bebbington, P., Brugha, T., Farrell, M., Coid, J., Fryers, S. Weich, S. Singleton, N. & Meltzer, H. (2008). Debt, income and mental disorder in the general population. *Psychological Medicine*, 38(10), 1485–1493.

Jianakoplos, N. A., & Bernasek, A. (1998). Are women more risk averse? *Economic inquiry*, 36(4), 620.

Johnson, E. J., & Weber, E. U. (2009). Mindful judgment and decision making. *Annual review of psychology*, 60, 53.

Kelly, S., & Gong, H. (2010). Saving tomorrow: the savings and spending patterns of Australians.

Kunnanatt, J. T., & Emiline, M. (2012). Investment strategies and gender: a study of emerging patterns in India. *Journal of Gender Studies*, 21(4), 345–363.

Lange, C., & Byrd, M. (1998). The relationship between perceptions of financial distress and feelings of psychological well-being in New Zealand university students. *International Journal of Adolescence and Youth*, 7(3), 193–209.

Lusardi, A., & Mitchell, O. S. (2008). Planning and financial literacy: How do women fare? (No. w13750). *National Bureau of Economic Research.*

Lusardi, A., & Mitchell, O. S. (2011). Financial literacy around the world: an overview. *Journal of Pension Economics and Finance*, 10(04), 497–508.

Menkhoff, L., Schmidt, U., & Brozynski, T. (2006). The impact of experience on risk taking, overconfidence, and herding of fund managers: Complementary survey evidence. *European Economic Review*, 50(7), 1753–1766.

Norvilitis, J. M., Szablicki, P. B., & Wilson, S. D. (2003). Factors Influencing Levels of Credit-Card Debt in College Students1. *Journal of Applied Social Psychology*, 33(5), 935–947.

Novailitis, J. M., Merwin, M. M., Osberg, T. M., Roehling, P. V., Young, P., & Kamas, M. M. (2006). Personality factors, money attitudes, financial knowledge, and credit-card debt in college students1. *Journal of Applied Social Psychology*, 36(6), 1395–1413.

OECD (2013). Financial literacy and inclusion: Results oF OECD/INFE survey across countrIes and by gender, vol.VI.OECDPublishing,Pisahttp://dx. doi.org/10.1787/http://www.oecd.org/daf/fin/financialeducation/TrustFund 2013_OECD_INFE_Fin_Lit_and_Incl_SurveyResults_by_Country_and_ Gender.pdf

Olsen, R. A., & Cox, C. M. (2001). The influence of gender on the perception and response to investment risk: The case of professional investors. *The Journal of Psychology and Financial Markets*, 2(1), 29–36.

Pacini, R., & Epstein, S. (1999). The relation of rational and experiential information processing styles to personality, basic beliefs, and the ratio-bias phenomenon. *Journal of Personality and Social Psychology*, 76, 972–987.

Powell, M., & Ansic, D. (1997). Gender differences in risk behaviour in financial decision-making: An experimental analysis. *Journal of economic psychology*, 18(6), 605–628.

Sapienza, P., Zingales, L., & Maestripieri, D. (2009). Gender differences in financial risk aversion and career choices are affected by testosterone. *Proceedings of the National Academy of Sciences*, 106(36), 15268–15273.

Schmidt, L., & Sevak, P. (2006). Gender, marriage, and asset accumulation in the United States. *Feminist Economics*, 12(1–2), 139–166.

Schubert, R., Brown, M., Gysler, M., & Brachinger, H. W. (1999). Financial decision-making: are women really more risk-averse? *American Economic Review*, 381–385.

Schubert, R., Brown, M., Gysler, M., & Brachinger, H. W. (2000). *Gender specific attitudes towards risk and ambiguity: an experimental investigation.* Institut für Wirtschaftsforschung, Eidgenössische Technische Hochschule.

Sekita, S. (2011). Financial literacy and retirement planning in Japan. *Journal of Pension Economics and Finance*, 10(04), 637–656.

Sierminska, E. M., Frick, J. R., & Grabka, M. M. (2010). Examining the gender wealth gap. *Oxford Economic Papers*, gpq007.

Siva, S. (2012). A study on Gender Difference in Investment Choice & Risk–Taking. *IJAR BAE*, 1(1), 01–06.

Sladek, R. M., Bond, M. J., & Phillips, P. A. (2010). Age and gender differences in preferences for rational and experiential thinking. *Personality and Individual Differences*, 49(8), 907–911.

Thaler, R. H., & Benartzi, S. (2004). Save more tomorrow™: Using behavioral economics to increase employee saving. *Journal of political Economy*, 112(S1), S164–S187.

Watson, J., & McNaughton, M. (2007). Gender differences in risk aversion and expected retirement benefits. *Financial Analysts Journal*, 63(4), 52–62.

Webster, R. L., & Ellis, T. S. (1996). Men's and women's self-confidence in performing financial analysis. *Psychological Reports*, 79(3f), 1251–1254.

Willows, G., & West, D. (2015). Differential Investment Performance In South Africa Based On Gender And Age. *International Business & Economics Research Journal (IBER)*, 14(3), 537–560.

Wong, K. F. E., Kwong, J. Y. Y., & Ng, C. K. (2008). When thinking rationally increases biases: The role of rational thinking style in escalation of commitment. *Applied Psychology*, 57(2), 246–271.

Zinkhan, G. M., & Karande, K. W. (1991). Cultural and gender differences in risk-taking behavior among American and Spanish decision makers. *The Journal of Social Psychology*, 131(5), 741–742.

Zissimopoulos, J. M., Karney, B., & Rauer, A. (2008). Marital histories and economic well-being. *Michigan Retirement Research Center Research Paper* No. WP, 180.

Appendix A

An Example Screen of Debt Management Game

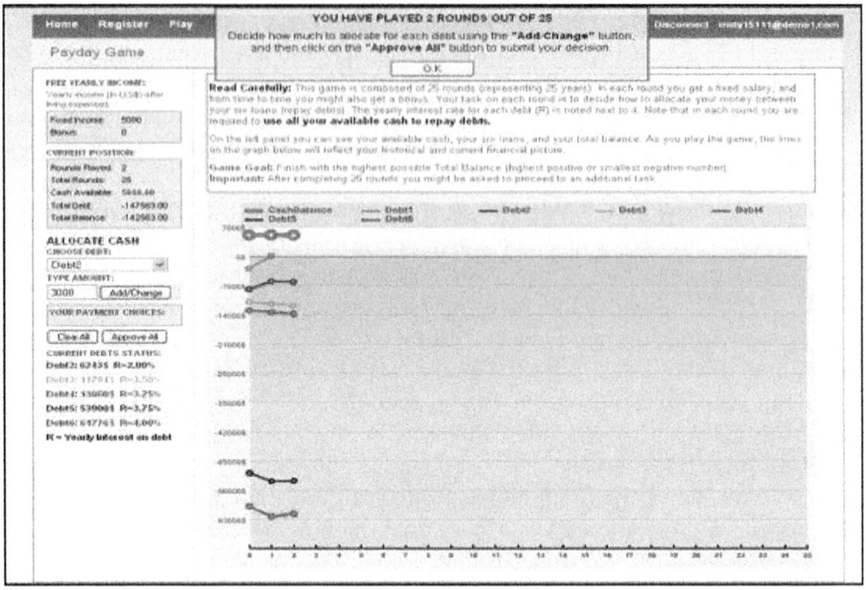

Appendix B

Final Screen of Debt Management Game for a Financially Optimal Player

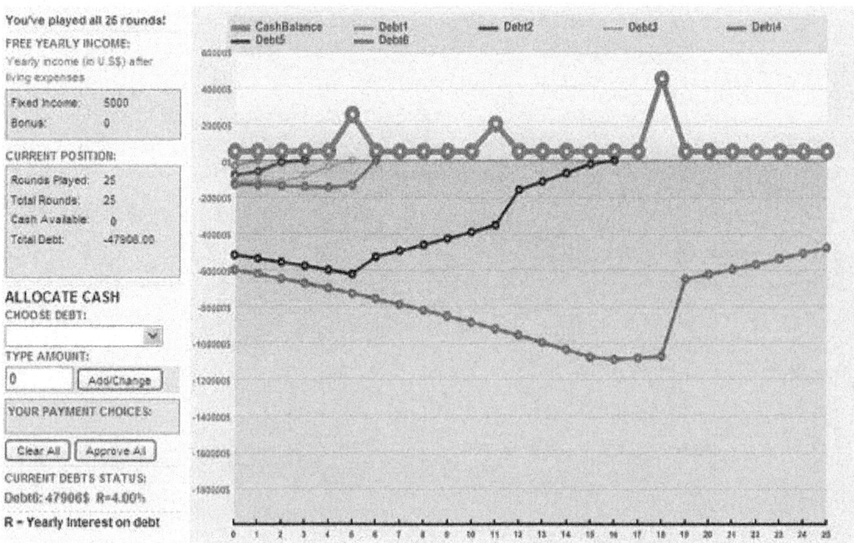

Part IV

Finance and the Media

Chapter 8

The Role of Emotions in Decision Making: Theory, Evidence, and Examples from Media Psychology

Gregory Gurevich* and Doron Kliger†

Abstract

Converging evidence from diverse areas of research suggests that emotions take an active part in decision making. We survey some of the ample work done on emotion research, in the fields of behavioral economics, cognitive neuroscience, and neuropsychology. Further, we discuss relevant theoretical and empirical studies in media psychology. The emerging picture shows that emotions and affective states constitute an integral part of decision making, often assuming the important role of informational mediators, primarily in social contexts.

Keywords: Decision making, Emotions, Media

JEL Classification: A12, D03, D87

1. Introduction and Background

Traditionally, decision making in economics has been described as an activity which is performed in isolation from any potential disturbances. Economic wisdom suggested that if emotions are at all relevant in this respect, then only as something to be avoided. However, the actual state of affairs appears to be more complex. For instance, consider an interaction-based decision making problem whose general structure can be represented by a well-defined outcome scheme, sterile and devoid of any situation-specific content. The scheme states the payoffs obtained by the opponents under every possible combination of their respective actions. Traditional

*Faculty of Social Sciences, University of Haifa, Israel
†Department of Economics, University of Haifa, Israel

economic theory relies on rational models, according to which decision makers arrive at decisions using general rules of logic and inference. Any details other than the payoffs, such as relationships between the opponents, their moods, circumstances of the interaction, etc., are irrelevant. Yet, often these particular details which are ignored by the standard approach may in fact bear essential importance for the decision makers. For instance, subjects may be sensitive to social aspects, such as interpersonal relations (e.g., degree of acquaintance or kinship with the opponent, valence of previous interactions, identification, etc.). As the importance of the social sphere is hard to doubt, it seems plausible that it should be taken into account in a systematic manner. This line of reasoning leads to some important questions of practical nature, for instance: What is the exact route by which the interacting participants access social content? How does the processing of this content take place? And, finally, how does the result of this processing affect the final outcome? For an abstract scheme such as a monetary (or utilitarian) payoff table, the rational process is rather clear: technical details, viz., all possible actions and corresponding outcomes, are evaluated and processed by intellectual machinery according to the rules of logic and inference, up to the point when a preferable course of action can be stated; this may be considered as 'sterile' decision making. The question is, whether also the additional data, particularly the social context of the situation, are processed in a similar way, i.e., manipulated according to the rules of logic and inference.

As we argue in the following pages, it is unlikely for social data to be processed in the same way as the abstract monetary/utilitarian scheme, much as it is unlikely for these data to be completely ignored. Instead, social aspects of the situation are expected to find their way of influencing actions of decision makers via their feelings and emotions. Apparently, feelings and emotions take an active part in about all regular human activity, and not as a disturbance factor, as it is often maintained, but as a necessary element of purposeful and often efficient behavior.[1]

Indications from all related areas of research suggest that explaining emotions should take into account their influence on information

[1]The strategic role of emotions as exposed by, e.g., Frank (1988), lends strong support to the view that emotions comprise much more than a mere by-product of human interactional activity.

processing and resulting decision making and behavior. Accordingly, we suggest that the social context of situations of choice makes its way to decision makers via their emotions and affective states, which therefore may be viewed in this regard as social information transmitters.[2] Various approaches provided by emotion research make it possible to predict which situational characteristics are expected to evoke specific emotions; which affective reactions can be expected after these emotions are evoked; and, finally, what influence on behavior is to be expected given these affective reactions.

The idea that emotions, feelings, moods, and affect exert systematic influence on decision making is familiar to cognitive science and economics. Elster (1998), Loewenstein (2000), and Hirshleifer and Shumway (2003) are some prominent examples from an extensive body of studies documenting this influence. It is by now generally accepted that factors such as moods induced by weather can systematically influence the ostensibly 'sterile' economic activity, such as that of the stock market (e.g., Hirshleifer and Shumway, 2003; Kliger and Levy, 2003a, 2003b, 2008; Kliger and Kudryavtsev, 2014); seasonal mood fluctuations have been shown to substantially influence the stock exchange performance of Initial Public Offerings (Kliger, Gurevich and Haim, 2012); and general relations between economic decision making and emotions and their neurological correlates have been addressed by a range of studies (Reimann and Bechara, 2010). It would therefore be natural to assume that emotions involved in social life and interpersonal relations exert systematic influence on decision making. Indeed, emotions associated with social life seem to constitute much more than just occasional or insignificant stimuli, taking as they are a ubiquitous and prominent part in most everyday decision making activities. The influence exerted by socially-induced emotions is successfully dealt with by established emotion accounts, such as Attribution Theory (Weiner, 1985; more details below).

The following pages offer a survey of relevant research. Starting from basic definitions, we proceed to outline some approaches to modeling

[2]Approaches such as *mood-as-information* or *feelings-as-information* (Clore, 1992; Schwarz, 1990; more details below) explicitly suggest that moods and emotions act as information carriers or transmitters.

the nature of emotions, sketch out theory and evidence, and conclude by referring to examples of emotion research in the domain of media psychology.

2. Emotions: Basic Definitions and Components

To begin examining the findings related to emotions, one has to define first, what is meant by the term *emotion*. While there is no universally accepted definition of this term, for the purpose of this chapter we employ a general and essentially descriptive definition, asserting that in general, *emotions* refer to *internal mental states that are primarily focused on affect, the latter denoting positive or negative valence of the experience* (Ortony, Clore and Foss, 1987; Clore, Schwartz and Conway, 1994). As a preliminary clarification, we observe that the states denoted as emotions are characterized as necessarily *mental*. The reason is that, while terms referred to exclusively bodily states are not generally considered emotions (as, for example, *tired*; cf. Clore et al., 1994), they often contain a somatic component but are not primarily defined by its presence. Even less the definition is likely to exclusively concentrate on behavioral aspects, which are nonetheless an important outward expression of emotions. Thus, while mainly stressing the mental aspect, most of the existing emotion accounts agree that there are three main components involved in emotion: *somatic* (as expressed in bodily reactions such as skin coloration and conductance, pulse rate, eye pupil dilation, etc.); *behavioral* (facial expression, voice modulation, gesticulation, etc.); and *cognitive* (mental representation, appraisal, valence evaluation). As the most prominent modern approaches to emotion show, all these three components are to be taken as organic parts of an integral whole for the purpose of comprehensive analysis of the nature of emotions.

3. Neuropsychological Evidence and Related Theories

One of the most dramatic accounts of emotions as active participants of regular mind activities is presented in Damasio (1994). Taking a neuropsychological perspective, the research describes general ways of emotions operating in a normal organism, and proceeds to show how, besides providing a background for the regular functioning, emotions and feelings comprise signals which actively guide decision making and behavior. In developing the Somatic Marker Hypothesis (hereafter SMH), Damasio distinguished between *primary* and *secondary* emotions, while making a case that the latter take an active part in everyday decision making by providing cues termed *somatic markers*, as explained by the author:

"Somatic markers probably increase the accuracy and efficiency of the decision process .... In short, *somatic markers are a special instance of feelings generated from secondary emotions.* Those emotions and feelings *have been connected, by learning, to predicted future outcomes of certain scenarios.* When a negative somatic marker is juxtaposed to a particular future outcome, the combination functions as an alarm bell. When a positive somatic marker is juxtaposed instead, it becomes a beacon of incentive" (pp. 173–174; italics original).[3]

The general point brought by Damasio is that the common assumption of the reason's independence of feelings is inherently incorrect:

"This is Descartes' error: the abyssal separation between body and mind, between the sizable, dimensioned, mechanically operated, infinitely divisible body stuff, on the one hand, and the unsizable, undimensioned, un-pushpullable, nondivisible mind stuff ... Specifically: the separation of the most refined operations of mind from the structure and operation of a biological organism" (pp. 249–250).

As a support for these claims, Damasio offers impressive evidence of how the damage or malfunction of certain brain areas produces behavioral failures which are strongly associated with emotional deficiencies. The story of Phineas Gage (pp. 3–10), a railroad construction foreman who had survived a grave brain injury with unexpected consequences, serves as a classical example showing that "...there were systems in the human brain dedicated more to reasoning than to anything else, and in particular, to the personal and social dimensions of reasoning. The observance of previously acquired social convention and ethical rules could be lost as a result of brain damage, even when neither basic intellect nor language seemed compromised" (p. 10).

---

[3]The distinction between primary and secondary emotions is found in virtually all current emotion accounts, under slightly varying labels of *basic* versus *component* emotions and similar terms.

The Phineas Gage story may be viewed as evidence supporting Mind Modularity Hypothesis (hereafter MMH; Fodor, 1983; Cosmides and Tooby, 1992), a theory suggesting that the human brain uses different ways of functioning for different purposes, e.g., for resolution of a social situation as opposed to solving a logical problem. This intriguing case shows how the ability for the former, but not the latter, can be compromised as a result of brain impairment. The central argument in Damasio (1994) is that the absence of emotional cues (somatic markers) renders inefficient the whole decision making mechanism.

A more recent study by Bechara and Damasio (2005) lends strong support to SMH by comparing economic decision making of healthy subjects to that of patients suffering from damage to certain brain areas which are associated with emotional deficits such as the absence of *anticipatory feelings* (a notion close to the 'gut feelings' in everyday usage). They show significant qualitative difference between decisions made by the two groups, leading to the conclusion that emotions play a key role in the interaction between environmental conditions and human decision processes, with the emotional systems providing valuable implicit or explicit knowledge for making fast and advantageous decisions.

In the domain of decision making under risk, Loewenstein, Hsee, Weber and Welch (2001) suggested the Risk-as-Feelings Hypothesis (hereafter RFH), which also makes explicit use of the notion of anticipatory feelings and their influence on decisions. According to the authors, RFH "...postulates that responses to risky situations (including decision making) result in part from direct (i.e., not cortically mediated) emotional influences" (p. 270); furthermore, the authors suggest that the emotional states at the time of decision play the role of informational inputs into decision making. A range of related studies reviewed in Loewenstein *et al.* (2001), including those conducted by the authors, lend strong support to the RFH argument that gut feelings experienced at the decision making moment play a role in the choices individuals eventually make.

Evolutionary psychology has also an interesting say about the interaction between emotions and decision making. As Cosmides and Tooby (2000) suggest, emotions essentially comprise adaptive computational algorithms, specialized to deal with distinctive real-life situations that have recurred many times over the species' evolutionary past. According to this view, the human cognitive architecture is multi-modular, with emotions comprising information processing 'programs' which have similar purpose to the rational cognition algorithms; the function of both is information processing, albeit performed in different (to some extent, complementary) ways.

Ostensibly conflicting accounts of emotion offered by evolutionary psychologists and advocates of some alternative views (e.g. Johnson-Laird and Oatley, 2000; see below) share the understanding that emotions comprise basically information-related phenomena. A question posed by Clore and Ortony (2000) addresses the issue of general role of cognition in emotion. Starting from the common and seemingly unquestionable view of emotion and cognition as totally separate phenomena, they proceed to show how close and inseparable these prove to be in practice, thereby suggesting a strong advantage of studying emotion from the perspective of cognitive neuroscience. Regarding the central question posed by their study, the authors conclude: "... Taken together, we think that the arguments we have presented provide a compelling answer to the question we set out to address in this chapter: When is cognition implicated in emotion? Always, sometimes, or never? Our answer, of course, is always" (p. 53).

The Mood-as-Information Approach (hereafter MIA; e.g., Schwartz and Clore, 1983; Clore, 1992) is related to the accounts just discussed. It states that people often treat their affective feelings as providing important cues related to the situation at hand, which can be viewed as a particular case of SMH with somatic markers being consciously interpreted, subconscious effect also being possible.[4] It is interesting to note that the central assertions of both MIA and Damasio (1994) share common ground with MMH with respect to the present context, while also conforming with the approach usually construed as an alternative to MMH (e.g., Johnson-Laird and Oatley, 2000). The alternative view maintains that there is no conclusive evidence for specialized modules in the human brain. Instead, it argues that the brain function depends upon two different systems, one for

[4]The approach is equally concerned with moods, feelings, and emotions as separate notions, which are generally referred to as "affective states," while the approach itself is interchangeably referred to as *mood-as-information* (Clore, 1992) or *feelings-as-information* (Schwarz, 1990).

reasoning and another for emotions (cf. Dual-Process theories discussed in, e.g., Sloman, 1996). Evidently, the final objective of both conjectured systems is the same: information processing and action/decision making. According to this approach, "...emotions should be guides to life, and so should interact with the human capacity for reasoning and planning" (Johnson-Laird and Oatley, 2000, 462).[5] The same general contention is clearly reflected in summarizing statements of MIA advocates, such as the following: "...Rather than being idle by-products of information processing, affective and cognitive feelings I argue are gainfully employed in the constructions of everyday social judgments" (Clore, 1992, 133). It seems that Damasio (1994) provides evidence fitting both MMH and MIA but also the two-system hypothesis of Johnson-Laird and Oatley (2000), insofar as all these theories rely on emotions as information-related agents. Both two-system view and MMH refer to *affective* as opposed to *rule-based* or *analytic* reasoning, while the difference may be viewed as due to the kind and intensity of the affect involved (again, the relation of both views to Dual-Process accounts is immediate). This may hint at the possibility that the two alternative views are not so opposite as it may seem on the surface: in general, both speak of different *modes* employed by the brain, and assuming that the modes differ by their respective emotional load (for which Damasio, 1994, presents abundant and impressive evidence), the presupposed operational difference between the two theories seems more like a matter of definition (of course, the basic neural circuitry implied by the two views may still be quite different). Then, MMH account can be construed not as an alternative to, but as a refinement of the two-system view, suggesting further subdivision of the latter's affective system. How serious the differences are is not as important for our present purpose, however, as the point of convergence of the two views, namely, that emotions

[5]Closely connected to this approach are accounts developed in the domain of *emotional intelligence* research (see Salovey and Mayer, 1990). Some of the basic assertions of this framework are immediately relevant to presently reviewed accounts, as suggested by Salovey and Mayer (1990): "...there is a set of conceptually related mental processes involving emotional information" (p. 190); furthermore, "...Moods and emotions subtly but systematically influence some of the components and strategies involved in problem solving" (p. 198); and moreover, emotional intelligence in general is considered a "subset of social intelligence" (p. 189).

can be construed as information transmitters, communicating essential data regarding the situation at hand to the decision maker. A question may be raised as of how efficiently this information is represented and processed, by analogy with the intellectual ability and its natural limits' questions in regard to the 'regular' information processing. It probably could be argued that, according to the evolutionary accounts such as that of Cosmides and Tooby (1992), the efficiency has to be quite substantial, in fact as high as to allow for the development of social adaptations involving emotions along millennia. The general point we presently would prefer to make is, however, much better reflected in the following citation: "...Although the practice of basing judgments on momentary feelings and passing thoughts sometimes leads to suboptimal outcomes, the main lesson from the evidence is not so much that such feelings and intuitions lead us astray, but that they are utterly basic to whatever it is that we mean by human judgment" (Clore, 1992, 156).

4. Social Cognition Perspective

By no means less important than the neuropsychological evidence and related theories, are the accounts suggested by emotion research studies in social cognition.[6] One of the key issues addressed by emotion research is a possible structure of emotional differentiation. A noteworthy part of the social cognition approach is fundamentally concerned with cognitive features of emotion, and consequently deals with that aspect of emotion which can be construed as informational. For instance, consider the emotion structure theory proposed by Ortony, Clore and Collins (1988; hereafter OCC). Generally, according to OCC emotions arise as a result of the subject's attending to certain aspects of the environment, while possible aspects can be grouped under the broad categories of *events*, *actions* and *objects*. It is the subject's evaluation of, e.g., consequences of events, that may

[6]Some of the points from this domain have been already presented above, like those related to Clore (1992). In what follows, no attempt at comprehensive review of this important domain is made, nor an in-depth analysis of any specific approach is undertaken; instead, we sketch out some of the most successful accounts with emphasis on aspects particularly relevant to our present topic.

give rise to a positive emotion once the consequences are judged desirable, and a negative emotion otherwise.

According to OCC, emotions arise as a result of appraisals formed with respect to one's goals, standards, and attitudes, so that emotional reaction reflects the information about the environment. More specifically, it is maintained that far from being just a passive reflection, emotions pass the information regarding the environment to the subject, providing the material on which judgment and decision making mechanism subsequently works. The following citations outline the essential position of OCC: "...That approach suggests the view...that the function of emotions is to represent in a conscious and insistent way (through distinctive feelings and cognitions) the personally significant aspects of construed situations" (p. 192); "...like the role of touch in allowing one to locate an object in a drawer without looking, affective experience allows one to navigate the interpersonal world" (Clore, 1992, 138). It is worth noting that "navigating the interpersonal world" in the last citation is directly related to our current argument, as it explicitly suggests the role of emotions as primarily *social* information transmitters.[7]

Higgins (1987) suggested another seminal hypothesis concerned with emotion formation, according to which emotions arise as a result of self-discrepancy, perceived as the gap between the way one is (*actual self*) versus the way one would like to be (*ideal self*) or the way one thinks one should be (*ought self*). According to this account, emotional reactions arise in the process of trying to follow ways leading to the ideal and/or ought self (*self-guides*). Similarly to the OCC account, also here emotions can be viewed as conveying information on one's current state or providing a feedback for one's actions, including data on self-discrepancy, its magnitude, importance, rate of change, etc.

Another important approach for decision making and behavior focused on emotions is suggested by Attribution Theory (hereafter AT; Weiner, 1985). This account is concerned, inter alia, with situations involving achievement, viz., success or failure as outcomes of one's actions.

[7] Evidently, also non-social events may give rise to emotions and especially moods, as for example in Hirshleifer & Shumway (2003); what is argued here is that the *main* arena where emotions operate is the social/interpersonal world, a view supported by, e.g., Simon (1967).

AT suggests that when such outcomes appear, a likely consequence is the subject's inclination to engage in a search for possible causes, seeking to retain those for success or eliminate those for failure; furthermore, a three-dimensional structure of causality is used to analyze the perceived cause; finally, subsequently experienced emotions influence action (behavior and decisions). The main causal dimensions of AT are *locus* (whether the perceived cause is internal or external to the subject), *stability* (whether it is stable over time), and *controllability* (whether it is controllable by the subject). Thus, for example, a student failing an exam and attributing the failure to his or her temporary illness suggests a cause that is internal, unstable, and uncontrollable. According to AT, internal uncontrollable causes of failure tend to give rise to emotions such as shame, whereas those perceived as internal controllable may give rise to guilt. Besides the ample evidence confirming AT in social psychology (see e.g., Weiner, 1986), the theory has been shown to explain economic decision making, for instance sharing gains or splitting profits (Gurevich, Kliger and Weiner, 2012) and financial assistance (Gurevich and Kliger, 2013), where causal attributions and accompanying emotions have exerted influence on economic decisions in accordance with AT predictions. Moreover, in both studies the attributional approach has been shown to help clarifying behavior unexplained by standard economic models. Specifically, in Gurevich *et al.* (2012), attributions and corresponding emotions were successfully employed to examine the rationale behind allocation decisions in the game of ultimatum (e.g., Guth, Schmittberger and Schwarze, 1982), while in Gurevich and Kliger (2013) attributional analysis was effectively used to elucidate one-shot Prisoner's Dilemma (see Luce and Raiffa, 1957) decisions made by the participants of a high-stake TV game show and a laboratory experiment. Relevant to the present point and similarly to OCC and self-discrepancy accounts, emotions can be thus regarded as information-carrying agents, in this instance conveying information concerning attributional aspect of social situation involving economic decisions. An extended attributional approach (Liu, Karasawa and Weiner, 1992) explores the observation that negative emotions are more likely to call for action, while the dispositional attribution itself is performed more often when negative rather than positive emotions are experienced. Evidently, this approach lends additional support to the view of emotions as information-loaded agents providing decision makers with practically useful data calling for action or otherwise, depending on particular circumstances. The approach is also definitely compatible with MIA mentioned earlier, as clearly outlined in the following citation: "...it is argued that negative affective states, which inform the organism that its current situation is problematic, foster the use of effortful, detail-oriented, analytical processing strategies, whereas positive affective states foster the use of less effortful heuristic strategies" (Schwarz, 1990, 527). Returning to the hypothesis advanced in this last research, it is worth noting that it is brought out as alternative to the account according to which the main role of emotions is the influence they exert on the kind and valence of data retrieved from memory (the latter suggested as the main source of information employed in decision making). Even this kind of supposedly vicarious function of emotion still reflects some of its informational role, while Schwarz (1990) presents substantial empirical evidence of emotions most often directly, rather than via memory pathways, serving information-related functions, influence evaluative judgments, and affect information processing strategies.

Another related structural approach to emotion is offered by Roseman (1984) and further developed in Roseman, Antoniou and Jose (1992). According to this account, different combinations of a number of basic appraisals give rise to different emotions, while basic appraisals are concerned with such data as *source of causality* of events (circumstance versus other person or self-caused), *motivation of actions* (appetitive versus aversive), and *control by the subject* (high versus low control potential). It is easy to see that also here the source of emotion formation is a multidimensional analysis of environment performed by the subject, whereas emotion, once formed, contains information regarding the most salient features of the situation, and so may serve as a guide for, or at least exert substantial influence on, subsequent actions, decisions, and judgments. Following Frijda (1988), "...emotions exist for the sake of signaling states of the world that have to be responded to, or that no longer need response and action" (p. 354). Evidently, this last point is shared by all of the accounts presented above, and is generally characteristic of most if not all current theories concerned with the cognitive (appraisal) aspect of emotions. Moreover, the view of emotions as state signals or information carriers is evidently compatible with many examples of emotion studies in important practical contexts, one of those being media domain, discussed next.[8]

5. Emotions and Media Psychology

The role of emotions in the media, including the film and radio realms, has been studied by now for no less than a hundred years (Nabi and Wirth, 2008).[9] While definitely not free from controversies, the work in this domain has resulted in remarkable advancements in dealing with many nontrivial challenges. For instance, Frome (2006) offers a lucid yet deep comparison of alternative theories aimed to explain emotions elicited by the works of art communicated through different media, including paintings, books, theatre, movies, and videogames. Essential to all alternative theories is the cognitive element of the process: emotional responses result from the mind, taken as a whole in some models (*the illusion* and *the pretend* accounts) or as an array of specific mental systems in others (*multi-level approach*), adequately attending to different situational characteristics of actual or fictional reality. In general, the impressive body of theory and data accumulated by media psychology leaves no doubt as to whether emotions can be considered an integral and systematic factor in decision making. Modern media psychology explores the impact of pre-existing emotions of the audience on message engagement as well as the influence of emotions stimulated by media exposure on message processing. In both respects, the view of emotions as essential part of information processing is evident. Below we review several examples of recent developments in media psychology that lend support to the view of emotions as information carriers.

---

[8]Media psychology is but one area of study concerned with emotions and their influence on behavior and judgment. Other relevant areas include attitude research; consumer and marketing studies; cultural history; and philosophy of mind (see Bartsch *et al.*, 2008). Furthermore, within media psychology, a wide range of contexts is related to emotions, including politics, entertainment, education, online communication, and more (Nabi and Wirth, 2008). Here we only briefly sketch out some select topics, with no attempt to compile a comprehensive review of the literature.

[9]For a broad survey of emotion research in media psychology, see e.g., Wirth and Schramm (2005).

One instance of emotions assuming the role of mediators is amply demonstrated in the empirical study of *media indignation* by Hwang, Pan and Sun (2008). In this research, the authors show that media content perceived as conflicting with one's personal view on some controversial issue (the so-called *hostile*, or *biased media perception*) tends to provoke the negative emotion of indignation, which in turn stimulates one's willingness to correct the situation, e.g., by engaging in discursive activities such as public discussions of the issue and voicing one's opinion. Note that according to this result, emotion, in this case indignation plays the mediating role between perception and subsequent behavior, a point also explicitly made by the authors. Interestingly, this study reports practical superiority, in terms of explanatory power, of mediating effects of emotion over cognition, as the resulting impact of media indignation seems to win over that of the cognitive pathway. More specifically, the impact of explicit, deliberate analysis of subjects' position versus media content on subsequent reaction was found non-significant across all three controversial issues tested in the study, in contrast to that of media indignation whose impact was found significant in all tested cases. Viewing emotion as just another data channel, as we suggest here, eliminates the apparent paradox and once again stresses out the importance of emotions as information carriers.

Another study exploring mediating effects of emotions in the media is reported by Holbert and Hansen (2008) in their paper focused on political communication. In this case, the authors have examined a number of related issues, one of them being the point that in the modern world, multiple and often conflicting communication messages may compete for our attention at the same time. Evidently in political context, but also in commercial, health- and science-related, and many other spheres, complex dynamics may arise as a result of the simultaneous exposure to conflicting messages, and according to the authors, non-media variables, notably emotions, serve as mediators of the process. For instance, the authors report the emotional reactions of *anger* experienced by the subjects exposed to a political documentary and their subsequent perceptions of debate superiority among candidates mentioned, as well as not mentioned in the film. The last point is specifically stressed by the authors who suggest that emotional reactions go beyond the message specificity, exerting influence on judgment and attitude not limited by the subject at the focus of the given message. These results can be considered as a more general evidence of emotions serving as information-loaded agents guiding decision making and judgment.

On a still more advanced level, Bartsch *et al.* (2008) explain how appraisal theories of emotions have led to the development of the relatively new concept of *meta-emotion*, viewed as "...a process that monitors and appraises emotions and recruits affective responses toward them, which results in a motivation to maintain and approach emotions, or to control and avoid them" (p. 7). As mentioned above, systematic approach to emotion appraisal and the insights provided by some modern emotion theories suggest that emotions indeed can (and, according to the emotional intelligence research by Salovey and Mayer (1990) and others, often, *should*) be managed. Meta-emotions are, essentially, feelings about emotions, including the anticipatory aspect which is especially important in selective media usage. According to Bartsch *et al.* (2008), meta-emotions serve regulating function with respect to the emotions experienced, inter alia, by media users, and may help explaining such phenomena as meta-mood, need for affect, and fear of emotions. As a construct providing conceptual basis for emotion regulation, meta-emotion enables better understanding of media selection processes, while stressing the cognitive component of emotions in this framework once again emphasizes their mediating role, this time in a still broader sense.

The studies sketched out above comprise only a select fraction of the ongoing, wide-ranging research of emotions in media psychology, whose results repeatedly lend support to our current argument. Other examples include, but are not limited to, the studies of media entertainment and the functional and adaptive role of emotions both as antecedents of and responses to entertainment (Tan, 2008); investigation of the role of emotions in health communication, including the impact of emotions on persuasion, risk perceptions, and behavioral responses (Dunlop, Wakefield and Kashima, 2008); studying the influence of emotions on judgement, message attention and processing with focus on humor and satire in political context (Young, 2008); and more. By clarifying the mediating role of emotions across different contexts, the research in media psychology makes evident the role of emotions in decision making and lends further support to the view of emotions as information carriers.

6. Summary and Conclusion

To summarize, a bulk of evidence originating in diverse domains of research leads to the conclusion that emotions constitute an integral part of decision making, often assuming an important role of informational mediators of social content. Converging evidence from emotion research, neurophysiology and cognitive neuroscience, social cognition, as well as theoretical and empirical studies in media psychology, indicates that under a wide range of circumstances, social content of the situation makes its way to individuals' decision making via their emotions and affective states, which therefore may be viewed in this respect as social information carriers. Given the ubiquitous nature of emotions and their considerable impact across different (primarily but not exclusively social) contexts, as aforementioned and many other studies demonstrate, the importance of emotions' role in decision making cannot be exaggerated.

References

Bartsch, A., Vorderer, P., Mangold, R. & Viehoff, R. (2008). Appraisal of Emotions in Media Use: Toward a Process Model of Meta-Emotion and Emotion Regulation. *Media Psychology*, 11:1, 7–27.

Bechara, A. & Damasio, A.R. (2005). The Somatic Marker Hypothesis: A Neural Theory of Economic Decision. *Games and Economic Behavior*, 52, 336–372.

Clore, G.L. (1992). Cognitive Phenomenology: Feelings and the Construction of Judgment. In Martin, L.L. & Tessler, A. (eds.), *The Construction of Social Judgment*, 133–164, Hillsdale, New York: Erlbaum.

Clore, G.L., & Ortony, A. (2000). Cognition in Emotion: Always, Sometimes, or Never? In Lane, R.D. & Nadel, L. (eds.), *Cognitive Neuroscience of Emotion*, 24–83, New York: Oxford University Press.

Clore, G.L., Schwarz, N. & Conway, M. (1994). Affective Causes and Consequences of Social Information Processing. In Wyer, R.S. & Srull, T.K. (eds.), *Handbook of Social Cognition*, 2nd ed., vol. 1, 323–417, Hillsdale, New Jersey: Erlbaum.

Cosmides L. & Tooby, J. (1992). Cognitive Adaptations for Social Exchange. In Barkow, J., Cosmides, L. & Tooby, J. (eds.), *The Adapted Mind: Evolutionary Psychology and the Generation of Culture*, 163–228, New York: Oxford University Press.

Cosmides L. & Tooby, J. (2000). Evolutionary Psychology and the Emotions. In Lewis, M. & Haviland-Jones, J.M. (eds.), *Handbook of Emotions*, 2nd ed., 91–115, New York: The Guilford Press.

Damasio, A.R. (1994). *Descartes' Error: Emotion, Reason, and the Human Brain.* New York: Putnam.

Dunlop, S., Wakefield, M. & Kashima, Y. (2008). Can You Feel It? Negative Emotion, Risk, and Narrative in Health Communication. *Media Psychology*, 11:1, 52–75.

Elster, J. (1998). Emotions and Economic Theory. *Journal of Economic Literature*, 36:1, 47–74.

Fodor, J.A. (1983). *The Modularity of Mind: An Essay on Faculty Psychology.* Cambridge, MA: MIT Press.

Frank, R.H. (1988). *Passions within Reason: The Strategic Role of the Emotions.* W.W. Norton & Company.

Frijda, N.H. (1988). The Laws of Emotion. *American Psychologist*, 43, 349–358.

Frome, J. (2006). Representation, Reality, and Emotions across Media. *Film Studies*, 8, 12–25.

Gurevich, G. & Kliger, D. (2013). The Manipulation: Socio-economic Decision Making. *Journal of Economic Psychology*, 39, 171–184.

Gurevich, G., Kliger, D. & Weiner, B. (2012). The Role of Attribution of Causality in Economic Decision Making. *The Journal of Socio-Economics*, 41, 439–444.

Guth, W., Schmittberger, R. & Schwarze, B. (1982). An experimental analysis of ultimatum bargaining. *Journal of Economic Behavior and Organization*, 3, 367–388.

Higgins, E.T. (1987). Self-Discrepancy Theory: A Theory Relating Self and Affect. *Psychological Review*, 94, 319–340.

Hirshleifer, D. & Shumway, T. (2003). Good Day Sunshine: Stock Returns and the Weather. *Journal of Finance*, 58:3, 1009–1032.

Holbert, R.L. & Hansen, G.J. (2008). Stepping beyond Message Specificity in the Study of Emotion as Mediator and Inter-Emotion Associations across Attitude Objects: Fahrenheit 9/11, Anger, and Debate Superiority. *Media Psychology*, 11:1, 98–118.

Hwang, H., Pan, Z. & Sun, Y. (2008). Influence of Hostile Media Perception on Willingness to Engage in Discursive Activities: An Examination of Mediating Role of Media Indignation. *Media Psychology*, 11:1, 76–97.

Johnson-Laird, P.N. & Oatley, K. (2000). Cognitive and Social Construction in Emotions. In Lewis, M. & Haviland-Jones, J.M. (eds.), *Handbook of Emotions*, 2nd ed., 458–475, New York: The Guilford Press.

Kliger, D., Gurevich, G., & Haim, A. (2012). When Chronobiology Met Economics: Seasonal Affective Disorder and the Demand for Initial Public Offerings. *Journal of Neuroscience, Psychology, and Economics*, 5:3, 131–151.

Kliger, D., Levy, O. (2003a). Mood and Judgment of Subjective Probabilities: Evidence from the U.S. Index Option Market. *European Finance Review*, 7, 235–248.

Kliger, D., Levy, O. (2003b). Mood-Induced Variation in Risk Preferences. *Journal of Economic Behavior and Organization*, 52, 573–584.

Kliger, D., Levy, O. (2008). Mood Impacts on Probability Weighting Functions: "Large-Gamble" Evidence. *Journal of Socio-Economics*, 37, 1397–1411.

Kliger, D., Kudryavtsev, A. (2014). Out of the Blue: Mood Maintenance Hypothesis and Seasonal Effects on Investors' Reaction to News. *Quantitative Finance*, 14:4, 629–640.

Liu, J.H., Karasawa, K. & Weiner, B. (1992). Inferences about the Causes of Positive and Negative Emotions. *Personality and Social Psychology Bulletin*, 18, 603–615.

Loewenstein, G.F. (2000). Emotions in Economic Theory and Economic Behavior. *American Economic Review*, 90:2, 426–432.

Loewenstein, G.F., Hsee, C.K., Weber, E.U. & Welch, N. (2001). Risk as Feelings. *Psychological Bulletin*, 127:2, 267–286.

Luce, R.D. & Raiffa, H. (1957). *Games and Decisions*. New York: Wiley.

Nabi, R.L. & Wirth, W. (2008). Exploring the Role of Emotion in Media Effects: An Introduction to the Special Issue. *Media Psychology*, 11:1, 1–6.

Ortony, A., Clore, G.L. & Collins, A. (1988). *The Cognitive Structure of Emotions*. New York: Cambridge University Press.

Ortony, A., Clore, G.L. & Foss, M. (1987). The Referential Structure of the Affective Lexicon. *Cognitive Science*, 11, 361–384.

Reimann, M., & Bechara, A. (2010). The Somatic Marker Framework as a Neurological Theory of Decision-Making: Review, Conceptual Comparisons, and Future Neuroeconomics Research. *Journal of Economic Psychology*, 31, 767–776.

Roseman, I.J. (1984). Cognitive Determinants of Emotion: A Structural Theory. In Shaver, P. (ed.), *Review of Personality and Social Psychology: Vol. 5. Emotions, Relationships, and Health*, 11–36, Beverly Hills, CA: Sage.

Roseman, I.J., Antoniou, A.A. & Jose, P.E. (1992). Appraisal Determinants of Emotions: Revising Current Theories. Unpublished manuscript, University of California, Los Angeles.

Salovey, P., & Mayer, J.D. (1990). Emotional Intelligence. *Imagination, Cognition and Personality*, 9:3, 185–211.

Schwartz, N. (1990). Feelings as Information: Informational and Motivational Functions of Affective States. In Higgins, E.T. & Sorrentino, R. (eds.), *Handbook of Motivation and Cognition: Foundations of Social Behavior*, vol. 2, 527–561, New York: Guilford.

Schwartz, N. & Clore, G. L. (1983). Mood, Misattribution, and Judgments of Well-being: Informative and Directive Functions of Affective States. *Journal of Personality and Social Psychology*, 45, 513–523.

Simon, H. (1967). Motivational and Emotional Controls of Cognition. *Psychological Review* 74:1, 29–39.

Sloman, S.A. (1996). The Empirical Case for Two Systems of Reasoning. *Psychological Bulletin*, 119, 3–22.

Tan, E. S.-H. (2008). Entertainment is Emotion: The Functional Architecture of the Entertainment Experience. *Media Psychology*, 11:1, 28–51.

Weiner, B. (1985). An Attributional Theory of Achievement Motivation and Emotion. *Psychological Review*, 92:4, 548–573.

Weiner, B. (1986). *An Attributional Theory of Motivation and Emotion.* New York: Springer-Verlag.

Wirth, W. & Schramm, H. (2005). Media and Emotions. *A Quarterly Review of Communication Research*, 24:3, 3–39.

Young, D.G. (2008). The Privileged Role of the Late-Night Joke: Exploring Humor's Role in Disrupting Argument Scrutiny. *Media Psychology*, 11:1, 119–142.

Chapter 9

Firm Disclosure, Media, and the Capital Markets

Doron Kliger* and Smadar Siev†

Abstract

Timely and accurate corporate information is essential for financial market efficiency. Decreasing information asymmetry between insiders and the public contributes to better investment decisions. Numerous studies examined the extent to which asset prices change in response to the arrival of new information in the market. Here we portray the picture that emerges from literature regarding the impact of information on cost of equity, liquidity, and trading volume. We focus on the source of information (firm disclosure vs. external entities), and we differentiate between pricing-relevant and pricing-irrelevant information (the former is related to a firm's future prospects) and between hard and soft information. Further, we refer to the impact of news stories depending on their sentiment, and we examine the impact of printed publications versus online media. We also discuss the mere effect of the amount of disseminated information, regardless of its content.

Keywords: Firm disclosure, media coverage, social media publications, stock prices, stock returns, hard and soft information, sentiment, capital markets

JEL Classification: G14, M4

Introduction

Conventionally, the demand for a firm's disclosure stems from information asymmetry between insiders and the public. Timely and accurate corporate information is essential for market efficiency. It enhances transparency and decreases information asymmetry, thereby contributing to improved

*University of Haifa, Department of Economics

†Carmel Academic Center, School for Business & Management

investment decisions. Nowadays, investors are exposed, more than ever, to an enormous amount of public information. We focus on several characteristics, the first of which is the source of information. We differentiate between information that is supplied and controlled by the firm (disclosure), such as financial reports, and information published by entities external to the firm, such as media coverage, analyst reports, and free information on the web.

The information that arrives in the market can be characterized in additional ways: (i) pricing-relevant information, which is related to a firm's future prospects, such as agreements with customers, and pricing-irrelevant information, which does not shed light in this regard, such as a firm's participation in sports events; (ii) hard information, which is quantitative in nature and can be easily assimilated in the firm's earning forecast such as the volume of orders, and soft information, which is qualitative and hard to quantify such as the addition of new features to products; (iii) the tone or sentiment of news stories, namely whether the news is positive or negative; (iv) whether the disclosure is mandatory or voluntary; and (v) whether the information appears in printed publications versus online media. We also discuss the mere effect of the amount of information disseminated by the firm and the media, regardless of its content.

Numerous studies have attempted to examine the extent to which asset prices change in response to the arrival of new information in the market. Here, we portray the picture that emerges from literature regarding disclosure and media coverage, as well as the characterization of the information, as mentioned above, and the impact of these factors on stock prices. We also address other factors attributable to capital markets, such as liquidity, volatility, and trading volume. The paper is organized as follows: the first part reviews the effects of public disclosure; the second part focuses on information published by entities external to the firm; and the third part offers a conclusion.

1. Effects of Public Disclosure

A firm's public disclosure of information may be classified into two types: mandatory and voluntary. Mandatory disclosure, required by legislation, (such as financial reports) refers to material information that might impact the firm's share price.[1] Voluntary disclosure, which is subject to the firm's discretion, (such as earnings guidelines) refers to other types of information. This discretionary information is potentially valuable to investors because it may facilitate understanding of the business environment and the forecast for future prospects. While investors may benefit from additional disclosure, superfluous disclosure might harm the firm by revealing commercial secrets to its competitors. As a result, firms have to disclose with caution and discretion.

Discussion about a firm's disclosure and its impact on stock prices would not be complete without pointing out some managerial motivation for disclosure. In the next section, we describe two theoretical streams regarding the relationship between disclosure and cost of capital, and some related empirical studies. Because of the natural relationship between cost of capital and liquidity, we will mention some studies that deal with the relationship between disclosure and liquidity. We close this section with an example from the recent growing literature on textual analysis of news stories and the effect of such soft information on the firm's financial reports.

Managerial motivation for disclosure

A firm's management is obligated to disclose all substantial information that might affect trading decisions. The managers' motivation to increase voluntary disclosure may stem from their perception of the stock mispricing. They reveal "good news" to correct undervalued stocks (Verrecchia, 1983 and 1990). Managers also tend to increase disclosure to correct overpriced stocks. In such scenarios, they will disclose bad news to avoid potential lawsuits and enhance their credibility (Skinner, 1994). This provides investors with the rationale for employing the disclosed information to assess firm value.

Lang and Lundholm (2000) suggested that firms intentionally increase the level of disclosure in order to "hype the stock" and lower the firm's

[1] The Regulation Fair Disclosure requirement mandates companies to disclose all material information simultaneously to all investors. This regulation was adopted by the Securities and Exchange Commission (SEC) to prevent selective disclosure by firms. The regulator's goal was to eliminate selective disclosure to certain preferred analysts and institutional investors before exposing that information to the public.

cost of equity capital. They examined disclosure activity around seasonal equity offerings and found that firms that dramatically increased disclosure activity during the six months before the issuance, particularly in the categories of disclosure over which firms have the most discretion, enjoyed increases in their stock prices prior to the offering. However, these firms' stock prices experienced a large decline when the market revealed their intention to issue. Thus the market may have somewhat corrected the initial increase.

Fisman and Hagerty (1989) showed that theoretically, an increase in the efficiency of stock pricing might induce managers to make more efficient investment decisions. Achieving such efficiency gives firms the motivation to increase voluntary disclosure, which would belie the regulator's concern regarding not enough disclosure. Since the firms also compete for the attention of traders, the more informative the firm's disclosure, the more profitable it is for the traders to learn about and trade the firm's stock.

Disclosure level and cost of capital

Two streams of theoretical research support the hypothesis that greater disclosure is associated with lower cost of capital. The first stream suggests that greater disclosure increases liquidity, thus reducing the cost of equity capital through the reduction of transaction costs. The second stream suggests that greater disclosure may reduce the estimation risk attributed when determining the asset return parameters or the distribution of the firm's future free cash flows.

Regarding the first stream, Diamond and Verrecchia (1991) discussed the contribution of market makers to trading volume and their effect on stock prices. Their model suggests a negative correlation between disclosure and cost of capital. When firms disclose, the information asymmetry between them and market participants is reduced. This in turn may increase demand and reduce the cost of capital. The authors differentiate between small and large firms. Institutional investors are usually interested in stocks of large firms. The larger the firm is, the larger the reduction in cost of equity capital. If initial information asymmetry is large, reducing it will increase the current price of the security. However, the maximum price occurs with some asymmetry of information. Further, reduction of information asymmetry will stress the undesirable effect of exit from "market making", which reduces liquidity. Amihud and Mendelson (1986) suggested that the larger the bid-ask spread is, the larger the cost of capital, because investors request higher returns as compensation for the added transaction cost. Disclosing information helps firms to reduce the bid-ask spread and so reduce the cost of equity capital.

Regarding the second stream, Barry and Brown (1985) showed that securities for which there is relatively little information have relatively higher systematic risk when that risk is properly measured. As more information becomes available concerning a security, that information leads to lower estimation risk and to convergent expectations on the part of all observers. Handa and Linn (1993) established a linear relationship between expected return and the estimation risk. While this risk cannot be diversified away, it is not fully reflected in the betas, because they are not always assessed correctly.

Numerous empirical findings support the abovementioned theoretical claim that increased disclosure is associated with lower cost of equity capital (Botosan, 1997; Froidevaux, 2004; Siev, 2014), while others disprove it (Healy, Hutton and Palepu, 1999). Yet other studies demonstrate mixed results (Botosan and Plumlee, 2001; Kothari and Short, 2003). Note that the empirical literature faced a major challenge in that disclosure level is difficult to quantify. Botosan (1997) used a self-constructed gauge that was based on data items taken from financial reports. Miller (1999) constructed his own gauge based on the financial press and categorized disclosures according to their content. Lang and Lundholm (1996), Healy *et al.* (1999), and Botosan and Plumlee (2001) used the disclosure score given by the AIMR-FAF.[2] Kothary and Short (2003) sampled disclosures from various sources, such as SEC reports, financial press, and analyst reports, and then classified disclosure as favorable or unfavorable. Another disclosure measurement was introduced by Schrand and Verrecchia (2004), who classified disclosure as informative or uninformative according to its content.

A negative correlation between disclosure and cost of equity capital was found by Botosan (1997), who checked disclosure in annual financial

[2]AIMR-FAF is the Association for Investment Management Research Financial Analysts Federation.

reports and found that the relationship exists only for firms with low analyst coverage. Froidevaux (2004) also found a negative relationship between disclosure level on the companies' web sites (the investor relations section) and their cost of capital, implied in stock price. Schrand and Verrecchia (2004) argued that disclosure can reduce information asymmetry and showed that greater disclosure frequency is associated with the reduction of underpricing in initial public offerings (IPOs).

Healy *et al.* (1999) noted a positive relation between disclosure level and cost of equity capital. They found that firms with large and continuous increase in their voluntary disclosure enjoyed increased stock returns during the year of the increased disclosure and during the year after, as well as enhanced institutional ownership and analyst coverage, increased stock liquidity, and an increase in raising debt and equity.

Mixed results were found by Botosan and Plumlee (2001), who used the AIMR-FAF grade as their proxy for disclosure level. They found that the relationship between disclosure and cost of equity capital depended on the disclosure type. Specifically, increased disclosure in annual reports decreased the cost of capital, while increased disclosure in the quarterly financial reports and other voluntary disclosure increased it. Investor relations activities did not affect the cost of equity capital.

Kothari and Short (2003) also found mixed results regarding the relationship between disclosure and cost of equity capital. They distinguished disclosure by its source — the firm, analyst reports, or financial press — and classified the disclosure as favorable or unfavorable. Generally, favorable disclosure decreased cost of equity capital and stock volatility, while unfavorable disclosure increased them. When the source of the disclosure was the firm, the market discounted good (favorable) news, and the cost of equity capital did not change significantly. However, bad (unfavorable) news increased the cost of equity capital. Disclosure that was published in the financial press had the strongest effect on the cost of equity capital.

Press releases and cost of capital

One popular and common way for a firm to publicize its news is a press release (PR). The annual number of PRs varies substantially among firms, from a handful to hundreds per year. Regarding the latter, the question is do firms have informative news on a daily basis or does the high frequency of PR streaming may merely aim to enhance the firm's presence and prominence in the mind of the investors. Note that some of these PRs contain pricing irrelevant information. While reading a PR, one should keep in mind that a company' interest is to present past performance and future plans in a positive light.

This observation is of special importance, given that PRs are not directly subject to third-party scrutiny. Siev (2014) documented a gap in stock returns between firms that publish low and high numbers of PRs per annum (LPR and HPR, respectively), in favor of the former.[3] This gap (PR premium) was found for both the year of the PR publication and the following year, and its magnitude was 7–8% and 5–6%, respectively. The analysis also indicated that the average daily trading volume of HPR firms was three times higher than that of LPR firms. The difference in trading supports the notion that perceived company image can bias and boost financial trading activity. Applying the same logic, firms that produce a much smaller volume of annual PRs garner less public attention, which leads to underpricing and can ultimately yield higher returns.

The willingness of investors to be compensated with lower returns and the high trading volume of HPR firms' stocks can be explained using behavioral finance arguments. As psychology affects the behavior of market participants, not all decision-making is rational. Using PRs may be a sophisticated way to interrelate with the public. The bottom line of this research is that the PR volume may be an important factor in calculating future return.

Solomon (2012) examined how media coverage of a firm's PR, which is promoted by Investor Relation (IR) companies, affects stock prices and returns.[4] Solomon's findings indicated that IR firms use their relationships with reporters at local newspapers to selectively promote media coverage of their clients' positive PRs relative to their negative PRs. Since most of the PRs

---

[3]See Siev's dissertation (referenced herein), completed under the supervision of Kliger.

[4]An investor relations company serves as a bridge between a firm's clients and the community of investors. Its role is to communicate the firm's relevant information. This information helps investors to make informed decisions.

contain soft information (as opposed to financial statements, which contain hard information), the IR companies are able to spin their clients' news, supplying a particular interpretation of a vague news events. This positive media coverage increases investors' expectations of future profitability, temporarily increasing stock prices, and therefore returns, around time of the news publication. However, the pattern of excessively positive media coverage cannot be repeated around the time of (negative) earning announcements (when IR firms cannot spin the news), and therefore subsequent lower returns occur around the earning announcement.

Disclosure and liquidity

According to Amihud and Mendelson (1986), there is a negative association between disclosure levels and bid-ask spreads. Welker (1995) documented this relationship empirically and concluded that a firm's disclosure policy can reduce information asymmetry, which in turn enhances liquidity and the firm's value. Leuz & Verrecchia (2000) found that trading volume increased as the level of disclosure increased. This finding is consistent with the theory that firms with high levels of disclosure attract more investors because investors can be confident the stocks are traded at fair prices. They also documented that a firm's commitment to an increased level of disclosure was associated with a lower bid-ask spread and higher share turnover. And as mentioned above, Siev (2014) documented that the trading volume of firms who distributed a high number of PRs was three times higher than that of firms who distributed a low number of PRs.

Hard and soft information disclosure

A firm's earning announcements are probably among the most important and awaited disclosures, with potentially considerable impact on stock prices. They usually evoke high interest among investors and are targeted in analyst forecasts. Alongside the financial statements themselves (the hard information), the management's common practice is to publish additional and complementary information. Demers and Vega (2010) conducted an advanced textual analysis of quarterly earnings announcements to examine whether, and under which conditions, soft information embedded in financial reports affected the dynamics of stock prices. They constructed two quantitative measures of soft information: a proxy for management net optimism and a proxy for certainty. Their findings show that, on average, net optimism affected asset prices within the earning announcement event window for up to sixty trading days after the announcement. Demers and Vega also found that net optimism had the greatest impact on asset prices when the certainty of the information was larger. In terms of volatility, the level of uncertainty was inversely related to the idiosyncratic volatility during the announcement and also to the abnormal volatility during the post-announcement period.

2. Media Publications and Capital Markets

In addition to the public disclosure of information by the firms, discussed in the previous section, information related to firms is disseminated by the general and financial press, either online or in print. The additional information includes analyst recommendations, rating agency reports, and the like.

Most research on media and its effect on the capital markets relates to the overall impact of news stories, rather than the impact of a specific event on stock prices. In addition, most of the newspaper articles are qualitative (soft) in nature (as opposed to hard information contained in financial reports). The articles may convey positive information, implying the management's credibility and reducing uncertainty about the firm's products and markets, or they may convey negative information, such as legal actions taken against the company or the loss of market share. For these reasons, most studies analyzing media coverage did not deal with the informational content, but rather attempted to characterize their sentiment via textual analysis. The first subsection will focus on this research.

While the sentiment itself is important, it does not contain the informational content of the text. In order to give some consideration to the content, some researchers analyzed the sentiment conveyed in fundamental news, such as the financial report. We will discuss some examples of this research in the second subsection.

Research on media coverage and textual analysis rarely discusses how informative the text is. Most of them seem to assume that the content is informative. In the third subsection, we discuss if and how non-informative announcements affect asset prices, as well as how the mere amount of information, regardless of its specification, may affect asset prices. We close the review with research focused on information on the web.

Textual Analysis

The aim of textual analysis is to provide a quantitative measure characterizing the degree of a text's positivity or negativity. The analysis is based on counting the positive and negative words embedded in a text and grading its tone (sentiment) according to their relative frequency. Most studies of textual analysis build such a proxy and studied its relationship to the capital market. The underlined word list, and application of textual analysis vary among researches.

Studies have found a positive correlation between the tone of the text and its effect on pricing, returns, and trading volumes. For example, Kothari and Short (2003) found that generally favorable text decreased cost of equity capital and stock volatility, while unfavorable news increased them. Tetlock (2007) and Tetlock, Saar-Tsechansky, and Macskassy (2008) focused only on the effect of the negativity conveyed in media news stories on daily stock returns and trading volumes. Tetlock (2007) found that high levels of media pessimism predicted downward pressure on market prices. The negative returns following the negative sentiment reversed over the next few days of market activity. Furthermore, the price impact of pessimism appeared especially large and slow to reverse itself in small stocks. In addition, unusually high or low values of media pessimism forecasted high market trading volume. Tetlock *et al.* (2008) found that the negativity proxy had predictive power, although very small, for negative returns and abnormal returns one day after the publication.

The majority of textual analysis research focused on the United States stock market. Unique in this regard was the work of Ferguson *et al.* (2015), who conducted textual analysis research focused on the United Kingdom market. Their main finding was that tone had a significant impact on the next day's returns and abnormal returns. Specifically, positive (negative) tone had a positive (negative) effect on the next trading day's returns and abnormal returns. In more specific analysis, it was found that the effect of tone was significant only among companies with low visibility.[5] Initial price pressure on the day of the news story did not show significant evidence of reversal in the following trading week. Ferguson *et al.* (2015) assumed that if investors react more to prominent stocks, then the combined effect of tone and volume of media coverage should increase market reactions. They found that the impact was higher for firms with high media coverage but only for positive tone and only on the next day's abnormal returns.

Semi-strong market efficiency maintains that market prices adjust themselves with the arrival of new public information. Consequently, Boudoukh *et al.* (2012) focused on identifying the new information and studied to what extent it affect stock prices. In their study, each day was classified into: day without news coverage, day with unidentified (irrelevant) or identified (relevant) news. Advanced[6] textual analysis was performed only for identified days with new information. Interestingly, 57% of the trading days were days without news, and identified news appeared only on 13% of the total days. Roll (1988) argued that once the market's overall effect is removed from a given stock return, the remaining variation is attributed and idiosyncratic to that firm. Therefore, on days without news, R^2s should be much higher in contrast to R^2s of relevant news days. The authors' first findings validate Rolls (1988) argument. With tone as an explanatory variable, R^2 increased on days with identified news, meaning that tone was relevant. Stock volatility was similar in days without news and in unidentified news days. In contrast, on days with identified news, the volatility increased twofold.

Media coverage of earning announcements

Usually earning announcements of firms are emphasized by the media. Most studies found that the accompanying media coverage has an additional impact on stock prices. For example, Dyck and Zingales (2003) found that stock prices were most reactive to the type of earnings emphasized by

---

[5]Small companies and companies with a high book to market ratio are considered to have low visibility.

[6]The advanced text analysis was based on the TSS application. In addition to the common negative and positive word count, the application also analyzes the sentence patterns for more accurate characterization of the tone.

the press. The effect was stronger for companies with fewer analysts and when the media outlet was more credible. Ferguson *et al.* (2015) examined the effect of tone in media stories on stock's abnormal returns, following the publication of financial statements. Significance was found only for negative tone among medium-size firms. It seems that the market discounts the good news as was found in Kothary and Short (2003). Engelberg and Parsons (2011) found that local media coverage of earnings announcements strongly predicted local trading of these stocks. In comparing the effect of media coverage on the stock price in emerging and developing markets around the world, Griffin, Hirschey and Kelly (2011) found the greatest impact among the most developed markets. In contrast, in many emerging markets, the stock return volatility on the news days was similar to the volatility on non-news days. As to the earning forecast, Tetlock *et al.* (2008) found that negativity in fundamental news stories had statistically significant predictive power of quarterly earnings surprise and analysts forecast errors.

Analyst reports and stock prices

Recommendations of analysts with Wall Street brokerage houses are of interest to the investor community. These analyst reports and buy-and-sell recommendations receive extensive media coverage. Numerous studies document their influence on the stock market. Barber and Loeffler (1993) found that analyst recommendations triggered abnormal trading volume on the date the recommendation was published and positive abnormal return on the two days following the publication. The return was partly reversed within twenty-five trading days. The authors concluded that the permanent price change suggested that the analyst recommendations revealed relevant information for fundamental revaluation of the security. Stickel (1995) found that brokerage house recommendations affected stock prices. Specifically, sell (buy) recommendations were associated with price decline (increase). The magnitude of the price changes, which appeared to be a permanent effect of the information, was found to depend on the strength of the recommendation, the magnitude of the recommendation's change, and same-sign revisions in earnings forecasts. Stickel's finding that recommendations explained only a small part of the abnormal return is in line with his conclusion that this "is exactly what one should expect in an almost efficient capital market."

A textual analysis of analyst reports conducted by Kothari and Short (2003) found that analyst reports did not affect the cost of equity capital regardless of whether their tone was positive or negative. Loh and Stulz (2011) investigated whether changes in analyst recommendations affected stock abnormal return and turnover. They found that about 12% of recommendation changes were influential in returns and about 13% were influential in turnover. Stock volatility and turnover were much larger in the three months after an influential analyst change than in the preceding three months. The authors concluded that although the majority of recommendations were uninformative, analysts add value to financial markets because they produce influential recommendations.

Brown, Wei, and Wermers (2013) found that a change in the analyst consensus induced mutual fund managers to trade in line with the recommendation. This trade led to significant same-quarter price impact, followed by a sharp subsequent price reversal. They concluded that "this type of trading has become price destabilizing with the increasing level of mutual fund ownership of stocks."

Non-informative information and the amount of information *per se*

Most research did not examine how informative the news stories were, but merely studied their tone. The implicit assumption derived from these analyses is that the sentiment affects stock prices regardless of how informative the news story is. Literature findings demonstrate that non-informative information affects prices, as does the sheer amount of information, regardless of its content.

Corget, Sutan, and Ashta (2006) examined non-informative information. The authors attempted to explore whether central banks or other sources that are perceived as "financial gurus" could manipulate asset prices and affect market stability or stock market bubbles by sending non-informative announcements to investors. The conclusion of the authors' experiment was that asset prices strongly reacted to non-informative information, even if the sender's credibility was low and the information was not accurate. However, it was not always possible to determine the direction of the influence. They also found that if the sender of the information was more credible, the effect on price was bigger.

The effect of the volume of media coverage on stock returns was analyzed by Fang and Peress (2009). The authors built a proxy for the magnitude of media coverage in the US stock market. They found that a portfolio of stocks not covered by the media outperformed a portfolio of stocks with high media coverage by 3% per year following portfolio formation. In addition, the difference in the return was particularly large among small stocks, stocks with low analyst coverage, and stocks primarily owned by individuals. In their view, the "no media premium" may stem from limitations on trade or compensation for little or lack of information. The findings of Ferguson *et al.* (2015) followed a similar direction: the volume of media coverage had a significant negative effect on the next day's excess return for big companies.

Free information on the web

Traditional news channel platforms like financial press or analyst reports are characterize by a relatively small number of writers. The number of individual free writers on the web is much larger. These writers spend a considerable amount of time and effort creating posts on stock message boards and crafting opinions transmitted through social media outlets. The readership of these publications amounts to hundreds of thousands per day, and their popularity continues to increase. Researchers have wondered whether these messages and articles contain economically relevant information. Specifically, they studied whether there is a relationship between the number of posts/articles and their characteristics, such as sentiment, bullishness, or disagreement, and the capital market variables, including stock returns, trading volume, and volatility.

One of the earliest studies of Internet stock message boards was that of Wysocki (1998), who examined the firms whose stocks received the highest volume of posted messages. Wysocki found that the most attention-grabbing firms were characterized by extreme returns, high or low; high market value; high price- to-earnings ratio; high book-to-market ratio; high volatility; high trading volume; and high analyst coverage.

As to the effect of the number of posts, the results were mixed. Wysocki (1998) found that an increase in messages posted overnight led to positive abnormal returns and an increase in trading volume the next day, while Antweiler and Frank (2004) found that when many messages were posted on a given day, there was a negative return on the next day. This return is very small when one considers transaction costs. Das and Chen (2007) found a negative correlation between changes in the amount of messages and changes in the contemporaneous stock prices.

Regarding differing opinions among the posted messages, Antweiler and Frank (2004) found that disagreement was associated with more trades, especially for small transactions. However, there was a reversal on the next day. Namely, greater disagreement on one day predicted fewer trades on the next day, not more trades. Das and Chen (2007) found that there was no correlation between levels of disagreement and changes in volatility or stock prices. In addition, they found that sentiment on a given day had a weak effect on the next day's stock prices.

Internet message boards are, by design, open, unstructured, and characterized by very short posts. In contrast, social media platforms are characterized by more lengthy articles. These articles are generally reviewed by a panel and subject to editors' changes. The goal of these websites is to provide venues where private investors can express their opinions and share the results of their own financial analysis with peers. In response to these articles, interested followers can write commentary and share their own views on the company in question, affirming or refuting the opinion of the author.

Chen *et al.* (2014) estimated the negativity tone in articles that were published at a popular social media outlet and the reader responses to these articles. They found that the views expressed in both articles and commentaries predicted future stock returns for a period of three months after publication. In addition, negativity expressed in the articles and commentaries strongly predicted earnings surprises. In cases where the tone of the comments disagreed with the basic tone of the article, the tone of the comments more reliably predicted the stock market's performance.

Another analysis of the wisdom of the crowd was conducted by Bagnoli *et al.* (1999), who compared Wall Street analysts' forecasts of quarterly earnings to informal earnings forecasts voluntary posted by private investors (called whispers). The researchers found that whisper forecasts tended to be more accurate than the analysts' forecasts. That is, the whisper forecast error was typically smaller. Interestingly, analysts' forecast errors were positive (which means that the analysts' forecast was lower than the actual earnings per share) and the whisper forecast errors were negative. This finding shows that the analysts underestimated and the whispers had more optimism regarding earnings.

3. Summary

Theoretical research supports a negative relationship between disclosure level and the cost of equity capital, but empirical research presents mixed findings, depending on factors such as the sentiment of the disclosure, the type of disclosure, and accompanying analyst coverage. However, disclosure volume was found to be an important factor in explaining stock returns.

Conclusions from research on media publications and their impact on the capital markets should be drawn keeping several considerations in mind. First, many of the news stories are based on preceding firms' disseminated disclosures and therefore are not new information, though they are often accompanied by comparing and complementary information, interpretations, and insight. In addition, several published articles are merely replications of other previously published articles. As a result, the effect on stock prices should be traced back to two possible sources: information (news) and behavior (e.g., attention). Second, despite vast media coverage of firms' activities, the number of firms that are thoroughly covered by the press is relatively low. Fang and Peress (2009) made an important distinction between the magnitude of media coverage of NASDAQ and NYSE firms: "First, overall newspaper coverage is surprisingly low. Even among NYSE stocks, which are generally large, over 25% are not featured in press in a typical year. Coverage is even lower for NASDAQ stocks, which only 42% of them receive coverage in a given year. . . but the coverage statistics generally are three to four times larger for NYSE stocks than those for NASDAQ stocks". Similar findings regarding media coverage were reported by Siev (2014), in terms of the press releases of 500 firms whose stocks were traded on NASDAQ and NYSE from 2001 to 2007. As much as 81% of the sample firms had fewer than five media articles per year. The average annual number of PRs was roughly ten times higher than the average annual number of media articles.

In addition to the well-known proven effect of new information on stock prices, the aforementioned research also indicates the behavioral effect of firms receiving attention. Media coverage (which may not necessarily offer new information), the volume of posts, and the sentiment provoked by opinion columns in the mainstream financial press and free online platforms all were found to affect subsequent trading and as a result affect stock prices. Barber and Odean (2009) argued that individual investors (as opposed to institutional and professional investors) decide which stock to buy from a choice set that they construct from attention-grabbing stocks. Shares on the news grab investors' attention. It was found that the implied sentiment in these news stories/posts/articles contain valuable information that, as of the date of publication, was not fully reflected in the stock prices.

To summarize, multiple factors are known to explain stock returns. Risk, firm size, momentum, and book-to-market ratio are all well-documented examples. The research described above demonstrates that disclosure level, disclosure volume, media coverage volume, and the sentiment conveyed by news stories, including free information on the web, are other possible factors that explain stock returns.

References

Amihud, Y., & Mendelson, H. (1986). Asset Pricing and the Bid-Ask Spread. *Journal of Financial Economics*, 17, 223–249.

Antweiler, W., & Frank, M. Z. (2004). Is All That Talk Just Noise? The Information Content of Internet Stock Message Boards. *Journal of Finance*, 59, 1259–1293.

Bagnoli, M., Beneish, M.D., & Watts, S. G. (1999). Whisper Forecasts of Quarterly Earnings Per Share. *Journal of Accounting and Economics*, 28(1) 27–50.

Barber, B. M., & Odean, T. (2008). All That Glitters: The Effect of Attention and News on the Buying Behavior of Individual and Institutional Investors. *Review of Financial Studies*, 21(2), 785–818.

Barber, B. M., & Loeffler, D. (1993). The "Dartboard" Column: Second-Hand Information and Price Pressure. *Journal of Financial and Quantitative Analysis*, 28(02), 273–284.

Barry, C. B., & Brown, S. J. (1985). Differential Information and Security Market Equilibrium. *Journal of Financial and Quantitative Analysis*, 20(04), 407–422.

Botosan, C. (1997). Disclosure Level and the Cost of Equity Capital. *The Accounting Review*, 72(3), 323–350.

Botosan, C., & Plumlee, M. (2001). A Re-examination of Disclosure Level and the Expected Cost of Equity Capital. *Journal of Accounting Research*, 21–40.

Boudoukh, J., Feldman, R., Kogan, S., & Richardson, M. (2012). Which News Moves Stock Prices?A Textual Analysis. *National Bureau of Economic Research*, No. w18725.

Brown, N. C., Wei, K. D., & Wermers, R. (2013). Analyst Recommendations, Mutual Fund Herding, and Overreaction in Stock Prices. *Management Science*, 60(1), 1–20.

Chen, H., De, P., Hu, Y. J., & Hwang, B. H. (2014). Wisdom of Crowds: The Value of Stock Opinions Transmitted through Social Media. *Review of Financial Studies*, *27*(5), 1367–1403.

Corget, B., Sutan, A., & Ashta, A. (2006). The Power of Words in Financial Markets. Paper provided by University of Siena in its series Labsi Experimental Economics Laboratory University of Siena.

Das, S. R., & Chen, M. Y. (2007). Yahoo! For Amazon: Sentiment Extraction from Small Talk on the Web. *Management Science*, 53, 1375–1388.

Diamond, D., & Verrecchia, R. (1991). Disclosure, Liquidity and the Cost of Equity Capital. *Journal of Finance.*

Demers, E., & Vega, C. (2010). Soft Information in Earnings Announcements: News or Noise? Federal Reserve Board.

Dyck, A., & Zingales, L. (2003). The Media and Asset Prices. Working paper, Harvard Business School.

Engelberg, J. E., & Parsons, C. A. (2011). The Causal Impact of Media in Financial Markets. *The Journal of Finance*, 66(1), 67–97.

Fang, L., & Peress, J., (2009). Media Coverage and the Cross-Section of Stock Returns. *The Journal of Finance*, Vol. LXIV, No. 5.

Ferguson, N. J., Philip, D., Lam, H. Y. T., & Guo, M. (2015). Media Content and Stock Returns: The Predictive Power of Press. *Multinational Finance Journal*, 19(1), 1–31.

Fishman, M., & Hagerty, K. (1989). Disclosure Decisions by Firms and the Competition for Price Efficiency. *The Journal of Finance.*

Froidevaux, E. A. (2004). Investor relation internet disclosure and the cost of equity capital (Doctoral dissertation, Université de Fribourg).

Griffin, J. M., Hirschey, N. H., & Kelly, P. J. (2011). How Important Is the Financial Media in Global Markets? *Review of Financial Studies*, hhr099.

Handa, P., & Linn, S. C. (1993). Arbitrage Pricing with Estimation Risk. *Journal of Financial and Quantitative Analysis*, 28(01), 81–100.

Healy, P. M., Hutton, A. P., & Palepu, K. G. (1999). Stock Performance and Intermediation Change Surrounding Sustained Increase in Disclosure. *Contemporary Accounting Research*, 485–518.

Healy, P. M., & Palepu, K. G. (2001). Information Asymmetry, Corporate Disclosure, and the Capital Markets: A Review of the Empirical Disclosure Literature. *Journal of Accounting and Economics*, 31(1), 405–440.

Kothari, S. P., Short, J. (2003). The Effect of Disclosure by Management, Analysts, and Financial Press on the Equity Cost of Capital. eBusiness@MIT.

Lang, M. H., & Lundholm, R. J. (1996). Corporate Disclosure Policy and Analyst Behavior. *Accounting Review*, 467–492.

Lang, M., & Lundholm R. (2000). Voluntary Disclosure and Equity Offerings: Reducing Information Asymmetry or Hyping the Stock? *Contemporary Accounting Research*, 17(4), 623–662.

Leuz, C., Verrecchia, R. (2000). The Economic Consequences of Increased Disclosure. *Journal of Accounting Research*, 38: 91–124.

Loh, R. K., & Stulz, R. M. (2011). When Are Analyst Recommendation Changes Influential? *Review of Financial Studies*, 24(2), 593–627.

Miller, G. (1999). Financial Statement Disclosures for Hong Kong H-Shares: Purposes, Subject and Number. *Asian Review of Accounting*, *7*(1), 1–19.

Roll, R., 1988, R2, Journal of Finance 43, 541–566.

Siev, S. (2014). The PR Premium. *Journal of Behavioral Finance*, 15(1), 43–55.

Schrand, C., Verrecchia, E. R. (2004). Disclosure Choice and the Cost of Capital: Evidence from Under Pricing in IPO. Working paper series, www.ssrn.com.

Skinner, D. J. (1994). Why Firms Voluntarily Disclose Bad News. *Journal of Accounting Research*, 38–60.

Solomon, D. H. (2012). Selective Publicity and Stock Prices. *The Journal of Finance*, 67(2), 599–638.

Stickel, S. E. (1995). The Anatomy of Buy and Sell Recommendations. *Financial Analysts Journal*, 51, 25–39

Tetlock, P. C. (2007). Giving Content to Investor Sentiment: The Role of Media in the Stock Market. *Journal of Finance*, 62, 1139–1168.

Tetlock, P. C., Saar-Tsechansky, M., & Macskassy, S. (2008). More than Words: Quantifying Language to Measure Firms' Fundamentals. *Journal of Finance*, 63, 1437–1467.

Verrecchia, R. (1983). Discretionary Disclosure. *Journal of Accounting and Economics*, 5(1), 179.

Verrecchia, R. E. (1990). Information Quality and Discretionary Disclosure. *Journal of Accounting and Economics*, 12(4), 365–380.

Welker, M. (1995). Disclosure Policy, Information Asymmetry and Liquidity in Equity Markets. *Contemporary Accounting Research*, 11, 801–828.

Wysocki, P. (1998). Cheap Talk on the Web: The Determinants of Postings on Stock Message Boards. Working Paper 98025, University of Michigan Business School.

Xiao-Xuan, Y. (2013). The Market Reaction to Stock Splits Used As Dividends. *Technology and Investment*, 4(1), 42.

Part V

Heuristics and Experiments in Finance

Chapter 10

Heuristics and Biases in the Israeli Mortgage Market

Moran Ofir*, Yevgeny Mugerman† and Zvi Wiener‡

Abstract

This research examines the three seminal heuristics that are employed in decision-making under uncertainty: availability; representativeness; and anchoring and adjustment; and their appearance in the Israeli mortgage market. We argue that the standard economic criteria are sometimes inadequate to explain household's choices, which may be motivated by heuristic principles which reduce the complex task of choosing a mortgage. More specifically, we focus on the households' choice between fixed rate mortgages (FRM) and adjustable rate mortgages (ARM). We empirically examine the effect of these heuristics on the decision between ARM and FRM using a unique data provided to us by the Bank of Israel, which contains detailed information on the household's decision between fixed and adjustable rate mortgage contracts in Israel in the past decade. The results of our analysis demonstrate a significant effect of availability and representativeness heuristics on households' decision. In addition, we show that regulatory provisions regarding the loan division between FRM and ARM may serve as a possible anchor to the borrowers.

Keywords: Heuristics and biases, mortgage decision making, household finance, adjustable and fixed rate mortgages

JEL Classification: D10, D14, G21, R2

*Radzyner School of Law, Interdisciplinary Center (IDC), Herzliya; mofir@idc.ac.il.

†Finance Department, School of Business Administration, The Hebrew University of Jerusalem; The Federmann Center for the Study of Rationality; and COLMAN; mugi@huji.ac.il.

‡Finance Department, School of Business Administration, The Hebrew University of Jerusalem; zvi.wiener@huji.ac.il.

1. Introduction

This paper examines the three seminal heuristics that are employed in decision making under uncertainty described in Tversky and Kahneman (1974) and their appearance in the Israeli mortgage market. The three heuristics are: (i) representativeness, which is usually employed when decision makers are asked to judge that an event belongs to class of events; (ii) availability, which is often employed when decision makers are asked to assess the plausibility of a particular development; and (iii) anchoring and adjustment, which is usually employed when an initial value to some aspects of the decision is available.

Since, housing is the most important asset in the portfolio of most households, the effect of each individual heuristic may lead decision makers to systematic errors which, in turn, can cause a substantive loss of economic value. A better understanding of the effect of these heuristics on mortgage borrowers' decisions can improve the design of market reforms in this area in order to maximize market efficiency and to minimize households' economic loss.

There is mounting of theoretical literature focusing on determining what factors contribute to the optimal choice in housing finance. Most of them examining the decision between Fixed Rate Mortgages (FRM) and Adjustable Rate Mortgages (ARM). Researchers have found that the relative attractiveness of a specific type of contract should depend on individual circumstances, such as the borrower's income, borrowing constraints, the probability of pre-paying the loans, and on macro-economic measures such as inflation of housing prices (Baesel and Biger, 1980; Statman, 1982; Alm and Follain, 1984; Stanton and Wallace, 1999; and Koijen *et al.*, 2009).

Despite it, there is little empirical evidence about the optimality of mortgage decision making. Campbell and Cocco (2003) show that mortgage borrowers sub-optimally choose between ARM and FRM contracts. Campbell (2006) use the American Housing Survey to show evidence that mortgage borrowers make several mistakes that leads to important implications for equilibrium in the mortgage market. Agarwal, Rosen and Yao (2012) show that mortgage borrowers sub-optimally refinance their mortgage and Agarwal, Ben-David and Yao (2014) show that mortgage borrowers exhibit the sunk cost fallacy.

In this paper we focus on the behavioral aspects of housing finance decisions. Understanding the mechanism through which these decisions are made is very significant in terms of housing in general and mortgage market implications in particular.

More specifically, we focus on the decision of homeowners to choose between fixed rate mortgages (FRM) and adjustable rate mortgages (ARM). Making the decision between FRM and ARM is difficult for most home owners, many of whom lack formal economic education or knowledge and are not sophisticated finance decision makers or mortgage borrowers.

Decisions about housing finance are based on beliefs concerning uncertain events which are employed to assess probabilities and to predict values. Tversky and Kahneman's (1974) seminal paper found that decision makers rely on a limited number of heuristic principles which reduce the complex task of assessing probabilities and predicting values to simpler judgmental operations. In general, these heuristics are useful, but can also lead to systematic errors. In our setting, an implication of these heuristics on making the decision between FRM and ARM can explain our empirical findings.

When faced with the difficult task of choosing between FRM and ARM (usually not having previous experience, and relevant knowledge), individuals employ a limited number of heuristics to simplify this decision. We hypothesize that decision makers are bounded by the *availability* of information the market provides through its general media and judging this information by its *representativeness.* Moreover they may be influenced by *anchoring and adjustment* taking into account regulation provisions limiting the ARM/FRM share out of the entire loan.

We tested the effect of these three heuristics using unique data provided to us by the Bank of Israel (Israel's central bank) which contains information on the choices households made between fixed and adjustable rate mortgage contracts in Israel during the past decade.[1] Overall, our analysis the

[1]At the single household level it could be either an FRM or ARM contract or some combinations between them. The Israeli market still has a strict distinction in FRM-ARM products. Moreover, while in most other markets switching (refinancing) is not so expensive; a key feature of the Israeli market is that the initial choice is essentially definitive. In order to switch FRM to ARM, an interest rate differential (IRD) of the entire remaining mortgage balance must be paid. This IRD represents the present value of interest differentials, which

results of our analysis demonstrate a significant effect of availability and representativeness heuristics on households' decision. In addition, we show that regulatory provisions regarding the loan division between FRM and ARM may serve as a possible anchor to the borrowers.

The paper proceeds as follows: Section 2 describes the data. Section 3 describes the tested heuristics. Section 4 provides the design. Section 5 presents our results, and finally, Section 6 discusses the findings and conclusions.

2. Data

Our main body of data comes from the Israeli Central Bank data on mortgage loans between the years 2002–2011. The Israeli mortgage market has undergone numerous changes in recent years due to the decline in inflation rates and structural reforms. As a result of the continuing decrease in inflation, the short interest rates of the Bank of Israel[2] have dropped in the last decade from two-digit settings to a "stable" low rate, as seen in Figure 1 (presents monthly commercial banks short term interest rates from November 2002 to April 2011).

The magnitude of the market for housing finance of households in Israel (see Figure 2, which shows monthly mortgage volumes from July 2003 to April 2011) and in most developed countries has risen substantially over the past decade.

In recent years, we have witnessed a significant increase in housing prices, which were already considered to be high even in historical perspective. Between 2008 and 2010, prices rose by 41% in real terms, significantly faster than the 1.5% increase in real terms starting in 1973, as displayed in Figure 3.

Most of the price increase, up to the last quarter of 2010, is attributed to interest rates dropping in response to the global economic crisis in

could be significant. A household has an option to switch FRM to ARM (this option can be phrased as a put option), while the option cost of this decision is already incorporated in the FRM terms.

[2]The short interest rate of the Bank of Israel is published on the last Monday of each month, for the upcoming month; this decision is widely discussed throughout the media.

Figure 1: Commercial Banks Prime Interest Rates (November 2002–April 2011, monthly figures)

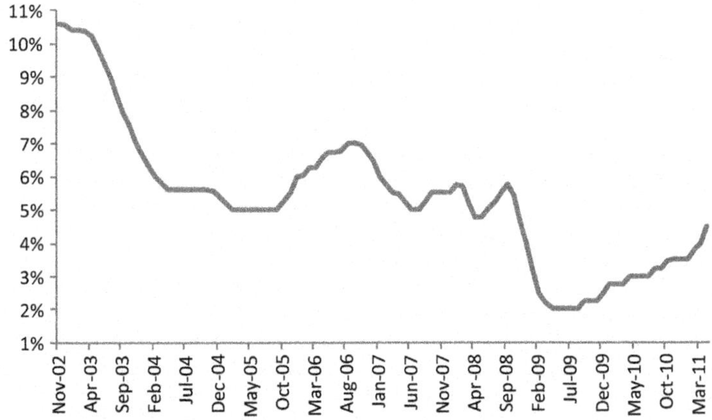

Figure 2: Mortgage volumes (Thousands NIS) (July 2003–April 2011, monthly figures)

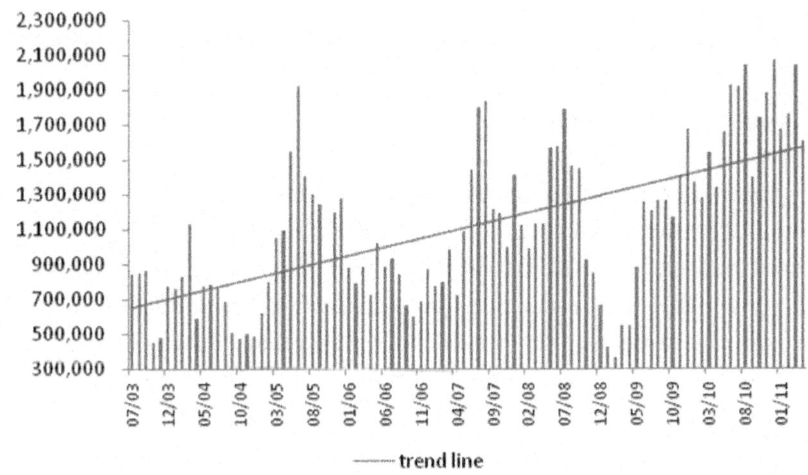

2008–2009. The reduction of interest rates also triggered a climb in inflation expectations, which subsequently increased housing acquisitions as a protective measure against inflation.

Moreover, changes in housing pricing are part of long-term price cycles, originating in previous price changes. In fact, from the mid-1990s to early 2008, real housing prices declined continuously, with an aggregate drop in

Figure 3: The Real House pricing (in comparison with the Consumer Price Index) (January 1973–January 2012, monthly figures, January 2000 = 1)

Source: bank of Israel

prices of over 20%, therefore implying that recent price changes represent a correction over the price decline of the past decade.

Another part of that increase is due to investors' activity, which was enhanced by housing loans financed by high leverage rates. Real mortgage interest rates declined, due to the drop in interest rates, generated investors' activity which led to housing price increases well beyond housing rental prices in the same period[3] (a 41% increase in real housing in 2008–2010, compared to a 15.8% real price increase in rent). In view of the fact that both the prices of purchasing housing and rental prices decreased in 2002–2007, the rapid increase in housing prices since 2008 strongly supports the claim of a correction over the real price decline of the past decade.

In light of these changes and in view of the inherent risk of housing loans with high leverage rates, the Bank of Israel adopted stabilizing measures in 2011 and in 2013. This policy limited leverage rates, including

[3]Theoretically, housing and rent are substitute products, and consequently should be correlated with price changes. However, since housing rentals do not grant ownership, they cannot produce capital gains for investors.

restraints on the ARM share of the total mortgage, parallel to government measures, especially implementing higher limitations for investors' activity. These limitations emphasize the importance of the FRM-ARM decision in the Israel mortgage market, and the crucial role Israeli regulators attribute to this decision. So, additional information regarding FRM-ARM decisions was collected from January 2012 to June 2015, around the major regulatory restriction of September 2013 — restricting a housing loan ARM share to 66.7% (two-thirds) of the total, applying to all durations.

3. Heuristics

Decisions about housing finance are based on beliefs concerning uncertain events which are employed to assess probabilities and to predict values. Tversky and Kahneman's (1974) seminal paper found that decision makers rely on a limited number of heuristic principles which reduce the complex task of assessing probabilities and predicting values to simpler judgmental operations. These heuristics can be useful, but can also lead to systematic errors. However, the implication of these heuristics on making the decision between FRM and ARM can explain our empirical findings.

(i) Availability

The *availability* heuristic uses strength of association as a basis for the judgment of frequency (Tversky and Kahneman, 1973). If the availability heuristic is applied, unrelated factors will affect the perceived frequency of classes and the subjective probability of events. Consequently, the use of the availability heuristic leads to systematic errors. Change in the short term interest rate occurs frequently and is therefore, highly available. Mortgage borrowers, find this frequent event easier to recall and to imagine, and it affects their long term interest rate decision embedded in choosing the mortgage type.

While a tremendous amount of research in social cognition is dealing with the availability heuristic (see Sherman and Corty, 1984; Schwatz *et al.*, 1991 for reviews), a few papers examine the influence of the availability heuristic in financial decision making. Shiller (1998) finds that investors' attention to different types of investment alternatives (as stocks, bonds, real estate, etc.) may be affected by the availability of these types of investment alternatives to the public attention. Barber and Odean (2008) find that when choosing which stock to buy, investors prefer the stock that has been recently available to them. Kliger and Kudryavtsev (2010) test the availability effect on investors' reactions to analysts' recommendation revisions and find a significant effect.

(ii) Representativeness

According to the *representativeness* heuristic, probabilities are evaluated by the degree to which A is representative of B. In other words, when judging the probability of an event by representativeness, one compare the essential features of the event to those of the structure form which it originates (Kahneman and Tversky, 1972). Therefore, by this heuristic, one estimates probability by assessing similarity or connotative distance. This approach, leads to serious errors, because similarity, or representativeness, is not influenced by several factors that should affect the judgment.

Representativeness in financial markets suggests that investors will infer past prices trends naively (Daniel, Hirshleifer and Teoh (2002)). In other words, investors use past performance as an indicator of future performance in managed funds and stock purchase decisions. For example, Sirri and Tufano (1998) find that purchase decisions in mutual funds are concentrated among the funds which have had high performance. This decision is in contrast with the empirical evidence that shows that there is no persistence in performance (Grinblatt *et al.*, 1995; Carhart, 1997). In another type of financial decision, Benartzi (2001) finds that employees allocate 401(K) retirement savings to investment in their own firm's stock based on how well that stock has done over the last 10 years. Here, as in the mutual funds context, these allocations do not predict future performance.

(iii) Anchoring and Adjustment

The anchoring effect is one of the most examined and tested behavioral heuristics. The anchoring effect is a highly robust heuristic, and in addition, carries a variety of implications to financial decision making as well as to non- financial decision making. The anchoring and adjustment heuristics, first introduced by Tversky and Kahneman (1974) seminal paper. As they explain, decision makers make estimates by starting from an initial value that is adjusted to yield the final answer, but the adjustments are typically insufficient. In their words "different starting points yield different estimates, which are biased toward the initial values".

As Furnham and Boo (2011) review, following Tversky and Kahneman's study, a significant number of studies have illustrated the prevalence of anchoring heuristic in human decision making processes (Plous, 1989; Chapman and Johnson, 1999; Epley and Gilovich, 2001; Mussweiler and Englich, 2005; McElroy and Dowd, 2007; and more). Most of the studies were conducted with university students in laboratory settings and a list of questions that the students may not have naturally used for decision making. Fewer studies faced the subjects with real life situations (such as Ariely *et al.*, 2003; Englich *et al.*, 2005; Critcher and Gilovich, 2008). However, these studies have shown the heuristic to be a robust one.

Moreover, regarding to the volume of the anchoring heuristics, the literature shows that the higher the ambiguity, the lower the familiarity, relevance or personal involvement with the problem, the stronger the anchoring effect (Van Exel *et al.*, 2006). In addition, the literature shows that informational relevance of values may play a role in affecting decision makers' susceptibility to the anchoring effect (Hastie *et al.*, 1999; Marti and Wissler, 2000; Englich *et al.*, 2005). More specifically, Strack and Musswieler (1997) show that anchor values similar or identical in judgmental dimensions to the estimates, yield significant effect on the volume of anchoring.

4. Design

In order to examine the effect of representativeness and availability heuristics on the mechanism that reflects the criteria by which home owners choose between FRM and ARM, we use detailed information on the decision households made between fixed and adjustable rate mortgage contracts[4] in Israel on a monthly basis during the period of November 2002 through April 2011.

The choice between FRM and ARM is estimated using the following linear model of the monthly differences ($t\text{-}t_{-1}$):

$$(1)\quad Slvi_t = \alpha + F(P_t, RW_t, RHpi_t, RBpi_t, (Lfi - Lvi)_t, Einf_t, Ld_t) + \varepsilon_t$$

[4]For decades, most of the mortgage loans taken by households in Israel consisted of mortgages linked to consumer price index, while unlinked mortgages only began to expand in recent years.

$Slvi_t$ denotes the dependent variable, representing the change of the share of adjustable (variable) rate linked mortgages contracts amount signed in period t (t = 1,2,...,101 — representing months), out of the total amount of linked mortgages contracts signed in that period. In other words, this variable represents the change in ratio of ARM/(ARM+FRM) of linked mortgages.

The independent variables are:[5]

P_t	Denote the change of Israel commercial banks' prime interest rate in period t
RW_t	Denote the change of average real wage per employee per month in period t (deducted of market inflation influence)
$RHpi_t$	Denote the change of housing price index in period t, deducted of market inflation influence
$RBpi_t$	Denote the change of building construction price index in period t, deducted of market inflation influence
$(Lfi - Lvi)_t$	Denote the change of the difference between reference rates for fixed and adjustable rate linked mortgages, as reported by Israeli central bank
$Einf_t$	Denote the change of the expected yearly inflation rate for the next 12 months, derived out of capital market expectations
Ld_t	Denote the change of the duration of linked FRM mortgages, as reported by Israeli central bank

Our main concern is the P_t coefficient, capturing the change of the short term interest rate influence. Since the latest change in the short-term interest rate should not influence long term loan decision, it can serve as proxy to the effect of heuristics and biases on the mortgage decision.

[5]Although the difference between FRM and ARM rates $(Lfi - Lvi)_t$ could be prone to selection bias: one does only observe the outcome-rate (either ARM or FRM) and not the alternative offered (and non-chosen) one. We test this possible issue by applying a yield curve approach, since it has a similar effect to that of the interest rate differential. Our analyses indicate similar results with the use of each of the two variables.

In order to examine the effect of anchoring and adjustment heuristic on the mechanism that reflects the criteria by which home owners choose between FRM and ARM, we use detailed information on the decision households made between fixed and adjustable rate mortgage contracts in Israel on a monthly basis during the period of January 2012 through June 2015. We chose this specific period since the major regulatory amendment dealing with the choice between FRM and ARM, took place at September 2013. We examine whether the regulatory restriction serve as an anchor to mortgage borrowers, and if so we further test the adjustment process.

5. Results

First, we estimate three regressions, with regard to the equation (1), marked as columns (1)–(3) in Table 1. Column (1) demonstrates the change of ARM share as a function of prime interest changes, while column (2) includes the full equation with the described controls. In column (3) we add yearly fixed effects into the equation, while in column (4) we subtracted prime interest changes from the full equation, including year fixed effects.

Column (1) of Table 1 illustrates a significant association between FRM preference and prime rates reduction, while column (2) demonstrates almost the same association between FRM preference and prime rates reduction, even after adding controls. As seen in column (3) results, year fixed effects added had no apparent influence in comparison to column (2). Column (4) illustrates that after taking out prime rate changes from the equation, none of the controls, which are commonly used in the literature, explains FRM preference. This supports our findings concerning FRM preference with prime rates reduction. The results of these four tests firmly demonstrate a significant association between FRM preference and prime rates reduction in the described period, above the beyond the other variables and yearly fixed effects.

Decision makers find the change in short term interest rates representative of the absolute level of interest rates. More precisely, a recent increase in short term interest rates is representative of a high level of interest rates and therefore, home owners prefer choosing ARM in this case. Accordingly, a recent decrease in short term interest rates is representative of a low level of interest rates and therefore, mortgage borrowers prefer FRM in this case. Figure 4 visually illustrates the results.

Table 1: ARM–FRM Share Decision in Linked Mortgages

	The change in ratio of ARM/ (ARM+FRM) of linked mortgages			
	(1)	(2)	(3)	(4)
Change of prime interest rate in period t	0.818***	0.812***	0.803***	
	(0.209)	(0.209)	(0.240)	
Change of monthly real wage in period t		−0.298	−0.281	−0.491
		(0.349)	(0.359)	(0.377)
Change of real housing price index in period t		1.013	0.258	−0.482
		(1.148)	(1.312)	(1.921)
Change of real construction price index in period t		−2.052	−1.328	−1.381
		(1.658)	(1.803)	(1.803)
Change of the difference between reference interest rates for FRM and ARM in period t		0.021	0.022	0.033
		(0.021)	(0.020)	(0.022)
Change of the expected yearly inflation rate in period t		−0.134**	−0.118*	−0.089
		(0.063)	(0.071)	(0.075)
Change of linked FRM duration in period t		−0.651	−0.614	−0.493
		(0.414)	(0.431)	(0.458)
Constant	0.009	0.004	0.008	0.019
	(0.012)	(0.013)	(0.122)	(0.130)
Observations	101	92	92	92
R^2	0.133	0.236	0.320	0.218

Notes: OLS regressions are reported in the panel, where each of the three columns represents an independent regression. The dependent variable includes is in the columns' title. Column (1) demonstrates the change of ARM share as a function of prime interest changes, while column (2) includes the full equation with the described controls. In column (3) we add year fixed effects into the equation, and in column (4) we subtracted prime interest changes variable. Standard errors are in parentheses. *** =Significant at the 1% level.** =Significant at the 5% level. * =Significant at the 10% level.

Figure 4: Changes in Prime Interest Rates (LN P) and Adjustable Interest Rates Mortgage Share (LN Slvi)(November 2002–April 2011, monthly figures)

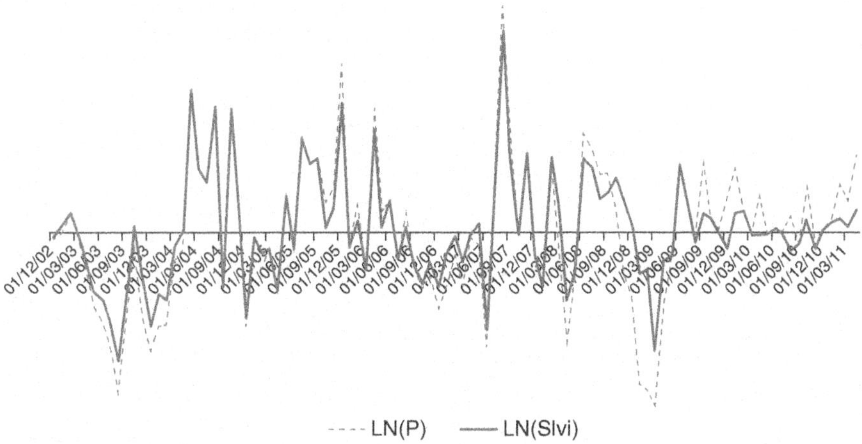

In the early part of the last decade, short term interest rates were double digit, followed by consecutive years of high interest rates, a remainder of the hyper-inflationary economy heritage of former years. The association between FRM preference and prime rates reduction may be more prominent in the early part of the last decade, since high interest rate environment is more salient and more available to the borrowers.

To check the influence of the interest rates environment on the FRM-ARM decision, we performed four additional regressions, dividing our sample into two (almost) equal periods.[6] The first period begins in November 2002 and ends in January 2007; the second period begins in February 2007 and ends in April 2011. The first period represents a high interest rate environment, and the second period represents a low interest rate environment.

The results are presented in Table 2. Column (1) demonstrates the change of ARM mortgages as a function of prime interest, without adding more controls in the first period, while column (2) includes controls and year fixed effects in the equation. Column (3) and column (4) repeat the same tests, as the first two columns, only in the second period.

[6]The first group contains 50 consecutive observations, while the second group contains 51 consecutive observations.

Table 2: ARM-FRM Share Decision in Linked Mortgages, by Time Periods

	The change in ratio of ARM/(ARM+FRM) of linked mortgages			
	(1)	(2)	(3)	(4)
	Period 1		Period 2	
Change of prime interest rate in period t	3.120***	2.939***	0.525**	0.579**
	(0.710)	(0.862)	(0.201)	(0.213)
Change of monthly real wage in period t		0.136		−0.469
		(0.676)		(0.406)
Change of real housing price index in period t		1.125		−0.403
		(2.752)		(1.445)
Change of real construction price index in period t		−1.746		−0.991
		(2.702)		(2.473)
Change of the difference between reference interest rates for FRM and ARM in period t		0.032		0.006
		(0.030)		(0.029)
Change of the expected yearly inflation rate in period t		−0.096		−0.152**
		(0.198)		(0.074)
Change of linked FRM duration in period t		−0.624		−0.840
		(0.600)		(0.684)
Constant	−0.010	−0.018	−0.005	0.063**
	(0.128)	(0.151)	(0.051)	(0.030)
Observations	50	46	51	46
R^2	0.396	0.404	0.196	0.377

Notes: OLS regressions are reported in the panel, where each of the four columns represents an independent regression. The dependent variable is in the columns' title. Columns (1) and (2) include period 1 observations, while columns (3) and (4) include period 2 observations. Standard errors are in parentheses.

The first period begins in November 2002 and ends in January 2007; the second period begins in February 2007 and ends in April 2011

*** =Significant at the 1% level. ** =Significant at the 5% level. * =Significant at the 10% level.

As Table 2 illustrates, one's initial notion could possibly be justified. The described association between FRM preference and prime rate reduction is more dominant in the early part of the last decade, and weakens in the later period. Dividing our sample into two periods, we found that the magnitude of our general findings is higher in the period which was represented in a high interest rate environment.

In other words, the change in the short term interest rate is more salient to the borrowers in periods of a high interest rate environment. This finding indicates that availability and representativeness are more influential in a high interest rate environment, in which those heuristics can be obtained more easily.

In order to decide whether the described association between FRM preferences is attributed to availability, or to expected prime rate changes, we examined the same test used in Table 2 by using future change of prime rates in observation $t + 1$ instead of observation t, which represents the foreseen change of prime rates rather than available and known prime rates. As Table 3 illustrates, the results are showing a significant difference between the effect of the available recent change to the effect of the expected change. The association between FRM preferences and prime rates is much less substantial in both periods, and only partially statistically significant.[7] The dramatic change between Table 2 and Table 3 demonstrates the availability influence of prime rate changes, which play an important role, compared to the general tendency of prime rate levels.

An alternative explanation for FRM preferences could refer to the mortgage leverage ratio. If an increase in the mortgage leverage ratio occurs, mortgages become riskier. This could induce favoring FRM. Hence, if this argument is valid, we would expect it to be more prevalent in the early part of the last decade (period 1), where FRM preference was more dominant. As seen in Figure 5, however, mortgage leverage ratio in the early part of the last decade was fairly constant, and, therefore, could not have created such an influence. In fact, mortgage leverage ratio actually increased in recent years, where FRM preferences were less dominant, while the repayment

[7]We also tested the use of prime rates in observation $t + 2$ instead of observation t; the association between FRM preferences and prime rates was even less substantial than with $t + 1$.

Table 3: ARM-FRM Share Decision in Linked Mortgages, in sequential time observation (T+1), by time periods

	The change in ratio of ARM/(ARM+FRM) of linked mortgages			
	(1)	(2)	(3)	(4)
	Period 1		Period 2	
Change of prime interest rate in period t+1	1.640**	1.530*	0.208	0.482*
	(0.809)	(0.850)	(0.201)	(0.244)
Change of monthly real wage in period t		−0.133		−0.570
		(0.748)		(0.433)
Change of real housing price index in period t		0.790		−0.698
		(3.050)		(1.519)
Change of real construction price index in period t		−2.243		0.603
		(2.994)		(2.621)
Change of the difference between reference interest rates for FRM and ARM in period t		0.038		0.016
		(0.034)		(0.031)
Change of the expected yearly inflation rate in period t		−0.138		−0.192**
		(0.220)		(0.086)
Change of linked FRM duration in period t		−0.616		−0.746
		(0.671)		(0.724)
Constant	0.023	0.025	0.003	−0.016
	(0.148)	(0.167)	(0.064)	(0.061)
Observations	50	46	50	45
R^2	0.202	0.267	0.093	0.321

Notes: OLS regressions are reported in the panel, where each of the four columns represents an independent regression. The dependent variable is in the columns' title. Columns (1) and (2) include period 1 observations, while columns (3) and (4) include period 2 observations. Standard errors are in parentheses.

The first period begins in November 2002 and ends in January 2007; the second period begins in February 2007 and ends in April 2011

*** =Significant at the 1% level. ** =Significant at the 5% level. * =Significant at the 10% level.

Figure 5: Mortgage Leverage Ratio in Housing Loans[8] (Q1 2003–Q2 2010, quarterly figures)

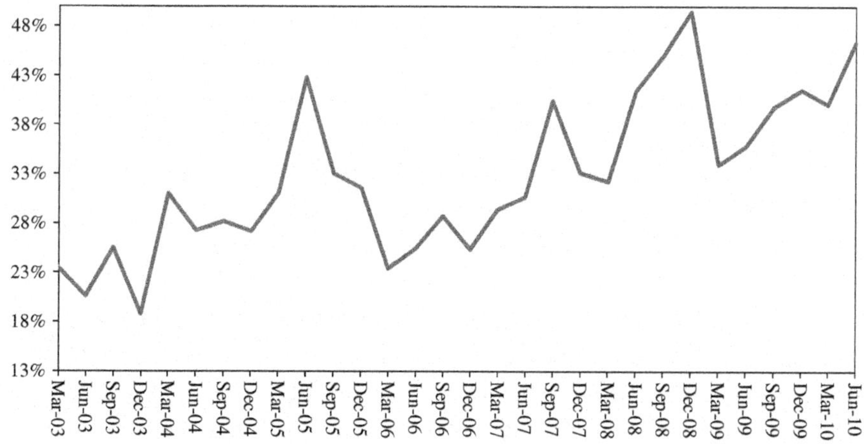

Figure 6: The Ratio of the Average House pricing to the Average Annual Wage (November 2002–April 2011, monthly figures)

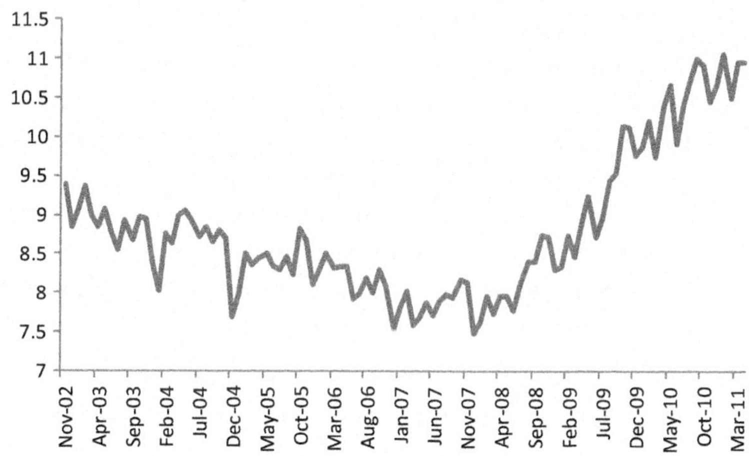

capacity of households did not change (see Figure 6 that demonstrates the ratio of the average home price to the average annual wage).

[8]The leverage rate is calculated as the ratio of total mortgages granted to the value of the homes purchased. The value of the homes is calculated as the product of the average transaction value by the number of transactions during the period (source: Bank of Israel).

A possible justification for the increased leverage ratio in recent years can account for a growing trend of investors' activity, exploiting low interest rate loans for short term profit, motivating high leverage ratio, and minimizing private capital exposure.[9] This may partially explain the influence in recent years, but does not suggest an explanation for initial FRM preference.

Similar to mortgage leverage ratio rationalization, a change in home-owners' repayment capacity can also potentially have an impact on the ARM–FRM decision. A decrease in the repayment capacity of homeowners could occur, which would encourage favoring FRM. Such a decrease may derive from an increase in real housing pricing, or, less likely, from a change in real wages. Thus, if this argument is valid, it would have been more prevalent in the early part of the last decade (period 1), where FRM preference was more dominant. However, as seen in Figure 5, repayment capacity in the early part of the last decades lightly improved. Real housing price increases only occurred in the second period, where favoring FRM was less dominant. As a result, neither leverage ratio nor repayment capacity can explain FRM preferences.

As shown in Table 1 and Table 2, neither does interest rate differential explain FRM preference. It is still possible, however, that our findings are partially influenced by the variety of mortgages of different maturities included in our sample. Consequently, we obtained additional data provided by the Bank of Israel, in which ARM–FRM share and the interest rate differential are calculated separately for each term.[10]

This data is divided into 16 term spreads,[11] where each of those has its own (calculated) interest rate differential. Accordingly, in order to test each

---

[9]In view of the inherent risk of housing loans with high leverage rates, the Bank of Israel adopted stabilizing measures in 2011 and in 2012 that take into accounts the mortgage characteristics and needs: rent unit housing enhancers and investors, halting massive hazardous housing loans. The Bank of Israel has limited leverage rates, including restraint on ARM share of total mortgage.

[10]The data is only available starting in July 2003, thus eliminating 8 observations (November 2002–June 2003) from our original sample.

[11]Mortgages with maturities as follows: (1) of up to one month , (2) of 1–3 months, (3) of 3–6 months (4) of 6–12 months (5) of 1 to 2 years (6) of 2 to 3 years (7) of 3 to 4 years (8) of 4 to 5 years (9) of 5 to 7 years (10) of 7 to 10 years (11) of 10 to 12 years (12) of 12 to 15 years (13) of 15 to 17 years (14) of 17 to 20 years (15) of 20 to 25 years (16) of more than 25 years.

period separately, we calculated the new dependent variable *Slvi* and the new independent variable *Lfi* – *Lvi* for each term spread.

We performed two separate regressions for each of the maturity terms — the first regression demonstrates the change of ARM share as a function of prime interest changes, while the second includes the full equation with the described controls and year fixed effects. Most of the term spreads do not obtain sufficient observations due to maturity distribution, which, incidentally, has remained fairly constant during the entire period. Figure 7 illustrates the scope of ARM and FRM lending volumes by maturity spread, in the entire period. Since ARM lending with a maturity greater than 15 years is rare, we concentrated on three term spreads, where sufficient data was found: 7–10 years of term maturity, 10–12 years of term maturity and 12–15 term maturity.

Consistent with the previous findings, the results shown in Table 4 illustrate a significant association between FRM preference and prime rates reduction. This association was found in each of the time periods.

That is, the availability and representativeness are more influential in a high interest rate environment, in which these heuristics can be obtained more easily.

For testing the anchoring and the adjustment effect we take the September's 2013 ARM share regulatory amendment and look closely on this share before and after the regulatory shock. In order to do so, we examine the data regarding the ARM share in the short period before the regulatory amendment (January 2012 to September 2013) and in short period after the regulatory amendment (September 2013 to June 2015). Longer period examination may be noisy and bear additional explanations to the borrowers' behavior, such as different interest rate environments or different regulatory amendments.

Before the regulator intervention, the ARM share remained stable for more than a year and a half (around 75%). As a respond to the September 2013 change, ARM share dropped to the new level, fluctuating between 56–58% for the following year.

Starting September 2014, as a possible result of the media campaign concerning the potential risk of the adjustable rate, ARM share began shrinking to the new 45% level as for mid-2015. The campaign was highly available throughout the media, as a part of the public discussion

Table 4: FRM-ARM Decision in Linked Mortgages for Various Terms, by Time Periods

	The change in ratio of ARM/(ARM+FRM) of linked mortgages	
	(1)	(2)
Change of prime interest rate in period t, in mortgages with term of 7 to 10 years	1.767***	1.651***
	(0.473)	(0.587)
	[0.133]	[0.278]
	{93}	{87}
Change of prime interest rate in period t, in mortgages with term of 10 to 12 years	2.419***	3.185***
	(0.921)	(1.185)
	[0.071]	[0.130]
	{93}	{87}
Change of prime interest rate in period t, in mortgages with term of 12 to 15 years	2.202***	1.796*
	(0.798)	(1.046)
	[0.077]	[0.134]
	{93}	{85}

Notes: OLS regressions are reported in the panel, where each cell represents an independent regression. The dependent variable is in the columns' title. Column (1) demonstrates the change of ARM share as a function of prime interest changes, in different maturities, while column (2) includes the full equation with the described controls and year fixed effects. Standard errors are in parentheses. R-squared is in square brackets. The number of observations is in braces.
*** =Significant at the 1% level. ** =Significant at the 5% level. * =Significant at the 10% level.

on the mortgage guarantee bill[12] first introduced to the Knesset (Israeli parliament). Figure 8 illustrates the results.

The immediate drop in the ARM share can be the effect of anchor caused by the regulatory new restrictions. The fluctuations in the ARM share in the following period may be a result of an adjustment process, influenced the households' decisions.

[12]The bill, if passed as a law, enables first-time apartment purchasers to receive a mortgage loan of up to 90% loan-to-value (LTV), by allowing the state to become a third party guarantee on mortgage loans taken by eligible citizens.

Figure 7: FRM and ARM Mortgage volumes (Thousands NIS), by Maturity (in years) (July 2003–April 2011, Average of monthly figures)

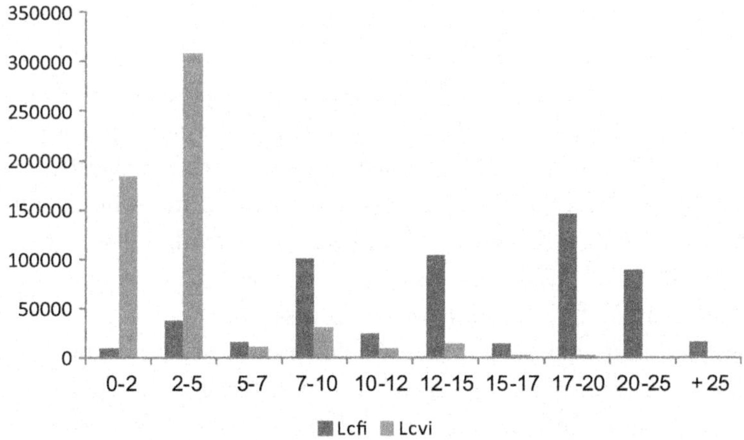

Figure 8: ARM share (January 2012–May 2015, monthly figures)

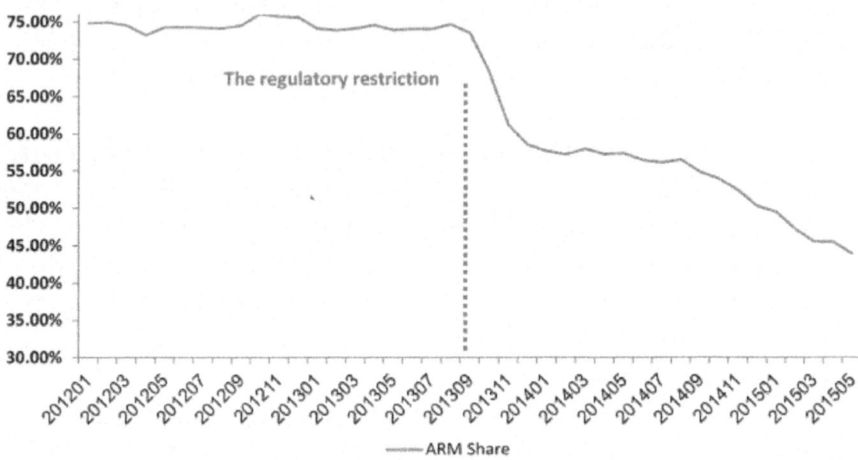

6. Discussion and Conclusion

This paper examines the three seminal heuristics that are employed in decision making under uncertainty: availability; representativeness; and anchoring and adjustment; and their appearance in the Israeli mortgage market. We focus on the households' choice between fixed rate mortgages

(FRM) and adjustable rate mortgages (ARM) and on the ARM share fluctuations out of the entire loan.

We empirically examine the effect of these heuristics on the decision between ARM and FRM using a unique data provided to us by the Bank of Israel, which contains detailed information on the household's decision between fixed and adjustable rate mortgage contracts in Israel in the past decade. The results of our analysis demonstrate a significant effect of availability and representativeness heuristics on households' decision. In addition, we show that regulatory provisions regarding the loan division between FRM and ARM may serve as a possible anchor to the borrowers and may lead to a further adjustment process.

We find that changes in the short-term interest rate occur frequently and therefore, are highly available for mortgage borrowers. In addition, decision makers find the recent change in short term interest rates representative of the absolute level of interest rates. In other words, a recent increase in short-term interest rates is representative of an absolute high level of interest rates and therefore, mortgage borrowers prefer ARM. Accordingly, a recent decrease in short-term interest rates is representative of an absolute low level of interest rates and therefore, mortgage borrowers prefer FRM.

Furthermore, we find that the recent changes in the short-term interest rate is more salient to the borrowers in periods of a high interest rate environment than in periods of low interest rate environment. This finding can be attributed to the phenomenon that the availability and representativeness heuristics are more influential in a high interest rate environment, because the interest rate levels are more salient in this environment to the borrowers.

In addition, we examine whether a regulatory restriction of the ARM share serve as an anchor to the blend choice between ARM and FRM. We do find a significant drop in the ARM share as a result of the regulatory restriction and a fluctuation in the share in the following year. These changes may be due to the effect of the anchoring and adjustment heuristic.

To conclude, our empirical analysis of the decision between FRM and ARM is an example of a possible implication of cognitive bias theory on the housing finance decisions. We suggest that common economic principles are sometimes inadequate to explain homeowner's choices. We show that this choice is motivated by psychological factors. Campbell (2013) argues that to understand mortgage markets we need a much broader perspective that integrates insights from across disciplines. Our paper contributes to our understanding of how the decision making process functions by demonstrating the linkage between FRM and ARM decisions and behavioral aspects such as availability, representativeness, anchoring and adjustment.

Examining the influence of regulatory restriction on decision makers' behavior, we believe that our paper can contribute significantly to the understanding of market functioning in *practice* beyond the theoretical predictions. Our findings concerning this functioning should be further investigated, especially in light of the implications of the recent stabilizing measures adopted by the Bank of Israel.

Acknowledgments

We are thankful to Alon Tubul and Ido Krakowsky for excellent research assistance. We have also beneficiated from helpful comments by Linda Allen, Simon Benninga, Ronen Elul, Avner Kalay, Eugene Kandel, Itzhak Venezia, Avi Wohl, Fernando Zapatero, and Ro'i Zultan. We further thank participants of the 2013 American Real Estate and Urban Economics Association International Conference, the 2014 Behavioral Legal Studies — Cognition, Motivation, and Moral Judgment, Research Workshop of the Israel Science Foundation, the 2014 Real Estate and Urban Economics Research Workshop of the Israel Science Foundation, the 15th International Association of Consumer Law Conference, and the 2015 the First Israel Behavioral Finance Conference. For financial support we thank the Fishman–J.E.C. Center for Finance, Entrepreneurship, and Real Estate, Maurice Falk Institute for Economic Research, the Krueger Center at the Hebrew University and Gazit Globe Real Estate Institute at IDC Herzliya. We thank the Bank of Israel for the data on household mortgages.

References

Agarwal, S., Ben-David I. and Yao, V., 2014. Systematic Mistakes of Borrowers in the Mortgage Markets, *Working Paper.*

Agarwal, S., Rosen, R. and Yao, V., 2012. Why Do Borrowers Make Mortgage Refinancing Mistakes? *Working Paper*, Federal Reserve Bank of Chicago.

Alm, J., Follain, J.R., 1984. Alternative Mortgage Instruments, the Tilt Problem, and Consumer Welfare. Journal of Financial and Quantitative Analysis 19, 113–126.

Ariely, D., Loewenstein, G., Prelec, D., 2003. "Coherent Arbitrariness": Stable Demand Curves without Stable Preferences. The Quarterly Journal of Economics 118, 73–105.

Baesel, J.B., Biger, N., 1980. The Allocation of Risk: Some Implications of Fixed Versus Index-Linked Mortgages. Journal of Financial and Quantitative Analysis 15, 457–468.

Barber, B.M., Odean, T., 2008. All that Glitters: The Effect of Attention and News on the Buying Behavior of Individual and Institutional Investors. Review of Financial Studies 21, 785–818.

Benartzi, S., 2001. Excessive Extrapolation and the Allocation of 401(k) Accounts to Company Stock. Journal of Finance 56, 1747–1764.

Campbell, J., 2006. Household Finance. Journal of Finance 61, 1553–1604.

Campbell, J., 2013. Mortgage Market Design. Review of Finance 17, 1–33.

Campbell, J., Cocco J., 2003. Household Risk Management and Optimal Mortgage Choice. Quarterly Journal of Economics 118, 1449–1494.

Carhart, M.M., 1997. On Persistence in Mutual Fund Performance. Journal of Finance 52, 57–82.

Chapman, G.B., Johnson, E.J., 1999, Anchoring, Activation, and the Construction of Values. Organizational Behavior and Human Decision Process 79, 1–39.

Critcher, C.R., Gilovich, T., 2008. Incidental Environmental Anchors. Journal of Behavioral Decision Making 21, 241–251.

Daniel, K., Hirshleifer D., Teoh, S.H., 2002. Investor Psychology in Capital Markets: Evidence and Policy Implications, Journal of Monetary Economics 49, 139–209.

Englich, B., Mussweiler, T., Strack, F., 2005. The Last Word in Court — A Hidden Disadvantage for the Defense. Law and Human Behavior 29, 705–722.

Epley, N., Gilovich, T., 2001. Putting Adjustment Back into the Anchoring and Adjustment Heuristic: Differential Processing of Self-generated and Experimenter-provided Anchors, Psychological Science 12, 391–396.

Furnham, A., Boo, H.C., 2011. A Literature Review of the Anchoring Effect. The Journal of Socio-Economics 40, 35–42.

Grinblatt, M., Titman, S., Wermers, R., 1995. Momentum Investment Strategies, Portfolio Performance and Herding: A Study of Mutual Fund Behavior. American Economic Review 85, 1088–1105.

Hastie, R., Schkade, D.A., Payne, J.W., 1999. Juror Judgment in Civil Cases: Effects of Plaintiff's Requests and Plaintiff's Identity on Punitive Damages Awards. Law and Human Behavior 23, 445–470.

Kahneman, D., Tversky, A., 1972. Subjective Probability: A Judgment of Representativeness. Cognitive Psychology, 3, 430–454

Kliger, D., Kudryavtsev, A., 2010. The Availability Heuristic and Investors' Reaction to Company-Specific Events. The Journal of Behavioral Finance 11, 50–65.

Koijen, R. S. J., Van Hemert O., Van Nieuwerburgh S., 2009. Mortgage Timing, Journal of Financial Economics 93, 292–324.

Marti, M.W., Wissler, R.L., 2000. Be Careful what You Ask for: The Effect of Anchors on Personal Injury Damages Awards. Journal of Experimental Psychology: Applied 6, 91–103.

McElroy, T., Dowd, K., 2007. Susceptibility to Anchoring Effects: How Openness-to-experience Influences Responses to Anchoring Cues. Judgement and Decision Making 2, 48–53.

Mussweiler, T., Englich, B., 2005. Subliminal Anchoring: Judgmental Consequences and Underlying Mechanisms. Organizational Behavior and Human Decision Processes 98, 133–143.

Plous, S., 1989. Thinking the Unthinkable: The Effects of Anchoring on Likelihood Estimates of Nuclear War. Journal of Applied Social Psychology 19, 67–91.

Schwarz, N., Bless, H., Strack, F., Klumpp, G., Rittenauer-Schatka, H., Simons, A., 1991. Ease of Retrieval as Information: Another Look at the Availability Heuristic. Journal of Personality and Social psychology, 61(2), 195–202.

Sherman, S.J., Corty, E., 1984. Cognitive Heuristics. In R.S. Wyer and T.K. Srull (Eds.), Handbook of Social Cognition 1, 189–286, Hillsdale, NJ: Erlbaum.

Shiller, R.J., 1998. Human Behavior and the Efficiency of the Financial System. Working Paper, NBER.

Sirri, E.R., Tufane, P., 1998. Costly Search and Mutual Fund Flows. Journal of Finance 53, 1589–1622.

Stanton, R., Wallace N., 1999. Anatomy of an ARM: The Interest-Rate Risk of Adjustable-Rate Mortgages. Journal of Real Estate Finance and Economics, 19, 49–67.

Statman, M., 1982. Fixed rate or Index-linked Mortgages from the Borrower's point of view: A Note. Journal of Financial and Quantitative Analysis 17, 451–457.

Strack, F., Mussweiler, T., 1997. Explaining the Enigmatic Anchoring Effect: Mechanisms of Selective Accessibility. Journal of Personality and Social Psychology 73, 437–446.

Tversky A, Kahneman D., 1973. Availability: A Heuristic for Judging Frequency and Probability. Cognitive Psychology 4, 207–232.

Tversky A, Kahneman D., 1974. Judgment under Uncertainty: Heuristics and Biases, Science. New Series Vol. 185, No. 4157, 1124–1131.

Van Exel, N., Brouwer, W., van den Berg, B., Koopmanschap, M., 2006. With Little Help from an Anchor. Discussion and Evidence of Anchoring Effects in Contingent Valuation. Journal of Socio-Economics 35, 836–853.

Chapter 11

The Availability Heuristic and other Psychological Aspects of Investors' Reactions to Company-Specific Events

Doron Kliger* and Andrey Kudryavtsev†

Abstract

Stock price reactions to company-specific events are supposed to reflect the effect of the events on the companies' expected future financial performance. Yet, it is difficult to estimate the effect an event may exert on a given company and, along with rational considerations, investors' reactions to company-specific events may also be affected by various psychological factors. In this chapter, we sketch the picture emerging from three studies of ours dealing with psychological aspects of investors' reactions to analyst recommendation revisions. These studies demonstrate that stock price reactions to recommendation revisions may depend on a number of factors, such as: (i) contemporaneous stock market index returns; (ii) contemporaneous changes in the value of VIX index; and (iii) daylight duration. We attribute the findings to the effects of the availability heuristic and mood on investors' behavior.

Keywords: Analyst recommendation revisions, availability heuristic, behavioral finance, financial market sentiment, mood maintenance hypothesis, seasonal affective disorder, VIX

JEL Classification: D81, D84, G11, G14, G19

1. Introduction

The importance of various psychological factors in the decision-making process has been documented in numerous research works in economics and finance. In particular, psychological processes that may result in systematic deviations from rationality are of continuously growing interest

*University of Haifa

†Yezreel Valley Academic College

in that literature. The overall conclusion of this research seems to be that analyst recommendation revisions contain useful investment information for investors. Though investors may be aware of some aspects in a company's current situation that lead the analysts to change their view on the company, still it is documented that analyst recommendations result in abnormal stock returns in the days surrounding their announcements. Yet, beyond the relevant information embedded in the recommendations, investors' valuations may be affected by psychological factors.

In this chapter, we concentrate on financial decision-making and sketch the picture emerging from three studies of ours dealing with psychological aspects of investors' reactions to company-specific events. As an example of such events, we employ analysts' recommendation revisions for the stocks of publicly traded companies.

Stock analysts form an integral part of capital market activity. They provide stock related research for their clients and, by doing so, take part in the information dissemination process at financial markets. The popular press awaits analysts' stock recommendations with keen anticipation; the recommendations are also posted prominently on popular financial websites.

In our studies, we analyze ways in which stock price reactions to analyst recommendation revisions are affected by two psychological factors: the availability heuristic, representing a decision-making rule in which a person determines the likelihood of an event according to the ease with which she can recall or imagine instances matching it (Tversky and Kahneman, 1973); and mood, involving a wide range of emotions and feelings. We employ a number of empirical proxies for these psychological factors and document that both exert economically and statistically significant effects on event-driven stock returns. These findings shed some more light on the functioning of stock markets and may have a series of practical implications.

The rest of the chapter is structured as follows. In Sections 2 and 3, we review the literature on psychological aspects and financial applications of the availability heuristic and mood, respectively. In Sections 4 and 5, we sketch and analyze some of the main findings of our studies dealing with the effects of these psychological factors on investors' reactions to company-specific events. In Section 6, we discuss the results and their potential implications for further research.

2. The Availability Heuristic: Definition, Psychological Evidence and Financial Effects

2.1. *Definition and Psychological Evidence*

People often tend to look for decision-making rules that would help taking into account the "input data" of a problem and simplify the process of solving it. Employing such rules of thumb, known as *heuristics*, may in many cases oversimplify the problem and lead to behavior which is not fully rational. Employing heuristics may cause overestimating the importance of certain facts, while underweighting others.

The term "availability heuristic", dubbed by Tversky and Kahneman (1973), refers to the phenomenon when people determine the likelihood of an event according to the easiness of recalling similar or related instances. As a result, vividly described and emotionally-charged possibilities will be perceived as being more likely than those that are harder to picture or difficult to understand. Tversky and Kahneman carry a series of psychological experiments and document that people's behavior is commensurate with the availability heuristic.

Tversky and Kahneman (1974) find that familiarity of an object (having personal acquaintance of it), and its salience (a state when the features of the object are highlighted) both enhance the easiness of recalling the instances related to that object. Furthermore, they argue that recent occurrences are likely to be relatively more available than earlier experiences (p. 1127), and, therefore, people tend to estimate probabilities by placing relatively more weight on the recent information.

The "recency" aspect of the availability heuristic is closely connected to *priming*: an unconscious remembering process, occurring when a certain stimulus or event increases the availability of (primes) a specific contemporaneous informative category. Priming may affect information processing and, thus, also decision-making (Baron and Byrne, 1997). A vast branch of literature documents and discusses the occurrence of the priming effect, which is considered an important aspect of social thought (e.g., Higgins *et al.*, 1977, Higgins and King, 1981).

Another aspect affecting availability is "imagery" or vividness. Sherman *et al.* (2002) find that people who are given more easily-imagined symptoms of a disease are much more inclined to believe that they might get that disease. Keller *et al.* (2005b) document that subjects who look at photographs showing houses in a flood zone provide higher evaluations of potential flooding risk with respect to those who look at neutral photographs.

2.2. *Financial Effects of the Availability Heuristic*

A number of papers discuss the effects of the availability heuristic in the context of market investors' behavior. Shiller (1998) asserts that alternating waves of public attention may affect investors' view on different investment categories (e.g., stocks versus bonds or real estate; investing abroad versus investing at home). Similarly, Barber and Odean (2008) document that when making a decision to buy a stock, investors tend to consider only those stocks that have recently caught their attention (e.g., stocks with extreme one day returns, stocks in the news, stocks experiencing high abnormal trading volume). This behavioral pattern leads to a systematic bias, which is stronger pronounced for individual investors who are net buyers on the days characterized by high attention. Gilad and Kliger (2008) and Kliger and Gilad (2012) analyze the influence of priming on financial decision-making, and conclude that priming manipulations have a significant effect on investors' risk attitudes and, hence, on their investment decisions.

Daniel *et al.* (2002) argue that investors and analysts are on average too credulous: when examining an informative event or a value indicator, they do not adequately take into account the incentives other people may have to manipulate this signal. Such behavior may be explained by limited attention and the fact that availability of a stimulus increases the weight it receives in the decision making process. Frieder (2003) detects that stock traders prefer to buy stocks after large positive earnings surprises (defined with respect to analysts' consensus estimates) and sell them after large negative earnings surprises, and explains this pattern by the availability heuristic, assuming that the more salient is an earnings surprise, the greater is its magnitude. Chiodo *et al.* (2003) construct a theoretical model of belief formation based on the assumption that it is easier for people to recall recent information, and therefore, investors tend to overreact to it. They discuss a number of economic phenomena, for example, the fact that stocks with very high levels of press coverage yield lower returns in the subsequent two years, and provide explanations based on heuristics.

The availability heuristic is also found to modify market analysts' behavior. Ganzach (2001) provides empirical support for his theoretical model in which analysts' judgments of risk and return for "unfamiliar" stocks are based upon global attitude. That is, if stocks are perceived as good, they are judged to have high return and low risk, whereas if they are perceived as bad, they are judged to be low in return and high in risk. Lee *et al.* (2005) discuss the phenomenon dubbed "recency bias", representing the tendency of people to make judgments about the likelihood of future events as a function of their recent experience. They document that analysts' forecasts of firms' long-term growth in earnings per share tend to be relatively optimistic (with respect to the earnings actually registered) if provided during the periods when the economy in general is expanding and relatively pessimistic if provided during the periods when the economy in general is contracting. This finding is in line with the availability heuristic, demonstrating that forecasters may overweight current state of the economy in making long-term growth predictions. The authors argue that this result may not be explained by any adaptive forecasting behavior that would take into account systematic characteristics of past growth.

3. Mood: Definition, Psychological Evidence and Financial Effects

3.1. *Definition and Psychological Evidence*

Hilgard's Introduction to Psychology (Hilgard, 2000) defines mood as an "enduring emotional state that affects people's evaluation of other people and inanimate objects". Mood also affects judgments about the frequency of various risks. Often, being in good (bad) mood, people see risks as less (more) likely. The world seems more dangerous when people are in bad mood. The influence of mood on people's perceptions and decisions is the focus of a vast body of psychological research. One of the main conclusions in this respect is that people in positive mood tend to make more optimistic judgments, while in negative mood they tend to make more pessimistic judgments (e.g., Isen *et al.*, 1978; Johnson and Tversky, 1983; Forgas, 1992; Schwarz and Clore, 1983; Kahneman and Riis, 2006). Furthermore, Schwarz (1990) finds that individuals in good mood are more likely to employ simplifying heuristics in making decisions, and subsequently, Isen

(2000) states that positive mood increases cognitive flexibility. On the other hand, Schwarz (1990) argues that bad mood stimulates people to engage in detailed analytical activity, and subsequently, Schwarz (2002) asserts that negative mood is related to more search of new alternatives, increased attention, and a more thorough processing of all available information.

A number of psychological studies focus on the relationship between people's feelings and emotions and their contemporaneous subjective evaluations of potential future risks. Constans and Mathews (1993) indicate that people's mood is negatively correlated with subjective probabilities they assign to various future risks. Wright and Bower (1992) argue that people's mood affects their judgments with respect to uncertain future events, by documenting that people in good (bad) mood estimate positive future events to be more (less) likely and negative future events to be less (more) likely. Loewenstein *et al.* (2001) construct "risk-as-feelings" model and incorporate in it the fact that the emotions people experience at the time of making a decision influence their eventual decisions. They suggest that the feelings of the decision-maker may significantly affect various aspects of the decision-making process, in particular, those involving risk and uncertainty.

People's mood is influenced by numerous factors and plays a considerable role in their decisions and actions, sometimes resulting in deviations from fully rational behavior. One of the factors routinely affecting the mood of a large number of people is the so-called Seasonal Affective Disorder (SAD, Rosenthal *et al.*, 1984). This term is related to seasonal states of depression experienced by a significant number of people during fall and winter, due to lack of daylight. Numerous psychological and clinical studies document the existence of SAD (e.g., Rosen *et al.*, 1990; Oren and Rosenthal, 1992; Dam *et al.*, 1998; Saeed and Bruce, 1998; Keller *et al.*, 2005a). According to the general findings of these studies, 4–6% of the general population experience seasonal depression, another 10–20% have subsyndromal features, and about half of the population manifests SAD symptoms at least to some degree. Common symptoms of SAD include depression, anxiety, sleep problems, fatigue, lethargy, social problems, feelings of hopelessness, difficulty concentrating, irritability and sadness, and mood changes. Molin *et al.* (1996) and Young *et al.* (1997) provide evidence that seasonal depression is related to hours of daylight, and hence the effects of SAD are more pronounced in countries at more extreme latitudes where fall and winter days are relatively shorter. Palinkas *et al.* (1996) and Palinkas and Houseeal (2000) demonstrate that SAD may be asymmetric around winter solstice.

One of the well-known psychological theories describing the mechanism of mood formation is the Mood Maintenance Hypothesis (MMH, Isen, 1984, 2000). It is based on the observation that people are psychologically motivated to maintain positive mood states. Therefore, according to MMH, positive moods are associated with risk-aversion, while negative moods cause people to behave in a risk-seeking way. In other words, people in a positive mood are reluctant to take risks because potential loss might diminish their good mood, while people in a negative mood do take risk because of the feeling that "they have got nothing to lose" (Isen *et al.*, 1988). Additionally, according to MMH, people in positive tend to analyze the available data in a more superficial way, because they feel that detailed information processing might undermine their pleasant mood states (e.g., Mackie and Worth, 1989; Schwarz, 2001). MMH is widely documented in various experimental and real-world settings. Isen and Patrick (1983) experimentally induce positive mood by giving some of the participants a gift certificate, and find that when the probability of risk in their simulated lottery is high, participants in the positive mood condition place fewer bets than those in the neutral mood condition. Similarly, Isen and Geva (1987) induce positive mood by giving some of the participants a gift prior to playing a roulette game, and document that persons who have been given a gift set a higher minimum probability level (i.e., lower level of risk) than those in the control group. Isen *et al.* (1988) detect that individuals in positive mood show more negative subjective utility in situations of potential meaningful loss than individuals in a neutral mood. They interpret these findings as indicating that individuals in a good mood state evaluate losses more negatively and are more sensitive to losses than individuals in a neutral mood state.

3.2. *Financial Effects of Mood*

The effects of mood on financial markets are widely-documented in recent literature. Bad mood, being expressed by a number of psychologically motivated proxies, like high levels of cloudiness (e.g., Saunders, 1993; Hirshleifer and Shumway, 2003; Kliger and Levy, 2003a, 2003b), high temperatures (Cao and Wei, 2005), heightened geomagnetic storms (Krivelyova and Robotti, 2003), cycles of full moon (Dichev and Janes, 2003; Yuan *et al.*, 2006), Daylight Savings Time Changes (Kamstra *et al.*, 2000), and small number of daylight hours (Kamstra *et al.*, 2003), results in significantly lower stock returns. In addition, Mehra and Sah (2002) indicate that investors' mood may exert an effect on equity prices if it affects investors' 'subjective parameters' (such as level of risk aversion and judgment of the appropriate discount factor). Baker and Wurgler (2006) find that high volatility stocks, unprofitable stocks, younger stocks, small stocks, non-dividend paying stocks, extreme growth stocks, and distressed stocks, or in other words, stocks that are attractive to optimists and speculators and at the same time unattractive to arbitrageurs are especially likely to be disproportionately sensitive to broad waves of investor sentiment. Kliger and Levy (2003a) employ option price data to recover risk preferences, documenting that good (bad) mood is associated with investors being less (more) willing to tolerate risk, and Kliger and Levy (2003b) find that bad mood, proxied by high cloudiness and large precipitation volume, is characterized by investors placing higher-than-usual probabilities on adverse events.

Several economic studies employ seasonal mood-related factors. Kamstra *et al.* (2003) analyze the effect of SAD on stock market indexes of several countries, documenting systematic seasonal patterns in the index returns. Garrett *et al.* (2005) explore the SAD effect in the context of an equilibrium asset pricing model to establish whether the seasonality can be explained using a conditional version of the CAPM that allows the price of risk to vary over time. They document that a conditional CAPM allowing the price of risk to vary with seasonal variation in the length of day fully captures the SAD effect. Kramer and Weber (2012) detect that people who suffer from SAD symptoms display financial risk aversion that varies across the seasons, and namely, that the SAD-sufferers have significantly stronger preferences for safe choices during the winter than non-SAD-sufferers, while they do not differ from non-SAD-sufferers during the summer. Kamstra *et al.* (2011) explore the correlation between investment flows in mutual funds and the onset and recovery from SAD, and show that, consistently with the nature of SAD, substantial amounts of money move from US equity to US government money market mutual funds in the fall and then back to the equity funds in the spring. Moreover, they conclude that there is a stronger seasonality in Canadian fund flows, which is in line with Canada's more northerly location and higher incidence of SAD, and a reverse seasonality in flows in Australian funds, consistent with the opposite southern hemisphere seasons. Kliger and Levy (2009) employ option data to elicit investors' preferences and expectations, and empirically document prospect theory characteristics, such as nonlinear Probability Weighting Functions (PWFs), loss aversion and diminishing marginal sensitivity. Kliger and Levy (2008) integrate the considerations of mood into non-expected utility theories, concluding that SAD factors cause investors to systematically distort their PWFs. Kliger *et al.* (2012) find that in the short run, stocks issued in "depressing" daylight conditions earn lower returns than stocks issued in 'cheerful' periods, and that in the long-run, the stocks issued in the "cheerful" periods relatively underperform and, subsequently, possibly revert to average IPO underperformance.

In line with MMH, Mano (1992) documents that people in an induced negative mood are willing to pay more for lottery tickets and also show a tendency to choose more lottery tickets with lower probability of winning a large prize. Williams *et al.* (2003) discover that managers with positive emotions view risk-related uncertainty more optimistically, but are not more willing to seek risks in real situations, while for the reverse situation they are more willing to take risks because they feel they have nothing to lose.

4. Effects of the Availability Heuristic on Investors' Reactions to Company-Specific Events

In Kliger and Kudryavtsev (2010), we analyze a well-known category of events whose influence on stock returns has been widely studied, namely, analyst recommendation revisions. Analyst recommendations represent an important means of transmitting company-specific information to market investors. Numerous research papers have documented that analyst recommendation upgrades are surrounded by abnormally high stock returns, while the downgrades are accompanied by abnormally low stock returns (e.g., Stickel, 1995; Womack, 1996; Jegadeesh and Kim, 2006;

Sorescu and Subrahmanyam, 2006; Mikhail *et al.*, 2007). These abnormal returns are in the focus of our research, where we attempt to understand the role of the availability heuristic in affecting them.

4.1. *Outcome Availability Effect*

A wide range of social, economic, political, and environmental factors affect people's perceptions and, therefore, the availability of different outcomes, on a daily basis. Specifically, we argue that when positive investment outcomes are highly available, it would be easier for the investors to imagine scenarios leading to gains, and the converse holds as well, to wit, when negative investment outcomes are highly available, it would be easier for the investors to imagine scenarios leading to losses. Further, we argue that the availability of investment outcomes is positively related to the market returns. This leads to the hypothesis that the information content of recommendation upgrades, would be perceived more saliently, resulting in amplified stock price reactions, when the market goes up, and that of downgrades would be perceived more saliently, when the market goes down.

For the empirical analysis, we construct a sample of analyst recommendation revisions employing all the companies that were listed on NYSE at the end of 2006. Our sample includes 1373 firms, for each of which we sample one recommendation upgrade and one recommendation downgrade. We employ the daily NYSE Composite Index returns around recommendation revisions as a proxy for the contemporaneous availability of the respective outcomes. The reasoning behind this proxy is twofold: first, positive (negative) market returns may reflect latent positive (negative) factors for which the investors may have been exposed to; second, the mere direction of the market may be perceived by the investors as such a factor.

Acting together or separately, both schemes result in the same prediction that stock price reactions to recommendation revisions would be amplified on days when the direction of change in the stock market index corresponds with the direction of the revision. Thus, by testing for stock price reactions to recommendation revisions conditioned on the sign of index returns, we are able to identify the effect of outcome availability on the perception of company-specific events by the investors.

We define the announcement day of each recommendation revision as day 0. Measuring the daily market returns (MRs) by the NYSE

Table 1: Average Event-day ARs by Upgrades and Downgrades and the Sign of Respective Contemporaneous Market Returns

	Average event-day AR		
Type of recommendation revision	MR0>0	MR0<0	Difference
Upgrades	2.82%	1.89%	***0.93%
Downgrades	−1.82%	−3.04%	***1.22%

Three asterisks (***) denote 2-tailed p-values < 0.01.

Composite Index, we calculate abnormal returns (ARs) for each event (recommendation revision) *i*, using Market Model Adjusted Returns (MMAR).[1] Table 1 presents the average ARs of upgraded and downgraded stocks conditioned on the sign of their respective contemporaneous MRs and the differences within upgrades and downgrades by the sign of the contemporaneous MRs.[2]

The results provide strong support for the existence of the outcome availability effect on the ARs related to the analyst recommendation revisions. All the estimated differences are positive and highly significant, meaning that event-driven ARs are higher for upgrades if the contemporaneous daily MRs are positive, and lower for downgrades if the contemporaneous daily MRs are negative. We note also that the availability-driven AR differences are larger for downgrades than for upgrades.

We also consider the cumulative stock price reactions to recommendation revisions over days −1 and 0 conditioned on the sign of the cumulative MRs over the same event period. We find that if the cumulative MRs corresponding to days −1 and 0 are positive (negative), then the cumulative average ARs over these two days following recommendation upgrades equal 3.16% (2.40%), and following recommendation downgrades equal −2.08% (−3.14%), the respective AR differences being highly significant.

In addition, we analyze the magnitude of the outcome availability effect by firms' size (market capitalization), stock beta, and historical volatility.

[1] Employing Market Adjusted Returns (MAR), i.e., return differences from the market index, instead of MMAR, for our analysis, we obtain the results that are qualitatively similar to those described below.

[2] Detailed results may be found in Kliger and Kudryavtsev (2010). Similar results to those presented in this and subsequent table were obtained when inspecting day −1.

Consistently with Baker and Wurgler (2006), who argue that stocks of low capitalization, growth, and highly volatile stocks are especially likely to be disproportionately sensitive to broad waves of investor sentiment, we document that the effect of outcome availability tends to decrease with market capitalization and to increase with stock beta and historical stock volatility. To wit, the prices of low market capitalization stocks and stocks characterized by higher volatility and higher sensitivity to market fluctuations are more affected by the availability heuristic, possibly due to the reduced amount of information on these stocks.

Furthermore we check the persistence of the outcome availability effect controlling for additional firm-specific and event-specific factors, by running multivariate regressions, with a *MR_dumit*, a dummy variable taking the value 1 if the market return corresponding to day *t* for event *i* is positive, and 0 otherwise. The controls (normalized in the cross section) consist of *MCapi*, the natural logarithm of the firm's market capitalization corresponding to event *i*; *betai*, the estimated CAPM beta for event *i*; *SR_volati*, the standard deviation of stock returns over the days −251 to −2 corresponding to event *i*; and *AR_30_2i*, the cumulative abnormal return over the days −30 to −2 corresponding to event *i*. The regressions also control for the properties of the recommendation revision, by including *Magnitudei*, the number of categories changed in the revision; and *fromsi*, dummies for the initial rating category before the recommendation revision.

Table 2 depicts the essence of the regression results. As expected, the company-specific, stock-specific and event-specific factors significantly affect ARs following recommendation revisions, but importantly, the effect of the sign of contemporaneous market returns remains significant after controlling for all these factors, providing an additional support for the robustness of the outcome availability effect.

Henceforth, we analyze the effect of outcome availability on event-driven trading volumes. Trading volume may result from dispersion in prior investors' expectations and idiosyncratic interpretations of information events, so that an increase in trading volume may be positively correlated with the information "surprise" (e.g., Copeland, 1976; Pfleiderer, 1984; Varian, 1985; Karpoff, 1986). For each recommendation revision, we calculate day-0 abnormal trading volume as the difference between the

Table 2: Multifactor Regression Analysis of Event-Driven ARs: Effect of Outcome Availability

Explanatory variables	Coefficient estimates	
	Upgrades	Downgrades
MR_dum	***0.88	***1.06
MCap	***−0.70	***0.62
beta	−0.12	0.01
SR_volat	***0.36	***−0.49
AR_30_2	*−0.15	0.10

Asterisks denote 2-tailed p-values: $^{*}p < 0.10$; $^{**}p < 0.05$; $^{***}p < 0.01$.

actual trading volume and the average trading volume for the respective stock over days −251 to −2 divided by the standard deviation of the trading volume over the same time window, and detect that the average event-day abnormal volumes following upgrades taking place on the days of positive market returns equal 1.91, compared to 1.55 on the days of negative market returns, and the average event-day abnormal volumes following downgrades taking place on the days of negative market returns equal 2.13, compared to 1.50 on the days of positive market returns, both abnormal volume differences being significant. Thus, we may suggest that on the days when the quality of news corresponds to the sign of contemporaneous market returns, the outcome availability makes an event more salient, that is, increases its "surprise" component, and leads to stronger average changes in investors' expectations, which results in increased trading volume.

4.2. *Risk Availability Effect*

Along with expected returns, the degree of financial risk represents a central parameter of any financial investment. In the previous Subsection, we have observed the effect of outcome (return) availability on investors' reactions to analyst recommendation revisions, and we suggest that the latter may be also influenced by risk availability.

Numerous studies (e.g., Slovic *et al.*, 1991; Alhakami and Slovic, 1994; McDaniels *et al.*, 1997) document negative correlation between perceived risks and benefits. Erb *et al.* (2002) demonstrate that priming affects people's risk preferences, and that judgments that go against the prime are made with less confidence. Furthermore, Gilad and Kliger (2008) and Kliger and Gilad (2012) establish that investors' awareness of financial risk, as well as their risk attitude, might be affected by environmental factors.

Following this line of research and employing the same sample of analyst recommendation revisions, we define the days of substantial changes in stock market index as the days when the absolute value of market return was larger than half standard deviation of the market's returns measured over the total sampling period (2001–2006).[3] In our sample, we have 1111 recommendation revisions taking place on the days of substantial MRs, of which 630 on the days of substantially positive returns and 481 on the days of substantially negative returns. We find that if the recommendation revisions take place on the days characterized by substantial (non-substantial) market moves, then the day-0 average ARs following recommendation upgrades equal 2.26% (2.59%), and following recommendation downgrades equal −2.61% (−2.24%), the respective AR differences being statistically significant.

These results are consistent with the existence of the effect of risk availability on stock price reactions to recommendation revisions. We may suggest that contemporaneous volatility of stock market index may prime risky scenarios, or in other words, create risk availability, and that on days, when risky scenarios are made available to investors or, alternatively, when investors' risk aversion is increased, they treat the "uncertainty ingredient" of any recommendation revision with more precaution, which results in lower stock returns around the revision. In this respect, our results demonstrate that on such "risky" days, the positive price reactions to upgrades are reduced, while the negative price reactions to downgrades are amplified.

Similarly to the case of the outcome availability, we henceforth analyze the effect of risk availability on the event-driven trading volumes and document that the average day-0 abnormal volumes following upgrades taking place on the days of substantial market moves equal 1.66, compared to 1.86 on the days of non-substantial market moves, and the average day-0 abnormal volumes following downgrades taking place on the days of

---

[3]This method of defining the days of substantial changes in stock market index is similar to the one employed by Fabozzi and Francis (1977).

substantial market moves equal 1.97, compared to 1.68 on the days of non-substantial market moves, both abnormal volume differences being significant. Therefore, we may suggest that on the days when the "risky" investment scenarios are made available, recommendation upgrades, regarded as good news, are made less salient, while recommendation downgrades, regarded as bad news, are made more salient.

4.3. *Combined Effect of the Outcome and Risk Availability*

Finally, in order to test for the combined effect of both above-analyzed kinds of availability on investors' reactions to company-specific events, for day 0, and separately for upgrades and downgrades, we run the regressions with *MR_dumit*, the dummy variable taking the value 1 if the market return corresponding to day *t* for event *i* is positive, and 0 otherwise; and *Subreti*, a dummy variable taking the value 1 if the absolute value of the day-0 MR corresponding to event *i* exceeds half standard deviation of the MRs over the sample period, and 0 otherwise.

According to the results, both availability effects remain significant when jointly considered and amplify each other. That is: (i) after controlling for the substantial stock market moves, the contemporaneous rises in the market index increase investors' positive reactions to upgrades, and the contemporaneous declines in the market index increase investors' negative reactions to downgrades; (ii) after controlling for the direction of change in the market index, substantial contemporaneous market moves decrease investors' positive reactions to upgrades, and increase investors' negative reactions to downgrades. In other words, stock price reactions to recommendation upgrades (downgrades) are the most positive (the least negative) if the latter take place on the days when the stock market index moderately increases, and the least positive (the most negative) if the latter take place on the days when the stock market index substantially decreases.

5. Effects of Mood on Investors' Reactions to Company-Specific Events

5.1. *The Effect of VIX*

In Kliger and Kudryavtsev (2013), we shed light on effects of mood on stock price reactions to analyst recommendation revisions. Previous literature indicates that mood is negatively correlated with subjective risk evaluations (e.g., Johnson and Tversky, 1983; Constans and Mathews, 1993; Kliger and Levy, 2003b). Consequently, we employ the implied volatility index (VIX), introduced by Whaley (1993) and launched by the Chicago Board Options Exchange (CBOE) in 1993 as a measure that captures investors' market volatility (or in other words, risk) expectations, and correspondingly, as a proxy for their contemporaneous mood.

VIX is based on the prices of S&P 500 index options, thus providing a benchmark for the expected future market volatility over the next month. The index is calculated in real-time and is continuously disseminated throughout each trading day. VIX is widely followed and has been cited in numerous news articles in leading financial publications. Since VIX represents an implied measure of expected future volatility, it is regarded as an indicator of future economic conditions. Yet, it is also widely-known as the investors' 'fear gauge' (e.g., Whaley, 2000 and 2008). According to this interpretation, though there are other factors affecting this index, in most cases, high VIX reflects increased investors' fear, while low VIX suggests complacency. Whaley (2008) documents daily S&P 500 index returns and VIX changes are negatively correlated, and interprets this fact as an indication that changes in the VIX are partially driven by investors demanding portfolio insurance in times of high current market volatility.

For the empirical analysis, we construct a sample of analyst recommendation revisions for NYSE-listed companies, in the years 2002 to 2011. We analyze a sample of 1,480 firms, of which 1,403 (1,422) have at least one upgrade (downgrade) event, resulting in a total of 25,214 events, or 12,723 (12,491) upgrades (downgrades).

We suggest that contemporaneous investors' mood may be reflected by daily changes in the values of VIX, which reflect changes in macroeconomic fundamentals and the general state of the stock market. Therefore, in order to test for the existence of the effect of VIX on investors' reactions to analyst recommendation revisions, we calculate the event-driven stock ARs (using the MMAR approach), and condition them on the direction of contemporaneous changes in the value of VIX. Table 3 comprises the average ARs on the event day, by direction of recommendation revision, separately for the cases when the contemporaneous value of VIX increases ($\Delta VIXit > 0$) or decreases ($\Delta VIXit<0$), where $\Delta VIXit$ is the continuously

Table 3: Average Event-day ARs by Upgrades and Downgrades and the Sign of Contemporaneous Daily Changes in VIX

	Average AR		
Type of recommendation revision	ΔVIX > 0	ΔVIX < 0	Difference (t-statistic)
Upgrades	2.31%	2.46%	**−0.15%
Downgrades	−2.74%	−2.62%	***−0.12%

Asterisks denote 2-tailed p-values: $^{**}p < 0.05$; $^{***}p < 0.01$.

compounded VIX return corresponding to day *t* for event *i*, their respective differences, and statistical significance levels.[4]

The results demonstrate that contemporaneous VIX changes do have an effect on ARs around recommendation revisions. Namely, we document (the effect of VIX suggesting) that on both days −1 and 0, positive event-driven ARs are significantly higher for upgrades if the contemporaneous daily value of VIX decreases, and negative event-driven ARs are significantly lower for downgrades if the contemporaneous daily value of VIX increases, or in other words, that positive (negative) stock price reactions to good (bad) company-specific news are weaker (stronger) on the days when the value of VIX increases, suggesting an increase in investors' stock market volatility expectations.

One possible explanation for the detected VIX effect is based on rational argumentation, according to which VIX may be regarded as an indicator of future economic conditions. That is, investors react more positively (negatively) to recommendation upgrades (downgrades) when the latter are accompanied by daily VIX decreases (increases), because, under these circumstances, the investors see the future economic conditions in a more (less) favorable way. Noting, however, that we document the VIX effect while employing abnormal daily stock returns (i.e., stock returns in excess of contemporaneous market index movements) as a measure of the stock price reactions, we may suggest that the results may be driven by more than mere changes in investors' expectations with respect to economic fundamentals. Therefore, we consider another possible explanation, which is consistent

[4]Detailed results may be found in Kliger and Kudryavtsev (2013). Similar results to those presented in this table were obtained when inspecting day -1.

with the growing literature connecting VIX and mood and indicating that mood is negatively correlated with subjective risk evaluations. Namely, we may suggest that the effect of VIX is driven by the fact that investors' mood mediates their reactions to analyst recommendation revisions. To wit, investors in good (bad) mood perceive positive (negative) future financial outcomes as more probable (whether indicative of future occurrences or not) and react more strongly to analyst recommendation upgrades (downgrades).

We also analyze the cumulative stock price reactions to recommendation revisions over days −1 and 0 conditioned on the direction of the cumulative change in the value of VIX over the same event period, and get additional supportive evidence for the existence of VIX effect. We detect that if the contemporaneous value of VIX increases (decreases) over the period corresponding to days −1 and 0, then the cumulative average ARs over these two days following recommendation upgrades equal 2.40% (2.69%), and following recommendation downgrades equal −3.18% (− 2.79%), the respective AR differences being highly significant.

5.2. *Seasonal Effects of Mood*

In Kliger and Kudryavtsev (2014), we explore seasonal effects of mood on investors' reactions to analyst recommendation revisions. Our empirical analysis is based on the Mood Maintenance Hypothesis (MMH, Isen, 1984, 2000), which is a widely-discussed psychological pattern indicating that people behave so that to maintain positive mood states. According to MMH, people in a positive mood avoid taking risks because their current mood is good so that they are not willing to put it in danger of being undermined as a result of potential loss, while negative mood causes people to engage in risk-taking behavior in order to improve their current (negative) subjective state.

Based on this line of reasoning, we expect investors' reactions to company-specific news to be influenced by two psychological (mood-driven) effects:[5]

- "Out of the blue" effect: Negative news arriving at the market in good mood periods (i.e., out of the blue) should have a stronger effect on stock prices than negative news arriving in other periods.

[5] The names of the effects are dubbed by us in Kliger and Kudryavtsev (2014).

- "Sunray on a cloudy day" effect: Positive news arriving at the market in bad mood periods (i.e., like a sunshine ray arriving on a cloudy day) should have a stronger effect on stock prices than positive news arriving in other periods.

Another conclusion arising from MMH is that positive mood causes people to analyze data and information more superficially, because they feel that more detailed information processing might undermine their pleasant mood states (e.g., Mackie and Worth, 1989; Kuykendall and Keating, 1990; Erber and Tesser, 1992; Schwarz, 2001). Accordingly, we predict an additional mood-driven effect on investors' reactions to company-specific news:

- "Shallow thinking" effect: All kinds of news arriving at the market in good mood periods (i.e., in the periods characterized by investors' shallow thinking) should have a stronger effect on stock prices than news arriving in other periods.

We note that "out of the blue" and "shallow thinking" effects are expected to act in the same direction for the bad news, increasing the respective negative stock price reactions during periods characterized by positive mood, while for the good news, the "shallow thinking" effect, which may be expected to increase positive stock price reactions to good news during periods characterized by positive mood, offsets the "sunray on a cloudy day" effect, which may be expected to increase positive stock price reactions to good news during periods characterized by negative mood.

In order to arrive at an empirical proxy for the periods of positive and negative mood, we employ the widely-documented phenomenon of Seasonal Affective Disorder (SAD, Rosenthal *et al.*, 1984), which is related to seasonal states of depression experienced by a considerable number of people due to lack of daylight during fall and winter (e.g., Rosen *et al.*, 1990; Oren and Rosenthal, 1992; Dam *et al.*, 1998; Saeed and Bruce, 1998; Keller *et al.*, 2005). A large number of recent studies employ seasonal mood-related factors based on SAD and document their effects on the capital markets (e.g., Kamstra *et al.*, 2003; Garrett *et al.*, 2005; Dowling and Lucey, 2008; Kramer and Weber, 2012; Kliger *et al.*, 2012). In this context, we suggest that investors' mood should be, ceteris paribus, more positive during the periods when daylight duration increases, that is, during the periods from winter till summer solstice (December 23–June 22), than during the periods when daylight duration decreases, that is, during the periods from summer till winter solstice (June 23–December 22).

For our empirical analysis, we employ the same sample of analyst recommendation revisions as in Section 4. In order to account for seasonal effects of mood, we partition the sample according to the daylight condition period relevant for the date of each recommendation revision. Table 4 presents average ARs following the recommendation revisions, separately for the Day Increase (DI) and the Day Decrease (DD) periods, for a number of event windows, as well as the respective AR differences and their statistical significance.

As predicted, for the downgrades, event-driven ARs are significantly lower during DI periods (when investors' mood is supposed to be better) than during DD periods, revealing a significant accumulated influence of the "out of the blue" and "shallow thinking" effects on stock returns.

Moreover, as we expand the event window, the seasonal effect is pronounced more strongly: for day 0, the average AR is lower during DI than during DD periods by 0.54%, while for the windows 0 to 2, and 0 to 30, the respective difference is already of 0.93%, 1 and 2.27%, all the differences being highly significant. On the other hand, for the upgrades, we get some mixed evidence. For different trading days around the events, ARs are either insignificantly higher or insignificantly lower during DI, than during DD periods, manifesting offsetting influence of the "sunray on a cloudy day" and "shallow thinking" effects.

Henceforth, we use an alternative measure to quantify the seasonally-related SAD effect on investors' reactions to news. Namely, we employ the account of SAD incidences onset and recovery (OR), based on the data on hundreds of SAD-patients compiled by Lam (1998), consequently developed by Kamstra *et al.* (2011), and used also by Kliger *et al.* (2012), as a proxy for the SAD influence on market participants. For each month, this measure is equal to the number of SAD-sufferers who have begun experiencing symptoms (cumulated starting in late summer when only a small proportion of SAD patients have been diagnosed with onset) minus the number of SAD-sufferers who have fully recovered from SAD. In other words, the OR variable is defined as the monthly change in the incidence

Table 4: Average Abnormal Returns (ARs) Around Recommendation Revisions, by Daylight Conditions

Days relative to event	Average AR							
	Downgrades				Upgrades			
	Total sample	DI (386 events)	DD (987 events)	Difference	Total sample	DI (550 events)	DD (823 events)	Difference
0	***−2.38%	***−2.77%	***−2.23%	***−0.54%	***2.45%	***2.61%	***2.34%	0.27%
0 to 2	***−2.74%	***−3.41%	***−2.48%	***−0.93%	***2.48%	***2.60%	***2.39%	0.21%
0 to 30	***−3.45%	***−5.07%	***−2.80%	***−2.27%	***2.83%	***2.48%	***3.06%	−0.58%

Asterisks denote 2-tailed p-values: $^{*}p < 0.10$; $^{**}p < 0.05$; $^{***}p < 0.01$.

variable. According to Kamstra *et al.* (2011), the OR values by month, starting with January are −5, −51, −42, −21, −5, 0, 3, 15, 38, 30, 8, 1. It is worth noting that OR is highly negatively correlated with the number of daylight hours and even more with the changes in the number of daylight hours. Following Kliger *et al.* (2012), we normalize OR variable to range from 0 to 1, so that the estimated coefficient would measure the effect on ARs between March and September (the months with the lowest and the highest OR values, respectively).

To quantify the SAD effect, we regress stock ARs around the downgrades and the upgrades on the OR variable, that is, for each event window, and separately for downgrades and upgrades, we run the following regression:

$$AR_i = \gamma_0 + \gamma_1 OR_i + \varepsilon_i \tag{11.1}$$

where: AR_i represents the abnormal stock returns related to event i, for each of the event windows; OR_i is the normalized monthly OR value corresponding to the day when event i took place.

Table 5 reports the regressions' coefficients. The results are in line with those reported in Table 4. For the downgrades, the OR coefficients are positive, suggesting that the negative stock price reactions to the downgrades are stronger for the periods characterized by lower OR values, that is for the periods of relatively good mood, and weaker for the periods of relatively bad mood, which is consistent with both "out of the blue" and "shallow thinking" effects. Similarly to the results presented in Table 4, the

Table 5: Regression Analysis of Abnormal Returns (ARs) Around Recommendation Revisions: The Effect of Monthly Assigned SAD Onset/Recovery (OR) Variable

	Coefficient estimates			
	Downgrades		Upgrades	
Days relative to event	Intercept	OR	Intercept	OR
0	***−2.77%	*0.65%	***2.82%	*−0.65%
0 to 2	***−3.43%	**1.14%	***2.70%	−0.39%
0 to 30	***−5.91%	***4.08%	***2.36%	0.82%

Asterisks denote 2-tailed p-values: $^*p < 0.10$; $^{**}p < 0.05$; $^{***}p < 0.01$.

magnitude and the significance of the effect increase as we expand the event window to after day 0. On the other hand, for the upgrades, we once again get some mixed evidence with the signs of OR coefficients being different for different event windows, which suggests that "sunray on a cloudy day" and "shallow thinking" effects offset each other. Now, we are also able to quantify the effects in a more detailed way and to state that day-0 abnormal negative stock price reactions to downgrades taking place in March are predicted to be stronger by 0.65% than day-0 abnormal negative stock price reactions to downgrades taking place in September, with the reactions for the rest of the months being predicted to increase with the decrease in OR values.

Moreover, we observe that for the downgrades taking place during low-OR (i.e., good-mood) periods, there is a significant drift during the first month following the event, compared to the downgrades taking place during high-OR periods. For example, the predicted difference between the cumulative (day 0 to 30) ARs following the downgrades taking place in March and September grows to impressive 4.08%.

6. Discussion and Potential Directions for Further Research

In this chapter, we have presented the picture emerging from the findings of three of our studies concentrating on the effects of the availability heuristic and mood on stock price reactions to analyst recommendation revisions. We have seen that, in addition to incorporating the effect of incoming news, abnormal event-driven stock returns may be influenced by various factors, such as the sign and magnitude of contemporaneous market returns (capturing the outcome and risk availability effects, respectively), the direction of contemporaneous change in the value of VIX (reflecting momentary changes in investors' volatility expectations, which may be correlated with their momentary mood), and the season of the year when the recommendation revision takes place (connected, as well, with contemporaneous investors' mood). Taking account of these findings may prove to be valuable for both financial theoreticians in the analysis of stock market efficiency and practitioners in the search of potentially profitable investment strategies.

The strand of research dealing with different psychological effects on the stock markets is rapidly growing, and it is clear that a lot of additional effects are still waiting to be discovered and documented. In particular, a lot still has to be done with respect to analyzing the effects of the availability heuristic and mood on investors' reactions to company-specific events. We suggest a few potential directions for further research in the field:

- To repeat the analysis for other countries/stock exchanges: Different populations may exhibit different psychological aspects, and this fact may be reflected in their reactions to company-specific information. In particular, it might be interesting to test for the existence and magnitude of mood-driven effects in countries with less hours of daylight in the winter and in the countries from the southern hemisphere.
- To repeat the analysis for other categories of company-specific events: Analyst recommendation revisions represent just an example, and there are a lot of other company-specific events producing significant effects on stock prices that may be affected by psychological factors.
- To compare the effects for different groups of investors: If the data for individual investors are available, it would be important to analyze what categories of investors are most influenced by the psychological effects when making their investment decisions.
- To analyze intradaily stock data: It might be useful to check if the above-described effects exist and are stronger or weaker if one looks at intradaily stock price reactions to company-specific events, conditioned on the contemporaneous changes in the stock market and VIX indexes.
- To employ other proxies for the availability heuristic and mood: With respect to the availability heuristic, it might be interesting to define availability proxies for certain (longer) time periods, rather than for separate trading days. With respect to mood, different weather-based proxies may be employed (cloudiness, precipitation, temperature, etc.). If these proxies also appear relevant for stock price reactions to company-specific news, they may provide some grounds for formulating potential investment strategies based on company-specific information and weather forecasts.
- To look for potential over- or under-reactions to news driven by psychological factors: If stock price reactions to company-specific events are systematically affected by the psychological factors, it might mean that in certain cases, stock prices systematically overreact (underreact) to new information, creating potential subsequent stock price reversals (drifts).

- To perform similar analysis during periods of financial crises: It might be important to establish if during periods of major financial distress, investors' decisions are more affected by psychological factors.
- To analyze combined effects of the availability heuristic and mood on investors' behavior: Such kind of analysis might serve as an important generalization of previous results. Moreover, additional psychological factors might be also employed in order to arrive, as close as possible, at the "general picture" of the psychological effects on investors' reactions to company-specific events.

References

Alhakami, A.S., and P. Slovic, 1994, A Psychological Study of the Inverse Relationship between Perceived Risk and Perceived Benefit, *Risk Analysis*, 14(6), 1085–1096.

Baker, M., and J. Wurgler, 2006, Investor Sentiment and the Cross-Section of Stock Returns, *Journal of Finance*, 61(4), 1645–1680.

Barber, B.M., and T. Odean, 2007, All that Glitters: The Effect of Attention and News on the Buying behavior of Individual and Institutional Investors, *Review of Financial Studies*, 21(2), 785–818.

Baron R.A., and D. Byrne, 1997, *Social Psychology*, 8TH Edition.

Cao, M., and J. Wei, 2005, Stock Market Returns: A Note on Temperature Anomaly, *Journal of Banking and Finance*, 29(6), 1559–1573.

Chiodo, A.J., M. Guidolin, M.T. Owyang, and M. Shimoji, 2003, Subjective Probabilities: Psychological Evidence and Economic Applications, The Federal Reserve Bank of St. Louis Working Paper.

Constans, J.I., and A.M. Mathews, 1993, Mood and Subjective Risk of Future Events, *Cognition and Emotion*, 7(6), 545–560.

Copeland, T.E., 1976, A Model of Asset Trading Under the Assumption of Sequential Information Arrival, *Journal of Finance*, 31(4), 1149–1168.

Dam, H., K. Jakobsen, and E. Mellerap, 1998, Prevalence of Winter Depression in Denmark, *Acta Psychiatrica Scandinavica*, 97(1), 1–4.

Daniel, K., D. Hirshleifer, and S.H. Teoh, 2002, Investor Psychology in Capital Markets: Evidence and Policy Implications, *Journal of Monetary Economics*, 49(1), 139–209.

Dichev, I.D., and T.D. Janes, 2003, Lunar Cycle Effects in Stock Returns, *Journal of Private Equity*, 6(4), 8–29.

Erb H.-P., A. Bioy, and D.J. Hilton, 2002, Choice Preference without Inferences: Subconscious Priming on Risk Attitude. *Journal of Behavioral Decision Making*, 15(3), 251–262.

Erber, R., and A. Tesser, 1992, Task Effort and the Regulation of Mood: The Absorption Hypothesis, *Journal of Experimental Social Psychology*, 28, 339–359.

Fabozzi, F.J., and J.C. Francis, 1977, Stability Tests for Alphas and Betas over Bull and Bear Market Conditions, *Journal of Finance*, 32(4), 1093–1099.

Forgas, J.P., 1992, Affect in Social Judgment and Decisions: A Multi-Process Model, *Advances in Experimental Psychology*, 25, 227–275.

Frieder, L., 2003, Evidence on Behavioral Biases in Trading Activity, Unpublished Paper, UCLA, The Anderson School.

Ganzach, Y., 2001, Judging Risk and Return of Financial Assets, *Organizational Behavior and Human Decision Processes*, 83(2), 353–370.

Garrett, I., M.J. Kamstra, and L.A. Kramer, 2005, Winter Blues and Time Variation in the Price of Risk, *Journal of Empirical Finance*, 12(2), 291–316.

Gilad, D., and D. Kliger, 2008, Priming the Risk Attitudes of Professionals in Financial Decision Making, *Review of Finance*, 12(3), 567–586.

Higgins E.T., and G. King, 1981, Accessibility of Social Constructs: Information Processing Consequences of Individual and Contextual variability. In N. Cantor & J. Kihlstrom (Eds.), *Personality, cognition and social interaction*, 69–121. Hillsdale, NJ, Erlbaum.

Higgins E.T., W.S. Rohles, and C.R. Jones, 1977, Category Accessibility and Impression formation, *Journal of Experimental Social Psychology*, 13, 141–154.

Hilgard's Introduction to Psychology, Thirteenth Edition, 2000, R.L. Atkinson, R.C. Atkinson, E.E. Smith, D.J. Bern and S. Nolen-Hoeksema, Harcourt College Publishers.

Hirshleifer, D., and T. Shumway, 2003, Good Day Sunshine: Stock Returns and the Weather, *Journal of Finance*, 58(3), 1009–1032.

Isen, A.M., 1984, Toward Understanding the Role of Affect in Cognition. In R.S. Wyer and T. K. Srull (Eds.), *Handbook of Social Cognition*, Hillsdale, NJ: Erlbaum, 179–236.

Isen, A.M., 2000, Positive Affect and Decision Making, In M. Lewis & J. M. Havieland (Eds.), *Handbook of Emotions*, 2, 417–435, London: Guilford.

Isen, A.M., and N. Geva, 1987, The Influence of Positive Affect on Acceptable Level of Risk: The Person With a Large Canoe Has a Large Worry, *Organizational Behavior and Human Decision Processes*, 39, 145–154.

Isen, A.M., T.E. Nygren, and F.G. Ashby, 1988, The Influence of Positive Affect on the Subjective Utility of Gains and Losses: It's Just not Worth the Risk, *Journal of Personality and Social Psychology*, 55(5), 710–717.

Isen, A. M., and R. Patrick, 1983, The Effect of Positive Feelings on Risk-Taking: When the Chips are Down, *Organizational Behavior and Human Performance*, 31, 194–202.

Isen, A.M., T.E. Shalker, M. Clark, and L. Karp, 1978, Affect, Accessibility of Material in Memory, and Behavior: A cognitive Loop? *Journal of Personality and Social Psychology*, 36 (1), 1–12.

Jegadeesh, N., and W. Kim, 2006, Value of Analyst Recommendations: International Evidence, *Journal of Financial Markets*, 9(3), 274–309.

Johnson, E.J., and A. Tversky, 1983, Affect, Generalization, and the Perception of Risk, *Journal of Personality and Social Psychology*, 45(1), 20–31.

Kahneman, D., and J. Riis, 2006, Living and Thinking About it: Two Perspectives on Life, *The Science of Well-Being*, F. Huppert, B. Keverne, & N. Baylis (Eds.), Oxford University Press.

Kamstra, M.J., L.A. Kramer, and M.D. Levi, 2000, Losing Sleep at the Market: The Daylight-Savings Anomaly, *American Economic Review*, 90(4), 1005–1011.

Kamstra, M.J., L.A. Kramer, and M.D. Levi, 2003, Winter Blues: A Sad Stock Market Cycle, *American Economic Review*, 93(1), 324–343.

Kamstra, M.J., L.A. Kramer, M.D. Levi, and R. Wermers, 2011, Seasonal Asset Allocation: Evidence from Mutual Fund Flows, Working paper, University of Maryland.

Karpoff, J.M., 1986, A Theory of Trading Volume, *Journal of Finance*, 41(5), 1069–1087.

Keller, C.M., B.L. Fredrickson, O. Ybarra, S. Cote, K. Johnson, J. Mikels, A. Conway, and T. Wager, 2005a, A Warm Heart and a Clear Head, *Psychological Science*, 16(9), 724–731.

Keller, C., M. Siegrist, and H. Gutscher, 2005b, The Role of Affect and Availability Heuristics in Risk Communication, The University of Zurich Working Paper.

Kliger, D., and D. Gilad, 2012, Red Light, Green Light: Color Priming in Financial Decisions, *Journal of Socio-Economics*, 41(5), 738–745.

Kliger, D., G. Gurevich, and A. Haim, 2012, When Chronobiology Met Economics — Seasonal Affective Disorder and the Demand for Initial Public Offerings, *Journal of Neuroscience, Psychology and Economics*, 5(3), 131–151.

Kliger, D., and A. Kudryavtsev, 2010, The Availability Heuristic and Investors' Reaction to Company-Specific Events, *Journal of Behavioral Finance*, 11(1), 50–65.

Kliger, D., and A. Kudryavtsev, 2013, Volatility Expectations and the Reaction to Analyst Recommendations, *Journal of Economic Psychology*, 37, 1–6.

Kliger, D., and A. Kudryavtsev, 2014, Out of the Blue: Mood Maintenance Hypothesis and Seasonal Effects on Investors' Reaction to News, *Quantitative Finance*, 14(4), 629–640.

Kliger, D., and O. Levy, 2003a, Mood-induced Variation in Risk Preferences, *Journal of Economic Behavior and Organization*, 52(4), 573–584.

Kliger, D., and O. Levy, 2003b, Mood and Judgment of Subjective Probabilities: Evidence from the U.S. Index Option Market, *European Finance Review*, 7(2), 235–248.

Kliger, D., and O. Levy, 2008, Mood Impacts on Probability Weighting Functions: "Large-gamble" Evidence, *Journal of Socio-Economics*, 37(4), 1397–1411.

Kliger, D., and O. Levy, 2009, Theories of Choice under Risk: Insights from Financial Markets, *Journal of Economic Behavior and Organization*, 71(2), 330–346.

Kramer, L.A., and J.M. Weber, 2012, This is Your Portfolio on Winter: Seasonal Affective Disorder and Risk Aversion in Financial Decision Making, *Social, Psychological and Personality Science*, 3(2), 193–199.

Krivelyova, A., and C. Robotti, 2003, Playing the Field: Geomagnetic Storms and International Stock Returns, Federal Reserve Bank of Atlanta, Working Paper 2003–5a.

Kuykendall, D., and J.P. Keating, 1990, Mood and Persuasion: Evidence for the Differential Impact of Positive and Negative States, *Psychology and Marketing*, 7(1), 1–9.

Lam, R.W., 1998, Seasonal Affective Disorder and Beyond: Diagnosis and Management, *Primary Care Psychiatry*, 4, 63–74.

Lee, B., J. O'Brien, and K. Sivaramakrishnan, 2005, An Analysis of Financial Analysts' Optimism in Long-Term Growth Forecasts, NEP Working Paper.

Loewenstein, G.F., C.K. Hsee, E.U. Weber, and N. Welch, 2001, Risk as Feelings, *Psychological Bulletin*, 127(2), 267–286.

Mackie, D.M., and L.T. Worth, 1989, Processing Deficits and the Mediation of Positive Affect in Persuasion, *Journal of Personality and Social Psychology*, 57(1), 27–40.

Mano, H., 1992, Judgments under Distress: Assessing the Role of Unpleasantness and Arousal in Judgment Formation, *Organization Behavior and Human Decision Processes*, 52, 216–246.

McDaniels, T.L., L.J. Axelrod, N.S. Cavanagh, and P. Slovic, 1997, Perception of Ecological Risk to Water Environments, *Risk Analysis*, 17(3), 341–352.

Mehra, R., and R. Sah, 2002, Mood Fluctuations, Projection Bias, and Volatility of Equity Prices, *Journal of Economic Dynamics and Control*, 26(5), 869–887.

Mikhail, M.B., B.R. Walther, and R.H. Willis, 2007, When Security Analysts Talk, Who Listens? *Accounting Review*, 82(5), 1227–1254.

Molin, J., E. Mellerup, P. Bolwig, T. Scheike, and H. Dam, 1996, The Influence of Climate on Development of Winter Depression, *Journal of Affective Disorders*, 37(2), 151–155.

Oren, D.A., and N.E. Rosenthal, 1992, Seasonal Affective Disorders, in Paykel, E.S., ed. Handbook of Affective Disorders, 2d ed. London: Churchill Livingstone, 551–567.

Palinkas, L.A., M. Houseal, and N.E. Rosenthal, 1996, Subsyndromal Seasonal Affective Disorder in Antarctica, *Journal of Nervous and Mental Disease*, 184(9), 530–534.

Palinkas, L.A., and M. Houseal, 2000, Sleep and Mood during a Winter in Antarctica, *International Journal of Circumpolar Health*, 59(1), 63–73.

Pfleiderer, P., 1984, The Volume of Trade and the Variability of Prices: A Framework for Analysis in Noisy Rational Expectations Equilibria, Stanford University, Working Paper.

Rosen, L.N., S.D. Targum, M. Terman, M.T. Bryant, H. Hoffman, S.F. Kasper, R. Hamovit, J.P. Docherty, B. Welch, and N.E. Rosenthal, 1990, Prevalence of Seasonal Affective Disorder at Four Latitudes, *Psychiatry Research*, 31(2), 131–144.

Rosenthal, N.E., D.A. Sack, J.C. Gillin, A.J. Lewy, F.K. Goodwin, Y. Davenport, P.S. Mueller, D.A. Newsome, and T.A. Wehr, 1984, Seasonal Affective Disorder: A Description of the Syndrome and Preliminary Findings with Light Therapy, *Archives of General Psychiatry*, 41(1), 72–80.

Saeed, S.A., and T.J. Bruce, 1998, Seasonal Affective Disorders, *American Family Physician*, 57(6), 1340–1346.

Saunders, E.M., 1993, Stock Prices and Wall Street Weather, *American Economic Review*, 83, 1137–1145.

Schwarz, N., 1990, Feelings as Information. Informational and Motivational Functions of Affective States, in R. Sorrentino and E.T Higgins, eds.: *Handbook of Motivation and Cognition* (Guilford Press, New York).

Schwarz, N., 2001, Feelings as Information: Implications for Affective Influences on Information Processing, In L.L. Martin and G.L. Clore (eds.), *Theories of Mood and Cognition: A User's Guidebook* (159–176), Mahwah, NJ: Erlbaum.

Schwarz, N., 2002, Feelings as Information: Moods Influence Judgments and Processing Strategies, In T. Gilovich, D. Griffin & D. Kahneman (Eds.). *Heuristics and Biases: The Psychology of Intuitive Judgment*, 534–547, New York: Cambridge University Press.

Schwarz, N., and G.L. Clore, 1983, Mood, Missatribution, and Judgments of Well-Being: Informative and Directive Functions of Affective States, *Journal of Personality and Social Psychology*, 45(3), 513–523.

Sherman, S.J., R.B. Cialdini, D.F. Schwartzman, and K.D. Reynolds, 2002, Imagining Can Heighten or Lower the Perceived Likelihood of Contracting a Disease: The Mediating Effect of Ease of Imagery, in *Heuristics and Biases: The Psychology of Intuitive Judgment*, edited by T. Gilovich, D. Griffin, and Daniel Kahneman. New York: Cambridge University Press.

Shiller, R.J., 1998, Human Behavior and the Efficiency of the Financial System, NBER Working Paper.

Slovic, P., N. Kraus, H. Lappe, and M. Major, 1991, Risk Perception of Prescription Drugs: Report on a Survey in Canada, *Canadian Journal of Public Health*, 82, S15-S20.

Sorescu, S., and A. Subrahmanyam, 2006, The Cross-Section of Analyst Recommendations, *Journal of Financial and Quantitative Analysis*, 41(1), 139–168.

Stickel, S.E., 1995, The Anatomy of the Performance of Buy and Sell Recommendations, *Financial Analysts Journal*, 51(5), 25–39.

Tversky, A., and D. Kahneman, 1973, Availability: A Heuristic for Judging Frequency and Probability, *Cognitive Psychology*, 4, 207–232.

Tversky, A., and D. Kahneman, 1974, Judgment under Uncertainty: Heuristics and Biases, *Science*, 185, 1124–1131.

Varian, Hal R., 1985, Divergence of Opinion in Complete Markets: A Note, *Journal of Finance*, 40(1), 309–317.

Whaley, R.E., 1993, Derivatives on Market Volatility: Hedging Tools Long Overdue, *Journal of Derivatives*, 1, 71–84.

Whaley, R.E., 2000, The Investor Fear Gauge, *Journal of Portfolio Management*, 26(3), 12–17.

Whaley, R.E., 2008, Understanding VIX, Working Paper, Vanderbilt University.

Williams, S., M. Zainuba, and R. Jackson, 2003, Affective Influences on Risk Perceptions and Risk Intention, *Journal of Managerial Psychology*, 18(2), 126–138.

Womack, K.L., 1996, Do Brokerage Analysts Recommendations Have Investment Value? *Journal of Finance*, 51(1), 137–167.

Wright, W.F., and G.H. Bower, 1992, Mood Effects on Subjective Probability Assessment, *Organizational Behavior and Human Decision Processes*, 52(2), 276–291.

Young, M.A., P.M. Meaden, F.L. Fogg, E.A. Cherin, and C.A. Eastman, 1997, Which Environmental Variables are Related to the Onset of Seasonal Affective Disorder?, *Journal of Abnormal Psychology*, 106(4), 554–562.

Yuan, K., L. Zheng, and Q. Zhu, 2006, Are Investors Moonstruck? Lunar Phases and Stock Returns, *Journal of Empirical Finance*, 13(1), 1–23.

Chapter 12

Uniform or Discriminatory Auctions: Endogenizing Bidder's Choice in Divisible Goods Auctions*

Menachem Brenner[†], Dan Galai[‡] and Orly Sade[§]

Abstract

The objective of this paper is to investigate the preferences of potential bidders in choosing between uniform and discriminatory auction pricing methods. Many financial assets, particularly government bonds, are issued in an auction. Uniform and discriminatory pricing constitute the two most popular mechanisms used in public auctions. Theoretical

---

*A substantial part of this paper was previously distributed under the title: "Auctioning Financial Assets: Discriminatory Vs Uniform, which Method is Preferred." In the process of conducting the surveys we have benefited from the help of Sari Carp, Ken Froewiss, Marti Subrahmanyam, Bernie Yeung, Zvi Wiener and Avraham Haim (Abe) from Leumi Bank. We thank Moran Ofir for her excellent research assistance. We also benefited from discussions with Bill Allen, Peter Cramton, Kenneth Garbade, Eugene Kandel, Avner Kalay, Michal Passerman, Jesus M. Salas, Raghu Sundaram, Avi Wohl, Yishay Yafeh, Zehavit Yosef and Jaime Zender. We would also like to thank the participants of the 2006 European Finance Association Meeting in Zurich, MTS 2006 in Istanbul, FUR XIII 2006 in Rome and the 2009 APESA meeting in Haifa. We also benefited from comments received from the participants of seminars at Tel-Aviv University, IDC (Israel), NYU, the University of Colorado at Boulder, University of Massachusetts at Amherst, University of Houston, University of Utah University of Montana and the Federal Reserve Bank of NY. We thank "The Caesarea Edmond Benjamin de Rothschild Center for Capital Markets and Risk" at IDC, the Krueger Center for Finance and the Zagagi Center at the Hebrew University of Jerusalem for partial financial support.

[†]Stern School of Business, New York University
Email: mbrenner@stern.nyu.edu

[‡]Jerusalem School of Business, Hebrew University of Jerusalem
And the College for Academic Studies, Or Yehuda
Email: dan.galai@huji.ac.il

[§]Jerusalem School of Business, Hebrew University of Jerusalem
orlysade@mscc.huji.ac.il

papers have not been able to provide an unequivocal preference of one mechanism over the other. This study investigates both bidder choice and the impact of that choice on the pricing outcome of the auction by allowing bidders to choose between the two alternative systems. The majority of the bidders in the survey prefer uniform pricing. Those preferring uniform auctions tend to bid more aggressively than those preferring discriminatory. On average, the proceeds to the issuer were higher under the uniform price mechanism.

Keywords: Uniform auction, discriminatory auction, Treasury bonds, T-bills

JEL Classification: G1, F3

1. Introduction

The recent financial crisis was followed by a potential sovereign debt crisis. During the crisis, the debt of several countries, some from the Euro-zone, were downgraded. The discussion around these events highlighted the importance of the process of sovereign debt issuance. Many financial assets such as treasury bonds, corporate bonds and stocks are issued to the public via auctions.[1] No consensus currently exists, either in the academic literature or in practice, as to the most appropriate method of the auction pricing mechanism. The question whether uniform or discriminatory pricing should be used remains unresolved.[2]

The impact of market design on the level of participation and prices in financial markets is a key issue in the literature on financial market micro-structure. A vast body of research focuses on this issue, particularly within

[1] For a discussion of the treasury bond market around the globe see Brenner, Galai and Sade (2009) for the discussion of the European central bank repo auctions see Bindeseil, Nyborg and Srabulaev (2009) for a discussion on the attempt of using auctions to price employee stock option see Mazumdar, Nanda and Surana (2009).

[2] In uniform price auctions (also known as single price auction), all bidders bidding above the market clearing price are awarded the entire amount, while those bidding at the clearing price are awarded on a pro-rata basis. All winners pay the same price, the market clearing price, for the entire quantity that they are awarded, regardless of the price submitted on their bid. In a discriminatory price auction (also known as multiple- price or pay-as-you-bid auction), bidders bidding above the market clearing price are awarded their bids. Each bidder, however, pays the price/s submitted in the bid.

the context of secondary financial markets.[3] Our study, while part of this literature, deals with auction design in primary bond markets and its affect on participation and pricing.

This study is the first to investigate in a controlled environment the connection between the design of the auction and its potential impact on the participation in the offering and its outcome.

So far the academic literature in financial economics viewed the issuer of sovereign bonds as a monopolist and hence ignored the preferences of the buyers. While this view was more appropriate in the past where markets were more segmented, especially in less developed financial markets, it is less appropriate now when financial markets are more integrated and participants invest globally. For example, when 60% of Greece's debt in the second quarter of 2005 was held by foreign investors (IMF report 2006), it is hard to argue that the Greek's Treasury can ignore the preferences of foreign institutional investors.[4]

As barriers to investment in foreign countries decrease, investors have many options to choose from. A US-based investor, for example, who is seeking to invest in highly rated sovereign bonds, linked to the euro, can choose to participate in the German or French government bond auctions that use discriminatory price auctions or in Finland's auctions that use the uniform price mechanism. He also can choose to buy Austrian bonds that use none of these auction methods (see Brenner, Galai and Sade, 2009). Though these bonds differ by their characteristics there is no doubt that one can find several which are close substitutes. In addition, it is important to note that auctions are not only used for sovereign debt, but also for the issuance of corporate debt. In Israel, for example, a particular corporation can sell its debt using a discriminatory auction or a uniform one. An investor can decide which bonds to purchase.

In this paper we try to uncover the preferences of participants for a particular auction design; the discriminatory price auction or the uniform one. This paper analyzes the results of an experiment conducted among bidders (students and professionals). It is essentially impossible to collect

[3] For a survey of the literature see Biais, Glosten, and Spatt (2005).

[4] The IMF report also indicates that foreign investments in emerging markets have doubled from 2000 to 2005.

relevant data regarding bidders' actions and their preferences for specific auction mechanisms, while controlling for other factors. Therefore, we surveyed potential bidders and ask them to participate in an experiment to learn about their preferences in choosing between alternative pricing mechanisms. To the best of our knowledge, our study is the first in which participants are offered a choice, albeit simulated, between alternative multi-unit (identical) goods auction systems.[5]

We conducted an experiment with no monetary rewards (hereafter "survey") among a variety of potential bidders, including financial professionals, business students, MBAs with a few years of work experience and executive MBAs in seven countries (US, Israel, Norway, South Africa, Luxembourg, Switzerland and the Netherlands.)[6,7] We initially received 220 qualified answers. Most surveys were conducted during 2004–5 (220 participants,) and our statistical results are mainly based on these surveys. A control group of 22 participants was used in a questionnaire given in March 2009. The survey focused on their preference for either a uniform or a discriminatory price auction.

The main findings are: (a) 90.9% of the participants are *not indifferent* with respect to the pricing rule of the auction. (b) 65.5% of those with a definite preference prefer to participate in a *uniform* price auction. This finding transcends country of origin and educational/professional background (MBAs, executive MBAs, undergraduates or professionals) and gender. Not only are the participants in our study preferring, on average, the uniform price mechanism, they also submit more aggressive bids under the uniform price mechanism (consistent with previous experimental work) and as result they are willing to pay, on average, a higher price. We do not

---

[5]There have been attempts, in the single unit auction literature, to empirically and experimentally examine bidder preferences among existing mechanisms and to theoretically incorporate the notion that issuers may need to compete for bidders. See, for example, Ivanova-Stenzel and Salmon (2004), McAfee (1993), Levin and Smith (1994).

[6]All the university students that participated in our survey attended advance finance courses and have a background in economics and statistics. They came from more than 20 countries.

[7]Camerer and Hogarth (1999) in their review paper about incentives in economics experiment also documented that: "The studies show that the effects of incentives are mixed and complicated." (page 8)

investigate the reasons for their choices, but, concentrate on their revealed preferences as reflected in their answers.

Milton Friedman (1960) has argued that in the context of Treasury auctions, discriminatory pricing drives out uninformed participants because of the danger of over-bidding, the so-called "winner's curse". As a result, discriminatory pricing attracts the better informed, typically large players, and may be more susceptible to collusion than uniform pricing. Hence, he predicts that by limiting the pool of bidders, discriminatory auctions lead to lower proceeds from the offering. Our paper provides experimental support to Friedman's hypothesis.

More recent work in the theory of divisible-unit auctions investigates trade-offs that policy makers face in the deployment of alternative pricing mechanisms.[8] These papers raise the following question: Given a set number of exogenous participants (N) at the time the rules are set, which mechanism will maximize proceeds from the auction? They show that a non-cooperative equilibrium exists under the uniform-price format, which supports collusive outcomes and is sub-optimal from the issuer's standpoint. These theoretical studies also show that collusive outcomes are not evident in discriminatory auctions, in contrast to Friedman's conjecture. They also claim that the uniform price mechanism may result in multiple equilibria.

In sum, in the case of divisible units, the theory is inconclusive. Also, there is no consensus as to which of the two methods will generate larger proceeds. Thus, the choice of the auction mechanism remains an empirical issue.

There is a growing strand of research in experimental economics investigating divisible good auctions.[9] The methodology employed in this research enables us to compare alternative pricing mechanisms in a

[8] See, for example, Wilson (1979), Back and Zender (1993), Ausubel and Cramton (2002) and Wang and Zender (2002) for theoretical discussions on strategic bidding in multi-unit auctions. A survey article on auction theory by Das and Sundaram (1996) discusses the implications of theoretical models for Treasury securities auctions and presents some empirical evidence.

[9] Starting from the early papers by Smith (1967), Miller and Plott (1985), Cox, Smith and Walker (1985) to the more recent papers by Goswami, Noe, and Rebello (1996) and Sade, Schnitzlein and Zender (2006).

controlled environment. In these controlled experiments, the number of participants in each mechanism was set in advance and bidders were asked to participate in a specific pre-determined auction.

While these experiments are able to gauge the potential impact of auction structure on pricing, the inability of participants to choose between the auction types may limit the applicability of these findings to financial markets. In actual auctions, the outcome depends on both price quotes and participation. Hence, no conclusions can be drawn regarding the impact of the auction mechanism without considering the number of participating bidders for each of the alternative pricing systems.[10]

Consistent with previous empirical research based on event studies our survey results suggest that by using the uniform price mechanism issuers may obtain higher revenues since the combination of the large number of bidders with their aggressive bidding strategies should yield larger proceeds.[11,12]

In addition to its contribution to the academic literature on auction mechanisms, our research has practical implications as well. Given that financial markets have become more global,[13] issuers, including sovereign governments, seeking to attract global participation, can no longer act as monopolists in their respective markets and must take into account preferences of potential bidders. Moreover, the degree of participation in the initial auction is likely to have a positive effect on the liquidity of the secondary market.

---

[10] See, for example, Engelbrecht-Wiggans, List, and Reiley (2006) and Bulow, and Klemperer (1996).

[11] Our results are consistent with the empirical investigation of Umlauf (1993) who examined Mexican T-bill auctions, with Feldman and Reinhart (1995) who studied the International Monetary Fund's auction of gold and with Tenorio (1993) who studied Zambia's weekly foreign exchange auctions. See also Nyborg and Sundaresan (1996), Malvey and Archibald (1998) and Goldreich (2007) for the U.S. experiment.

[12] The experimental work by Goswami, Noe, and Rebello (1996) shows that discriminatory auctions yield higher proceeds than do uniform auctions.

[13] See, for example, the evidence from Finland: "The introduction of the euro has boosted market volumes as well as numbers of active counterparties and final investors. Already during the first year of the euro, domestic banks lost much of their earlier dominant position as the share of foreign demand increased to 75%, and the share is still increasing", Salavirta and Taipalus (2003, pp 44).

Our paper joins the strand of literature that uses both professionals and students in experimental/survey settings.[14] Within the context of financial market decision-making, several experimental papers have examined the choice of professional versus student subjects and found that the behavior of professional decision-makers does not qualitatively differ from that exhibited by the students.[15] Our paper joins the discussion in the experimental economics literature (Guala, 2005) about the need of monetary rewards in experiments. We show that we obtain consistent results in our experiments that involve no monetary rewards with previous experiments that had monetary rewards.

The rest of the paper is organized as follows. Section 2 describes the hypotheses relating to bidders' choice and discusses the design of the survey. In Section 3, we summarize and discuss the survey results. Section 4 provides concluding remarks.

2. Hypotheses about Bidders' Choices

As discussed above, the existing theory does not provide us with a definitive answer regarding the pricing rule that an issuer of financial assets should choose in designing an auction. One possible alternative is to try to get a reading on the preferences of potential bidders. An experiment conducted by the US Treasury between 1992 and 1996 compared the two auction systems. The results (see Malvey, Archibald and Flynn, 1995; and Malvey and Archibald, 1998) are marginally in favor of the uniform price mechanism when the total revenues generated by the two methods are compared. In the uniform price mechanism, the experiment also gave indications of wider participation and less concentration.

The purpose of our study is to shed some light on the preference of potential market participants regarding the pricing mechanism in public auctions. Unable to measure these preferences directly from market data,

---

[14]Friedman and Sunder (1994) provide a detailed discussion on the choice of subjects for experimental economics and survey studies of different economic decisions.

[15]See, for example, DeJong, Forsythe and Uecker (1988), Dyer, Kagel and Levin (1989), Plott (1988) and Smith, Suchanek and Williams (1988).

and believing that they should have an impact on the propensity of investors to participate in auctions, we provide evidence obtained from surveys of potential bidders. These estimates are then entered into a model comparing the proceeds generated from uniform and discriminatory auctions, to render a more realistic analysis of how market design may affect the functioning of primary markets.

The first question to be addressed in the survey is whether in fact auction participants have a preference (or are they indifferent) to a specific type of pricing mechanism, be it uniform (UPA) or discriminatory (DA). Second, we tried to discover if the choice of mechanism affected bidding behavior. Is the bidding similar in either mechanisms or does one mechanism encourage more aggressive bidding? Third, we investigate the total impact of participation and bidding aggressiveness to find out if there is a significant difference in proceeds that the issuer collects.

3. Survey Design

3.1. *Methodology*

The responses to the surveys, which were conducted among different groups in several countries, constitute our source of data. Designing an effective survey is a challenging task since one needs to express a complicated realistic situation in a relatively short survey and elicit honest replies. We decided to adopt the experimental design of SSZ (2006) as the base case of our survey. This enables us to check the consistency of our survey ("one shot game") with a multi-round experiment. Moreover it enables us to check the consistency of the results of two methods, an unpaid survey versus a paid lab experiment.[16] In the design of the specific survey questions that are asked we used standard techniques to minimize potential biases. In addition, we applied IRB constraints. A copy of the survey is provided in Appendix A.

In order to keep the identity of the participants confidential the survey does not ask for specific individual identification such as name, birth date, or social security number other than gender. Yet, in order to incorporate

---

[16]For an elaborate discussion on the effects of financial incentives on performance in experimental tasks see Camerer and Hogarth (1999).

the potential impact of financial experience, particularly financial auction experience, we do ask questions about experience in financial markets and previous participation in financial auctions.

The first part of the survey describes the objectives of the research and provides a detailed example of the two auction mechanisms. The second part consists of the questionnaire, including questions regarding the participants' experience.

3.2. *Survey Questions and the Main Example*

In our survey (see Appendix A) the participants were asked to imagine that the market consists of 10 participants and each participant can decide in which auction mechanism to participate. As in reality, the decision of each member of the group affects the number of bidders that he or she will eventually be bidding against. In other words, if more participants will choose the uniform price mechanism the total amount of bidders that they will compete with, in a given auction, will be larger. The parameters of the problem are based on SSZ (2006), which is described below.

In their study there are $N = 5$ bidders in each auction mechanism (5 in the uniform and 5 in the discriminatory) who compete for $Q = 26$ units of a good. The after-market value of a unit is known in advance and is equal to 20.[17] Prices are discrete and the "tick size" is 1. In particular, bids were submitted for quantity orders at four distinct prices contained in the set {17, 18, 19, 20}. Quantities are in integers and the aggregate quantity demanded by each bidder is 26. Each quantity order is an offer to purchase the specified number of units at a given price (or below in the case of the uniform-price auction). The stop-out price is determined as the highest price at which demand equals or exceeds the supply of $Q = 26$ units. Winning bids are those submitted at or above the stop-out price. All quantities demanded at prices strictly above the stop-out price are filled while orders bid at the stop-out price are rationed on a pro-rata basis.

---

[17] Since a known post-auction price was employed by SSZ (2006), there is a legitimate concern about this design decision. One motivation was to avoid the potential bidder bankruptcy, a factor we cannot control for in our survey. Another consideration was that, given a fairly liquid Treasury bond market, the reissuance of the same bonds occurs in a market with continuously observed prices.

Given this structure, SSZ (2006) describes the Nash equilibria of the one-shot auctions. While the uniform price mechanism supports multiple equilibria (at all possible prices), the discriminatory price mechanism supports only one equilibrium at the auction price of 19.

In our setting, the experimental design which allocates five bidders to each mechanism can be thought of as a special case where either all the 10 participants choose to be indifferent between the two auction mechanisms or 50% of them choose to participate in a uniform price mechanism and the other 50% choose the discriminatory price mechanism. It should be noted that the equlibria described in the case where 10 players are divided into two groups of five each is not necessarily the equilibria obtained in other possible division of the 10 players. If, for example, only one participant decided to choose the uniform price mechanism, while the rest (9) decided to choose the discriminatory price mechanism, then the only equilibrium in the uniform price mechanism is 17.

In our survey the participants are presented with two identical firms which try to issue debt via an auction. The only difference between the two firms is the auction mechanism; one firm opts for uniform pricing, while the other uses discriminatory pricing.[18]

We asked the participants which, if any, preference they have, or whether they are indifferent to the pricing mechanism. Given their choice, they were asked to submit a schedule of bids. We also asked them which mechanism (if any) they thought most of the other participants would choose. We did not reward the participants with monetary prizes and participation in the survey was strictly voluntary. In the control group from 2009 we also asked them, using the same initial survey, to write the reasons for their choice.

3.3. *Survey Sample*

We conducted the survey in six countries in 2004–2005.[19] Our final sample consists of 220 participants. (USA (43.2%), Israel (22.7%), Switzerland

---

[18]It is important to note that while the participants in our survey choose between two firms, we could have replaced the word "firm" with the word "country". Since we wanted the participants to be unbiased by the common practice of their own home country, we chose firms as the auctioning (offering) entity.

[19]We excluded a few cases of participants that either did not respond to the question of mechanism choice, did not submit bids, or submitted bids for more than 26 units in the sample.

(8.2%), Luxembourg (12.3%), Norway (7.7%) and South Africa (5.9%). The participants (see Table 1) consisted of bankers from South Africa attending a risk management course, financial professionals from one of the leading financial institutions in Israel, business undergraduates from the US, MBA students from the US, Israel, Luxemburg and Switzerland, as well as executive MBA students, primarily financial professionals, from Israel and Norway.[20]

The participants in our sample have on average 2.33 years of experience in financial markets (the maximum is 25 and the minimum is zero). 11.4% indicated that they had previously participated in financial asset auctions. Given the strand of literature that argues that gender may have an affect on various aspects of the decision making process, we also controlled for gender. Our sample included 21.8% female subjects.

We also conducted a robustness test (March, 2009) among risk managers in a major bank and an insurance company in the Netherlands and among Executive MBA students in Luxembourg with work experience in banks and financial institutions. Altogether, 22 students answered the questionnaire. This is our control group.

4. Analysis of the Findings

4.1. *Choice of Pricing Mechanism*

The first major finding is that 91% of the participants indicated a definite preference for a given pricing mechanism. 65.5% of those with a preference chose to participate in the uniform price auction. This finding persisted across countries and across types of education/professional experience (Executive MBA versus MBA versus Undergraduates) (see Table 1 for detailed results). In other words, the majority of the participants in each country and in each education group *preferred uniform pricing.*

What may affect bidders' choice? Some of the potential factors are information/knowledge, risk preference, behavioral biases, culture, or strategic behavior. As a proxy for information/knowledge we asked the participants to indicate the years of work experience in financial markets

---

[20]Many of the students in the classes in Switzerland and Luxembourg are citizen of other countries such as Germany, France, Belgium and Holland.

Table 1: Bidders Choices between the Auction Methods

Participants	Month and Year	Number	% Uniform	% Discriminatory	% Indifferent
Executive MBA and Executive Courses	June 2004 and April 2005	18	55.56%	38.89%	5.56%
Israel-Hebrew U-Executive MBA-Finance					
South Africa-Bankers	June 2004	13	46.15%	30.77%	23.08%
Norway — Executive MBA at BI	May 2005	17	76.47%	17.65%	5.88%
MBA					
Luxembourg — School of Finance	February 2004 and January 2005	27	70.37%	25.93%	3.70%
Switzerland-Lausanne-MBA Finance	May 2004	18	50.00%	33.33%	16.67%
Israel — Hebrew U — Advanced MBA — Finance	November 2004	10	40.00%	60.00%	0.00%
NYU–MBA 2–3 year part time MBA	December 2004	24	66.67%	20.83%	12.5%
NYU — full time 2nd year MBA	December 2004	40	62.50%	32.50%	5.00%
NYU — 2nd year MBA-Investment Banking, Business & Law School	December 2004	19	52.63%	31.58%	15.79%
Advanced Undergraduate					
NYU-Business Undergraduate — Seniors	December 2004	12	41.67%	33.33%	25.00%
Professionals					
Financial professionals from a leading financial institution in Israel	January 2005	22	63.64%	36.36%	0.00%
TOTAL		***220***	***90.91%***		***9.09%***
TOTAL		***220***	***59.55%***	***31.36%***	***9.09%***

This table summarizes the responses of participants in a survey conducted during 2004 and 2005. Participants specify the location, academic institution, type of education or occupation. "Month and Year" specifies the date the survey was conducted. "Number" indicates the qualified answers from this sub-group. " %Uniform" denotes the percentage of the qualified answers preferring uniform pricing, while "%Discriminatory" indicates the percentage of the qualified answers preferring discriminatory pricing and "% Indifferent" indicates the percentage of the qualified answers stating indifference between the two alternative price mechanisms.

and if they had prior experience in financial auctions. Since there is indication in the academic literature that risk attitudes is related to gender and risk attitude may affect the mechanism choice, we also gathered information on the gender of the participants. As a proxy for potential culture difference we control for the US versus other countries where the survey took place.

Table 2 presents the univariate relationship between, gender, length of work experience in the financial industry and exposure to financial auctions and their pricing method. Those preferring uniform pricing have, on average (p=0.057), greater professional experience in the financial industry than those favoring discriminatory pricing (2.7, and 1.8 years respectively). While the proportion of those that had previous exposure to financial auctions is higher among the group preferring discriminatory pricing, the difference is not significant. Neither gender nor location (i.e., most surveys that were conducted in the US) was statistically significant.

To investigate this question further in a multivariate context we estimated the following logit (probit) equations on the sample of participants who had a specific preference ("not indifferent") and answered all the

Table 2: Univariate Analysis — Bidders Characteristics and Preferences

	Uniform	Discriminatory
Mean — Years of Financial Work Experience	2.72*	1.79*[21]
Median — Years of Financial Work Experience	0.67	0.25
% of Female	22%	25%
% of Previous Financial Auctions Experience	11%	14%
% of US Responses	43%	41%

This table summarizes the descriptive statistics of participant responses to a survey conducted during 2004 and 2005 according to mechanism of choice. *indicates that the variable is statistically significant at 10% confidence level (the p-value of the t-test was calculated assuming unequal variance and a two tail test.)

[21] P-value equals 0.057

essential questions (n=194):[22,23]

$$\text{UPM} = \alpha + \beta_1\text{YE} + \beta_2\text{Dummy(AE)} \tag{12.1}$$

$$\begin{aligned}\text{UPM} = \alpha + \beta_1\text{YE} + \beta_2\text{Dummy(AE)}\\ + \beta_3\text{Dummy(G)} + \text{Dummy(US)}\end{aligned} \tag{12.2}$$

Where:

UPM (Uniform Price Mechanism) is a dummy variable that gets the value 1 if the participant chooses the uniform price mechanism and 0 if the participant chooses the discriminatory price mechanism.

YE is years of experience that the participant has in the financial industry.

Dummy (AE) is a dummy variable that gets the value 1 if the participant had experience with financial asset auctions.

Dummy (G) is a dummy variable that equals 1 if the participant is a female and 0 if he is a male.

Dummy (US) is a dummy variable that equals 1 if the survey was done in the US and 0 elsewhere.

The results obtained from estimating the above logit (probit) equations are consistent with the univariate analysis as follows: From equation (1) we find that the preference for the uniform price mechanism is positively correlated with years of financial market experience but it is barely significant (p=0.08 for the logit and 0.07 for the probit). Exposure to financial asset auctions has a non-significant negative correlation with auction choice. The pseudo R-square is rather low (0.017 for the logit and 0.018 for the probit) indicating that we are explaining a very small part of the variation in the auction choice. The basic result and the explanatory power of the model do not change when we add a dummy for gender or a dummy for the US location as control variables (equation 2).[24] These two control variables were both insignificant.

---

[22]We also conducted a multinomial logit test that included the "indifferent" group The results were essentially the same.

[23]In five cases the participants did not indicate the years of experience. They were excluded from the analysis.

[24]The P value of the chi-square test for the model is also insignificant.

Figure 1: Mechanism Preference and Experience in Financial Markets

Figure 1 describes the distribution of choices of the participants among the pricing mechanism as a function of their years of work experience in the financial markets. "No Experience" represents the group of participant with no work experience in the financial markets. "Up to (including) Two Years" represents the group of participants that have positive work experience in financial markets that is less than (including) two years. "Above Two Years" represents the group of participants with above two years of work experience in financial markets.

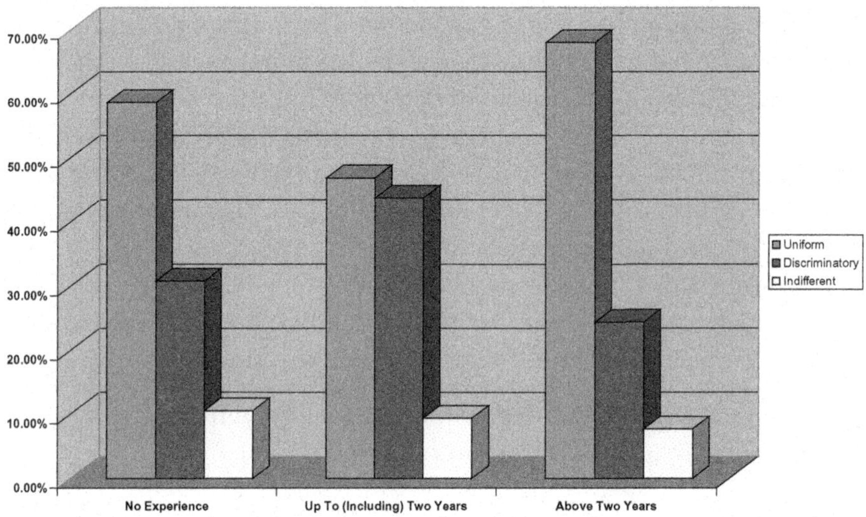

We next divided the sample of participants into three groups according to their reported years of experience in the financial markets: The first group reported no experience in financial markets (n = 104), the second group is the group that reported experience of up to (including) two years (n = 32) and the last group is the group that reported experience of more than two years (n = 78). Figure 1 shows the preference of the participants for each of the three groups. Though all three groups show a preference for the uniform mechanism, the relatively strongest support for this mechanism is provided by the participants who reported to have financial market experience of over two years.[25]

[25]It is interesting to note that the preference for the uniform mechanism is only slightly greater than for the discriminatory mechanism among those that have approximately two-years work experience.

4.2. *Bidding Startegy*

After observing that most bidders prefer the uniform price mechanism, the next question we examined was whether there is a difference in the bidding strategy among those that prefer uniform pricing compared with those that prefer discriminatory pricing and how that is translated to the revenue obtained by the issuer.

We find that not only do most bidders prefer uniform pricing, they are also willing to bid more aggressively under the uniform price mechanism. The weighted average (by quantity demanded) of the price submitted by bidders that chose the uniform price mechanism is 18.72 while the weighted average of the price submitted by bidders that chose the discriminatory price mechanism is 18.59. This result is statistically significant at the 10% level and is consistent with the finding of SSZ (2006).[26]

To test whether the difference between the weighted average price that was bid in the two auctions is statistically significant, while controlling for relevant variables, we use the following Tobit regression[27]

$$\begin{aligned} \text{AP} = \alpha &+ \beta_1 \text{YE} + \beta_2 \text{Dummy(AE)} + \beta_3 \text{Dummy(G)} \\ &+ \beta_4 \text{Dummy(UPM)} + \beta_4 \text{Dummy(DPM)} \end{aligned}$$

Where:

AP is the weighted average of the price submitted by bidders calculated as:

$$\text{AP} = \frac{\sum_{i=17,18,19,20} i * Qi}{\sum_{i=17,18,19,20} Qi}$$

Where Qi represents the quantity demanded at that price.

Dummy (UPM) is a dummy variable that receives the value 1 if the participant chose the uniform price mechanism and 0 if the participant chose the discriminatory price mechanism or was indifferent. Dummy (DPM) is a dummy variable that receives the value 1 if the participant

---

[26] It is important to note that in SSZ(2006) experiments students were motivated by monetary rewards and professional were not. We find similar results in an experiment with no monetary result. This add to the recent debate described by Guala (2005) about the need of monetary rewards in experiments.

[27] We use Tobit since the bidding prices in the survey are limited to the range between 17 and 20.

chose the discriminatory price mechanism and 0 if the participant chose the uniform price mechanism or was indifferent. YE is the amount of experience in round years that the participant had in the financial industry. Dummy (AE) is a dummy variable that receives the value of 1 if the participant had experience with financial assets auctions. Dummy (G) is a dummy variable that equals 1 if the participant was a female and 0 if he was a male. Dummy (US) is a dummy variable that equals 1 if the survey was done in the US and 0 elsewhere.

The only significant variable at the 10% level (P=0.07) is UPM and its coefficient is positive, which gives additional support to the hypothesis that those opting for the uniform price mechanism bid more aggressively on average.

In order to investigate which mechanism will yield greater proceeds to the issuer, given the participants' choices, we randomly assigned the 220 participants answers to twenty two groups of ten each. In each group we divided the participants' answers according to their mechanism choice; either discriminatory or uniform. Participants expressing indifference between the two mechanisms were randomly assigned. We calculated the auction price for the two mechanisms for each of the 22 groups. On average, the uniform price mechanism leads to significantly higher proceeds when compared to the discriminatory price mechanism (t=2.95 paired test). Consistent with SSZ (2006) we also find that there is higher variation in the proceeds obtained under the uniform price mechanism than under the discriminatory price mechanism. Table 3 shows the proceeds for each of the 22 groups. In most groups, the uniform bids resulted in much higher proceeds (14 out of 22 groups). In thirteen cases, the uniform bids actually yielded the highest possible proceeds of 520. The highest proceeds for the discriminatory bidders was 514.

4.3. *What Drives Bidders Preferences?*

What is driving our results? Do bidders project correctly choices of other bidders? In our survey we asked the participants which method will be mostly chosen by others? About 20% of our sample did not answer this question. Hence, the relevant sample decreased to 175. Out of them 10.3% predicted that most participants will be indifferent, 66.3% predicted that most participants will choose the uniform price mechanism and

Table 3: Proceeds for Each Random Group for Uniform and Discriminatory Bidders

Market	U	D	U–D
1	520	508	12
2	520	481	39
3	494	507	−13
4	520	494	26
5	520	495	25
6	520	494	26
7	520	478	42
8	520	496	24
9	520	495	25
10	520	494	26
11	494	497	−3
12	494	496	−2
13	520	494	26
14	494	494	0
15	520	500	20
16	494	513	−19
17	520	504	16
18	494	514	−20
19	494	495	−1
20	494	499	−5
21	520	505	15
22	494	495	−1
AVG	**509.36**	**497.64**	**11.73**

"U" and "D" denote proceeds from the simulated uniform and discriminatory price auctions respectively. "U-D" represents the difference in proceeds obtained under the uniform price mechanism versus those obtained under discriminatory pricing. "Avg" indicates the average of each of the variables.

23.4% predicted that most participants will choose the discriminatory price mechanism. Overall, the predictions of our participants were in line with the actual responses. Most thought that the majority will choose the uniform price mechanism and in fact, most did. It is interesting to note that 76.6% of the participants thought that most participants will choose the same mechanism that they chose. It is an interesting observation because participating in the mechanism that most players choose is not necessarily an optimal choice.

While focusing on the bidders' choice one may ask how our survey results fit into the paradigm of a general equilibrium. In a world with open financial markets and (relatively) free access to a variety of different auctions of close substitutes, shouldn't there be some kind of an irrelevance result that applies to any country? Under this paradigm, if bidders are rational and only concerned with paying the lowest price they will look for the best value across auctions taking into account their ability to extract rents from the seller and the anticipated participation in each auction.

To learn more about what drives bidders preferences we conducted two additional surveys with different groups in the early months of 2009. The first group that consisted of 13 risk managers in a major bank and an insurance company in the Netherlands and the second that consisted of 14 Executive MBA students in Luxembourg with work experience in banks and financial institutions. In addition to the questions presented before, the two groups were explicitly asked to answer why they chose a particular mechanism. Not all participant were willing to disclose their mechanism choice (four did not). Of those that did, the majority chose the uniform price mechanism. We got varied responses from those that picked the uniform price mechanism (equality of the price, risk, clarity of the mechanism and the luck of the winner curse) and we could not single out a clearly dominant reason that explains the mechanism choice. Our results, admittedly on a relatively limited sample, are consistent with the previous literature, and suggest that although price plays a major role in the preference of the uniform mechanism, it seems that there are other considerations as well. For example, the uniform price mechanism is associated with "fairness".

In designing the initial survey, we focused on documenting the subjects' actions and demographic differences rather than asking their opinions and reasoning for their actions. We made this experimental choice in order to avoid some of the biases that may otherwise occur in the answers of the respondents. Only in the control group we also asked the subjects for the reasoning for their choices. What is clear from our exercise is that even though different bidders are driven by different reasons, such as fairness, complexity of the market or the illusion of expertise, the outcome is consistent with the bidders' preference for the uniform price mechanism.

5. Summary and Conclusions

Most governments and some corporations use auctions when offering securities and other financial assets to the public. The most common types of auctions for financial assets use either a uniform pricing mechanism or a discriminatory (multiple) one. Existing theoretical and empirical work is ambivalent about which method is optimal for issuer. Experiments designed to compare the two mechanisms examine the impact of the auction's structure on pricing assume, however, that the level of investor participation under each pricing system will be equal. This assumption does not necessarily reflect market reality. In general investors are not indifferent to the design specifics of the auction. In order to more accurately compare between pricing mechanisms, the propensity of bidders to participate must be taken into account.

For the first time in the academic literature this paper provides survey evidence on the preference that potential bidders may have regarding uniform versus discriminatory pricing. We surveyed over 200 financial professionals, executives and business students in order to learn about their preferences between the two auction mechanisms. Our survey revealed that an overwhelming majority of potential participants are not indifferent between auction mechanisms and the majority *prefers uniform pricing.* The only variable that we found to be positively correlated to the choice of auction mechanism is years of experience in financial markets. Other factors, such as country of origin, education level (undergraduate versus MBA versus executive MBA), previous exposure to financial auctions and gender had no bearing on bidder's preference.

Our study provides evidence consistent with the results of the US experiment and suggests that issuers, including sovereign governments, seeking broader-based participation in securities auctions, should consider using the uniform price mechanism.

References

Ausubel, L., and P. Cramton, 2002, *Demand Reduction and Inefficiency in Multi-Unit Auctions,* University of Maryland working paper.

Back, K., and J. F. Zender, 1993, "Auctions of Divisible Goods: On the Rationale for the Treasury Experiment," *Review of Financial Studies,* 6, 733–764.

Biais, B., L. Glosten, and C. Spatt, 2005, "Market Microstructure: A Survey of Microfoundations, Empirical Results, and Policy Implications", *Journal of Financial Markets*, 8(2), 217–264

Bindseil, U., Nyborg, K. G. and Strebulaev, I. A., 2009, "Repo Auctions and the Market for Liquidity". *Journal of Money, Credit and Banking*, 41: 1391–1421.

Brenner M., D. Galai and O. Sade, 2009, "Sovereign Debt Auctions: Uniform or discriminatory?", *Journal of Monetary Economics*, vol. 56, issue 2, pages 267–274.

Bulow, J I. and P. D. Klemperer. 1996, "Auctions vs Negotiations," *American Economic Review*, 86, 180–94.

Camerer C.F, and R.M Hogarth, 1999, "The Effects of Financial Incentives in Experiments: A Review and Capital-Labor-Production Framework" *Journal of Risk and Uncertainty*, 19: 1–3, 7–42.

Cox C. J, L. V. Smith and J. M. Walker, 1985, "Expected Revenue in Discriminative and Uniform Price Sealed Bid Auction", in Smith L. Vernon (ed), *Research in Experimental Economics*, a research annual, Vol. 3, JAI Press INC, 183–232.

Das, S. R., and Sundaram R. K. 1996, "Auction Theory: A Survey with Applications to Treasury Markets", *Financial Markets, Institutions and Instruments*, Vol.5, No.5, 1–36.

DeJong, D., R. Forsythe and W. Uecker, 1988, "A Note on the Use of Businessmen as Subject in Sealed Offer Markets", *Journal of Economics Behavior and Organization*, 9, 87–100.

Dyer, D., J. Kagel, and D. Levin, 1989, "A Comparison of Naive and Experienced Bidders in Common Value Offer Auctions: A Laboratory Analysis", *Economic Journal*, 99, 108–115.

Engelbrecht-Wiggans R, A.J. List and D. H. Reiley, 2006, "Demand Reduction in Multi-unit Auctions with Varying Numbers of Bidders: Theory and Field Experiments", *International Economic Review*, 47(1), 203–231.

Feldman, R. A and V. R. Reinhart, 1995, *Flexible Estimation of Demand Schedules and Revenue under Different Auction Formats*, IMF–Working Paper No. 95/116.

Friedman D and S Sunder, 1994, Experimental *Methods: A Primer for Economists*, Cambridge University Press.

Friedman, M., 1960, *A Program for Monetary Stability*, Fordham University Press, New York.

Goldreich D, (2007) "Underpricing in Discriminatory and Uniform-Price Treasury Auctions,"*Journal of Financial and Quantitative Analysis*, 42 (2), 443–466.

Goswami, G., T. Noe, and M. Rebello, 1996, "Collusion in Uniform-Price Auctions: Experimental Evidence and Implications for Treasury Auctions," *Review of Financial Studies*, 9, 757–785.

Guala Francesco, (2005), "The Methodology of Experimental Economics", Cambridge University Press

Ivanova-Stenzel Radosveta and Timothy C. Salmon, 2004, "Bidder Preferences among Auction Institutions", *Economic Inquiry*, 42, 2, 223–236.

Jagadeesh N, 1993 "Treasury Auction Bids and the Salomon Squeeze" *The Journal of Finance*, Vol. 48, No. 4. 1403–1419.

Levin, D. and J.L. Smith, 1994, "Equilibrium in Auctions with Entry" *American Economic Review*, 84, 585–99.

Malvey, P. F., C. M. Archibald, and S. T. Flynn, 1995, *Uniform-Price Auctions: Evaluation of the Treasury Experience*, Office of Market Finance, U.S. Treasury.

Malvey, P. F., and C. M. Archibald, 1998, *Uniform-Price Auctions: Update of the Treasury Experience*, Office of Market Finance, US Treasury.

Mazumdar C.S, Nanda V. and R Surana 2009, Using Auctions to Price Employee Stock Options: The Case of Zions Bancorporation ESOARS, *Financial Analyst Journal*, 65(6), 79–99.

McAfee R. P, 1993, "Mechanism Design by Competing Sellers", *Econometrica*, 61(6), 1281–1312.

Miller J. G. and Plott R. C., 1985, "Revenue Generating Properties of Sealed-Bid Auctions; An Experiment Analysis of One-Price and Discriminative Process", in Smith L. Vernon (ed), *Research in Experimental Economics* a research annual, Editor, Vol. 3, JAI Press INC, 159–182.

Nyborg, K., and Sundaresan, S., 1996, "Discriminatory versus Uniform Treasury Auctions: Evidence from When-Issued Transactions," *Journal of Financial Economics*, Vol. 42, 63–104.

Plott, C, 1988, *Research on Pricing a Gas Transportation Network*, Office of Economic Policy Technical Report No 88-2. Federal Energy Regulatory Commission, Washington DC.

Sade O., C. Schnitzlein and J. F. Zender, 2006, "Competition and Cooperation in Divisible Good Auctions: An Experimental Examination" *Review of Financial Studies* 19(1), 195–235.

Salavirta E and K. Taipalus, 2003, "Money and Capital Markets, Finnish Financial Markets 2002", in Heikki Koskenkylä (ed), *Bank of Finland Studies* A: 105, 37–65.

Smith V., G Suchanek and A. Williams, 1988, "Bubbles, Crashes, and Endogenous Expectations in Experimental Spot Markets", *Econometrica*, 56, 1119–1151.

Smith L. V., 1967, "Experimental Studies of Discrimination versus Competition in Sealed-Bid Auction Markets", *Journal of Business*, 40, 56–84.

Tenorio, R., 1993, "Revenue Equivalence and Bidding Behavior in a Multi-unit Auction Market: An Empirical Analysis" *Review of Economics and Statistics*, vol.75, pp.302–314.

Umlauf, S., 1993, "An Empirical Study of the Mexican Treasury Bill Auction," *Journal of Financial Economics*, 33, 313–340.

Wang and Zender, 2002, "Auctioning Divisible Goods" *Economic Theory*, 19, 673–705.

Wilson, R., 1979, "Auctions of Shares," *Quarterly Journal of Economics*, 93, 675–698.

Appendix A — Survey (Experiment) Submitted to Individuals

Professor Dan Galai and Dr. Orly Sade *from the Finance Department at the School of Business Administration, Hebrew University of Jerusalem and* ***Professor Menachem Brenner*** *from the Finance department at New York University* ***Stern School of Business*** *are conducting academic research in an attempt to better understand auction design mechanism. For the purpose of this research we would like you to answer a few questions. Everything contained in these instructions and everything you hear in this session is an accurate representation of this research. Be sure to ask any questions that you may have during the instruction period, and ask for assistance, if needed, at any time. All subjects receive the same instructions.* (***No minors are allowed to participate***).

Your identity will be confidential with regard to the participation in this study. The survey does not ask for specific individual identification. The survey responses will be combined, and results will be presented only in aggregated form. Participation in this study is strictly voluntary. Omitting answers to specific questions is at the participant's discretion.

This Survey includes:

1. Case description
2. Examples
3. Survey

1. Case Description:

Two identical firms decided to issue bonds and to sell them via auctions. Each of the firms is going to sell 26 units. The economic value of each of the bonds in the secondary market is known with certainty and is equal to 20. The minimum price that can be submitted in the auction is 17. Bids can be made only in integers. Each participant can participate only in one of the auctions. The only difference between the two firms is the auction mechanism that is used: Firm "A" uses uniform price auction while firm "B" uses discriminatory (pay your bid) price auction. Each participant can bid for 26 units at most.

Firm "A"

This firm is going to issue bonds and sell them via "Uniform Price Auction".

The Auction Method:

There will be **26** units available for sale. You can submit bids for up to 26 units. Your resale value for each unit is **20**. (This means that after the auction your profit will be 20 for each unit that you hold, less what you paid for each unit). Prior to the auction, you are required to submit a schedule of bids. This schedule indicates the number of units you are willing to buy (including zero units) at each possible price level. The possible price levels will be 17, 18, 19, and 20. The sum of all of your bids may not exceed 26 units.

Once all participants have submitted their bids, the auctioneer will calculate the highest price at which all 26 bonds can be sold and will allocate units to players that submit bids that are equal to or higher than this price (if needed, the units will be allocated proportionally to the units demanded at the clearing price). *The price paid for each bond will be equal to the clearing price. The market-clearing price will be the highest price at which the total demand for bonds summed across all bidders is equal to 26.* If the total demand will be smaller than 26 at any of the suggested prices, the maximum total demand will be sold. A numerical example that illustrates this type of auction will be presented.

Firm "B"

This firm is going to issue bonds and sell them via "Discriminatory (Pay Your Bid) Price Auction".

The Auction Method:

There will be **26** units available for sale. You can submit bids for up to 26 units. Your resale value for each unit is **20.** (This means that after the auction your profit will be 20 francs for each unit that you hold, less what you paid for each unit). Prior to the auction, you are required to submit a schedule of bids. This schedule indicates the number of units you are willing to buy (including zero units) at each possible price level. The possible price levels will be 17, 18, 19, and 20. The sum of all of your bids may not exceed 26 units.

Once all participants have submitted their schedule of bids, the auctioneer will calculate the highest price at which all 26 bonds can be sold, and will allocate units to players that submit bids that are equal to or higher than this price (if needed, the units will be allocated proportionally to the units demanded at the clearing price). *The price you pay for each unit you receive, is equal to the price that you bid for that particular unit.* This means that it is possible that you will pay different prices for the bonds you buy, and it is possible that different bidders will receive bonds at different prices. If the total demand will be smaller than 26 at any of the suggested prices, the maximum total demand will be sold. A numerical example that illustrates this type of auction will be presented.

You will randomly be assigned to a group that contains 10 participants, you will not know in advance who are the members of your group. You must choose your preferred auction mechanism. Then, you will participate in the chosen mechanism and submit your bids accordingly. At the time that you submit your bids you will not know how many of your group members decided to play the type of auction as you have decided upon.

The number of units allocated to you and the price per unit will be determined based on the results of the auction mechanism of your choice and the bids submitted for that mechanism by members of your group.

The profits are calculated as: number of bonds purchased $*$ 20 – total purchase cost

2. Examples

The following examples are for illustration purposes only. They are not intended to be suggested as "best" strategies and simply demonstrate the implications of a possible set of actions.

In the examples, for simplicity, we assume that five participants decided to choose the Uniform Price Auction and five participants decided to choose the Discriminatory Price Auction.

2.1 Results for the Uniform Price auction

Uniform Price Auction Example

(Numbers in the table are units)

Price	Participants A	B	C	D	E	Demand	Aggregate Demand	Supply
20	11	0	5	0	0	16	16	26
19	5	0	3	2	0	10	26	26
18	5	0	8	6	18	37	63	26
17	5	26	10	18	8	67	130	26

The demand at each price is the sum of the demands of bidders A, B, C, D, and E. For example the demand at price 20 is equal to $11 + 0 + 5 + 0 + 0 = 16$. The aggregate demand is equal to the total demand at that price and all higher prices. For example the aggregate demand at the price of 19 is 26: (Demand at 20) + (Demand at 19) = 26 units. The clearing price is the highest price at which the cumulative demand equals the supply. In this case, the cumulative demand equals the supply at price equal 19.

The allocations in units and profits of the participants is as follows:

Price	Participants A	B	C	D	E
Allocation	16	0	8	2	0
	16∗	0	8∗	2∗	0
Profit	(20 – 19) = 16		(20 – 19) = 8	(20 – 19) = 2	

Since the resale value of the bond for each player is 20, each player makes a positive profit for each unit that he/she buys at a price below 20. The equilibrium price is 19 hence each player will profit one for each unit allocated.

2.1 Results for the Discriminatory Price auction

Discriminatory Price Auction Example

(Numbers in the table are units)

Price	Participants A	B	C	D	E	Demand	Aggregate Demand	Supply
20	1	0	0	0	0	1	1	26
19	20	0	3	2	0	25	26	26
18	0	0	13	6	18	37	63	26
17	5	26	10	18	8	67	130	26

The demand at each price is the sum of the demands of bidders A, B, C, D, and E. For example the demand at price 20 is equal to $+1+0+0+0 = 1$. The aggregate demand is equal to the total demand at that price and all higher prices. For example the aggregate demand at the price of 19 is 26: (Demand at 20) + (Demand at 19) = 26 units. The clearing price is the highest price at which the cumulative demand equals the supply. In this case, the cumulative demand equals the supply at price equal 19.

The allocations and profits of the participants are as follows:

	Participants				
Price	A	B	C	D	E
Allocation	21	0	3	2	0
Profit	$1 * 0 + 20 * 1 = 20$	0	$1 * 3 = 3$	$2 * 1 = 2$	0

Since the resale value of the bond for each player is 20, each player makes a positive profit for each unit that he/she buys at a price below 20. Player A receives one unit that he demanded at price 20 and pays 20 for it, and receives 20 units at price 19, and hence his profit is 20.

Questionnaire

1. I choose to participate in the auction of firm: (circle the appropriate answer)
    a. "A" Uniform Price Mechanism
    b. "B" Discriminatory Price Mechanism

c. I am totally indifferent between participating in each of the two mechanisms
d. I prefer not to participate in any of the suggested mechanism.

If your answer is either *a* or *b* please continue to question number 3 if your answer is *c* please continue to question 2 and if your answer is *d* please continue to question 4.

2. Please randomly select between the mechanisms. Your random selection is

____

Now continue to question 3

3. My bids are:

Price	Quantity Demanded
20	
19	
18	
17	

4. I believe that most of the participant will choose: A/B/indifferent
5. Gender:
   a. Female
   b. Male
6. Did you ever participate in financial assets' auction?
   a. Yes
   b. No
7. Years of work experience in financial markets_______________

Chapter 13

Factors Affecting The Impact of Investors' Horizon on Asset Allocation Decisions: An Experimental Exploration

Moty Amar* and Yoram Kroll†

Abstract

For 50 years, there has been a theoretical and practical debate concerning the effect of an investment horizon on the optimal proportion of risky assets. One side claims that expected-utility investors should or can be myopic because under a set of plausible assumptions, an investment horizon is irrelevant to selecting the optimal proportion of risky assets. The supporters of the other side assume different utility functions under which an investment horizon should have a crucial effect on risk-taking decisions, but many of those who support this approach claim that investors do invest myopically and that this can explain the well-known equity premium puzzle (EPP). Using an incentive-compatible multi-stage investment, game we explore the factors that affect the impact of horizon on the allocation decision.

The results indicate that participants' behaved myopically and that this behavior depends on their initial risk entering level "*status quo*". Specifically, only participants with an initially low risk-taking level behaved myopically. In addition, the level of education had a significant effect on the allocation decision while the gender, age and wealth were did not had such effect.

*Ono College Israel
kroll504@bezeqint.net

†Ono College Israel and Ruppin Academic Center-Israel

The authors would like to thank Ono Research Institute in Finance (ORIF) for their financial support and the behavioral lab of Ono academic College. This research was also supported by an Israel Science Foundation (ISF) Grant # 1566/2012 to MA.

Keywords: Time diversification, myopic loss aversion, EPP, investment games, status quo

JEL Classification: C91, G11, G23

1. Introduction

Perhaps the most important attempt to behaviorally elucidate Mehra and Prescott's 1985 equity premium puzzle (EPP)[1] was made by Benartzi and Thaler (1995), who argued that the puzzle's roots are related to myopic loss aversion.[2] They argued that if the investors have loss-averse preferences, then if they do not invest myopically in the long run they should increase their relative investment in equity as suggested by Mehra and Prescott. However, a myopic loss-aversive investor who computes the value of a portfolio frequently (primarily annually) would find investing in stocks less attractive relatively to the long time period (many years as the short-term timely uncorrelated fluctuations cancel one another out.[3]

Somewhat separable from the above alternative EPP explanations to Benartzi and Thaler's myopic loss aversion is the *status quo* theory, which states that individuals irrationally tend to prefer remaining in the current state of affairs. The current position (or *status quo*) is taken as a reference point, and any change from that position is perceived as a loss.

A large body of research has reported evidence of an irrational preference for the *status quo*, affecting decision making in many fields. For example, in finance, Samuelson and Zeckhauser (1988) document substantial *status quo* bias in a wide range of decision-making scenarios, including investment situations. They observe that the allocation of pension reserves to TIAA and CREF tend to be very stable from year to year despite

[1]According to the EPP, the historically higher rates of return on equity relative to those of bonds are inconsistent with the high weight of bonds in the portfolios of rational, risk-averse investors.

[2]Loss aversion plays a central role in Kahneman and Tversky's (1979) descriptive theory of decision-making under uncertainty. It refers to the tendency of individuals to be more sensitive to reductions in their level of well-being than to increases.

[3]Benartzi and Thaler's explanation of EPP has since been supported by many additional papers (see a review and additional tests of MLA by Gneezy *et al.* 2003; and Mayhew and Vitalis, 2014).

the large variation in the rate of return. A similar effect is reported by Agnew, Balduzzi, and Sunden (2003), who examine the pension accounts of US investors.

Possible evidence of *status quo* bias in the EPP is that individuals who initially do not invest in stocks (or who invest only a very limited amount of their savings in stocks) and have a strong tendency to remain in a *status quo* will prefer to keep their money in risk-free financial instruments, such as government bonds, rather than investing in stocks.

In light of this theoretical and practical debate concerning the effect of an investment horizon on the optimal proportion of risky assets, the current research explores the factors that affect the impact of the horizon on the investors' allocation.

We hypothesize that subjects are myopic and thus will not invest more in equity when their horizon is longer. Namely, we assume that difference between the optimal proportion of equity and the actual proportion will be much higher for longer horizons than for shorter horizons. We also assumed that subjects would prefer to avoid changing their portfolios and sticking the *status quo*. Therefore, one of the most dominant factors affecting their allocation decision in any round is their decisions in the previous rounds starting from the first round. In addition, we examine potential factors, which might influence participants' allocation decision, specifically, gender, age, education and wealth.

To address the questions raised above, we developed risky remunerating incentive-compatible portfolio management games for the laboratory. The game aimed to identify the main factors that affect participants' consecutive allocation decisions to invest in stocks or bonds.

2. The Portfolio Management Games

We constructed experiment to understand participants' myopic behavior. The experiment was composed of 30 game rounds, representing 30 years. In each round, subjects had to allocate their investment between bonds and equity (appendix A shows screenshots of the game). Subjects were able to hold equity between 0% and 100%. Following their allocation decision, the returns of bonds and equity were determined by randomly selecting one year out the 49 years from 1958–2006, the return of the portfolio in that year was calculated and the subjects obtained those returns.[4] In each of these years, the actual returns on bonds and equity from the CPI-indexed government bonds and all stock indexes on the Tel Aviv Stock Exchange (TASE) were used. These annual real returns are provided in appendix B. The 30-year annual average geometric return obtained after 30 rounds (minus 20% tax plus 2% participation bonus) was added (or subtracted in the case of a negative return) to the grade of the student in the course in which the game was played. Note that in a real-life portfolio decision, the goal is the terminal wealth at the end of an investment horizon and not the geometric mean.[5] Later, we show that manipulation of remuneration according to the geometric mean return leads to a long run high relative investment in equity by rational expected-utility investors, whereas it does not manifest when the goal is terminal wealth.

Before submitting and confirming each of the 30 rounds' decisions, participants were presented with a performance status chart illustrating the portfolio's current cumulative yield of bonds, stocks and their portfolio (an example can be found in Appendix A). In addition to this chart, participants were also presented with a tabular summary of the running geometric average yields for stocks, bonds, the portfolio, the after-tax portfolio average (an example can be found in Appendix C), and their bonus, provided that they finalized the game. They were also informed that their performance in terms of the geometric mean would not change. The historic yields table, from which a random year was drafted for each round, was constantly available for reference.

In each round, the subjects were told that they would actually receive the calculated bonus only if they completed all 30 rounds. Subjects with interim positive geometric mean returns who did not complete all 30 games received a zero bonus to their grade. For subjects with interim negative geometric mean returns who did not complete the 30 games, the interim after-tax negative geometric mean return was subtracted from their grade.

---

[4]Although the experiments were run in the years 2010–2012, we avoided the traumatic data of 2008.

[5]In the case of a logarithmic utility function, maximizing the geometric mean is equivalent to maximizing terminal wealth.

Under these conditions, it is not surprising that all subjects who started the game also completed all 30 rounds.

The option to invest only in bonds and the 2% bonus guaranteed an almost risk-free addition to the grade (4.4% addition to the grade with only 0.72% SD), and almost all students who were invited to play the game voluntarily did indeed play the game.

The experiment aimed to identify the main factors that affect participants' consecutive allocation decisions to invest in stocks or bonds. The experiment conducted at an Israeli university.

Optimal allocation decisions in each round for various non myopic assumed utility functions are calculated by simulations of 5,000 steps that replicate the conditions of the experiments. These optimal decisions are then compared with the actual decisions of the subjects.

3. The Returns

The annual statistics for 1958–2006 are exhibited in Figure 1 and Table 1.

The one-year horizon average return in 1958–2006 is 3.1% for bonds and 14.1% for stocks. These expected returns and standard deviations are relevant only in the case of ten years horizon. However, when the horizon increases the geometric average return of the stock index and its standard deviation will go down. Five thousands simulations expose that the geometric average returns of stocks goes down almost monotonically from one year horizon to 30 years horizon from 14.6% to 8.4%. The standard deviations of the risky returns also go down dramatically and

Figure 1: Annual Returns on Bonds and Stocks, 1958–2006

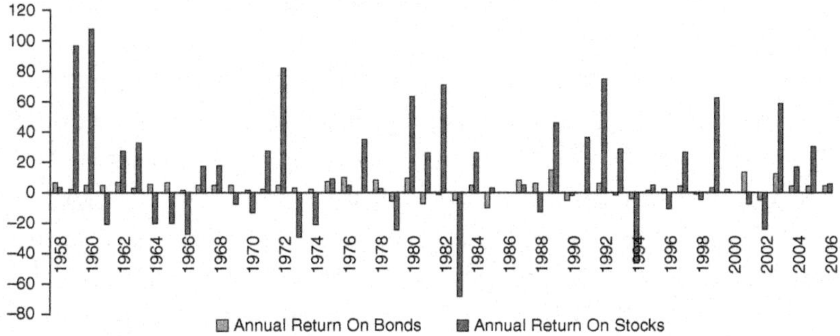

Table 1: Statistics of the Real Annual Return on the Indexes of Governmental Bonds and All Stocks in Tel-Aviv, 1958–2006

	1958–2006		1983–2006		1958–1982	
	Bond	Stock	Bond	Stock	Bond	Stock
Average annual return	3.1%	14.1%	2.6%	10.4%	3.6%	17.6%
Annual geometric mean	3.0%	8.2%	2.4%	4.6%	3.6%	11.7%
Standard deviation	5.1%	36.1%	6.0%	32.3%	4.1%	39.1%
Correlations between annual returns of bonds and stocks	28.4%		48.8%		5.4%	

monotonically from 35.5% for one year horizon to 6.8% for 30 years horizon. Thus the coefficient of variance (the ratio of standard deviation to average return) of the risky return also goes down from 2.43 for one year horizon to 0.88 for 30 years horizon. On the other hand the average return on the bonds is very close to 3% regardless of the horizon. These results indicate that in case of our data set and in case the compensation is based on average geometric return, the subjects should prefer more equity when their horizon is longer. Note that in reality investors are compensated according to their terminal wealth and not according to average return as in our game. Samuelson (1963), Merton (1969) and Bodie (1995) concluded that if the investors maximize the expected utility of terminal wealth than the proportion of their investment in equity may not goes up with the horizon. In the next section we use our simulated data set to examine this claim and our claim that in case the remuneration is based on average return the optimal proportion in equity will go up with the horizon, increases.

Simulated Optimal Decision of Rational Non Myopic Expected Utility Investors

To cover the quite wide range of reasonable utility functions, we examine the optimal decision of various types of utility function, assuming different levels of risk aversion in each. The simulated optimal portfolios of bonds and equity are calculated for two alternative goals. The first goal is the expected utility of the terminal wealth for the given horizons (for horizons from 1 year to 30 years). This goal is considered by economists to be the one that reflects reality. The second goal is the manipulated goal, in which the goal is set to maximize the expected utility from the geometric mean return for each given single year up to 30-year horizons. This goal is the one that the subjects faced in our game. The two alternative goals yield the same optimization results only in the case of one period (year) horizon for all utility functions besides the log utility function in which for all the horizons the optimum for the terminal wealth goal is the same as for the geometric mean goal (see Merton and Samuelson, 1974).

We also assumed that under the two alternative goals, investors could revise their decision each year. This assumption fits the conditions in which the subjects played the investment game. Accordingly, the optimization process is a backward process. Specifically, we start the optimization at the end of the 29th year which is the final round in the game and there is a horizon of only one year. At this one-year investment horizon, the investor allocates his/her optimal portfolio. Then, the investor moves backward to the end of the 28th year. At that time, the investor must determine his/her optimal portfolio for the 29th year, whereas the allocation of the assets for the 30th year has been already determined in the previous step. Following this procedure, we move backward to the start of the first period, when the investor has a horizon of 30 years. According to the above optimization process, we assume that there are no myopic constraints and that investors have no annual restrictions on revising their portfolio as it actually is in our games.

The results of the simulations fit the well-known theoretical findings. Specifically, when the goal is to maximize the expected utility of the geometric mean for all utility functions (besides the $LN(1+r)$), the optimal level of equity increases with the horizon of the investment. However, when the goal is the expected utility from terminal wealth (and according to our empirical data, the expected terminal wealth increases with the horizon), we find that the effect of the horizon on the proportion of equity depends either on the effect of wealth on the relative risk aversion or the specific unique structure of the assumed utility function. Let us know present the optimal decision for the specific utility functions.

The results of the optimization for the function[6] $U = E(1 + r) - K\sigma^2$ are provided in Figure 2.

---

[6]This is a practical function widely used by practitioners. This equation is used as a recommended scoring tool by the Association of Investment Management and Research (AIMR). The average empirical K is approximately 2 (see Bodie, Kane, and Marcus (2002), p. 157). Additionally, note that this function is only an approximation of expected utility because it is composed of only the first two terms of the Tailor expansion of the expected utility arrowed the mean.

Figure 2: Optimal portfolios for the function $U = E(r) - K\sigma^2$ for K=8, 4, 2. The maximum goals are the expected terminal wealth (MAX EU(TW)) and maximum geometric mean (MAX EU(GM))

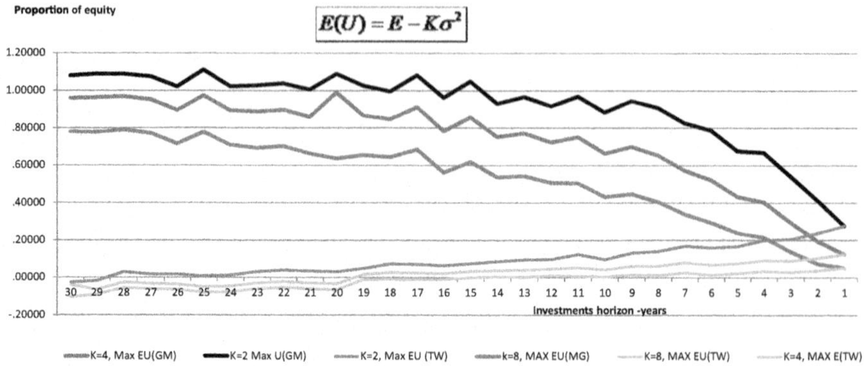

In the case of the one-year horizon, we obtain for risk aversion levels (k) of 8, 4, and 2, an optimal investment in equity of 5.2%, 12.4% and 27.6%, respectively. When the horizon increases to 30 and the goal is the maximization of expected utility from the geometric mean, investments in equity increase (with jumps due to sampling errors[7]) to 77.9%, 95.8% and 107.7%, respectively. However, when the expected utility over the terminal wealth is considered, then the investment in equity decreases to −4.1%, −2.5% and −3.5%, respectively. It seems that the "practitioners" utility function does not fit long-term terminal wealth considerations.

The optimal allocation in the case of the second function[8] $U = 1 - e^{-a(1+r)}$ is provided in Figure 3.

Once again, when the optimization is related to the expected utility of the geometric mean, the optimal level of equity for risk aversion parameters of a = 8, 4 and 2 increases from 13.1%, 29.1% and 61.3%, respectively, for a one-year horizon to 96.3%, 107.9% and 114.7%, respectively, for horizon of 30 years. However, when the optimization is over terminal wealth , for a = 8, 4 and 2, the optimal investment in equity decreases from 13.1%,

[7]Note that, due to sampling errors, there are jumps up and down in the results of all of the simulations. The jumps are due to the high sensitivity of the results to extreme sampling.

[8]This function has Constant absolute risk aversion measure with respect to wealth and increasing relative risk aversion with respect to wealth

Figure 3: Optimal portfolios for the function $U = 1 - e^{-a(1+r)}$ for a=8, 4, 2. The maximum goals are the expected terminal wealth (MAX EU(TW)) and maximum geometric mean (MAX EU(GM))

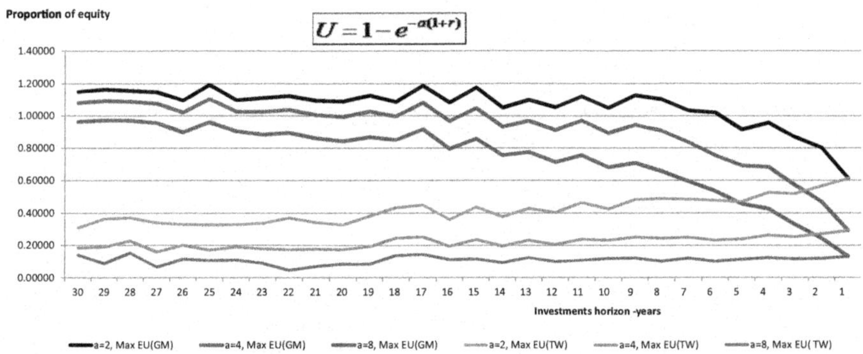

29.1% and 61.3%, respectively, in the case of a one-year horizon, to 13.9%, 18.3% and 31.0% in the case of a 30-year horizon.[9]

The Optimal level of equity when the utility function[10] is $U = \frac{(1+r)^{1-\alpha}}{1-\alpha}$ is given in Figure 4.

Once again, the optimal level of equity increases with the horizon when the goal is the expected utility from the geometric mean. However, because the relative risk aversion of this utility function is constant with respect to wealth, in our simulations the horizon does not change the simulated level of optimal investment in equity.

When the utility function is $U(1+r) = LN(1+r)$, then as is expected theoretically, the optimal investment is not affected by the horizon, and maximization of the expected utility of terminal wealth yields the same

[9]The relative risk aversion for the utility function $U = 1 - e^{-a(1+r)}$ is increasing with wealth. Thus since in our game the terminal average wealth increases with the horizon, we find that when the goal is the expected utility from terminal wealth, the optimal proportion of equity decreases with the horizon.

[10]The power utility function reveals the two acceptable properties of decreasing absolute risk aversion (DARA) and constant relative risk aversion (CRRA). Higher wealth does not change the optimal proportion of risky assets in the optimal portfolio (due to CRRA). This function was used by Merton and Samuelson in their proof of the fallacy of time diversification and by Mehra, R., & Prescott for showing the Equity premium puzzle (EPP).

Figure 4: Optimal portfolios for the function $U = \frac{(1+r)^{1-\alpha}}{1-\alpha}$ for $\alpha = 10, 5, 2$. The maximum goals are the expected terminal wealth (MAX EU(TW)) and maximum geometric mean (MAX EU(GM))

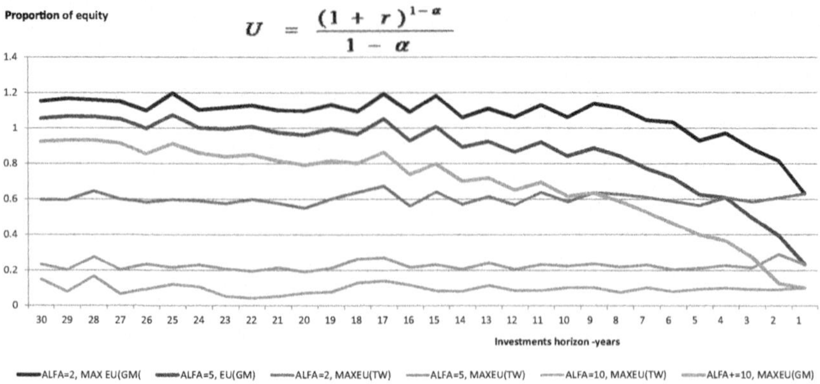

results as maximization of expected utility from the geometric mean. This result should be obtained according to Merton and Samuelson (1974). In our case, the optimal level of equity is approximately 120% percent (See Figure 5)

Figure 5 also exposes the optimal investment according to the loss-aversion utility function $U(r) = \begin{cases} R^{\alpha} & \text{if } r \geq 0 \\ -\lambda(-r)^{\beta} & \text{if } r \leq 0 \end{cases}$ of Kahneman and Tversky (1979). Based on our empirical simulated data regardless of the selected goal, the optimal investment in equity increases with the horizon. However, when the goal is the expected utility from terminal wealth and the selected parameters of the utility are $\alpha = \beta = 0.88$ *and* $\lambda = 2.25$, which are suggested by Kahneman and Tversky, then the one-year optimal investment in equity is 74.5%, and the two-year optimal level is 154%. Because of default cases in our 5000 step simulation, it was not possible to obtain valid results for these parameters for horizons of three years or more.[11] When we changed the loss-aversion parameters toward a higher loss aversion of $\alpha = \beta = 0.5$ *and* $\lambda = 3$, we obtained an optimal level of equity of 6.8% for a one-year horizon and 104.0% and 135.8% for a 30-year horizon when the

[11]Defaults may accrue at an investment in equity of more than 100% when the return on bond is above that of equity and the investor is short on bond.

Figure 5: Optimal portfolios for the functions $U = ln(1 + r)$ and $U(r) = \begin{cases} R^{\alpha} & if\ r \geq 0 \\ -\lambda(-r)^{\beta} & if\ r \leq 0 \end{cases}$. The maximum goals are the expected terminal wealth (MAX EU(TW)) and maximum geometric mean (MAX EU(GM)).

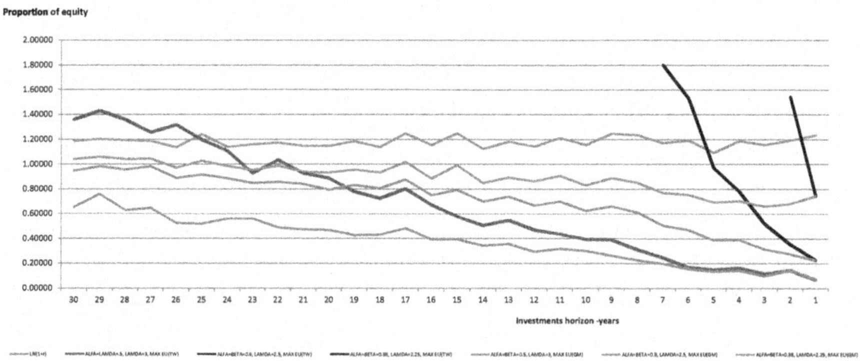

goals are maximization of expected utility of terminal wealth and geometric mean, respectively.

In summary, our empirically based simulated results of the optimal allocations of equity and fixed income clearly indicate that rational investors who hold all of our assumed utility function and maximize the expected utility from the geometric mean should not have a lower proportion of equity when the horizon increases. Moreover, in almost all cases beside the logarithmic utility function, they should increase their proportion of equity with the horizon. Our experiments examine whether the above conclusions are valid for our subjects.

4. Experimental Exploration of Factors that Affect the Impact of Horizon on the Allocation Decision

Overview and Procedure

The aim of the experiment was to identify the main factors that influence participants' allocation decision, specifically, the decision to invest in stocks or bonds, throughout the 30 rounds.

Sixty-six undergraduate finance students were asked to volunteer to play the 30-round (years) risky/riskless portfolio allocation game. They were paid according to their game performance via a bonus to their course grade. The experiment was performed in a computer lab and took an average of 30 minutes; each participant was tested individually. The dependent variable in this experiment was the proportion of allocation to stocks in each round.

Approximately half of the participants were female, and the average age was 26. The annual geometric mean return of the 30 periods that was gained (or lost) plus a 2% participation bonus for completing the experiment was added to the percentage grade of the students in the finance course. The performance of the equity, bonds, and portfolio and the average annual return was calculated at the end of each interim round and given to the student. If a student with a positive interim average annual return quit the game without completing all 30 rounds, zero was added to the student's course grade. If the interim annual average return was negative upon quitting the game, then this negative value (after tax return) was subtracted from the student's grade. Under these conditions, all students who decided to participate in the experiment (and almost all students who were invited to participate did opt to participate) completed all 30 rounds.

The expected annual average return on stocks in the 30 rounds was 8.4% (Table 2). Thus, the expected bonus to the course grade for a player who allocated 100% of his capital to stocks in all rounds, considering 20% tax and a 2% completion bonus, was $0.8 * 8.4\% + 2\% = 8.72\%$. The expected almost-riskless bonus for a player who invested only in bonds was $0.8 * 3.0\% + 2\% = 4.4\%$. Thus, the risk premium in the game is $8.72\% - 4.4\% = 4.72\%$. To raise participants' awareness of the risk premium, we emphasized in the instructions the risk involved with selecting stocks and the option to avoid risk by allocating 100% to bonds in all rounds.

To understand the subjective perceived risk involved in the game, we first conducted a short survey. In this survey, 29 participants from the population of the first experiment were asked to write the amount of money they are willing to pay to add 10 points to their final course grade on a piece of paper, which was then sealed in an envelope. The average amount was 677 NIS (approximately 170 USD) with M = 677 and SD = 621. This result supports the notion that our game involves realistic, risky decision-making and provides an approximation of the decisions participants had

Table 2: Mean, std, skewness, kurtosis, maximum and minimum 5000 simulated returns

Period	1	2	4	6	8	10	12	14	16	18	20	22	24	26	28	30
Part A: Stocks																
Mean return	14.6%	11.2%	9.6%	9.3%	9.0%	8.7%	8.5%	8.7%	8.6%	8.5%	8.5%	8.4%	8.4%	8.3%	8.2%	8.4%
Standard deviation	35.5%	24.6%	17.8%	15.3%	12.5%	11.6%	10.5%	9.7%	9.1%	8.6%	8.5%	7.8%	7.7%	7.3%	7.2%	6.8%
Coefficient of variance	243.4%	220.3%	185.6%	164.5%	138.6%	133.3%	123.2%	111.8%	106.6%	101.0%	99.5%	92.9%	91.7%	88.0%	87.9%	81.3%
Skewness	60.9%	31.7%	19.4%	20.9%	10.6%	14.7%	−0.6%	3.1%	−11.2%	14.8%	15.2%	10.0%	12.5%	23.5%	4.4%	6.4%
Kurtosis	0.1	0.3	0.3	0.3	−11.4%	27.8%	−0.9%	19.3%	4.9%	15.4%	−15.1%	−4.9%	15.1%	56.1%	−7.5%	20.1%
Minimum return	−67.6%	−63.4%	−58.6%	−43.4%	−39.6%	−23.8%	−26.2%	−24.5%	−23.2%	−22.6%	−21.2%	−14.8%	−14.0%	−13.9%	−14.0%	−12.6%
Maximum return	107.2%	101.6%	78.7%	62.4%	53.1%	54.2%	46.7%	38.6%	39.5%	37.5%	37.3%	34.8%	34.6%	43.5%	30.6%	27.6%
Part B: Bonds																
Period	1	2	4	6	8	10	12	14	16	18	20	22	24	26	28	30
Mean return	3.1%	3.2%	3.1%	3.0%	3.0%	3.0%	3.0%	2.9%	2.9%	2.9%	2.9%	2.9%	3.0%	3.0%	3.0%	3.0%
Standard deviation	5.2%	3.6%	2.6%	2.1%	1.9%	1.6%	1.5%	1.3%	1.3%	1.2%	1.2%	1.1%	1.1%	1.0%	1.0%	0.9%
Coefficient of variance	169.1%	111.4%	83.7%	69.6%	61.9%	54.0%	49.1%	45.7%	44.5%	40.6%	39.8%	36.2%	36.2%	34.3%	32.6%	30.8%
Skewness	−21.2%	−9.3%	−19.2%	0.6%	−18.0%	−10.2%	−8.0%	−20.4%	−2.9%	−4.8%	4.9%	−6.7%	−21.7%	0.8%	−4.3%	6.3%
Kurtosis	0.2	0.0	0.3	−0.2	22.3%	7.0%	−0.9%	3.8%	7.7%	13.0%	−8.0%	20.8%	30.4%	5.3%	1.4%	−11.5%
Minimum return	−4.2%	−4.0	−2.4%	−4.0%	−2.4%	−3.8%	−2.3%	−1.8%	−2.0%	−1.1%	−1.6%	−1.2%	−1.1%	−0.6%	−0.3%	0.1%
Maximum return	5.0%	3.7%	5.9%	8.8%	8.2%	7.9%	9.0%	6.7%	8.4%	7.3%	6.8%	7.0%	6.2%	6.1%	5.9%	5.9%

to make in monetary terms. These results support the notion that our game actually involved risk taking.

5. Result of the Experiment

According to Figures 2–5, in the case of a 30-year horizon, even extremely high risk averters who consider the geometric mean had to invest in equity 78% if $U = E(1+r) - K\sigma^2$, 96% if $U = 1 - e^{-a(1+r)}$, 92% if $U = \frac{(1+r)^{1-\alpha}}{1-\alpha}$ and more than 100% for the other utility functions. Figure 6 shows the unsurprising[12] result that even in case of a horizon of 30 years, the average allocation in equity was 75%, which is high but quite less than 100% (In the first three rounds the average investment in equity was 78.3%).

However, Figure 6 demonstrates very clearly that the subjects tend to increase their allocation to equity as the horizon becomes longer; the effect of the round number was significant and negative ($\beta = -.032, t = -2.328, p < .01$). In the last 10 rounds, when the horizon was relatively short, the average allocation to equity was only 67.0%. In rounds 11–20, it was 71.6%, and in the first ten rounds when the horizon is relatively the longest, the average allocation was 75.8%, significantly higher. An ANOVA on the three round's groups (rounds 1–10, 11–20, and 21–30) revealed a significant effect ($F(1, 27) = 16.25, p < .001$), and a contrast test between

Figure 6: Average percent allocated to stocks in each round (experiment 1)

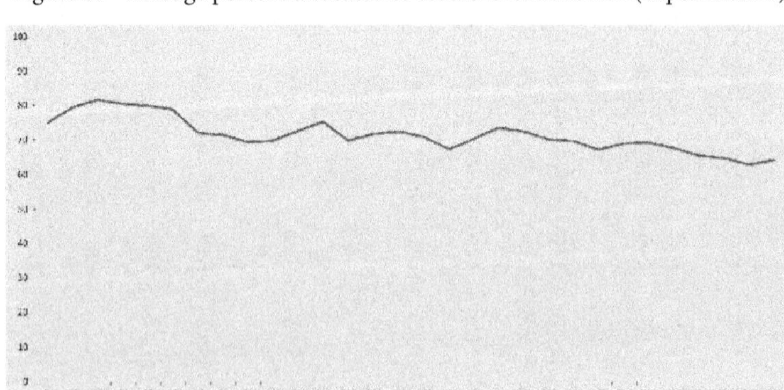

[12]This result is not surprising because the subjects were not allowed to hold more than 100% in equity.

rounds 21–30 and the other conditions reveals a significant difference ($t(27) = -4.99, p < .001$). A contrast test between the first 10 rounds and the other rounds revealed a significant difference ($t(27) = 4.88, p < .001$).

The above result indicates that myopic loss aversion is in fact only a bounded phenomenon.[13] However, according to our simulation models, for almost all utility functions and a goal based on the expected utility from the geometric mean, the optimal proportion of equity rises quite steeply with the horizon. For example, for the function $U = \frac{(1+r)^{1-\alpha}}{1-\alpha}$ and $\alpha = 5$, the one-year optimal level of equity is 23.2%, and when the horizon is 30 years, the optimal level is 105.6%. This is a convex increase of 87.4% or almost a 3% average increase per additional one horizon year. In the cases of all of the utility functions, the average convex increase per horizon year is from 1%–3%. However, in our experiment, the average proportion of equity increased almost monotonically from 64.1% when the horizon was one year to 75.0% for horizon of 30 years. This is a much lower average increase of approximately one-third percent per one horizon year. One may explain the difference between the theoretical simulated results and the experimental ones by partial myopic behavior by all of the subjects or at least by some of the subjects.

To understand better the factors that influenced the effect of the horizon on the allocation of equity by our subjects, we conducted a multi-factor regression analysis. Our dependent variable was the allocation to equity in a given round. Unsurprisingly, according to reasonable statues quo ideas, the main factor for the allocation in a given period was the allocation in a previous round ($\beta = .74, t = 46.79, p < .001$). The results of the regression also indicate that the effect of the initial proportion of equity, which can be considered the initial entering the game *status quo*, was very strong; it was the second most important and significant factor explaining allocation in all of the rounds ($\beta = .086, t = 5.50, p < .001$). The third most important and significant factor explaining allocation in all of the rounds was education

[13] Recall that because the goal of the subjects in our games is based on the geometric mean and not terminal wealth, the results of our experiments cannot explain either the EPP or other long-term investment such as the Chilean and life-cycle pension strategies. (For a review of the Chilean and life cycle models, see Cerda (2008). For a review and test of the lifecycle model, see Bikker *et al.* (2012).)

($\beta = -.083, \mathrm{t} = 5.41, p < .001$). The other important factor are the round number ($\beta = -.032, \mathrm{t} = -2.32, p < .05$), yield achieved in stocks in the previous round ($\beta = -.071, \mathrm{t} = 2.42, p < .05$), and total yield (achieved by investing in stocks and bonds together) ($\beta = -.091, \mathrm{t} = -3.02, p < .05$). The accumulated wealth of subjects in terms of the average annual return at the end of the previous round had no significant effect on the allocations.

To better understand the effect of the allocation in the first round on the allocations in the preceding steps, we divided the subjects in the experiments into two subgroups based on the median allocation to equity in the first round (greater and less than the median). Figure 7 shows the very surprising results about the initial investment in equity and the different behavior of the groups.

Participants who initially allocated heavily in equity were those most influenced by the investment horizon. As it became shorter, they significantly decreased their stock allocations ($\beta = -.058, \mathrm{t} = -3.05, p < .01$).

In the first three steps, when participants' investment horizons were 30–27 years, their allocation was 96.5% which is extremely high since they were not allowed to invest in equity more than 100%. However, this allocation fits well the theoretical 30-year average allocation of 99.1% in equity according to all our utility functions and risk-aversion levels. Then, the allocation to equity of this above median group decreased almost monotonically to 60.3% in the last three steps. For this group, one additional horizon year increases the investment in equity by more than 1%. That is,

Figure 7: Average percent allocated to stocks in each round (experiment 1), divided into two groups by the median allocation in the first round

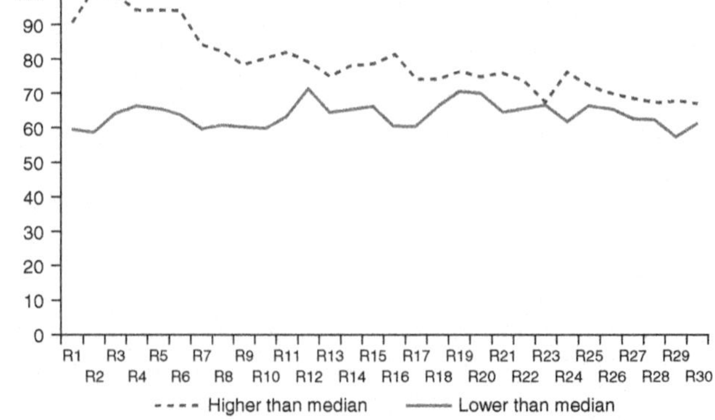

for the initially "relatively heavier" investors in equity, we find an investment behavior over time which fit very well the optimal simulated behavior of non-myopic investors.

Further statistical results for the above median investment group indicate an 89.6% average allocation in equity in the first ten rounds. In rounds 11–20, this group dramatically decreases its average allocation in equity to 77.3%, it then decreases to 70.5% in the last 10 rounds. An ANOVA between the three rounds groups (rounds 1–10, 11–20, and 21–30) revealed a significant effect ($F(1, 27) = 32.69, p < .001$), and a contrast test between rounds 1–10 and the other conditions reveals a significant difference ($\mathrm{t}(27) = 7.58, p < .001$). The contrast test between rounds 21–30 and the other conditions reveals a significant difference ($\mathrm{t}(27) = -6.23, p < .001$).

The second group of the initial below-median allocation to equity who initially deterred the risky equity markets were also most influenced by the allocation in the previous round ($\beta = .58, \mathrm{t} = 21.57, p < .001$). However, they tended to remain very close to the *status quo* of their initial allocations in all of the rounds, essentially ignoring their investment horizon; the effect of the round number on the allocation of equity was not significant ($\beta = .05, \mathrm{t} = .574, p < .556$). In rounds 1–10, they invested only 61.9% in equity on average. In rounds 11–20, when their horizon was shorter, the average allocation increased slightly (rather than decreased) to 65.8%, and in rounds 21–30, the average investment in equity decreased to 63.4%. An ANOVA of the three groups (rounds 1–10, 11–20, and 21–30) revealed a significant effect ($F(1, 27) = 3.77, p < .05$), and a contrast test between rounds 1-10 and the other conditions revealed a significant difference ($\mathrm{t}(27) = -2.21, p < .05$). The contrast test between the last 10 rounds and the other rounds revealed an insignificant difference ($\mathrm{t}(27) = -.315$, $p > .01$).

6. General Discussion

The aim of our research was to examine factors that will be helpful in explaining the effect of a horizon on investment in equity. In addition to the well-known myopic behavior in investment decisions, we suspected that participants' initial investment position could serve as a *status quo* position and be one of the factors that could explain the effect of the horizon on investment decisions in all of the rounds. It is not entirely surprising that the decision in the previous round is a significant factor, explaining 70.9% of the allocation in the following round (the dependent variable). It is much more surprising that the allocation in the first round explained 12.8% of our dependent variable, i.e., the percentage invested in stocks in the portfolio in all of the rounds. These findings are in line with our perception of a tendency for decision makers to avoid unnecessary changes in their allocation and retain the status quo from the previous round, even in the first allocation. When the entire population is analyzed, other factors, such as the accumulated and current yields of the portfolio, stocks in the previous round, age and gender, were not identified as significant factors. However, when divided into two groups by the median allocation in equity, we found myopic behavior only by some investors; investors whose initial equity allocations were greater than the median revealed a non-myopic investment behavior. Their allocation to equity in each round was very close to those that were simulated for the various assumed utility functions. Specifically, as suggested by the simulation, their actual initial investment in equity was very close to 100%, and their tendency was to reduce the investment in stocks because their horizon became shorter at a rate which is in line with the simulated suggested optimal rate (the allocation trend to equity in the rounds was significant; Figure 7). However, those who initially invested in equity below the median, maintained an allocation that was close to the initial one in all rounds. Their initial investment of only 60.3% in equity in the first three rounds is identical to that in the three ending rounds, the range of the invested capital in equity in all of the games is in the narrow range of 71.5%–50.6%, and the allocation trend to equity in the rounds was insignificant (Figure 7). It is very possible that the statues quo bias is nourishing the Benartzi and Thaler's (1995) myopic hypothesis, which together with the Kahneman and Tversky (1979) loss-aversion assumption, well explains the Mehra and Prescott, E. (1985) EPP finding. In our laboratory experiment, only the behavior of the below-median equity initial allocation group supports the hypothesis of a *status quo* bias/ myopic investment decision making.

Note that in this paper, we do not ask the important question of what determines the initial investment in equity. There can be many factors such as risk aversion, self-confidence, experience and probably other personal factors. We do claim that the difference between the two groups segregated by above and below the initial allocation in equity is not only due to different levels of risk aversion. According to our simulations, when the goal is based on the geometric mean, different levels of risk aversion generate greater differences in the optimal level of equity when the horizon is short. Namely, According to our simulations and when $E(U) = E - K\sigma^2$, difference between the lowest assumed risk aversion and the highest assumed risk aversion generates difference in the optimal allocation in equity for a one-year horizon of $27.5\% - 5.2\% = 22.3\%$. In the case of a 30-year horizon, this difference is reduced almost monotonically from 22.3% to only 6.9%, and for the other utility functions, the same ranges are reduced from 48.1% to 18.4%, from 53.1% to 22.7%, and from 67.7% to 38.6%. The experimental results show a completely opposite result for the below- and the above-median initial investment in equity. In the last three rounds, the above-median group average allocation to equity was 67.4%, and allocation of the below-median group was once again 60.3%. This is a very small difference of only 7.1%, in which the average difference in the first three rounds when the horizon was 27–30 years was $96.5\% - 60.3\% = 36.2\%$. According to our simulations, these results support our claim that the different initial allocations to equity in the first round are significantly affected by additional factors rather than only by the different level of risk aversion. Recall also that in the last rounds, there are no myopic considerations. In addition, in the last rounds, both groups already obtained the same experience with the game; thus, we can safely conclude that in the last rounds, primarily level of risk aversion explained the different allocations. In our experiment, the difference of the allocations in equity between the two groups in the last three rounds was only $67.4\% - 60.3\% = 7.4\%$, whereas according to the simulations, under our assumed utility functions, the optimal allocation to equity in the last step was only 22.3% when the risk aversion was the highest and 67.7% when the assumed risk aversion was the lowest. Thus, we conclude that the difference in risk aversion between the two experimental groups was much lower than what we obtained by the optimal expected utility considerations in the simulations and that differences in the level of risk aversion may provide at most a very partial explanation to the differences in the allocations to equity of the participants.

Limitations, Future Research and Implications

Our study has two basic limitations. First, the results of the investment game have limited implications with respect to realistic optimal allocation to equity and to horizon because, as in real life, the goal is the total wealth along the way to or at the end of a given horizon, whereas in our game, subjects were remunerated by the annual geometric mean of 30 years. We selected this manipulation of real life because only under it would the optimal allocation to equity by rational non-myopic investors increase with the horizon. Thus, due to this manipulation, we were able to compare theoretical optimal allocations with those in the experiments. In a future study, we would like to create a more realistic game in which subjects will also be remunerated by their terminal wealth.

Second, our research showed a significant effect of the first portfolio allocation. However, in this article, we only showed that risk aversion provides at most a partial explanation for the initial allocation; we did not investigate further the other root causes of this initial decision. Based on the current research results, we suggest that a future study should try to find the additional root causes of the first decision, which is denoted by us as the initial *status quo*.

References

Abel, A. B. (1990). Asset prices under habit formation and catching up with the Joneses. *The American Economic Review*, 80(2), 38–42.

Agnew, J., P. Balduzzi and A. Sunden (2003) Portfolio choice and trading in large 401(k) plan. *American Economic Review*, 93, 193–215.

Aiyagari, S. R., & Gertler, M. (1991). Asset returns with transactions costs and uninsured individual risk. *Journal of Monetary Economics*, 27(3), 311–331.

Allais, M. (1953). "Le comportement de l'homme rationnel devant le risque: critique des postulats et axiomes de l'école Américaine". *Econometrica*, 21 (4): 503–546.

Belsky, G. and Gilovich, T. (1999) Why smart people make big mistakes- and how to correct them; Lessons from the new science of behavioral economics.

Benartzi, S., & Thaler, R. H. (1995). Myopic loss aversion and the equity premium puzzle. *The quarterly journal of Economics*, 110(1), 73–92.

Benartzi, S., & Thaler, R. H. (1999). Risk aversion or myopia? Choices in repeated gambles and retirement investments. *Management science*, 45(3), 364–381.

Benartzi, S., & Thaler, R. H. (2001). Naive diversification strategies in defined contribution saving plans. *American economic review*, 79–98.

Bikker A., D. W. G. A Broeders, D. A. Hollanders and E. H. M. Ponds (2012). Pension Funds' Asset Allocation and Participant Age: A Test of the Life-Cycle Model. *Journal of Risk and Insurance*, 79(3), 595–618.

Bodie, Z. (1995) On the risk of Stocks in the long run, *Financial Analysts Journal*, 51(3), 18–22.

Brown, S. J., Goetzmann, W., Ibbotson, R. G., & Ross, S. A. (1992). Survivorship bias in performance studies. *Review of Financial Studies*, 5(4), 553–580.

Campbell, J. Y. (1999). John H. Cochrane. *By Force of Habit: A Consumption Based Explanation of Aggregate Stock Market Behavior, Journal of Political Economy*, 107(2), 205–251.

Cerda, R. A. (2008). The Chilean pension reform: A model to follow? *Journal of Policy Modeling*, 30(3), 541–558.

Chichilnisky, G.(2009) The topology of fear, *Journal of mathematical Economics*, 30, 1–10.

Constantinides, G. M. (1990). Habit formation: A resolution of the equity premium puzzle. *Journal of political Economy*, 98(3), 519–543.

Constantinides, G. M., & Duffie, D. (1996). Asset pricing with heterogeneous consumers. *Journal of Political economy*, 104(2), 219–240.

Ellsberg, D. (1961). Risk, ambiguity, and the Savage axioms. *The Quarterly Journal of Economics*, 75(4), 643–669.

Epstein, L. G., & Zin, S. E. (1991). Substitution, risk aversion, and the temporal behavior of consumption and asset returns: An empirical analysis. *Journal of Political Economy*, 99(2), 263–286.

Ewijk, C. V., & H. L. F. de Groot and C. Santig. (2010). A meta-Analysis of the Equity Premium *Tinbergen Institute Discussion Paper* TI2010-078/3.

Gneezy, U. and Potters, J., (1997) An experiment on risk taking and evaluation periods, *Quarterly Journal of economics*, 112, 631–645.

Gneezy, U., Kapteyn A. And Portters, J. (2003) evaluation periods and asset prices in market experiment. *Journal of Finance*, 58(2), 821–838.

Heaton, J., & Lucas, D. 1996. Evaluating the Effects of Incomplete Markets on Risk Sharing and Asset Pricing. *Journal of Political Economy*, vol. 104(3), 443–487.

Heaton, J., & Lucas, D. (1997). Market frictions, savings behavior, and portfolio choice. *Macroeconomic Dynamics*, 1, 76–101.

Ibbotson Associates. (2001). Stocks, Bonds, Bills, and Inflation. 2000 Yearbook. Chicago, IL

Kahneman, D., & Tversky, A. (1979). Prospect theory: An analysis of decision under risk. *Econometrica: Journal of the Econometric Society* 47(2), 263–292.

Kahneman, D., & Tversky, A. (2003). Experienced utility and objective happiness: A moment-based approach. The psychology of economic decisions, 1, 187–208.

Kroll, Y., Levy, H., and Markowitz, H. (1984) Mean–Variance Versus Direct Utility Maximization. *Journal of Finance*, 39, 47–61.

Mankiw, N. G. (1986). The equity premium and the concentration of aggregate shocks. *Journal of Financial Economics*, 17, 211–219.

Marcus, A. J., Bodie, Z., & Kane, A. (2002). *Investments*. McGraw Hill.

Mayhew, B. W. and Vitalis, A. (2014) Myopic Loss aversion and Market experience. *Journal of Economic Behavior& organization* 97, 113–125.

Mehra, R., & Prescott, E. C. (1985). The equity premium: A puzzle. *Journal of monetary Economics*, 15, 145–161.

Merton, R. C., (1969). Lifetime portfolio selection under uncertainty: The continuous-Time case, *Review of Economics and Statistics*, 51, 247–257.

Merton, R. C. and Samuelson P. A. (1974). The fallacy of the Log-Normal approximation to portfolio decision-making over many priods. *Journal of Financial Economics* 1, 67–94.

Mossin, J., (1968). Optimal multi-period portfolio policies, *Journal of Business*, 41, 215–229.

Pozzi, L., De Vries, C., & Zenhorst, J. (2010). World equity premium based risk aversion estimates.

Rietz, T. A. (1988). The equity risk premium a solution. *Journal of monetary Economics*, 22, 117–131.

Samuelson, P. A., (1963) Risk and uncertainty the fallacy of large numbers, *Scientia*, 98, 108–113.

Samuelson, P. A., (1969) Lifetime portfolioselection by dyanamic stochastic programming, *Review of Economics and Statistic*, 51, 239–246

Samuelson, W., & Zeckhauser, R. (1988). Status quo bias in decision making. *Journal of risk and uncertainty*, 1, 7–59.

Savage, L. J. (1954). The foundations of statistics. New York: Wiley

Siegel, J. J., & Thaler, R. H. (1997). Anomalies: the equity premium puzzle. *The Journal of Economic Perspectives*, 11(1), 191–200.

Thaler (1999). Mental accounting matters, *Journal of Behavioral decision making*, 12(3) 183–206.

Thaler, R. H., & Benartzi, S. (2004). Save more tomorrow™: Using behavioral economics to increase employee saving. *Journal of political Economy*, 112(S1), S164–S187.

Tversky, A., & Kahneman, D. (1992). Advances in prospect theory: Cumulative representation of uncertainty. *Journal of Risk and uncertainty*, 5(4), 297–323.

Van Ewijk, C., De Groot, H. L., & Santing, C. (2012). A meta-analysis of the equity premium. *Journal of Empirical Finance*, 19(5), 819–830.

Volokh, E. The mechanism of the slippery slope. *Harvard Law Review* 116, 1028–1037.

Appendix A: Example of the Final Screen of *Portfolio Management Game*

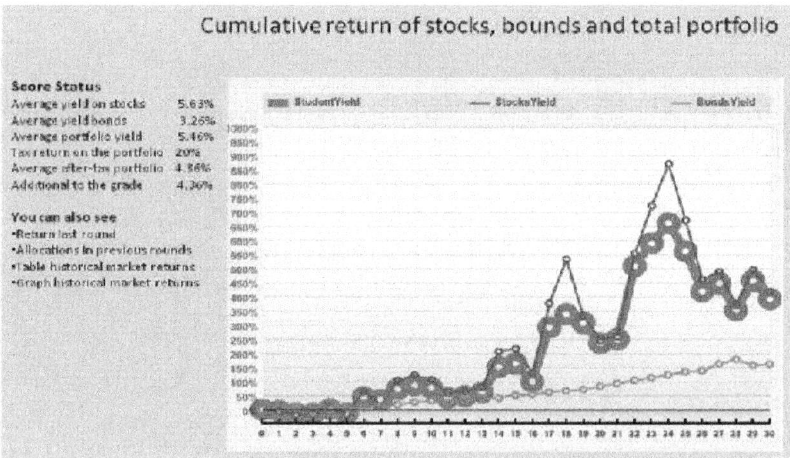

Appendix B

Historical market returns on bonds and stocks

PeriodNumber	PeriodName	BondsYield	StocksYield
1	1958	6.1	3.8
2	1959	2.4	96.1
3	1960	5	107.2
4	1961	4.6	-20.6
5	1962	6.2	27.7
6	1963	3.1	32.8
7	1964	5.7	-20.3
8	1965	6.4	-20
9	1966	1.3	-27.3
10	1967	5.2	17.5
11	1968	5.2	17.9
12	1969	4.2	-7.5
13	1970	1.5	-13
14	1971	2.1	28
15	1972	5.5	81.7
16	1973	3.3	-31.7
17	1974	1.9	-21.6
18	1975	7.8	9.5
19	1976	10.1	5
20	1977	-.1	34.6
21	1978	8	3.4
22	1979	-5.7	-23.7
23	1980	9.7	63.3
24	1981	-7.6	26.3
25	1982	-.9	71
26	1983	-4.2	-67.6
27	1984	4.6	26.4
28	1985	-9.6	3.3
29	1986	.4	.6
30	1987	8.1	5.2
31	1988	6.3	-12.4
32	1989	15.3	45.7
33	1990	-6.5	-1.5
34	1991	-.5	37.1
35	1992	6.2	75.2
36	1993	-1.5	28.7
37	1994	-3.8	-47
38	1995	1.1	5.4
39	1996	2.7	-10.5
40	1997	4.1	26.4
41	1998	-1.2	-5.1
42	1999	3.4	62.3
43	2000	2.1	.3
44	2001	13.5	-7.9
45	2002	-5.3	-24.8
46	2003	12.5	58.3
47	2004	4.3	16.2
48	2005	4.2	29.7
49	2006	4.4	5.9

Index

CPSIA information can be obtained at www.ICGtesting.com
Printed in the USA
BVOW06*0957211016

465547BV00003B/1/P

9 789813 100084